Herrington J. Bryce
School of Business Administration
The College of William and Mary

Financial and Strategic Management for Nonprofit Organizations

Prentice-Hall, Inc., Englewood Cliffs, N.J. 07632

Library of Congress Cataloging-in-Publication Data

BRYCE, HERRINGTON J.
   Financial and strategic management for nonprofit organizations.

   Includes bibliographies and index.
   1. Corporations, Nonprofit—Finance.
2. Corporations, Nonprofit—Management.
3. Strategic planning. I. Title.
HG4027.65.B78 1987   658'.049   86–30454
ISBN 0-13-316597-3

Editorial/production supervision
and interior design: PATRICK WALSH
Cover design: LUNDGREN GRAPHICS LTD.
Manufacturing buyer: CAROL J. BYSTROM

*The publisher offers discounts on this book when ordered
in bulk quantities. For information write:*
   Special Sales/College Marketing
   Prentice-Hall, Inc.
   College Technical and Reference Division
   Englewood Cliffs, N.J. 07632

Printed in the United States of America

10 9 8 7 6 5 4 3 2 1

ISBN 0-13-316597-3 025

Prentice-Hall International (UK) Limited, *London*
Prentice-Hall of Australia Pty. Limited, *Sydney*
Prentice-Hall Canada Inc., *Toronto*
Prentice-Hall Hispanoamericana, S.A., *Mexico*
Prentice-Hall of India Private Limited, *New Delhi*
Prentice-Hall of Japan, Inc., *Tokyo*
Prentice-Hall of Southeast Asia Pte. Ltd., *Singapore*
Editora Prentice-Hall do Brasil, Ltda., *Rio de Janeiro*

Dedicated to
SIMON J. BRYCE and MYRA BRYCE LAPORTE,
who gave more than their all

Contents

Preface

This book is intended to be used as a college-level text, as a training tool for managers and boards of directors of nonprofit organizations, and as a desk reference text for these officials. This book focuses at the heart of the problem faced by all nonprofit organizations—money. This book has a financial focus intended to assist the management of nonprofit organizations to broaden their financial bases and to carry out their financial responsibilities successfully. By management is meant members of the board of directors, chief executive officers, and all managers with staff responsibilities for the economic welfare of a nonprofit organization.

The book focuses on improving the flow of two streams of income into nonprofits: (a) those generated from within, through the sale of goods and services and through sophisticated cash management and investment strategies, and (b) those generated from without through sophisticated tools for attracting and accommodating large gifts and contributions. For most nonprofits, the first stream of income has been left unexplored. Yet, it is a potentially fruitful source. This type of income is ideal because its use is unrestricted by grantors. It may be used at the discretion of the management of the nonprofit so long as its use is consistent with the law.

The second stream of income with which this book deals comprises gifts and contributions from individuals and from corporations. While appealing to foundations through proposal writing and marketing is very commonly thought of as the most potentially productive source of funding, the fact is, as we shall show in this book, foundations have consistently accounted for only 5 to 8 percent of all contributions made from all sources to nonprofits. Furthermore, the contributions of foundations are highly concentrated in the fields of education, health agencies, and hospitals, with relatively little going to other types of nonprofits. With the government sector constantly retrenching and issuing not grants, but contracts for which a specific performance is required, the most fruitful strategies for most nonprofits would be (a) to generate their own business income which can be unrestricted in its use and is often nontaxable, (b) to generate a larger flow of contributions, from individuals and corporations, and (c) to improve cash management and investments. This book will show how.

Book Outline

The book begins with a discussion of the financial function in nonprofit organizations and shows how it differs from the financial function in government and in the business sector. The proper handling of the financial management function in any type of organization requires a good knowledge of the legal limitations and financial powers given to that institution by law. Thus, the second chapter of the book develops the theme of nonprofits as legal institutions and the limitations placed on them by state and federal laws. The chapter shows that in spite of these limitations, there are extensive financing powers explicitly given to nonprofits.

The third chapter develops one aspect of this financing power: the power to self-finance by operating as an economic institution with a community or public welfare mission. As such an institution, the nonprofit has appropriate productive roles in the market economy and can benefit from economic growth. Thus, chapters four and five present a framework for identifying market opportunities for nonprofits and give case examples of nonprofits that have done so successfully.

But nonprofits are distinguishable by law from for-profit firms operating in the economy. While this is true, the law does provide latitude for nonprofits to create profitable corporate structures, even on the level of a conglomerate. They may own, control, and operate their own profitable businesses. Chapters six and seven show how this can be done within the law and provide case examples.

Admittedly, the decision to go into business can be a complex investment decision. But such decisions are made every day and need not take the nonprofit far afield from what it is presently doing. Indeed, the legal definition of a related business is one that a nonprofit conducts as a part of its carrying out its charitable mission. Chapter 8 helps to remove the mystery of making an investment decision by walking the reader through the steps, raising the appropriate types of questions that the nonprofit management should ask.

Chapter 9, a transition chapter, is concerned with cost minimization as a financing responsibility. Some students of finance feel that minimizing costs is the major financial challenge before most nonprofits. Whether one agrees with this proposition or not, it is true that the cost of labor is a principal cost facing nonprofits. Hence, Chapter 9 addresses ways in which nonprofits can manage costs by the appropriate managing of employee benefits while yet maintaining a benefit structure that can attract good workers. As the management of nonprofits become increasingly exposed to suits, as is very common in hospitals, liability insurance is a benefit that must be considered.

A second avenue for financing nonprofits is by increasing gifts and contributions. To increase the productivity of fund-raising efforts, it is necessary to understand why gifts are made and some of the forms other than outright cash in which large gifts are usually made. Chapters 10 and 11 are dedicated to this understanding. Chapter 10 begins with a discussion of the motivation for giving, techniques used to appeal to potential corporate and individual donors, and the analysis of gifts. When is a gift a gift? When is a gift not worth taking? How can gifts be made?

Chapter 11 shows how trusts, wills, insurance and endowments can be used to set up intricate mechanisms for making large gifts. For example, it shows how a trust can be used to provide a donor and his spouse or children a lifetime income which may even be tax free. It can also give the donor a large tax deduction at the time the gift is made—all this at the same time it gives the nonprofit money it needs to finance its mission.

Managing the financial function of a nonprofit is more than raising funds. It is also about helping the organization to allocate its resources once the funds are obtained and to provide managerial control over their use. In this connection, it is necessary to know about budgeting which is the subject of Chapter 12. In this chapter, we are less concerned with budget processes than we are with understanding the kind of information in a good budget and how that information may be interpreted in providing managerial control.

But the budget is not singularly the most important financial document. The budget is a projection of expenses and receipts. Other financial documents are needed because they reveal the economic well-being of the organization and tell how efficiently the organization is operated from a financial point of view. Moreover, some reveal sources of cash that could be used to advance the mission or investment objectives of the organization. Chapter 13 teaches the reader how to interpret these other documents for identifying financial threats and opportunities.

The book closes with Chapter 14, which shows how all of the previous chapters are intertwined to create a financial planning and action loop. The ability to interpret the financial documents leads to the revelation of both the need for and potential sources of cash which can be obtained internally, by gifts and contributions, or through the operation of a profitable business. All of these revenues are available to advance the mission of the organization. This chapter discusses cash management to meet the organization's objectives.

Supplementary Use of the Book

This book may be used as a single text on the management or financing of nonprofits, or it may be used as a supplementary text. When used as a supplementary text, Chapters 1–5, may have applicability to courses dealing with strategic planning as applied to nonprofits. Chapters 1–6, 9, 12, 13, and 14 are applicable to courses dealing with the general (as opposed to the financial) management of nonprofits. Chapters 10, 11, and 14 will be useful in courses dealing with fund-raising. Chapters 1–5 would be applicable to courses dealing with the marketing of nonprofits.

Four Themes

Four themes underlie the discussions in this book. One is the emphasis placed on viewing nonprofits as economic organizations with welfare missions rather than as welfare organizations with welfare missions. It is shown that this emphasis is consistent and even encouraged by the law. New financing opportunities are revealed as this theme is explored.

A second theme is that there are severe legal penalties imposed on the organization as well as on the management (including the board) for the abuse and violation of the principles and laws discussed in each chapter. Many persons accept board membership in nonprofits without being conscious of their exposure to penalties attendant to violations by the organizations. These penalties may be imposed on the members and management even though they may have had no direct complicity in the violation.

A third theme is that making profits or surpluses is perfectly consistent with the legal authority of nonprofits. The critical points are how the profits are made, and in what proportion these profits, surpluses (excesses of revenues over expenditures) stand in respect to other sources of support. Nonprofit managers who do not understand the intricacies of this opportunity will constantly shy away from it, partly in the belief that zero profits and even deficits are unequivocal evidence that an organization is a nonprofit. Rather, this belief is an invitation to failure.

A fourth theme of this book is that the analogy between nonprofits and governments is misleading. Governments can tax, write laws and enforce them, declare and operate monopolies, legally restrict competition, give themselves a perpetual life long after the value of the service rendered has disappeared; and, in the case of the federal government, print money. Nonprofits, like firms, can do none of these. Neither has a constitutionally enforceable basis to assure its financial support. They cannot tax. They must raise money in a highly competitive environment.

Unlike government, both for-profit and nonprofit organizations are subject to the same market test: Do they satisfy their clients and donors (in the case of a nonprofit)? Stockholders and donors are similar in the basic sense that both seek results. Failure frequently means that firms and nonprofits go out of business. They die. Governments (as opposed to incumbents) do not die as a result of bad management; organizations do. But, like governments, nonprofits must also change financially uninformed leadership.

Style

This book is written with an appreciation that many students and in-service readers are often best served when the information can be imparted without the need for working through graphs, equations, and unfamiliar language. This book presents the technical material using the language and situations that a nonprofit manager would confront. For example, there is a discussion of present value, discounting, and the use of discount factors. Instead of dealing with these subjects in their pure technical form, the book presents questions that are familiar in nonprofit management and shows how all these questions can be answered using these principles. No equations are used. Moreover, the tables that are used already reflect any additions or divisions that would be necessary. Therefore, all answers can be gotten by multiplication, one single operation.

Furthermore, when technical terms are necessary—and they should not always be avoided—they are immediately defined so that there is no need for the reader to pause, define, memorize, read, and then understand. The appendices are used often to give a slightly more technical application of the information in the text. Accordingly, an arithmetic solution of the breakeven point is given in an appendix but with a direct application to a problem that a nonprofit organization would face. In short, the book is written such that it always answers the question: How does it apply?

To give realism to the discussion, newspaper clippings are used to illustrate some points. In addition, real case examples and court decisions are also given. Again, the driving force in this book is always to answer: How can you do it?

The Origin of the Book

This book is the outgrowth of 15 years of experience as a senior employee, as an officer, a member of the board, and as a consultant to a number of nonprofits large and small and as an officer of a for-profit corporation. It also grows out of years of teaching experiences in economics of the firm, public finance, cost administration, nonprofit finance and management, and as the director of a graduate program in budgeting, finance, and legal systems.

The major source cited in the book is The Internal Revenue Code of 1954 as amended in 1969. I began by reading all of the relevant sections of this law even in its tedious form. To bring this material up to date and to give it perspective, U.S. Treasury regulations, Revenue rulings, private letter rulings, General Counsel Memos, Tax Court rulings, decisions of District and Supreme Courts, and the publications of the IRS were read. The reader will frequently find references to these in the text. Reading these documents was tedious and often frustrating, but comparing the doctrines in these documents with popular notions about nonprofits even among so-called experts revealed how badly nonprofits are understood. Many of the popular notions about nonprofits, for example, the concepts of "charitable," "profits," "foundations," and that the profit and charitable motives are incompatible, have no basis in law, in fact, or in the practice of the most successful and charitable of nonprofits.

After reading these primary sources, I turned to academic journals. The reader will note several references to law journals and to journals on taxation. The inventory of social science research on nonprofits is very small and many of them deal with the econometric studies of giving and making contributions. Many of these studies are cited in the text.

This book avoids the common errors of believing that business techniques are readily transferable to nonprofits or that they are totally inapplicable to them. The real opportunity for increasing the efficiency of financial management in nonprofits lies in going beyond some of these popular views. Consequently, this book is less of a how-to-do-it manual than how-to-think-about-it, so that you may apply it to the very special situation in which your nonprofit finds itself.

Acknowledgements

I am particularly grateful to Beverly, Marisa, Herrington Simon, and Shauna Bryce for their patience, recommendations and encouragement; to the students I taught at the University of Maryland both in the Graduate School at the University College and in the Family and Community Development Department at College Park, to the Foundation Center Library in Washington, D.C. and the library at the University of Maryland; to Beverly Gray at the Library of Congress, to Ramona Edelin, Edward Wallace and Curtis McClinton, to the Freedom of Information Center, and to the Tax Exempt Office of the Internal Revenue Service in Washington, D.C.; to Donna and Michael Lenaghan who gave suggestions and to Dennis Young and John Murray who read the manuscript in its entirety. I am grateful to the School of Business Administration at the College of William and Mary for its support. My deepest thanks to Beverly Gaustad Bryce, and to the very many for-profit and nonprofit corporations that permitted the use of their literature.

Herrington J. Bryce

ONE

Objectives of Financial Planning and Strategic Management in Nonprofit Organizations

The management in a nonprofit organization has three basic responsibilities: (1) to uphold and advance the philosophical mission of the organization, (2) to advance its financial well-being, and (3) to oversee the performance of the organization's personnel. No single book can adequately deal with all of these tasks. This book concentrates on the second task, that of promoting the financial well-being of the organization.

This is an immense task made more difficult in recent years because of the decrease in government support to individual nonprofits,[1] the declining birth rate of private foundations,[2] the low rate of growth in giving by foundations,[3] the rise in the number of nonprofits competing for financial support,[4] and the rising costs of programs. Without additional money nonprofits cannot adequately operate no matter how worthy their missions. Thus,

> Private agencies caring for New York City's needy faced with reduced government aid and rising operating expenses, say they are beginning to scale back programs.
>
> The impact is far-reaching among the region's 6,000 nonprofit agencies, which include day-care centers, job-training services, the neighborhood "Y" and health programs for mothers and children. Others dealing with low-cost housing or legal services for the poor also are hard hit.
>
> Besides reduced Government aid, many of these private agencies say they are facing intense competition for the philanthropic dollar. They complain that they are struggling to find affordable rents as leases run out. Virtually all are confronted by escalating liability insurance costs.

> The Y.M.C.A. reported insurance premiums for all 32 sites in the city increased to $1.7 million, from $400,000.
>
> "As a consequence," said Walter I. Jacoby, senior vice president for operations, "we went into 1986 with a $600,000 deficit. Unless we raise more money privately, we will take fewer kids in our programs, give fewer scholarships for summer camp and reduce day care."
>
> New Jersey nonprofits are similarly affected, according to the Center for Non-Profit Corporations in Trenton, and some insurance costs there have gone up 2,000 percent.

Kathleen Teltsch, "Agencies Aiding Needy in New York Feel Cuts," *New York Times*, Sunday, March 2, 1986. p. 47. Copyright 1985 by The New York Times Company. Reprinted by permission.

> Hard pressed to do much more, however, are the nation's foundations. Because of the troubled stock market and what some critics describe as "federal regulatory overkill," the percentage of philanthropic dollars coming from foundations has dropped from 10 percent a decade ago to 5 percent now.
>
> Still, foundations are being barraged with requests. David F. Freeman, a New York foundation executive, says one project of the Gulf & Western Foundation had 870 applications for four or five awards sharing $500,000.

Jeannye Thornton, "The Challenge Facing Private Donors Now," *U.S. News and World Report,* January 11, 1982, p. 1.

As we shall see in Chapter 3, there are two streams of income that hold hope. One is income generated through the operation of the nonprofits including joint ventures with businesses, and the other is income generated through more sophisticated approaches to obtaining large gifts and contributions from businesses and from individuals. These two promising streams of income are analyzed and illustrated in this book. Whatever the source, each nonprofit can increase its resources by undertaking a good investment strategy. The book discusses investment strategies under capital budgeting and under cash and endowment management.

To put things into perspective, this chapter focuses on the role of the financial management function in nonprofit organizations and compares it to similar functions in government and in for-profit firms. These differences are significant and must be understood if the range of operation of nonprofits is to be successfully broadened.

THE FINANCIAL FUNCTION IN THE NONPROFIT ORGANIZATION

Unlike the task of upholding the philosophical purpose of the organization, the debates over financial matters do not rest principally on differences in beliefs or ideological commitments. These are taken as given. The principal focus of the task is to acquire, manage, and allocate dollars so that the philosophical mission of the organization—whatever it may be—can be discharged.

Unlike the task of overseeing the performance of the personnel of the organization, the debates over financial matters do not rest upon how personnel should be managed. It does not seek to determine who should be hired, how time should be allocated among projects, or who should supervise whom. Rather, it is concerned with finding and allocating the dollars needed to pay employees, to purchase necessary equipment, to pay the rental for the space in which they work, and to control the costs they generate.

Financial management is not the sole responsibility of the organization's president, controller, treasurer, accountant, or vice president of finance. Although, it is important to designate one person to be in charge of the financial well-being of the organization, ultimately the financial well-being of the organization is the responsibility of its managerial staff including the chief executive officer, each member of the board of directors, and any other officer of the organization who has decision-making responsibilities.

The Internal Revenue Service (IRS) regulations that govern nonprofit organizations state that any of these persons may be held liable for financial errors as long as there is sufficient evidence to presume that they should have known of such errors and could have acted to avoid them. The regulations do not state that the managers or officers have to participate in the decision or its implementation. All that is required is a reasonable presumption that the decision fell within their area of responsibility; and, as a consequence, they should have been aware.

In addition to the preservation of self, mastery of the information in this book will enable managers and directors to serve the financial needs of their organizations. Again, this includes managers in staff positions as well as members of the board of directors. Persons holding such positions have a responsibility for the organization as a whole and not just for particular programs.

Sources of Money and the Financial Function

A for-profit firm generates its income through the economic activity it conducts internally, i.e., from producing and selling goods and services and from its investments. On the other hand, a nonprofit may have an internal flow of funds in addition to the legally required external source, i.e., the inflow of money in the form of public support such as donations and membership fees. A nonprofit cannot legally have only internal funding.

But it behooves a nonprofit to develop a strong internal stream of funding because incomes generated from its internal economic operations and investments give the organization independence, make it less reliant on outside grant-making agencies, and are usually unrestricted. Unrestricted incomes are those over which the management may exercise greatest discretion in determining how they may be used in discharging the organization's mission.

The law does require a nonprofit to demonstrate external sources of support, however. Thus, fund raising and development serve an extremely important function not only in the diversification of the income stream of the organization, but in helping it to maintain its legal and tax status as a nonprofit.

Money raised externally may be unrestricted and can be used at the discretion of the organization in ways that would best advance its mission. But external sources often place restrictions on the use of their money. Proposal writers, grant managers, and program directors focus on grants and contracts for specific tasks. Only a small part of the funds raised in this manner can be used to take care of the financial needs of the organization as a whole. Most, if not all of the monies must be used to discharge the tasks agreed upon in the contract or the grant. In some cases, even shifts of monies from one line item to another within the contract may require approval from the contract source.

Financial Function and Fund Raising

The financial management function enables fund raising to be more successful by focusing on the financial techniques for raising large amounts of money from single donors. This can be accomplished through trusts, wills, insurance, annuities, and endowments—instruments that make large and complicated gifts possible. In addition, the financial management function carries out policies that bring high and acceptable rates of return on the investment of these funds. This must be done in a manner that is consistent with the philosophy of the organization and its money needs. Success with these efforts tends to generate additional gifts as fund-raisers are able to demonstrate to potential donors that their financial impact on the organization can be several times the size of the original gift.

By answering such questions as how much must be raised in the current period if the organization is to meet its various objectives, the financial management function helps in the setting of fund-raising targets. It also helps in the fund-raising effort by identifying the best instrument to meet a donor's situation. In a fund-raising campaign, it can help to speed up the time that the organization has access to the money pledged to it, and by so doing, earn interest on that money. It can do this by establishing relationships with regional banks that collect pledges, debiting the account of a donors, and immediately crediting the account of the organization. It can set up a lock box so that pledges are mailed directly to the bank and deposited in the account of the organization. These types of relationships reduce the time lost in mailing checks from the donor to the organization, for processing the checks in the organization, for the organization to deposit the checks in its own bank, and for the bank to collect payment before crediting it to the account of the organization. The financial function is in a position to perform these services since it has the responsibility for coordinating the organization's banking activities.

Financial Function and Program Management

The financial management function assists the program officers not only by providing them with funds and the support needed to write proposals, but by assisting them to use these same programs to generate income for individual units as well as for the organization as a whole. This can be accomplished through assisting these units in determining the full cost of running a project so that these costs may be passed on to the project sponsors rather than absorbed by the organization.

The charging of a program fee whether it be for tuition, patient care, or a mark up on a contract is a business and financial transaction. So too is the acceptance of a grant from a foundation. These, unlike a gift, are exchanges of money for the promise of specific performance by the nonprofit. Tuition are fees paid by prospective students based on the promise that the school will educate them. A grant is a payment from the foundation based on the promise that the organization will perform in the manner in which it represented itself to the foundation. A government contract is an agreement that the government will pay the organization based on its promise to perform a specific job. While it is the duty of the program or operations people in the organization to carry out the specific job and perform as promised, it is the responsibility of those in charge of the financial function to price the job to be done, to manage collection of the payments so as to accelerate the rate that payments are received, recorded and reported, and to allocate or invest payments received in the best interest of the organization in a manner consistent with the organization's policies and mission.

The Financial Function and Marketing

According to a leading scholar in marketing, "The marketer knows how to research and understand the needs of the other party; to design a valued offering to meet these needs; to communicate the offer effectively; and to present it at the right time and place."[5] From this statement it is clear all management activities, including financial management, involve some marketing.

In the financial function, marketing involves knowing the various ways in which a gift may be made and being able to select the best alternative for each potential donor. The principal marketing function of the financial director is "selling" the right type of instrument to make a gift possible. For this reason, much of this book is dedicated to understanding the "product" to be sold. It is a cardinal rule of marketing that the marketer knows the product.

Marketing and financial functions are distinctly different. The director of marketing is concerned with the intricacies of making the products and services of the organization attractive to clients, in developing client awareness, in disseminating information to stimulate sales and contributions, in studying potential markets and in designing programs for penetrating these markets successfully. The financial function is concerned with money management. As Kotler points out, in some organizations the marketing function is equal to the finance, personnel, and production functions. In others it might be subordinate or superior to these other functions.[6]

Although separate and distinct, the financial and marketing functions are related because the former assists in determining the final marketing budget of the latter. It also assists in the pricing of products, services, and proposals to be marketed and can also aid in designing effective strategies and instruments to meet the needs of potential donors.

The Financial Function and Strategic Management

The financial function is so central to the strategic management of the organization that we have chosen to entitle this book *Financial and Strategic Management of Nonprofit Organizations.* Strategic management refers to the determination of the organization's mission and value system, the setting of long-range targets, the identification of the organization's niche, and the charting of the course that will be followed in fulfilling the organization's mission. No matter how laudable a mission may be, it must be financed in order to be realized. It needs money and financial game plans for the short run (operating budget) and for the long run (capital budgets).

To the financial executive long-range planning is not visionary. It is dealing with objectives and expectations of future realities. For example, the acquisition of a building is a long-range objective. Once the decision is made to acquire a building, its actual acquisition must respect the conditions of present and future markets for money and real estate. Long-term commitments must be entered into well before the building is occupied. Similarly, the acquisition of a car is a long-term commitment to financing and maintenance costs.

In yet another way, the financial function is intricately tied to strategic management. Recall that strategic management involves considerations of the organization's values and philosophy. This value system influences the sources of support to which the organization may turn. It also influences the kinds of investments the organization makes and the image the organization wishes to portray.

Finally, the financial function and strategic management are intertwined because, as we shall see in this book, bad (although not necessarily illegal) financial decisions can lead to the loss of tax-exempt status and virtually terminate the organization's ability to meet its mission. Certain expenditures and revenue imbalances can also lead to termination.

THE FINANCIAL FUNCTION IN THE ORGANIZATIONAL CHART

Figure 1.1 shows one of many ways in which the financial function may be represented in the organizational chart of a nonprofit. Note that at the top of the organizational chart is the public. Nonprofits exist to advance public welfare and are fiduciaries of the public. Unlike a for-profit corporation, they are not owned by stockholders. The board answers to the public or community and much of the laws that govern nonprofit corporations are intended to assure that decisions made by the board of directors are aimed at advancing the public welfare. The board may be divided into several committees each having a responsibility to oversee a financial aspect of the organization; for example, there might be a budget committee, an investment committee, an audit committee, and a development committee with each possibly having several subcommittees. Committee members can be held personally liable for certain financial misdeeds of the organization. This is the law and some organizations such as the YWCA alert their trustees (See insert, p. 8). We shall refer to such liabilities throughout this book especially in Chapters 2, 6, 7, 9, and 14.

The chief financial officer may carry the rank of a vice president or senior vice president reporting directly to the president or chief executive officer of the organization. On the same rank as the chief financial officer may be vice

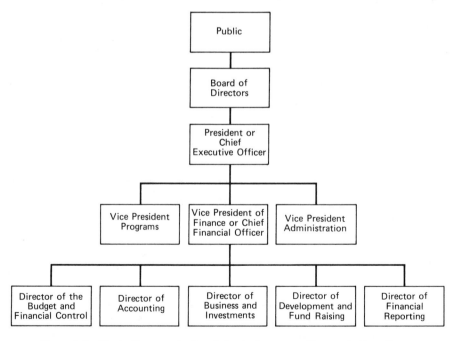

Figure 1.1 Illustrative organizational chart of a nonprofit organization. Source: Author.

Trustee of a Corporation

By the act of incorporating, a YWCA establishes itself as a legal entity subject to laws applicable to not-for-profit corporations. Boards of Directors are responsible for seeing that corporate duties defined by law and by its own corporate charter ("Articles of Incorporation" or "Articles of Association") are discharged, a responsibility shared with boards of trustees in states where the latter are required.

The standard for meeting this responsibility is that the Board member or trustee must discharge her/his duties in good faith and with the degree of diligence that an ordinarily prudent person would exercise in like circumstances. Failure to maintain this diligence may result in personal liability.

To meet her legal responsibilities a Board member should:

- Review and understand the Association's corporate charter

- Attend Board meetings regularly

  The power of a Board of Directors or Trustees rests in the group, acting together. No one Board member has the authority to control or make decisions for the Association, and members may not vote by proxy.

  If it is necessary for her to miss a meeting, she should take reasonable steps to learn of decisions made in her absence and, if necessary, register any opposing view at the first suitable opportunity.

Bring informed and objective judgment to the decisions the Board must make —

seeing that the power of the Board is employed for the greatest benefit to the program and to all of the members of the Association;

putting the Association's needs ahead of her own aspirations.

It is particularly important that the individual Board member avoid a conflict of interests. Preferably, she should have no personal interest in the business transactions of the Association. If this becomes necessary, statutory and charter limitations should be reviewed before action is taken, her interest should be made known to the Board, and she should not participate in the vote.

- Safeguard the Association's property and other assets —

  seeing that decisions concerning property reflect the Association's long-range program plans

  studying and making thoughtful judgments concerning the adequacy and type of the Association's funding

  protecting its tax-exempt status

  seeing that its tax obligations (employee income, FICA, etc.) are met.

- Monitor employer responsibilities, including implementation of an affirmative action plan

- See that written records of Board meetings are kept

- Seek expert advice before taking any action which the directors lack reasonable competence to handle.

"Trustee of a Corporation" Source *A YWCA Member* © National Board, YWCA, New York, p. 4.

presidents for administration including personnel and purchasing, and a vice president for programs who may be responsible for a number of operating programs.

Directly under the chief financial officer may be the office of budgeting and financial control which is responsible for preparing the budget for the organization, setting up all financial controls such as procedures for recording receipts and expenditures, scheduling of payments, regularly computing and comparing differences between actual and projected receipts and expenditures, preparing estimates of program costs and revenues for bidding on contracts, and so on. This office may also keep track of various costs such as employee benefits, equipment, and rental costs and compare the products of various benefits and equipment providers.

Also directly under the chief financial officer may be an accounting operation. These people will systematically classify and record actual income and expenditures of the organization. They keep systematic records of each type of expense such as payroll, supplies, transportation, and entertainment as well as records of receipts from fees, gifts and contributions, contracts, and so on. Moreover, this group must keep certain expenditures and receipts segregated from the general accounting of the organization. Certain funds are restricted by covenant, agreement, or contract to specific uses and may not become part of the general funds of the organization. Each building fund and scholarship fund, for example, must be accounted for separately. This is called fund accounting.

Also directly reporting to the chief financial officer may be a director of investments. Some nonprofits have sizeable portfolios and businesses that they own and operate. The person who heads this function may not necessarily be the one who makes investment decisions. Investment decisions may be made by the board of directors or through contract with an outside investment advisor. Similarly, each business operated by the organization may have its own manager. All of these may, however, report to one person who is responsible for coordinating and overseeing the entire spectrum of investment.

Fund raising is another function that may report directly to the chief financial officer. This function need not report directly to the chief financial officer. Organizations may have a vice president for development to whom fund raising is assigned. Even when this is the case, a chief financial officer has some direct responsibility for specific aspects of the fund-raising activity because so much of what is done here requires technical aspects of finance and goes beyond making and perpetuating financial contacts. Fund raising involves contribution campaigns, working with individual, corporate, or foundation donors, working with alumni, and using such technical instruments as wills, trusts, insurance, endowments, and noncash property.

Also reporting to the chief financial officer may be a director of financial reporting. This function covers preparing annual reports on financial matters of the organization, its donors and supporters, filing income tax forms, preparing and making available public reports which are sometimes required by law, and disseminating these reports.

The nature of the configuration that any single organization may take will depend upon the organization's complexity, the level of development, the mission (a hospital compared to a day care center), the size of the organization, and the management style of its leadership. In some organizations, administrative and financial functions may be combined. Some small organizations may have but one vice president and the financial officer may also oversee purchasing and acquisitions. In others the chief executive officer may carry on the function of chief financial officer. Organizations change structure when confronting new challenges; therefore, it is important to go beyond organizational structure and to focus on the content of certain central financial functions.

While certain configurations and assignments may change, the vice presidents are always responsible to a president or chief executive officer who is in turn responsible to the board. The board is responsible to the public on whose behalf the legal sytem acts. To reiterate, in the nonprofit world the financial function is conducted within a set of legal rules that is different from those in the public or for-profit sector. Violation of these rules jeopardizes the organization's existence. The management including the board of directors may be held personally liable. Hence, in the nonprofit organization the financial function involves more than the art of investment or politics. It is a specialized aspect of strategic management.

To summarize, the financial management function is a staff function. It assists management in setting realistic financial and performance targets. How much can reasonably be raised and, therefore, how much can reasonably be done? It makes recommendations about ways to increase the inflow of funds into the organization and it can improve the use of short-term investment techniques to turn idle cash balances into assets earning interest. It can also assist the organization in making long-term investments in such assets as bonds, land, equipment and buildings and in acquiring and managing its own business. All of these involve comparisons of income streams expected from alternative uses of the organization's money and the risks associated with investments, including that of losing the tax-exempt status of the organization.

In addition to assistance in fund raising and development and in the investment of the organization's money, financial management also assists in the assessment of the financial standing of the organization. This is accomplished by interpreting the financial statements prepared by the accountants. Good management must know how to read the three principal financial statements: the balance sheet, the statement of revenues and expense, and the statement of changes in the financial position of the organization. Not being accountants, it is not necessary for financial managers to master the details of fund accounting which is the accounting method used by nonprofits. However, the financial management function does require the ability to interpret the accounting data in light of the organization's objectives and to work out the alternatives available to management. Stated otherwise, the financial management function converts accounting data into a financial policy consistent with the organization's mission.

THE IMPORTANCE OF FINANCIAL INFORMATION

In today's highly specialized world, it is not expected that all managers, chief executives, and members of the board of directors of nonprofit organizations be financial wizards. What is important is that management has a working knowledge of the financial management function as it applies specifically to nonprofit organizations. Here is a list of what this necessitates.

1. The management has to broaden its perspective about what it means to be a nonprofit from a financial rather than philosophical point of view. Recall that the financial management function does not debate the philosophical merits of a mission. It takes that as a given and tries to solve the problem of how the mission will be financed. This means talking about money which is measurable. Thus, performance can be measured.

2. Management has to view its organization as a competitor for scarce dollars. To be financially successful, nonprofits must compete not only among themselves but among alternative ways in which potential donors have to use their money. Giving away money is not the only, and frequently it is the least attractive alternative that a person or corporation has. Competition is also involved in recruiting good staff persons and chief executive officers and in being able to retain them by providing good, but affordable benefits.

3. Management has to engage in the planning and the setting of attainable goals and strategies to carry out a mission successfully including the mission of raising money. From a financial perspective, programs must compete for a limited supply of money. The most profitable program may not always be chosen, but the questions of how much money a certain program can bring the organization or how much the program will cost, should never be treated trivially. Except in the cases of mercy and emergency which are rarities for most nonprofits, a program is not simply an exercise in benevolence. It is a vehicle to directly (through sales) or indirectly (through goodwill) raise money so that even more clients may be served by the organization. Admittedly, money making should not always be the most persuasive reason for choosing one program over the other. Indeed, some money-losers may be properly chosen, but the financial impact of such choices on the organization should be known—preferably in advance.

4. Management has to master an understanding of the major streams of revenues to nonprofit organizations: gifts and contributions. What are they? Where do they come from? When is a gift not a gift? When is a gift likely to be a disguised financial disaster? What are the limits to giving and receiving? What is the potential impact of tax reform on gifts and contributions? The more sophisticated management's knowledge of these streams is, the easier it is to tap them in an imaginative manner and to adjust to changes such as tax reform.

5. Mangement has to have a working knowledge of some of the more sophisticated tools for giving. How can a gift be arranged to provide income for the life of a potential donor or some other person and at the same time provide a handsome contribution to the nonprofit? How can a nonprofit get an annual income from a trust?

6. Mangement has to understand the legal boundaries placed on the organization and the hidden opportunities available to the imaginative managers. Often, the conclusion that "we can't do it because of our nonprofit status," is incorrect.

7. It is incumbent upon management to explore the opportunities to earn the most cherished form of revenues—those self-generating revenues over which the nonprofit management has full discretion. These opportunities lie in making good short- and long-term investments including the acquisition of profit-making enterprises.

8. Management has to be able to think through an investment decision. This can be done without being trapped by details or formulas that few managers will ever retain or calculate themselves. Yet, every manager should be able to understand the thinking and solution to such basic investment questions as: How do we know it is a good investment for our organization?

9. Management has to use the budget and the budgetary process as financial planning tools, as tools to coordinate or allocate resources among various programs, and as tools to control spending and the overall direction of the organization.

10. Management has to be able to read the critical financial statements. These are the balance sheet, the statement of revenues and expenses, and the statement of changes in the financial conditions of the organization. It is the ability to interpret these statements that will give early warning of financial disaster as well as the financial capacity to grow.

The chapters of this book deal with all these topics. They do not presume that the reader has prior knowledge of financial planning and do not try to make the reader a financial planner. The book tries to make the reader a competent and contributing member of the management staff of a nonprofit organization and of its board of directors. Such members know their potential liability and are capable of contributing to the growth and financial well-being of the organization. Why? Because such readers will have acquired a firm understanding of the basic blocks of knowledge of the nonprofit financial world and can proceed to institute imaginative and productive programs to make money.

UNIQUE CHALLENGES OF FINANCIAL MANAGEMENT IN NONPROFITS

From a financial management point of view, to equate nonprofits with government agencies is devastatingly wrong. Nonprofits are more like businesses. Government agencies can exist forever under the taxing powers of the state, local, or federal governments. A government can tax the earnings of every entity whether dead (through death taxes) or alive, domestic, or foreign. Nonprofits have no such powers. Like businesses, they may go bankrupt and close. Government agencies do not go bankrupt. Governments default (postpone payment of interest) and increase taxes to cover their debts. They do not close down and do not go bankrupt. Nonprofits do.

> Attendance at the aircraft carrier Intrepid, the floating museum at 46th Street and the Hudson River, has stabilized this summer and organizers say they are confident the three-year-old museum will survive its financial problems.
>
> To provide the museum with breathing room until revenues can be increased, its administrators filed for bankruptcy in late July, just a few days before bondholders were to receive a $1.2 million payment that would have depleted the museum's bank account.
>
> Without the interest payments, the museum's revenues are enough to pay operating expenses. But with the interest, the museum operated at a loss of $4.3 million in the fiscal year ending last April 30, up from $3 million two years earlier.

Michael Quint, "The Intrepid Museum Fighting to Weather a Financial Storm," The *New York Times,* Sunday, October 13, 1985, p. 59. Copyright 1985 by The New York Times Company. Reprinted by permission.

Another error in equating nonprofits with government agencies is the singular importance placed on the budget. In government, the budget is a legal document. When a budget is passed by a legislative body and signed by the executive, it becomes law. This is true on the state, local, and federal levels. In nonprofits, this is not the case. The budget is at best a plan. Nonprofits do not write laws.

To take this argument one step further, most states and local governments have a legal debt limit, a legal taxing limit of some kind, and are legally prohibited from running a deficit in their annual budget. All of these budgets are subject to public hearings. None of these rules applies to nonprofits. To the contrary, nonprofits run deficits year after year without sanction of any kind—except the possibility of bankruptcy.

In short, by focusing primarily on the budget, which is a financial plan, managers of nonprofit organizations may overlook more critical financial documents that do provide early warnings about potential financial problems of their organizations.

In another way, the financial function in a nonprofit organization is strikingly different from the same function in most government agencies. There are few chief executive or financial officers of government agencies who worry about raising revenues. The revenues of government agencies are allocated to them through a political process. The revenues of nonprofits are raised through the market process and through appealing to donors or supporters including persons, foundations, and corporations. Appealing to a legislative body is quite different than appealing to a foundation, individual or corporate donors, or to government agencies as clients.

All chief executive officers of nonprofits, even those such as the Smithsonian Institution that are funded by the government, must worry about revenues. In government agencies, revenues are allocated by legislative and executive bodies, and they are obtained through taxation. Nonprofit managers cannot tax and do not have legislative allocation of funds. They must raise funds from the public and private sectors. Consequently, their knowledge of money-raising techniques must be extensive and aggressive. They must learn about trusts, wills, endowments and the use of insurance to magnify small gifts. Neither the manager of a government agency nor the manager of a business has to be concerned with these instruments as ways of raising money.

Few chief executives or senior managers of government agencies need worry about how to invest the agency's dollars. But good managers of nonprofits must choose among various short- and long-term investments. Government executives worry about how to spend; that is, which programs to underwrite and how much to allocate to each, assuming that both the amount and the allocation are not already written into law. On the other hand, chief executives of nonprofits must not only worry about how much to allocate to each program, they must also worry about investing the organization's funds to maintain a desired stream of income. In the case of nonprofits, no program is mandated by law as in the case of a government agency or a government-created nonprofit.[7]

In a sense, the financial function in government agencies concentrates on financial reporting, on minimizing costs, and on helping to get a budget through the legislative and executive branches. Financial management in the nonprofit sector also concentrates on these factors, but getting a budget accepted by the board of directors is a substantially less formidable task than getting it through a legislative body or competing with other agencies for the priority of the executive branch. On the other hand, in the nonprofit sector there is greater emphasis on raising revenues. Revenues must come from a variety of sources and cannot be commanded by law as taxes are. Furthermore, the law requires that the revenues of nonprofits be mathematically balanced between external and internal sources.[8]

The financial functions in nonprofit and for-profit organizations also differ. In the latter, funds for growth and for financing new initiatives can be obtained from earnings retained from past years' profits, from selling stocks or new interests in the business, or from borrowing. Nonprofits cannot sell stocks because they cannot legally issue them. Consequently, the nonprofit manager has to rely on borrowing, new gifts and contributions, retained earnings or assessments of the membership. In short, the inability to sell stocks means that nonprofit managers cannot appeal to the desire of individuals to make monetary gains as a motive for giving. And it means that it is incumbent on those responsible for the financial function of nonprofits to be knowledgeable and imaginative in exploiting the options available to raise money.

The financial management functions in the for-profit and nonprofit sectors are different in yet another way. In the for-profit sector, the financial function is rarely so constrained that the very existence of the organization is legally threatened by certain types of revenues and expenditures. For example, in the non-profit sector, large contributors are prohibited from exercising control over the organization. In the for-profit sector the large investors own the organization and sometimes exercise total control. Therefore, a sense of power as well as of profits becomes a reason for being involved; not so in nonprofits. Large donors are asked to divorce themselves from control of the organization and of the gift once it is made. Failure to do this has dire consequences on the donor, on the organization, and on its management.

All for-profits do not have to maintain a critical balance in the structure of their revenues.[9] Nonprofits that are public charities must demonstrate that a high proportion of their revenues comes from public support or that they are owned by an organization that is publically supported. Violation of the critical balance in revenues by source can lead to loss of tax-exempt status.

Finally, in the nonprofit sector, there are likely to be prohibitions against making certain types of investments or in engaging in certain types of investment strategies. Nonprofits are less likely to be permitted either by state law or by their boards to deal in the commodity markets, or in buying and selling options on stocks. These are highly risky.

Contrary to a common belief that has inhibited many nonprofits and permeated the literature, the law does not prohibit nonprofits from making a profit. The profit might be sizeable. We shall point to nonprofits that operate for profit in all kinds of ventures, and we shall cite court and IRS decisions reaffirming that the law does permit nonprofits to make a profit.

There are those who would challenge the drawing of similarities between for-profits and nonprofits. One common claim is that nonprofits have multiple and complex objectives and for-profits do not. This statement is false. Unlike for-profit firms, nonprofits are legally restricted to one of eight objectives discussed in the next chapter. There are only eight missions or objectives that can be legally used to obtain a nonprofit tax-exempt status. Most nonprofits restrict themselves to one. The mission of a university is to educate. The missions of a hospital are health care and, in the case of a teaching hospital, education. The mission of a church is religion. As we shall see later on in this book, not only does the law define what it means by education, religion, and the like, the definitions are short and to the point. There is nothing complicated about them. Indeed, the more complexity or uncertainty a nonprofit uses to define its mission, the less likely it is to be awarded tax-exempt status. Triune was not denied tax-exempt status because it was not a religion but because it could not prove that its operation fit the strict rules set up by the IRS in its definition of what a nonprofit should be.

> Petitioner is dedicated to the doctrine of the Triune of Life. That doctrine has three components: intelligence, matter, and force. The sole sacrament currently administered by petitioner is that of spinology. The object of spinology is to restore human beings to harmonious unity of mind, spirit, and body for the fulfillment of life. Petitioner's doctrine teaches that, sometimes, when an individual is spiritually inhibited from expressing his or her full life potential, there is a physical manifestation. Spinology seeks to correct this spiritual problem by the physical sacrament of spinology, which involves a gentle laying of the hands on the person by a certified spinologist.

Triune of Life Church, Inc. Petitioner v. Commissioner of Internal Revenue, Respondent, T.C. 7/1/85.

But, as we shall show later, research as well as the award-winning work by students of American corporations have shown over and over again that for-profit firms do not have singular, easily defined objectives and often these multiple objectives clash. We should no longer tolerate claims of multiple objectives as reasons for excusing the failure of the management of a nonprofit to clearly articulate the mission of the organization. This is important because, as we shall show, those organizations that rise above these excuses have been very successful in penetrating profitable markets at the same time that they continue to carry on a worthwhile charitable mission.

Another common claim is that nonprofits cannot measure their output as for-profit firms do. This, too, has only a grain of truth. Ask the presidents of a private and a public university to compare their institutions. Both will talk about enrollments, student scores, number of undergraduates and graduates, the number of Ph.Ds on their faculties, and their endowments, capital programs, and operating budgets. These are all measurable, although not perfectly. They are also both comparable between a private and a public school. The fact that these indicators may not be perfect measures is no reason to accept excuses. Profits are not perfect measures and they are not the only measures; the same firm can show profits in a given year at several different levels depending on its accounting scheme, no single one of which is perfect. The point is that strategic and financial managements do not surrender to claims of impossibility because measures are imperfect. In the final analysis, every good manager settles on some measurable indicator. It does not always have to be dollars. Yet, financial management in for-profit and nonprofit organizations is basically about the same thing—money.

This is not to argue that there are no substantive differences between for-profit and nonprofit corporations and their financial functions. To reiterate, there are differences including *not* whether a profit can be made, but how the profits are used and their centrality to the corporate mission, the role of gifts and contributions, the involvement of the public as a source of financial support as well as in the discharging of the duties of the corporation, the cost of operation because of private and public subsidies such as volunteers and postal rates, the role of owners and donors and the legal constraints placed on the activities of the organization. These differences are rooted in law and are the critical distinctions which impact on the financial function in nonprofits and make this function substantively and legally different in the nonprofit as compared to government agencies or firms.

LEGAL AND ORGANIZATIONAL CONSTRAINTS ON FINANCIAL DECISIONS

As stated earlier, financial management of nonprofits is about money, and this theme underlies the entire financial management function. It does not mean that the financial function is unaffected by nonmonetary and ideological considerations. It means that those deliberations are done in a larger context and provide the constraints under which the financial planning function operates. Thus, the decision not to invest in South Africa is not a financial planning decision. It is made by the board of directors of an organization based upon its philosophical committments, and the financial manager is instructed that all relevant financial decisions must obey the basic policy direction set by the board of the organization.

There are also legal constraints on the financial management function. Unlike for-profit firms, nonprofits must obey stringent rules about investments, expenditures, and revenues. Violation of these rules can lead to a loss of tax-exempt status from the IRS and to the termination of the organization by the state. Therefore, it is critical that these rules be understood and this book focuses on them.

THE FINANCIAL IMPACT OF TAX REFORM

Tax reform has been on the national agenda of virtually every administration. The most significant tax reform concerning nonprofit organizations is the reform of 1969 which placed all tax-exempt nonprofits classified as 501 (c) (3) organizations into one of two major categories: private foundations and "others." Some private foundations are classified as private operating foundations. Among the "others" which are not private foundations are community foundations (those that give grants) and public charities (those that provide direct services or products to the community).

The reform of 1969 also stipulated limitations on the behavior of these groups. For example, noting that private foundations were potentially captives of their founders, the law limits the control and the relationships between the private foundations, their founders, supporters, management and any other persons or groups with which these supporters or founders may have a relationship. Thus, the law limits the relationship that the nonprofit may have with its founders and with the founder's business or family.

In recent years, a number of reforms have been proposed. Let us look at the most recent, some of which were made law in September 1986, and ask how each would affect the material in this book. How would each affect the financial and strategic management of nonprofits?

1. One recent proposal that is no longer being actively considered was proposed by the U.S. Treasury. It was to prohibit the deduction of charitable contributions to amounts over $2,000. This means that a taxpayer would have to give a minimum of $2,000 before he or she could deduct contributions. The new law disallows charitable deductions for those who do not itemize deductions. It is not certain how much giving would be affected since the obtaining of a tax deduction is only one of many reasons why people give. Part of the effect of this proposal would be to offset an earlier reform that permitted taxpayers who did not itemize their deductions (and, therefore, could not deduct donations) to deduct their charitable contributions.

2. A second proposal was to limit the valuation of property. Present law permits a donor to purchase a property, hold it until it has appreciated substantially, and then donate it. The amount that may be deducted is the fair market value on the date the gift is made. This makes it possible, for example, for a donor to purchase a property for $1,000, hold it until it has appreciated to perhaps $3,000, donate it, and deduct $3,000. The failed proposal was to restrict the amount that can be deducted to the original purchase price of the property, plus an amount of appreciation keyed to the rate of inflation. In simple terms, this would mean that if the rate of inflation was 10 percent and the property was held for one year, the most that could be deducted in such a case as described would be $1,100 even though within this period the property might have tripled (not unusual for stocks). The effect of this rule would be to dampen contributions particularly to hospitals, universities and museums—nonprofits which rely heavily on large appreciated gifts. Consequently, these organizations have lobbied heavily against this proposal.

3. Another proposal is to remove the special treatment that donations receive in calculating the alternative minimum tax. Several years ago, Congress decided that too many wealthy taxpayers were getting away with paying little or no taxes. Taxpayers did this partly by taking as many tax deductions as they could and by investing money in projects such as real estate, oil and gas, livestock and farming which give them paper losses that they could deduct from their sizeable incomes, thus reducing the amount of taxes they paid. To curb this practice, Congress instituted the alternative minimum tax. This law, as amended in 1982, requires taxpayers to compute their taxes two ways: (1) with all of the deductions they can legally take, and (2) alternatively, without some specified deductions. The second way, without certain deductions, tends more often to yield the higher of the two tax liabilities. The taxpayer is required to pay the higher of the two tax liabilities.

In computing the alternative tax, the taxpayer is permitted to continue to deduct charitable donations. However, the new law makes the amount by which the property has appreciated taxable when computing the alternative tax. Since the alternative tax is most often applicable to higher income taxpayers, the effect will be to decrease the tax incentive for their giving. By how much is unknown, for at least two factors will offset the dampening effect. One is that although the tax incentive is important, there are other motives for giving. Second, many taxpayers may offset this effect by better tax planning. Since the institution of the alternative tax, a considerable amount of financial planning effort has gone into avoiding it or minimizing its impact. This implies that when large gifts are anticipated from wealthy donors, seeking tax advice would be important.

4. The new law lowers individual and corporate tax rates. As we show in Chapter 12, empirical studies have repeatedly demonstrated that giving is related to taxes. People give more because they are able to deduct the donation from their taxes. The effect of this is to reduce the cost to them of making the gift. The lower the tax rate, the higher the cost of the gift is to the donors because the amount they can deduct from their taxes decreases. Thus, proposals to increase taxes should cause giving to rise as people seek more deductions; proposals to decrease taxes should cause people to reduce giving as they find less need for tax deductions. Again, these effects are offset by the nontax incentives for giving and what we may call the "income" effect of giving. This means that the greater the disposable income of the individual—that is, the more income the person has at his or her disposal due to a tax cut—the more charitable he or she may feel to make greater donations.

5. A fifth reform has to do with the valuation of donations to insure against cheating. It is alleged that taxpayers who give works of art, jewelry and other collectibles and rare items that are hard to appraise, generally overvalue them when giving to a charity. This overpricing increases the deduction the taxpayer can take. Under the new rules, donors who contribute property with a stated value of over $500 (the old rule was $5,000) must file Form IRS 8283. The form requires that the donor give the name of the charity and its address, a description of the donated property, the date of the contribution, the date the donor acquired the property, how it was acquired, the cost to the donor adjusted for any improvement, the fair market value of the property, and the method used to determine the fair market value.

If the value of the property exceeds $5,000 the donor must also provide an acknowledgment by the charity that it was received. Either the donor or the appraiser must provide information on the donated property and the appraiser must certify the appraisal given to the property. This reform is already on the books with the effect of reducing cheating. It may also reduce the urgency with which people give to museums, hospitals, universities, and to some thrift shops.

6. One future area of tax reform may arise from a recent Supreme Court decision, *United States, Petitioner* v. *American College of Physicians,* April 22, 1986. In this case which will be discussed later, the Supreme Court suggested that the current reading of the Treasury Regulations on advertising income particularly in medical journals may be too restrictive, leading to the taxation of such income. Chief Justice Warren Burger and Justice Lewis Powell argued in that decision that given the rapid expansion of medical knowledge, such advertising provides a "correspondence course" or "continuing education for physicians."

7. One other proposal that was considered might have affected the employee benefit packages. That proposal has to do with reducing the amount that an employee puts into the corporate retirement plan by the amount that is placed in an Individual Retirement Account. That is, if the employee puts $2,000 a year in an IRA, that amount must be deducted from the contributions to the corporate plan. However, this and other new IRA rulings have no bearing on our discussion. They change amounts, not the structure, of the discussion.

The new law lowering the maximum that an employee may contribute to some retirement funds will not change the arguments in Chapter 9. These strategies will remain.

8. A failed proposal has to do with taxing the amount of cash value that accumulates in a life insurance policy. This could make such policies less attractive as an instrument for accumulation by individuals. One possible short-run effect is that some existing policies could be donated because their tax value has been lost. Another effect is that fewer individuals would invest in these policies so that in the long run fewer would be available for giving.

9. The new law provides for taxing individuals for some amount of the premiums paid by their employers on life and health insurance policies not available to all employees. Employee life and health insurance are near necessary goods and a tax on them would hardly eliminate them.

10. The new law eliminates the distinction between short- and long-term capital gains, the 60 percent exclusion, and makes all capital gains subject to a maximum of 28 percent tax rate. Such a ruling may increase the tax paid by nonprofits when they obtain and dispose of properties subject to debt and may reduce the rate of return calculated on some gifts by donors. Only a few paragraphs in this book deal with capital gains.

The enactment of the new law means that references to short-term capital gains and the exclusions would be deleted. For taxpayers in the highest tax bracket, however, there would still be a maximum capital gain tax of 28 percent, meaning that the discussion about capital gains in this book would remain essentially correct.

11. The new law doing away with the investment tax credit and lengthening depreciation time may lower the rate at which businesses and individuals recover investment expenses and make gifts of used property.

12. The new law placing dollar limits on industrial development bonds will limit the ability of state and local governments to help nonprofits raise capital funds. Universities, hospitals, and housing agencies will experience higher borrowing costs.

The manager of a nonprofit should keep in mind that every year proposals concerning taxation are made. Few of these are seriously considered, fewer yet ever adopted. The shrewd manager should keep abreast of these matters and several sources provide timely information. These include the newspaper, trade and association journals and newsletters, *Revenue Rulings* (Rev. Rul.) from the IRS which give an explanation of IRS interpretation and application of laws, *General Counsels Memorandums* (GCM) which tell how the lawyers in the IRS advised the IRS Commissioner to rule on a specific question and the legal reasoning behind their recommendation, a private letter ruling which is a letter sent to the taxpayer relating the IRS conclusion concerning the legality of a specific question raised by that organization, Tax Court (T.C.) decisions which tell how the courts responded, and The Code of Federal Regulations, which gives details of new regulations. In addition, there is the basic law, the *Internal Revenue Code* (IRC) and decisions made by the Supreme Court. With the exceptions of journals, newspapers, and newsletters, all of these are primary sources.

THE FINANCIAL IMPACT OF NONTAX REFORM

There are two nontax reforms that will have significant impact on nonprofits but not on the substance of what is said in this book. Gramm-Rudman-Hollings mandates annual cuts in the federal budget in order to bring the two-trillion-dollar and growing federal debt under control. Technically, this means that all nonprofits receiving federal contracts or other forms of support are subject to unpredictable cuts every year into the 1990s. The impact of this law is all-encompassing since, with few exceptions such as defense and social security, the law applies across the board. Therefore, nonprofits such as those dealing with the handicap, social and community welfare, health, housing, employment and training, environment, work safety, publications, transportation, education and justice are particularly vulnerable. These areas are not only unprotected but are often political targets for budget cuts.

A second nontax development that is likely to affect nonprofits is a recent proposal by the federal Office of Personnel Management that certain groups will no longer be allowed to participate in the Combined Federal Campaign. These groups include those who spend more than 15 percent of their annual budgets on lawsuits, meaning that advocacy groups will become ineligible unless by special dispensation on a case-by-case basis. Only charities that conduct activities that, in the word of the decision, "help lessen the burdens of government" will be eligible to participate. These include groups dealing with drug addiction, community rehabilitation, aid to the poor and disaster assistance, health and education, and legal services to the poor.[10]

The Combined Federal Campaign is one in which employees of the federal government agree to give part of their earnings through payroll deductions to charity. The employee may designate a specific charity to which the deducted amount should go or, if a charity is not designated, the money goes into a pool and is divided among all charities on the list. The regulations not only make those charities cited in the previous paragraph ineligible, they also prohibit the employee from writing in names. Thus, only those names on the list can benefit from the Combined Federal Campaign.

The new proposal (if ever implemented) may mean that some employees may give less because their favorite charity is no longer eligible. More likely, however, these employees will continue to give at least the same amount but designate other charities on the list—if they designate at all. The proposed regulations surely mean that an increasing number of nonprofits will have to search for new sources of support.

REVENUE STREAMS AND THE PRACTICE OF FINANCIAL MANAGEMENT IN NONPROFIT ORGANIZATIONS

The concepts and strategies that form the core of this book are more than theory and philosophy. They are grounded in decades of legal opinions pronounced by the courts, in the regulatory practices of the IRS, and in the daily practices of the most successful of nonprofit organizations. Throughout this book we shall, with the permission of these organizations, cite some of their practices. We shall even analyze some of their financial statements, investment strategies, and business operations. Through these approaches we shall have a better understanding of the financial management challenge in the nonprofit world.

To appreciate the scope of this book as well as its practical orientation, the reader is directed to two pages taken from the 1985 Annual Report of the Colonial Williamsburg Foundation, which operates Colonial Williamsburg in Williamsburg, Virginia, a historic museum that attracted some 1,000,000 visitors in 1985.

Note that, unlike a business, this nonprofit cannot carry out its mission merely by relying on revenues from its business income; and, as in the case of many other nonprofits, it cannot rely purely upon grants and contributions. Notice also that, contrary to common belief, nonprofits do pay taxes. And, as we shall see when analyzing another large nonprofit, the well-run nonprofit strives for a positive fund balance and an operating surplus. (We shall describe

Financial Support Of Operations

Exhibition and historical programs of the Colonial Williamsburg Foundation are funded by a combination of admissions revenues, gifts and grants for operating purposes, endowment income, net income from hotel and restaurant properties, sales of Colonial Williamsburg products, and rental income from real estate the Foundation owns.

During 1985, costs associated with exhibitions and historical programs totaled $27.2 million. Admissions and related revenues of $16.2 million provided 60 percent of these costs, an increase from the 58 percent of costs provided by admissions revenues in 1984. Gifts and grants for operating purposes increased to $3.4 million, of which the Colonial Williamsburg Fund accounted for $2.5 million and other gifts $900,000.

The net income in 1985 from the Foundation's revenue-generating hotel, restaurant, products, and real estate operations was $3.3 million after a provision for income taxes of $600,000.

Withdrawals from endowment for general operations totaled $5.3 million, and interest on temporary investments totaled $1.4 million.

Consolidated total revenues of the Foundation and its wholly owned hotel and restaurant subsidiary totaled $93.9 million when investment income available for operations was included. This represented a 9.1 percent increase over 1984. Consolidated operating expenses totaled $92.7 million, a 12.2 percent increase over 1984. The more rapid growth of operating expenses relative to revenues was primarily a result of the recognition for accounting purposes of increased provisions for depreciation, retirement, and vacation benefits, none of which represents an immediate call on the Foundation's cash balances.

The operating results, together with major gifts pledged in previous years, permitted the Foundation to increase its 1985 capital expenditures for new and replacement buildings and equipment as well as for additions to the collections to $26.5 million from $22.4 million in 1984.

Major capital expenditures included work on the DeWitt Wallace Decorative Arts Gallery, the Carter's Grove Reception Center, acquisition of the Governor's Inn, and expansion of the Williamsburg Lodge.

The market value of the Consolidated Endowment Fund of the Foundation totaled $145.7 million at the end of 1985. The various accounts that make up the consolidated fund consist of both donor-restricted funds and unrestricted funds, which may be utilized for purposes approved by the trustees. Distributions from the endowment funds for general operating purposes and replacement of physical assets are governed by a policy that sets annual withdrawals at five percent of the average market value of the endowment funds over the previous three years.

Total assets on the Foundation's consolidated balance sheet at December 31, 1985, were $297.9 million. Total liabilities were $36.3 million, leaving a fund balance of $261.6 million.

Taxes

The Colonial Williamsburg Foundation, as a nonprofit educational organization, is exempt (except for certain hotel and restaurant operations and merchandise sales) from the payment of federal income taxes in accordance with Section 501 (c)(3) of the Internal Revenue Code. The organization is classified as a publicly supported foundation, in accordance with Section 509 (a)(2) of the Code. Gifts and contributions made to the Foundation are tax-deductible.

The Foundation pays real estate taxes to the City of Williamsburg, to James City County, and to York County on all properties it owns with the exception of the major exhibition buildings, which, together with the public greens, are exempt from taxation under Virginia law. Exempt properties are, however, subject to a service charge imposed by the City of Williamsburg, which amounted to $15,992 in 1985.

Taxes of $626,056 paid to the City of Williamsburg during the year totaled 20 percent of all real estate and personal property taxes collected in the city in 1985. Taxes paid to the adjoining counties of James City and York on properties of the Foundation were $72,996 for the year.

Audits

The books and records of the Foundation are audited annually. For 1985, the audit was performed by the independent public accounting firm of Cooper & Lybrand.

Financial Support of Operations, Colonial Williamsburg Foundation, 1985 Annual Report, p. 11.

both of these terms in later chapters.) They give the organizations an internal financial foundation and the internal ability to further their mission.

Notice also the role of endowments and their use not only to help in the operations of the organization but in its capital planning, for example, in the

Gifts, Grants, and Pledges

Gifts and grants to Colonial Williamsburg in 1985 totaled $8.9 million. In addition, $6.9 million in new pledges were recorded, bringing to $63.7 million the amount raised in gifts and pledges since the funds development program began in 1976.

The Colonial Williamsburg Fund, representing annual unrestricted gifts, exceeded $2.5 million from more than 29,000 donors. This was an increase of 21 percent in dollars and 25 percent in donors over 1984, and was the ninth consecutive annual increase for the Fund.

The Raleigh Tavern Society increased its membership to 139 in 1985. Members of the Society, who contribute $5,000 or more annually, contributed $545,000 in unrestricted gifts and another $436,000 in restricted gifts and tangible objects. "Keepers of the Key," a Raleigh Tavern membership category introduced in 1984, now has 19 participants who each give $10,000 or more annually to the Colonial Williamsburg Fund.

Major gifts and pledges were received from the DeWitt Wallace Fund for Colonial Williamsburg, a private foundation; Mr. and Mrs. Joseph Hennage; the National Endowment for the Arts; the J. Howard Pew Freedom Trust; and the Institute of Museum Services.

Fund-raising efforts are now under way to build an addition and to add to the endowment of the Abby Aldrich Rockefeller Folk Art Center (AARFAC). The total AARFAC campaign seeks to raise $9 million; $5 million for the expansion and $4 million for additional endowment. In September 1985, Colonial Williamsburg was notified of a prestigious $250,000 National Endow-

ment for the Arts Challenge Grant. Terms of the challenge grant require a 3:1 match for gifts to endowment. This commitment, combined with other gifts, puts the total raised for the AARFAC expansion at $1 million.

Endowed Funds

The Colonial Williamsburg Foundation encourages the establishment of named endowment funds. Funds may be created to support many different programs of the Foundation or may be established for unrestricted use. The funds appear permanently on the books of Colonial Williamsburg in recognition of their ongoing support of the work of the Foundation. Named endowment funds may be established for a gift of $100,000 or more and, once established, additions may be made at any time. Currently, the following funds support Colonial Williamsburg:

- Elizabeth R. and Miodrag R. Blagojevich Fund
- Mildred and J. B. Hickman Conservation Endowment Fund
- IBM Educational Endowment Fund
- William R. Kenan, Jr., Educational Endowment Fund
- Andrew W. Mellon Endowed Conservation Fund
- Carlisle H. Humelsine Endowed Chair for Curator of Collections
- Abby Aldrich Rockefeller Folk Art Fund
- Winthrop Rockefeller Endowment Fund for Carter's Grove Plantation

Gifts, Grants, Pledges, Colonial Williamsburg Foundation, 1985 Annual Report, p. 15.

construction of the Aldrich Rockefeller Folk Art Center. In this book we shall discuss the role of endowments, capital planning, and gifts.

The report also makes reference to the fact that the books of the Foundation have been audited. Audits are important for a variety of reasons, including the fact that they give confidence to the board of directors and to potential donors that the financial accounting of the organization is in keeping with acceptable accounting procedures. This book will discuss audits, their purposes, and characteristics.

Toward Diversification of Support

This book concerns itself with, in part, the diversification of financial support structures. The following statements by the YMCA illustrate this diversification and how critical it is to their fulfilling an enormous charitable mission.

A YMCA's programs are supported by fees that are affordable to people of all incomes in the community served. Those unable to pay full fees are subsidized by contributions—generally from individuals, corporations, and United Ways—as well as by revenues from programs that earn income. Such support also allows YMCAs to reach outside their buildings into the neighborhoods with innovative programs and services for those who need them.

With programs that meet community needs and effective management, the YMCA now serves 2 million more participants annually than it did five years ago. In 1985 we served 13 million people of all ages, abilities, and incomes. About half were female and half were under 18.

YMCA of the USA © National Council of Young Men's Christian Associations of the United States of America, 1986, p. 2.

Patterns of Y income vary from place to place. But taken as a whole, the sources of Y income are the fees people pay to take part in Y programs (33.3 percent); memberships fees (28.4 percent); United Way allocations to local Ys (10.3 percent); other charitable contributions, endowments, and bequests (5.6 percent); government grants (5.3 percent); return on investments (2.5 percent); and miscellaneous, including fees from room rentals at 251 Y residences (14.6 percent). Not all Ys receive United Way monies and not all receive government grants.

The YMCA national office is funded by dues from local Ys that range from 1 to 2 percent of a local Y's gross income. Local YMCAs raise and spend over $735 million yearly and have assets (including 1,858 buildings) that are worth $1.78 billion.

Discovering The YMCA National Council of Young Men's Christian Associations of the United States of America, 1984, p. 28.

The mix of support sources used by an organization depends upon a number of factors. Some organizations have a poor clientele and, even though they may be able to charge for some of their goods and services, these sales are likely to produce insufficient revenues. Other organizations have the kind of clientele—including members—who can afford to pay dues and fees for a wide variety of services provided by the organization. What is certain is that even the most charitable of charities needs the capacity to draw from more than one source of dollars to support its mission.

SUMMARY AND CONCLUSIONS

This chapter describes the role of the financial management function in a nonprofit organization and compares it with similar functions in the for-profit and government sectors. There are dissimilarities which are so important that to equate a nonprofit organization with a government agency, as is frequently done, leads to incorrect conclusions about what a nonprofit may or may not do in attempting to finance its mission and to conduct its financial function in a manner that is best for the organization.

There are several similarities between the financial function of the nonprofit and the for-profit firm. From a financial function point of view, both are concerned with money. As we shall see in this book, those nonprofits that appreciate the real differences and similarities between the nonprofit organization and the for-profit firm can exploit these in ways that significantly improve the financial well-being of their organizations without sacrificing the conducting of the organization's mission.

The conducting of the financial function of a business, as is the conducting of a nonprofit organization, is closely tied to tax laws. This chapter reviews the major tax reform proposals that have been considered and shows how each may affect nonprofit organizations.

NOTES

1. Lester Salamon and Alan Abramson, *The Federal Budget and the Nonprofit Sector* (Washington, D.C.: The Urban Institute, 1982).
2. See "The Declining Birth Rate of Foundations," *Research Reports Program on Nonprofit Organizations,* Institution for Social and Policy Studies. No. 5, Fall 1985, Yale University, p. 6.
3. Chapter 3 will show that foundations account for 5 to 8 percent of all contributions to nonprofits.
4. Chapter 2 will show the growth rate of nonprofits to be 3 to 5 percent per year.
5. Philip Kotler, *Marketing for Nonprofit Organizations,* 2nd ed. (Englewood Cliffs, New Jersey: Prentice-Hall, Inc., 1982), p. 6.
6. Philip Kotler, *Marketing Management,* 5th ed. (Englewood Cliffs, New Jersey: Prentice-Hall, Inc., 1984), p. 25.

7. As shown in Table 2.1, there are some nonprofits that are created by law, but these are very few.
8. We discuss the mathematical balance in Chapter 5.
9. Theoretically, there are limits on some for-profit firms that restrict their entry into certain industries.
10. Office of Personnel Management, *Solicitation of Federal Civilian and Uniformed Services Personnel for Contributions to Private Voluntary Organizations;* Final Rule, Federal Register 5 CFR Part 950 Friday April 4, 1986.

SUGGESTED READINGS

American Management Association, *The Financial Manager's Job* (New York: AMACOM, 1964).

"Commission on Stewardship," "Office of Finance and Services" and "Office of Personnel" in *Triennial Report. National Council of the Churches of Christ in the U.S.A., 1982–84* (New York, 1984).

ENGSTROM, JOHN H. and W. TIMOTHY O'KEEFE, "Staffing the Financial Function" in Tracy D. Connors and Christopher T. Callaghan, eds., *Financial Management for Nonprofit Organizations* (New York: American Management Association, AMACOM, 1982).

WORTMAN, JR., MAX S., "Strategic Management: Not-for-Profit Organizations," in Schendel, Dan E. and Charles W. Hofer, *Strategic Management: A New View of Business Policy and Planning* (Boston: Little, Brown and Company, 1979), pp. 353–373.

TWO

Legal Limits on the
Financial Activities
of Nonprofits

The nonprofit may be defined as an organization created under state law which does not have the conducting of a substantial commercial activity or the making of a profit as a principal purpose or mission. The largest group of nonprofits, those commonly called charities, are best defined as economic organizations with community or public welfare as their purpose or mission.

The purpose of the next two chapters is to elaborate on these two definitions. An understanding of these definitions will permit a more aggressive and imaginative program for financing nonprofits.

SCOPE OF FINANCIAL ACTIVITIES PERMITTED
BY STATE STATUTES

All nonprofits except those created by the United States Congress or a foreign government are legal creatures of a state. They are formed and organized according to state laws and must operate within the laws of the states in which they function (see insert, p. 29). The state in which the nonprofit is formed or organized confers certain legal purposes, powers and obligations on the organization and its officers. In this sense, nonprofits are no different from business firms. As creatures of the state, both may take the corporate form, and when they do, they are called corporations.[1]

All business corporations have the following characteristics: (1) Their principal purpose is to conduct a commercial activity and make a profit; (2) they have centralized management, meaning that management activities are carried out by only a few designated persons rather than having all associated persons

---

DEPARTMENTAL RESPONSIBILITIES

Primary Areas

As established by the State Constitution, the office of Commissioner of Charities and Corrections is charged with the responsibility of inspecting conditions and management of all state penal, correctional, and charitable institutions at least once a year. The further duty of inspecting all county and city jails on a regular basis has also been assigned to the Commissioner.

Collateral Duties

Charitable Organizations, professional fund raisers, and professional solicitors are required to register with the Commissioner of Charities and Corrections by the Oklahoma Solicitation of Charitable Contributions Act, 1959.

This act charges the Commissioner with the responsibility of registering any benevolent, philanthropic, patriotic, eleemosynary, educational, social, civic, recreational, religious, or any other individual group performing acts beneficial to the public.

The Commissioner is further charged with the responsibility of the collection of the annual fees required of these organizations and individuals. Registration information required of each organization is also maintained by the Commissioner and is available as a matter of public record. Each registrant must also file with the Commissioner each year a report of the activities regarding contributions and their solicitation that have occurred during the past year.

Special Investigations

The Commissioner of Charities and Corrections stands ready to undertake a special investigation regarding any documented complaint concerning care or treatment of patients or inmates in the institutions under his investigative jurisdiction.

Charities and Corrections, Annual Report, Fiscal Year 1972–1973
(Oklahoma City: Charities and Corrections, 1973), p. 7

participate in management decisions; (3) they have continuous life, meaning that the organization does not end due to the death of one of its principals; (4) ownership is easily transferrable so that one owner can easily transfer or sell his or her ownership interest to another person; and (5) there is limited liability, meaning that the organization is a separate legal entity and the personal assets of the owners and managers cannot be claimed if the organization is in trouble.

In no state does the single word "corporation" distinguish a business organization from a nonprofit. The key differences between the profit and the nonprofit organization are that the nonprofit may do business but cannot have profit-making as its major aim and cannot have a substantial part of its energies devoted to a commercial activity. Because there are no owners, stocks or stockholders of a nonprofit corporation, there can be no transfer of owner-ship. For this reason, nonprofits are called nonstock corporations. There are no individual owners of a nonprofit corporation.

A nonprofit or a business corporation is said to be domestic in the state in which it is incorporated. Nonprofit "X" is a domestic corporation in the state of Maryland if it is incorporated in that state. A nonprofit is called a foreign corporation when reference is being made to a state in which it is operating but is not incorporated. Nonprofit "X" is foreign to the state of Maryland if it operates in that state but is incorporated in another. A nonprofit is called alien if it is incorporated abroad. Nonprofit "X" is alien if it is incorporated in Canada but operates in Maryland. A nonprofit does not have to be incor-porated in each state. It is incorporated in only one but may need permission from each state in which it wishes to operate.

Both business and nonprofit corporations are governed by the corporate laws of each state. The charter must conform with the charter requirements of the state in which the corporation is formed and the organization must operate in conformity with the laws of each state in which it is located. Often a group of incorporators (those who form the nonprofit corporation) would purposely incorporate in one state in order to take advantage of some aspect of the law in that state, but operate in another because of a local or some other advan-tage. Businesses do the same. Many are incorporated in the state of Delaware but operate elsewhere. Many professional and other associations operate and have their headquarters in Washington D.C. to be close to the center of political and governmental power but are incorporated elsewhere.

The Corporate Charter and Bylaws

The document that describes the purpose, obligations and character of the corporation is called the charter. The bylaws govern the procedures of the organization. The state awards a certificate of incorporation to a new nonprofit once the state requirements for incorporation are met.

States differ in what they require a nonprofit to include in its charter and bylaws. The state of Maryland, a reasonably typical state, requires that the charter or bylaws of the nonprofit organization include the following:

1. A provision prohibiting the issuing of capital stock

2. A provision that no director's term may be shorter than the period be-tween annual meetings unless such directors are members and the condition of membership is shorter than the period between annual meetings

3. Provisions that describe the rights, duties, privileges and qualifications of members

4. Provisions that describe the manner of giving notices of meetings

5. Provisions that describe what consitutes a quorum

6. Provisions that deny or limit the rights of members to vote by proxy

7. Provisions that provide for voting by proxy

8. Provisions that provide that any action may be taken by some specified number or proportion of all members entitled to vote

These are merely some of the common provisions. There may be additional ones including the provision that a nonprofit corporation is subject to the same rules of a regular corporation unless specifically stated otherwise. Note that these specifications are important because they affect how the organization makes decisions—including financial decisions. The latter decisions often must be made by the board of directors or the membership. The charter or bylaws must state how these issues must be voted upon. Even the requirements of announcing meetings can be crucial. For example, the Maryland Section 5.206 provides that when a meeting is called and a quorum is absent, a new meeting may be called. As long as the meeting has been duly announced in the newspapers of the county where the organization has its principal office stating that decisions other than the ones that were originally being contemplated can be considered, then the persons constituting the new meeting (without regard to their numbers) may form a quorum and may make decisions in addition to those which were originally being considered.

Powers and Purposes of the Nonprofit Corporation

In their creative capacity, states specify the purpose for which a nonprofit must be intended if it is to acquire a nonprofit status in that state. In Washington, D.C., a popular location for both the chartering and location of nonprofits, the Section 29.504 provides that "Corporations may be organized. . .for any lawful purpose or purposes including but not limited to, one or more of the following purposes: benevolent; charitable; religious; missionary; educational; scientific; research; literary; musical; social; athletic; patriotic; political; civic; professional, commercial, industrial, business, or trade association; mutual improvement. . ." This broad scope is not unusual. Notice that the intent is not one of being created principally for making a profit. Yet, any of these activities can generate revenues. As we shall see later, once the intent is satisfied, it is the relative amount of revenues that comes from the sale of the goods or services and how they are used that matters—rather than the absence of such sales, revenues or profits or their magnitude.

States may also empower nonprofit corporations. The District of Columbia, Section 29.505, lists the following among the powers of nonprofits:

1. To sue and be sued

2. To purchase, take, receive, lease, take by gift, devise or bequest, or otherwise acquire, own, hold, improve, use, and otherwise deal in and with, real or personal property, or any interest therein, wherever situated

3. To sell, convey, mortgage, pledge, lease, exchange, transfer, and otherwise dispose of all or any part of its property and assets

4. To purchase, take, receive, subscribe for, or otherwise acquire, own, hold, vote, use, employ, sell, mortgage, loan, pledge, or otherwise dispose of, and otherwise use and deal in and with, shares or other interests in, or obligations of, other domestic or foreign corporations, whether for profit or not for profit, associations, partnerships, or individuals, or direct or indirect obligations of the United States, or of any other government, state, territory, governmental district, or municipality or of any instrumentality thereof

5. To make contracts and incur liabilities, borrow money at such rates of interest as the corporation may determine, issue its notes, bonds, and other obligations, and secure any of its obligations by mortgage or pledge of all or any of its property, franchises and income

6. To lend money for its corporate purposes, invest and reinvest its funds, and take and hold real and personal property as security for the payment of funds so loaned or invested

7. To conduct its affairs, carry on its operations, hold property, and have offices and exercise the powers granted by this chapter in any part of the world

8. To elect and appoint officers and agents of the corporation, and define their duties and fix their compensation

9. To make and alter bylaws not inconsistent with its articles of incorporation or with the laws of the District of Columbia, for the administration and regulation of the affairs of the corporation

10. Unless otherwise provided in the articles of incorporation, to make donations for the public welfare or for religious, charitable, scientific research, or educational purposes, or for other purposes for which the corporation is organized

11. To indemnify any director or officer or former director or officer of the corporation, or any person who may have served at its request as a director or officer of another corporation, whether for profit or not for profit, against expenses actually and necessarily incurred by him or her in connection with the defense of any action, suit, or proceeding in which he or she is made a party by reason of being or having been such director or officer, except in relation to matters as to which he or she shall be adjudged in such action, suit, or proceeding to be liable for negligence or misconduct in the performance of a duty.

Note that these powers give the nonprofit a wide range of financing authority including the making of loans, issuing of bonds and selling of goods and services, tangible and intangible. It only prohibits the sales of stocks and engagement in trade that is ordinarily illegal, such as the sale of marijuana. Thus, in the District of Columbia as in other jurisdictions, the major limits to financing by nonprofits is economic and financial imagination. The District of Columbia also uses its powers to issue bonds to raise funds to finance the capital project of some nonprofits. Note also that the general powers include indemnification. Trustees and managers may be held personally liable for the misconduct of their nonprofits.

A Plan of Dissolution

Because nonprofits are legal institutions, states also require that charters contain a plan of dissolution. This plan states the order in which claims against the assets of the nonprofit must be satisfied if the nonprofit is terminating. In the state of Maryland, a dissolution plan must provide that:

1. The assets must first be used to meet the outstanding liabilities of the organization; i.e., pay off its creditors.

2. The remaining assets must be distributed as is required by the contractual arrangements. For example, some assets are donated with the expressed agreement that the organization will, if necessary, dispose of them in a certain way such as to offer them to a specific other group.

3. The remaining assets not affected by the two previous conditions may be transferred to other charitable organizations (whether domestic or foreign as these terms have been defined earlier) which are connected to the dissolving organization or that have a similar purpose for being.

4. Other assets may be distributed to members as provided for by law.

5. The remainder, if any, may be transferred to other persons as provided in the bylaws.

The plan of dissolution is critical not only because it is required by the state and provides for an orderly and agreed upon manner of disposing of the assets of the organization, but because the federal government requires a specific plan before it confers tax-exempt status on the organization. The federal requirement must be met even if it conflicts with what individual states may allow. Unlike states, the federal government prohibits the transfer of assets to individuals if the organization is specifically seeking a 501(c)(3) status. In addition to giving the organization exemption from paying federal income taxes, this status permits donors to deduct gifts and contributions. Hence, Items 4 and 5 of the preceding list may be allowed by the state but may have to be disavowed or modified in trying to obtain a 501(c)(3) status.

Another item that the states may require in the charter relates to disposing of property through mergers. Generally, like for-profit firms, nonprofits may merge. Nonprofits may only merge, however, with other nonprofits.

Dissolution and merger are ways of dealing with financial difficulties. Liquidation, the selling of assets due to the termination of the organization as through bankruptcy, is also a way of dealing with financial difficulties. However, opportunities for asset acquisition by other nonprofits are provided because the law stipulates that upon dissolution of a nonprofit, the assets must be transferred to a similar nonprofit.

Unlike the creditors of business firms, creditors of nonprofits cannot initiate an act of involuntary bankruptcy against the nonprofit.[2] That is to say, if a business cannot pay its bills, it creditors may petition the courts to declare that the business is bankrupt. This cannot be done with a nonprofit. There is no involuntary bankruptcy; thus, the museum referred to in Chapter 1 cannot be declared by its creditors to be bankrupt. It must do so itself and then follow the rules of dissolution in determining how to distribute its assets. One possibility is to merge with another museum. A merger is a form of financing.

To summarize this section, the reader should recall that the nonprofit organization is a creation of the state and that in the exercise of its creative powers, the state imposes requirements for incorporation. Some typical requirements relate to the way the nonproft will conduct itself as an organization, how its assets may be disposed of, the kinds of powers that the organization may exercise, and its purpose for being.

SCOPE OF ACTIVITIES PERMITTED BY FEDERAL LAW

Nonprofit is a status conferred by each state according to its laws. The status refers to a corporation or trust that exists to perform one or more of the functions such as those enumerated in the District of Columbia's law referred to previously and without the intent of operating primarily for making a profit. The organization must also commit itself not to distribute its earnings to individuals as if they were owners, for there are no individual owners.

While states may designate those organizations that would be exempt from the state income tax, states may not give exemption from the federal income tax. If there is a dispute between the IRS and the organization, only the IRS or the courts may award federal tax-exempt status. As a rule, states honor the federal decision whether it is made by the IRS or by a court decision which the IRS follows. Thus, the key exemption comes from the IRS.

On one level, tax exemption means freedom from paying federal (and state) income taxes unless the income of the nonprofit falls into one of the categories to be described in later chapters. On a second level, tax exemption means that not only is the organization exempt from federal and state income taxes, but that contributions to it are deductible by the donor in calculating his or her federal and state income tax liabilities. Without this second benefit, many individuals would not have the incentive to give to certain organizations and these organizations would not then be able to finance their activities.

In order to be exempt from federal and state taxation, an organization must first be a legally created nonprofit. That is, it must meet the charter and bylaw requirements for nonprofits in the state in which it is created and must show the IRS evidence that it was created according to state law and was granted a nonprofit charter (in the case of a corporation) or a deed (in the case of a trust) by the state in which it is a domestic corporation. The IRS refers to the charter or deed as the organizing document.

To be exempt on both these levels, exemption from paying income tax and deductibility of gifts and contributions requires that the principal mission of the organization be one defined in Section 501(c)(3) of the Internal Revenue Code. This is called the organizational test. This section of the code identifies charitable, religious, educational, scientific, literary, testing for public safety, fostering national or international amateur sports competition (except the provision of athletic facilities or equipment), or the prevention of cruelty to children or animals as eligible missions.

The organizational test is not passed by merely asserting in the organization's application to the IRS that it is a religious, educational, charitable or some other title identified in Section 501(c)(3). The organization must demonstrate that the specific characteristics of its mission are consistent with the description used by the IRS. If a nonprofit applies for tax-exempt status by asserting that it is an educational institution, it should have the characteristics and mission of educational institutions as described under Section 501(c)(3). If it is a charitable organization, it should have the characteristics of charitable organizations as described by the *Code* and so on. These descriptions are set by the U.S. Congress and subject to the interpretation and enforcement of the IRS.

> The Senate, in the name of blocking government subsidies for witchcraft, has approved legislation giving the Internal Revenue Service unprecedented power to question the religious beliefs of groups claiming tax exemption as a church.
>
> With no debate, the Senate last week attached to an appropriations bill a provision denying a tax exemption to any group that promotes witchcraft or worship of the devil.

Jim Luther, "Senate Acts to Bar Tax Breaks for Witchcraft." Reprinted with permission of the Associated Press.

Because all of these functions could easily be conducted with a motive of making money for the organizers or the managers of the nonprofit organization, the IRS requires that the motive for conducting the mission not be one of advancing the private welfare of individuals. The motive must be charitable which means that the motive cannot be to make a profit or to benefit individuals as owners or managers. The beneficiaries must be the community or the public. (We shall return to this theme over and over again in this book.) Its understanding is central to how nonprofits can be financed. Unfortunately, it is an often misunderstood concept. For the time being, it is sufficient to know that the exclusive motive of the nonprofit has to be one of advancing community or public welfare; that is, it has to be charitable.

In order to be tax exempt on both levels, it is also necessary for the nonprofit to pass what is known as the asset test. To pass, the organizing document must prohibit the nonprofit from distributing any of its assets or income to individuals as owners or as managers except for fair compensation for services rendered. Further, the nonprofit may not be used for the personal benefits of the founders, supporters, managers, their relatives or personal or business associates. Moreover, the organizing document needs a dissolution plan similar to the one required by the state. However, the IRS insists that to satisfy its requirements, the plan should unequivocally prohibit the transfer of assets upon the termination of the organization to any person or entity that is not a tax-exempt nonprofit in the same sense as is the terminating nonprofit. The only exception to this rule is that the assets may be transferred to the state.

The long and the short of the matter is that the [Kneadmore Life Community Church] KLCC was operated for several purposes. We do not doubt that one purpose for which the KLCC was operated was to permit members to explore various religions so that each individual could find God in his own way.

However, other substantial purposes for which the KLCC was operated include to permit experimentation with lifestyles different from the ones community members grew up with, to permit like-minded individuals to live together at little or no cost, and to permit members to grow and eat organic food. While eating organic food may have acquired some religious significance along the way, it is clear that, on the whole, the KLCC was operated, to more than an insubstantial degree, for nonexempt purposes and that it afforded its members benefits which violated the "private inurement" test.

Canada v. Commissioner, 82 T.C. No. 73, June 1984.

Finally, to qualify under Section 501(c)(3), the nonprofit must pass a political test. The organizing document must forbid the nonprofit from participating in any political campaign on behalf of a candidate. Participation is meant to include the preparation and distribution of literature. This test does not prohibit voter education, but because such an activity can be broadly interpreted, it is wise to seek specific exemption from the IRS if a nonprofit is planning to be involved in political activities.

Once the 501(c)(3) status is awarded, the nonprofit is assigned a foundation status. It is either classified as a private foundation, a private operating foundation, or what is broadly referred to as a public charity. An essential difference between a public charity and the private foundation or private operating foundation is that it receives broad public support. Thus, we may say that a public charity is a nonprofit organization that is broadly supported (financially) by the public. Private foundations and private operating foundations are also nonprofits but they do not have to demonstrate the depth of public support required of public charities. In Chapter 6 we delve more into these distinctions.

Taxation of Nonprofits

It should be understood that being both nonprofit and tax exempt does not necessarily mean that an organization pays no taxes. It means simply that (1) the organization pays no taxes on gifts and contributions and income derived from conducting its mission, and (2) persons and corporations that make contributions to the organization may deduct it from their income taxes. Even though tax exempt at all levels, nonprofits must pay taxes on income derived from activities unrelated to their mission, on certain types of expenditures, and as penalties. These penalties may also be levied against the management of the nonprofit, including the board of directors. We discuss this in Chapter 6.

The Universe of Nonprofits

There are several types of tax-exempt nonprofit organizations. The most common way of classifying these organizations is according to the section of the *Internal Revenue Code* under which they fall. Each section describes a particular type of organization and is the basis of the type of tax exemption that the organization has.

Table 2.1 shows that there are 27 types of nonprofit, tax-exempt organizations according to the IRS classification scheme.[3] These range from churches to insurance companies, from fraternal societies to cemeteries, from labor unions to credit unions, from business leagues to civic leagues, and so on.

Table 2.1 also indicates that only six of these groups of organizations qualify to receive tax-deductible contributions. These include cemeteries, veterans' organizations, nonprofit corporations organized by Congress, fraternal and beneficiary associations, organizations of past and present members of the armed forces and that large group of 501(c)(3)s on which we focus. For these six groups, not only are contributions to them deductible by the donor, but the revenues of these organizations are also tax exempt. For the others, donors may not deduct contributions, but the income of the organization is tax exempt.

Of all 27 groups, only those that are defined under Section 501(c)(3) are commonly called organizations that aim at advancing public or community welfare. Most of the others tend to advance the welfare of more narrowly defined groups and are generally referred to as social welfare organizations, as differentiated from public or community welfare organizations.[4]

TABLE 2.1 The Universe of Nonprofits

Section of 1954 Code	Description of Organization	General Nature of Activities	Tax Deductible Contributions Allowable
501(c)(1)	Corporations Organized Under Act of Congress (including Federal Credit Unions)	Instrumentalities of the United States	Yes, if made for exclusively public purposes
501(c)(2)	Title Holding Corporation For Exempt Organization	Holding title to property of an exempt organization	No[1]
501(c)(3)	Religious, Educational, Charitable, Scientific, Literary, Testing for Public Safety, to Foster Certain National or International Amateur Sports Competition, or Prevention of Cruelty to Children or Animals Organizations	Activities of nature implied by description of class of organization	Generally, Yes[1]
501(c)(4)	Civic Leagues, Social Welfare Organizations, and Local Associations of Employees	Promotion of community welfare; Charitable, educational or recreational	Generally, No[1]
501(c)(5)	Labor, Agricultural, and Horticultural Organizations	Educational or instructive, the purpose being to improve conditions of work, and to improve products and efficiency	No[1]

Section	Description of organization	Description of activities	Deductibility of contributions
501(c)(6)	Business Leagues, Chambers of Commerce, Real Estate Boards, Etc.	Improvement of business conditions of one or more lines of business	No[1]
501(c)(7)	Social and Recreation Clubs	Pleasure, recreation, social activities	No[1]
501(c)(8)	Fraternal Beneficiary Societies and Associations	Lodge providing for payment of life, sickness, accident, or other benefits to members	Yes, if used for Sec. 501(c)(3) purposes
501(c)(9)	Voluntary Employees' Beneficiary Associations (Including Federal Employees' Voluntary Beneficiary Associations formerly covered by section 501(c)(10)	Providing for payment of life, sickness, accident or other benefits to members	No[1]
501(c)(10)	Domestic Fraternal Societies and Associations	Lodge devoting its net earnings to charitable, fraternal, and other specified purposes. No life, sickness, or accident benefits to members	Yes, if used for Sec. 501(c)(3) purposes
501(c)(11)	Teachers' Retirement Fund Associations	Teachers' association for payment of retirement benefits	No[1]
501(c)(12)	Benevolent Life Insurance Associations, Mutual Ditch or Irrigation Companies, Mutual or Cooperative Telephone Companies, Etc.	Activities of a mutually beneficial nature similar to those implied by the description of class of organization	No[1]

			Generally, Yes
501(c)(13)	Cemetery Companies	Burials and incidental activities	
501(c)(14)	State Chartered Credit Unions, Mutual Reserve Funds	Loans to members. Exemption as to building and loan associations and cooperative banks repealed by Revenue Act of 1951, affecting all years after 1951	No[1]
501(c)(15)	Mutual Insurance Companies or Associations	Providing insurance to members substantially at cost	No[1]
501(c)(16)	Cooperative Organizations to Finance Crop Operations	Financing crop operations in conjunction with activities of a marketing or purchasing association	No[1]
501(c)(17)	Supplemental Unemployment Benefit Trusts	Provides for payment of supplemental unemployment compensation benefits	No[1]
501(c)(18)	Employee Funded Pension Trust (created before June 25, 1959)	Payment of benefits under a pension plan funded by employees	No[1]
501(c)(19)	Post or Organization of War Veterans	Activities implied by nature of organization	Yes
501(c)(20)	Group Legal Services Plan Organizations	Legal services provided exclusively to employees	No

Section	Organization	Description	Deductible
501(c)(21)	Black Lung Benefit Trusts	Funded by coal mine operators to satisfy their liability for disability or death due to black lung diseases	No
501(c)(22)	Employer Liability Trusts	Established by plan sponsors	No
501(d)	Religious and Apostolic Associations	Regular business activities. Communal religious community	No[1]
501(e)	Cooperative Hospital Service Organizations	Performs cooperative services for hospitals	Yes
501(f)	Cooperative Service Organizations of Operating Educational Organizations	Performs collective investment services for educational organizations	Yes
521(a)	Farmers' Cooperative Associations	Cooperative marketing and purchasing for agricultural producers	No

[1] An organization exempt under a Subsection of Code Sec. 501 other than (c)(3), may establish a charitable fund, contributions to which are deductible. Such a fund must itself meet the requirements of section 501(c)(3) and the related notice requirements of section 508(a).

Source: Adapted from *Tax Exempt Status for Your Organization*, Publication 557 (Washington, D.C.: U.S. Government Printing Office, January 1982), p. 40.

TABLE 2.2 Number of Active Exempt Organizations

	1983	1984	1985
Section 501(c)			
(1) Corporations organized under act of Congress	24	24	24
(2) Titleholding corps.	5,567	5,679	5,758
(3) Religious, charitable, etc.	*335,757	*352,884	366,071
(4) Social welfare	129,209	130,344	131,250
(5) Labor, agriculture organizations	79,775	76,753	75,632
(6) Business leagues	51,714	53,303	54,217
(7) Social and recreation clubs	53,467	55,666	57,343
(8) Fraternal beneficiary societies	88,272	92,431	94,435
(9) Voluntary employees' beneficiary societies	9,303	10,145	10,668
(10) Domestic fraternal beneficiary societies	16,871	16,116	15,924
(11) Teachers' retirement funds	12	11	11
(12) Benevolent life insurance assns.	5,125	5,200	5,244
(13) Cemetary companies	6,412	6,845	7,239
(14) Credit unions	5,754	6,053	6,032
(15) Mutual insurance companies	1,017	998	967
(16) Corps. to finance crop operation	22	19	18
(17) Supplemental unemployment benefit trusts	771	747	726

(18)	Employee funded pension trusts	3	3	3
(19)	War veterans' organizations	22,130	22,100	23,062
(20)	Legal service organizations	116	140	167
(21)	Black lung trusts	12	14	15
501(d)	Religious and apostolic organizations	72	81	82
501(e)	Cooperative hospitals	90	90	82
501(f)	Coop. service orgs. of operating educational orgs.	0	0	0
521	Farmers' cooperatives	2,713	2,673	2,542
	Nonexempt charitable trusts	0	0	1,233
		31,248	32,905	27,913
	Total	$45,464	871,224	886,658

*All section 501(c)(3) organizations are not included because certain organizations, such as churches, integrated auxiliaries, subordinate units and conventions or associations of churches, need not apply for recognition of exemption unless they desire a ruling.

Source: Internal Revenue Service, Annual Report of Commissioner and Chief Consul (Washington, D.C.: U.S. Government Printing Office, 1984) p. 76 and 1985, p. 70.

Table 2.2 shows the number of each type of nonprofit tax-exempt organization that is in existence. In 1985, there were 886,658 nonprofit tax-exempt organizations that were included in the IRS files. The actual number of these organizations in existence well exceeds this figure because the only organizations that are included in this count are the ones which are required to file an application for tax-exempt status. The footnote to Table 2.2 states which organizations are not included in the figure. The actual number of tax-exempt nonprofits, including those omitted from the IRS count, may well exceed one million.

Table 2.2 also shows that the most numerous of the tax-exempt organizations are the ones falling under Section 501(c)(3) of the Code. These include the churches, schools, day-care centers, health facilities, research centers and most of the community and public welfare or service nonprofits groups and foundations, both large and small. Together they number in excess of 366,000 or roughly 42 percent of the total number of tax-exempt organizations in existence today. In actuality, there are countless more of these organizations in existence than the IRS is aware of because certain churches and auxiliaries of churches and associations do not have to apply or inform the IRS of their existence.

Table 2.3 shows the growth rate of these 501(c)(3) organizations over the past five years. With the exception of fiscal year 1982 when there was a decline, these organizations have grown in number at a healthy rate, thus intensifying the competition for financial support. In fact, they have accounted for the bulk of all of the growth in the nonprofit sector as a whole. Between 1983 and 1984 alone, they grew by about 20,000 from 335,757 to 352,884. Which was about one and two thirds times the growth of the entire nonprofit sector. At this pace, they will continue to be the largest type of tax-exempt organizations for the forseeable future.

TABLE 2.3   Annual Growth in the Number of 501(c)(3) Organizations and Total Number of Tax-Exempt Organizations, 1979–1985

| | 501(c)(3) | | All Tax Exempt | |
Year	Number	Growth (percent)	Number	Growth (percent)
1979	304315		824536	
1980	319942	5	846433	3
1981	327758	2	851012	1
1982	322826	− 1	841440	− 1
1983	335757	4	845464	.5
1984	352884	5	871224	3
1985	366071	4	886658	2

Source: Internal Revenue Service, Annual Report of Commissioner and Chief Consul (Washington, D.C.: U.S. Government Printing Office, various years). Calculation and compilations by author.

Community or Public Welfare Organizations

As stated earlier, the primary focus of this book is on the most numerous type of nonprofits, those under section 501(c)(3). These organizations exist to advance the public or community welfare by undertaking the following missions:

1. Religious
2. Education
3. Charitable
4. Scientific
5. Literary
6. Testing for public safety
7. Fostering certain national or international amateur sports competitions
8. Prevention of cruelty to children or animals

One condition that is common to all eight of these purposes is that an organization formed exclusively for one or more of these reasons is not considered tax exempt unless the intent is to serve a public purpose. Thus, in the words of the IRS:

> (ii) An organization is not organized or operated exclusively for one or more of the purposes specified in subdivision (i) of this subparagraph unless it serves a public rather than a private interest. Thus, to meet the requirement of this subdivision, it is necessary for an organization to establish that it is not organized or operated for the benefit of private interests such as designated individuals, the creator or his family, shareholders of the organization, or persons controlled, directly or indirectly, by such private interests.

> *Treasury Regulations, Section 1.501(c) (3)–1 (d)(1) (ii), 1980.*

The serving of a public purpose is equated to a community purpose. Thus, when the IRS writes of the conditions that would qualify an educational institution for tax exemption, it states:

> (3) *Educational defined*—(i) *In general.* The term "educational", as used in section 501(c)(3), relates to—
> (a) The instruction or training of the individual for the purpose of improving or developing his capabilities; or
> (b) The instruction of the public on subjects useful to the individual and beneficial to the community.

> *Treasury Regulations, Section 1.501(c) (3)–1 (d)(3)(i) 1980.*

And in *Church of the Chosen People* v. *U.S.,* a group teaching the single tenet that pairings between persons of the same sex (men with men and women with women) are acceptable in the eyes of God was denied exemption because the court held, among other reasons, that this group existed for the benefit of private individuals rather than for a public purpose.[5]

Several shorthand terms have been used in the literature to describe these organizations that fall under Section 501(c)(3). Sometimes they are referred to as nonprofit organizations because they must all be nonprofit. But as we saw earlier in the chapter, all nonprofits do not fall into these eight categories or under this section of the *Internal Revenue Code*. There is a universe of over 20 different types of nonprofits. Sometimes they are referred to as 501(c)(3) organizations, since this is the section of the *Internal Revenue Code* in which they are described. But merely knowing that a nonprofit is classified as a 501(c)(3) is insufficient to determine its foundation status and, therefore, its limits on financing, expenditures, investment, business relationship to its sponsors, managers and their relatives and associates and its corporate relationship to other nonprofits. We must know if the 501(c)(3) organization is a public charity, a private or private operating foundation. Each is subject to different financing rules, which we shall discuss.

Sometimes they are referred to as charitable oranizations; however, this is but one of the eight categories mentioned. Yet, the word "charitable" is often used by the courts or the IRS as the key word to describe these organizations. Basically what is meant by charity is that the nonprofit seeks to promote public or community welfare by providing a service that is not otherwise provided by the market and that the principal motive for providing the goods or services is not to make a profit. This concept is so central that we formally return to it in the next chapter.

Sometimes they are referred to as tax-exempt organizations because they are tax exempt on both levels described earlier. Other organizations are also tax exempt, but only in the sense that they do not pay income tax. A good example of this is a mutual fund. It is tax exempt not because it is charitable but because it distributes 95 percent of its earnings. Yet, contributions to them cannot be deducted. Like most of the other organizations in Table 2.1, they are tax exempt in a very different way and for a different purpose than the 501(c)(3) organizations.

Sometimes these 501(c)(3) organizations are referred to as public welfare or community welfare organizations, as opposed to social welfare organizations, to highlight that they all must exist to discharge a mission to improve community welfare rather than the welfare of a select group of individuals. This is their common and distinguishing feature.

In short, the distinguishing characteristic of this group is that although they are all nonprofits, they are tax exempt on both levels as described earlier and they undertake a mission or purpose that is to advance community or public welfare. Thus, we refer to them as nonprofits with a community or public mission. The single word that best describes community or public welfare is "charitable," even though the word is also used to describe a specific group of tax-exempt nonprofits.

SCOPE OF ACTIVITIES PERMITTED BY LOCAL LAWS

While state and federal laws are the basic laws affecting the formation and operation of nonprofits, local laws must also be obeyed. Local zoning laws and building codes affect the physical location of the nonprofit such as the design and location of its buildings and the physical safety of the building from fire. Local laws also affect solicitation and local governments may have special rules covering exemptions from property and sales taxes.

Local rules may supplement or be independent of state rules. For example, the City Council of New Orleans had to pass a special ordinance on solicitation even though the state has a law on solicitation. The reason is that the residents of the city were receiving telephone calls from a group selling light bulbs. The calls were made in such a way that the listener would associate them with a nonprofit group, the Lighthouse for the Blind. But the Lighthouse for the Blind does not sell bulbs. It sells brooms, mops, dust cloths and ironing board covers.[6]

SUMMARY AND CONCLUSIONS

In the next chapter we explore further the definition of charitable and what is meant by referring to these organizations as economic institutions with a community or public welfare mission or, alternatively, economic institutions with a charitable mission.

In this chapter we have established three points: (1) that nonprofits are legal institutions created in the image of state laws that define their responsibilities, purposes and powers, including the powers of financing; (2) that federal laws interpreted and enforced by the IRS and the courts determine the tax-exempt status of the nonprofit; and (3) that the common characteristics of the nonprofit organizations that are tax exempt so that the incomes they earn are not taxed and that the contributions to them are deductible by the donors is that these organizations exist to advance public or community welfare; that is, they are charitable.

In addition, we have reviewed state and federal laws related to the creation of nonprofits and the acquisition of tax-exempt status. States create nonprofits and define their powers including the powers that nonprofits have to finance themselves. State and federal laws also define how the assets and income of the organization may be distributed upon dissolution, bankruptcy, and merger of the organization. An unequivocal rule is that these assets and income may not be distributed to individuals as if they were owners. There are no individual owners of nonprofit corporations. This is consistent with the legal rule that the nonprofit, unlike the business firm, does not exist for the economic benefits of individuals; rather, they exist for advancing the welfare of the community or public.

In the next chapter we also explore two other aspects of the definitions of nonprofits with which this chapter opens. These other two aspects are the nonprofit as an economic institution, and the nonprofit not having profit making as a principal purpose and not conducting commercial activities as a substantial part of its mission. Again, understanding these notions is critical to aggressive and imaginative financing of nonprofits.

NOTES

1. See Section 303(a) of the United States Tax Code.
2. The corporate form of organization is not the only possibility. Nonprofits may also organize as trusts and for-profits may also organize as partnerships or sole proprietorships.
3. For a discussion of these various types of nonprofits, see Howard Godfrey, *Handbook on Tax-Exempt Organizations,* (Englewood Cliffs, New Jersey: Prentice-Hall Inc., 1983).
4. "IRS Denial of Charitable Status: A Social Welfare Organization Problem," *Michigan Law Review,* 82, no. 3 (December 1983), 508–36.
5. Church of the Chosen People v. U.S. U.S.D.C. Minn, Civil 4:81–311, 10/18/82, 82–2 U.S.T.C. Section 9646.
6. Lynn Cunningham, "Charity Law May Put End to False Calls" The Times Picayune, Tuesday, August 21, 1984. P. E1.

SUGGESTED READINGS

GODFREY, HOWARD, *Handbook on Tax-Exempt Organizations,* (Englewood Cliffs, New Jersey: Prentice-Hall, Inc. 1983).

Internal Revenue Service, Department of Treasury, *Tax Exempt Status for Your Organization,* Publication 557, Revised, February 1984 (Washington, D.C.: U.S. Government Printing Office, 1984).

_____*Tax Information for Private Foundations and Foundation Managers,* Publication 578, Revised October 1981, (Washington, D.C.: U.S. Government Printing Office, 1981).

THREE

Financing Opportunities for the Nonprofit Managed As An Economic Institution

In the previous chapter, we defined the nonprofit as a legal organization that does not conduct a substantial commercial activity and that has, as its principal purpose, an objective other than making profits. We noted that the single largest group of nonprofits are those that have community or public welfare as their mission. In this chapter we explore other aspects of these definitions and see that the definition does not prohibit nonprofits from making a profit or from engaging in commercial enterprises. Indeed, the profits may be quite large. "Charity" defines the mission, "economic" the organization.

THE NONPROFIT AS AN ECONOMIC INSTITUTION

Perhaps the most fundamental change in perspective that is needed to improve the financial management of nonprofits is to view them as economic institutions with charitable missions improving the public or community welfare, rather than as charitable institutions with charitable missions. This view broadens the scope in which the organization may profitably function.

As an economic institution, a nonprofit operates within the broader market system and aims at earning revenues to the extent that market conditions, the nonprofit's mission, and the law allow. Nonprofits are legal entities with financial powers and limitations defined by law. Violation of the legal limits can lead to the loss of the tax-exempt status of the organization and to severe penalties on the management including the board of directors.

Why Nonprofits Are Economic Institutions

Nonprofits are economic institutions because nonprofits are productive units as defined in economics. Such units acquire inputs of land, labor and capital and transform them through a productive process into goods and services that have value to society. In the case of a business firm, these values are measured in terms of the market price for which the goods and services are sold. In the case of nonprofits, the value is imputed, a term used by economists to mean approximated. Imputation is required because all of the goods and services produced by nonprofits are not sold for a price that truly reflects the value of the good or service to society. Many nonprofits charge no price or charge one that is well below the true market price of the good or service they produce. For others, their output is priceless.

Economists take the view of nonprofits as productive units so seriously that they annually impute the value of goods and services produced by nonprofits and include the imputations in their calculations of the gross national product of the country. The gross national product is the sum of goods and services produced by the economy of the country in any given year. It is the most comprehensive indicator of economic production and of the wealth of the nation. Thus, the value of the productive contribution of nonprofits to the gross national product (GNP) of the country is annually imputed.

Notice that what is central in the definition of the economic institution is the transformation of inputs into goods and services that have value. A school takes the input of teachers (labor) and capital (buildings and books) and land (the playground) and transforms these into something called an educated student who is valuable to society. Whether or not a price is charged for the good or service produced by the school is not what matters in the definition. The price serves to measure the value of the output of the institution rather than to determine if the institution is an economic entity. What makes the institution an economic entity is that it uses society's scarce resources (land, labor and capital) to produce a product or service of value.

The Purpose for Producing the Good or Service
Must Be to Improve Community or Public Welfare

As an economic institution, the nonprofit's purpose for producing the good or service must be to improve public or community welfare; to be motivated by community welfare rather than by private profits. Thus, it is commonly held that nonprofits cannot make profits because they are supposed to be charitable. What does charitable mean? The courts have historically maintained a loose definition of the term. This has been done to accommodate the fact that over time, the charitable needs of society change; that is, new needs are recognized.[1] In practice, the IRS and the courts use the following criteria to determine if a motive is charitable:[2]

> (2) *Charitable defined.* The term "charitable" is used in section 501(c)(3) in its generally accepted legal sense and is, therefore, not to be construed as limited by the separate enumeration in section 501(c)(3) of other tax-exempt purposes which may fall within the broad outlines of "charity" as developed by judicial decisions. Such term includes: Relief of the poor and distressed or of the underprivileged; advancement of religion; advancement of education or science; erection or maintenance of public buildings, monuments, or works; lessening of the burdens of Government; and promotion of social welfare by organizations designed to accomplish any of the above purposes, or (i) to lessen neighborhood tensions; (ii) to eliminate prejudice and discrimination; (iii) to defend human and civil rights secured by law; or (iv) to combat community deterioration and juvenile delinquency.

Treasury Regulations Section 1.501(c)(3)-1 (d)(1)(2), 1980.

1. The motive of the organization must be to meet a recognized need of the community or some segment thereof in a manner and level that are significantly different to what a for-profit firm would do.

2. The means used to meet the charitable purpose must be integrally related to satisfying the needs that have been identified as charitable.

3. There must be a clear manifestation of providing the service without seeking personal advantages for the providers or for the providing organization.

4. The charitable purpose must be consistent with public policy.

Using these principles, the IRS and the courts have awarded charitable status to nonprofits that specialize in otherwise commercial activities. The IRS has granted charitable status to an organization specializing in the making of loans to minority businesses that are located in distressed areas and that are unable to get loans from regular commercial sources.[3] Similarly, charitable status was awarded to an organization located in a rural area that made development loans to businesses unable to get loans from normal commercial sources and that were located in distressed parts of rural communities.[4]

And, although manufacturing is a for-profit activity, the IRS awarded charitable status to a job-training organization that also ran a toy manufacturing business. The organization hired, trained, gave job counseling and placed unskilled workers.[5]

In addition, although barber and beauty shops are traditionally for-profit businesses, a beauty and barber shop was given charitable status even though it operated for a profit. The IRS concluded that the shop operated at the convenience of elderly citizens and serving these citizens was a charitable mission.[6]

In the same vein, a medical and dental referral service was designated a charity even though it charges a price and makes a profit. The court held, among other things, that both the profits and salaries were kept reasonably low and that the purpose of the referral system was to improve medical service to the community and not to benefit the medical practitioners. Their benefits were incidental to those of the community.[7]

From these examples it should be clear that a nonprofit is an economic institution with a charitable mission, even if it charges a price and makes a profit. Unfortunately, even when described by their most ardent supporters, nonprofits are too often viewed as purely charitable organizations. A pure charity is defined as an organization that functions to meet benevolent objectives and does not sell its goods or services.[8] Importantly, the law does not restrict nonprofits to operating in this purely charitable mode. To view nonprofits in this purely charitable mode is to limit their money-making potential to seeking gifts and contributions.

What distinguishes nonprofits from other economic institutions is not that all nonprofits are pure charities. The fact is that most nonprofits, including churches, could not meet a stringent application of this test of not selling any good or service. Raffles, bargain sales, tuitions, and contributions related to the receipt of a specific good or service by the contributor are sales. It is not the inability to sell the good or service that is the distinguishing feature.

The distinguishing feature is that the organization must not have been *created* with the motive of selling its goods and services at a gain; in that case, it would merely be a for-profit firm. The word "created" is emphasized because the exclusive motive for creating and operating the nonprofit must be for community welfare or charity as measured by the four criteria previously stated. However, the nonprofit does not have to be a pure charity.

This point is well illustrated in a series of court cases. Thus, in *Fraternal Medical Specialist Services, Inc.* v. *Commissioner,*[9] the court stated:

In determining whether petitioner is operated exclusively for exempt purposes, or whether instead, petitioner is operated in furtherance of a substantial commercial purpose our inquiry must focus upon the purpose or purposes furthered by petitioner's activities, and not on the activities themselves. The fact that an organization's activities may even constitute a trade or business does not, of itself, disqualify it from classification under section 501(c)(3). . .The determination of whether petitioner is operated for a substantial commercial purpose is primarily a question of fact. . .Factors such as the particular manner in which the organization's activities are conducted, the commercial hue of those activities, and the existence and amount of annual or accumulated profits are relevant evidence of a proscribed commercial purpose.

Similarly, the Supreme Court has held that having a trade or business does not disqualify the organization from tax exemption.[10] On the other hand, the existence of a single nonexempt (commercial activity) that is a substantial part of the purpose for the existence of the organization would destroy its qualification as tax exempt regardless of how many tax-exempt purposes it has.[11] In short, the trade or business cannot be a substantial reason for the creation of the organization.

To illustrate, the training or educating of people is a recognized tax-exempt purpose—one that is beneficial to public welfare. But the training of dogs is not a recognized public purpose (although as we see in the next chapter, the neutering of dogs is). Thus, in a well-known case, the courts ruled:

> By contrast, petitioner has not shown that actually training a dog is necessary for teaching an individual how to train a dog. While it is clear that an infant needs custodial care when he or she is learning, it is not plain that an individual cannot be taught to train animals without the animal being present for the entire class time. Essentially, unlike in *San Francisco Infant School,* there are no facts in the administrative record regarding petitioner's curriculum, theories, or methods. While we know that the dogs receive degrees and awards, we do not know whether or how the individual's skills are evaluated.
>
> We find, therefore, that since the training of dogs is a substantial, if not the primary, purpose of petitioner, petitioner is not operated exclusively for one or more exempt purposes specified in section 501(c)(3).

Ann Arbor Dog Training Club, Inc. Petitioner v. Commissioner, T.C., 1974, pp. 207–212.

The existence of one substantial nonexempt purpose (the training of dogs) led to the denial of the tax-exempt status. Ironically, the status may have been awarded if the training of people were the substantial purpose for which this organization was formed, and the training of dogs only incidental to the training of people. This is what the court meant when it said "By contrast, petitioner has not shown that actually training a dog is necessary for teaching an individual how to train a dog."

In further illustrating this point of a community welfare or charitable motive, it should be noted that if the organization was created with the motive of making a gain (a profit) on its activities, the failure to realize this gain does not make the organization a nonprofit. It is merely a for-profit firm that has a loss or is breaking even. Similarly, if the organization was created with a motive of making a profit, its making large charitable contributions does not make it a nonprofit. In this case, it is simply a profit maker with a strong social conscience.

To the for-profit firm, charity may be important but is not essential to its existence; the charitable purpose is incidental. Accordingly, many for-profit firms have their own charitable foundations and make sizable charitable gifts to nonprofits. To the nonprofit, charity is the exclusive motive for existing and profits are incidental although important means for financing the charitable mission. Thus, as seen from these examples, nonprofits may run profitable businesses.

Profit Making as a Source of Finance

What is the legal history upon which the courts and the IRS have held that nonprofits may make a profit? The seminal case is *Trinidad v. Sagrada Orden.*[12] The Supreme Court stated that the law:

> . . .recognizes that a corporation may be organized and operated exclusively for religious, charitable, scientific or educational purposes, and yet have a net income [profits]. . .it says nothing about the source of the income, but makes the destination the ultimate exemption.

In several cases thereafter, the IRS and the courts have held that organizations dedicated to a charitable, educational, religious or other tax-exempt purpose could conduct profitable business activities without losing their exempt status and without paying taxes or penalties on these profits. An example is the ruling by the IRS that a tax-exempt museum engaging in the

> . . .sale of greeting cards displaying printed reproductions of art works contributes importantly to the achievement of the museum's exempt educational purposes by stimulating and enhancing public awareness, interest, and appreciation of art. Moreover, a broader segment of the public may be encouraged to visit the museum itself. . .as a result of the cards. The fact that the cards are promoted and sold in a clearly commercial manner at a profit and in competition with commercial greeting card publishers does not alter the fact of the activity's relatedness to the museum exempt purposes.[13]

Accordingly, the IRS concluded that not only should the engagement in these profitable sales by this museum not result in the loss of tax-exempt status, but the profits should not be taxed.

Similarly, in a recent decision in *American College of Physicians* vs. *U.S.,* the courts held that revenues from advertising in the *Annals of Internal Medicine* were related to its tax-exempt mission. Therefore, the advertising was not cause for the repeal of its tax-exempt status and the profits from the advertising were not taxable. In the words of the court:[14]

> That the primary purpose may have been commercial, however, does not preclude a finding that the activity is substantially related to an exempt function. . .While the educational function of the advertising may well have been secondary to the purpose of raising revenues, the evidence of record establishes that the advertising in *Annals* fulfilled an important educational function. . .The evidence of record establishes that the contribution of the advertisements to the exempt purpose is an important one.

Accordingly, the court continued, "We hold that the sales of advertising in *Annals* are substantially related to the exempt purpose of the College to educate internists and, therefore, are not taxable. . ." We shall return to this case. This is not the end of the story.

From these two cases, we see that the two ultimate authorities—the courts and the IRS—both sanction the making of profits by nonprofit organizations. A careful reading of the rulings indicate the separation of two levels of analysis by the courts and by the IRS: (1) Is the tax-exempt mission of the organization threatened or secondary to the for-profit activity? If it is, tax-exempt status is denied or revoked. If it is not, then (2) is the for-profit activity related to the carrying out of the tax-exempt mission? If it is not, the earnings from the business are taxed. If it is related, the earnings are not taxed.

In some cases, both the courts and the IRS rule that the organization may maintain its tax-exempt nonprofit status, but it must pay taxes on the profits. This is so when the business is unrelated to the tax-exempt mission of the organization. Thus, in another case involving a museum, the IRS ruled that an art museum was dealing in an unrelated business when it sold books dealing with science. In the eyes of the IRS, the sale of science books had nothing to do with art. In this case, the museum's tax-exempt status was not threatened, but it had to pay taxes on the profits from the sale of its scientific books but not on the sale of cards promoting art.[15]

To fully appreciate this point, let us go back to the case of the American College of Physicians. Not satisfied with the lower courts, the IRS appealed the case to the Supreme Court. On April 22, 1986, Justice Thurgood Marshall in *United States, Petitioner* v. *American College of Physicians,* rendered the unanimous decision of the Court. It held that the advertising in *The Annals of Internal Medicine* was unrelated business and that the American College of Physicians must pay taxes on the earnings from such advertising.

The case against the American College of Physicians turned on whether or not the advertising was conducted in a manner that showed that it was not substantially related to the tax-exempt mission of the organization. The Court pointed to an earlier focus of the Claims Court that:

> "The evidence is clear that plaintiff did not use the advertising to provide its readers a comprehensive or systematic presentation of any aspect of the goods or services publicized. Those companies willing to pay for advertising space got it; others did not. Moreover, some of the advertising was for established drugs or devices and was repeated from one month to another, undermining the suggestion that the advertising was principally designed to alert readers of recent developments [citing, as examples, ads for Valium, Insulin and Maalox]. Some ads even concerned matters that had no conceivable relationship to the College's tax-exempt purposes." 3 Cl. Ct.. at 534 (footnotes omitted).

Supreme Court of the United States, United States v. American College of Physicians, No. 84–1737, April 22, 1986, pp. 14–15.

Based on that finding the Supreme Court concluded:

> These facts find adequate support in the record. See, *e. g.,* App. 29a–30a, 59a. Considering them in light of the applicable legal standard, we are bound to conclude that the advertising in Annals does not contribute importantly to the journal's educational purposes. This is not to say that the College could not control its publication of advertisements in such a way as to reflect an intention to contribute importantly to its educational functions. By coordinating the content of the advertisements with the editorial content of the issue, or by publishing only advertisements reflecting new developments in the pharmaceutical market, for example, perhaps the College could satisfy the stringent standards erected by Congress and the Treasury. In this case, however, we have concluded that the Court of Appeals erroneously focused exclusively upon the information that is invariably conveyed by commercial advertising, and consequently failed to give effect to the governing statute and regulations. Its judgment, accordingly, is
>
> *Reversed.*

Supreme Court of the United States, United States v. American College of Physicians, No. 84–1737, April 22, 1986, p. 15.

Note several points from these quotations. First, the American College of Physicians did not lose its tax-exempt status. Second, it may continue a business of advertising for a profit although it must pay taxes on these profits like any other business. Third, the Court did not ban advertising and did not rule out that this could be a related business of a nonprofit and therefore free of taxes. Fourth, the Court suggested how the American College of Physicians may accomplish this objective.

It is important to appreciate the purpose of this unrelated business income tax. It is not intended to stop the nonprofit from making a profit. It is to make sure that if a nonprofit engages in a business unrelated to the promotion of its mission, the profits on that business are then taxed in the same way as all profit-making firms doing the same kind of business are taxed.

This thinking is revealed in the Congressional record on the legislation leading to the unrelated business tax on nonprofits:[16]

> The problem at which the tax on unrelated business income is directed is primarily that of unfair competition. The tax-free status of. . .organizations enables them to use their profits tax-free to expand operations, while their competitors can expand only with the profits remaining after taxes. Also, a number of examples have arisen where these organizations have, in effect, used their tax exemptions to buy an ordinary business. That is, they have acquired the business with little or no investment

> on their own part and paid for it in installments out of subsequent earnings—a procedure which usually could not be followed if the business were taxable.

And, the Congressional record continues:

> In neither. . .bill does this provision deny the exemption where the organizations are carrying on unrelated active business enterprises, nor require that they dispose of such businesses. Both provisions merely impose the same tax on income derived from an unrelated trade or business as is borne by their competitors. . .

In short, a nonprofit may make profits from engaging in a trade or business that is related to its tax-exempt mission without losing its tax-exempt status and without paying taxes on that profit. It may engage in profit-making businesses unrelated to its tax-exempt mission, but it must pay taxes on the profits earned. None of these two situations leads to a loss or denial of tax-exempt status.

The status is lost or denied when it appears to the IRS or the courts that the community or public welfare purpose claimed by the organization is nothing but a ruse for carrying on a commercial activity for profit and that the tax-exempt status is intended by the organization simply as a means to evade taxes or to gain a competitive advantage over for-profit firms. Thus, in *Piety, Inc.* v. *Commissioner,* the court held that an organization that did nothing but run bingo games was not tax exempt even though it fed its profits to a tax-exempt organization.[17]

The tax-exempt status is also denied or revoked if the benefits of the organization or the profits of its business inure to private persons. Thus, in *Church of Scientology of California* v. *Commissioner,* the court held that the tax-exempt status was to be revoked because the church was operated for a substantially commercial purpose, and its net earnings privately benefited its founder.[18]

To summarize, this section provides legal evidence that nonprofit organizations are allowed to make a profit (and the very word is used in the law). But if a nonprofit is allowed to make a profit, what distinguishes a for-profit firm from a nonprofit? Under what conditions will an organization that deems itself to be a nonprofit be considered just another for-profit firm in the eyes of the law and consequently be denied its tax-exempt status?

The critical factors, as we learn in this book, in avoiding revocation or denial of tax-exempt status are that (1) the organization must clearly and unequivocally be motivated by a community or public welfare purpose defined by the *Internal Revenue Code* as worthy of tax exemption; (2) the benefits must not inure to private individuals; (3) commercial activity must not be its primary purpose and must not diminish or rival the ability of the organization to conduct its tax-exempt mission; and (4) the activity could not easily be conducted by a commercial firm for a profit.

Note that the community or public welfare purpose to which the organization is exclusively dedicated must also be one that is both defined by law as tax exempt and is contained in the organization's charter. Accordingly, in the example of the second museum, the court held that the sale of scientific books would have been tax exempt to another organization that was scientific in its orientation, but not to an art museum. It is not simply the activity that counts, but the combination of considerations mentioned in the preceding paragraph. Thus, in the case of the American College of Physicians mentioned earlier, the fact that the principal objective of the advertising was to raise money, is not separated from whether the purposes served by the advertising are defined as tax-exempt. Is it education as defined?

To illustrate further, the community welfare purpose may be stated in the charter of the organization but is not defined as a tax-exempt activity by the law. Thus, in Society of Costa Rica Collectors, both the court and the IRS concluded that tax exemption was not warranted by the philatelic society that primarily engaged in sales that were indistinguishable from commercial sales. Merely the sale of philatelic materials is not by itself defined by law as a tax-exempt purpose.[19] And the training of dogs, as we saw earlier, is not recognized as a community or public welfare purpose (a charity) that is tax exempt.

The Use of the Profits Must Be to Advance Public or Community Welfare

A distinguishing characteristic between a nonprofit and a for-profit firm as an economic institution is that nonprofits may not distribute their assets, profits, or other benefits to individuals as owners. They may not advance private welfare but must only utilize profits to carry on their mission to improve public or community welfare. In this sense, there are the following important differences between a for-profit and a nonprofit:

1. The for-profit obtains revenues strictly from sales of assets, goods and services and from investments. There is no legally required balance among these sources of revenues. The profits may be distributed to individuals because they are the owners of the assets and earnings of the firm. A stock certificate is evidence of ownership and the payment of dividends to stockholders is a distribution of assets and earnings.

2. In contrast, the nonprofit can obtain revenues from the sale of assets, goods and services and investment, but there is an additional source—gifts and contributions. The nonprofit is legally required to maintain some balance among these sources of income. And, the nonprofit may not distribute its assets, income or earnings to individuals or to any other entity that is not a similar nonprofit except the state.

Costs and Revenue Perspectives of Being an Economic Institution

As an economic institution, nonprofits have expenses and revenues. A major cost is labor in the form of salaries and benefits. Salaries in some nonprofit organizations are very high because nonprofits must compete for labor.[20]

Rentals may also be high because nonprofits must compete for space. Neither gifts of labor nor space are deductible.

It is sometimes said that the word "voluntary" best distinguishes the nonprofit from the profit sector but this is not true. Workers in the nonprofit sector are not all volunteers. Even the most charitable of charities, religious organizations, pay their leaders.

The problem with the use of the word "voluntary" is best described by a long-time and well-respected observer of the nonprofit world. Alan Piper, writing for the Foundation Center, asserts:[21]

> The term itself is elusive. Theoretically, it includes not only all kinds of private enterprise, both nonprofit and for profit, but even the institutions of a democratic form of government as well—in short any activity by private citizens undertaken in concert and on their own volition.

True, membership in nonprofit associations is voluntary but most nonprofits are not membership organizations. Moreover, membership in many nonprofits such as labor, professional and trade associations are only nominally voluntary because failure to join is to deprive oneself of employment, advancement opportunities and information. Indeed, some associations have certifying powers and without being certified a person faces barriers to functioning.

True, some participation in a nonprofit is voluntary but this does not distinguish nonprofits from for-profit organizations or market transactions from transactions in the nonprofit sector. To illustrate, participation in the ownership of corporations is voluntary. All market transactions are voluntary. People are not coerced to buy or sell, as this is illegal. Producers and workers make voluntary decisions about all their activities in a market economy. Indeed, without voluntary initiatives, the market system would collapse. It is precisely the voluntary aspects of the market economy (to be described in the next chapter) that open money opportunities for nonprofits.

From a revenue perspective, nonprofits may charge a price for the assets or goods or services they sell. The range of prices a nonprofit may charge varies from nothing or free to the competitive price that is being charged by for-profit firms. What gives nonprofits this range is that they have one source of income that for-profit firms do not have—gifts and contributions.[22] For-profits do not have gifts and contributions and must sell at a price that absorbs all costs and make a profit for the owners. In contrast, nonprofits do not have owners and may not distribute profits to anyone.

For-profit firms do frequently charge below market price (discounted sales) and give products and services away (donations). The difference is that the nonprofit can sustain this behavior as modus operandi, and for-profit firms cannot. But nonprofits may sustain this type of operation only to the extent that they can pay their bills by turning to nonprice support such as gifts and contributions.

KIND OF BUSINESSES NONPROFIT ORGANIZATIONS MAY ENTER

What for-profit activities are nonprofits allowed to undertake? In keeping with the spirit of entreprenuership and free enterprise, there are no restrictions to the kinds of business ventures nonprofits may enter as long as the venture is legal and the rules discussed in this book are followed. Nonprofits have been known to legally own race tracks,[23] oil wells,[24] engage in the weapons business,[25] own and run hotels and undertake to legally sell condoms.[26]

The courts, as discussed in Chapter 2, have steadfastly held to the view that it is not the activity or the making of a profit that distinguishes a for-profit from a nonprofit corporation. It has never barred a nonprofit simply because it undertook a profitable venture. It is a matter of proportion that disturbs the courts. We shall see in Chapters 4 and 7 a number of examples of nonprofits running profitable businesses with the approval of the IRS and the courts. In Chapters 7 and 8 we get additional insight into nonprofit businesses.

We should not underestimate the extent to which nonprofits can penetrate the for-profit sector. A symposium on the competition between nonprofit and small business sectors sponsored by the Small Business Administration highlighted areas in which nonprofits have begun to penetrate aggressively.[27] These are:

1. The development, production and distribution of audio visual aid.

2. The conducting of analytic and laboratory testing in health and hygiene, soil and foilage.

3. Consulting in water quality, surveying, mapping, computer design and engineering.

4. Travel agencies selling airline tickets, tours, and offering travel consultation.

5. Tour operators conducting motorcoach tours both local and long distance.

6. Research services in all academic fields at universities, colleges and technical schools.

7. Computer services including remote data processing, systems integration, and software services.

8. Hearing aid production and distribution.

Successful business ventures are often the result of capitalizing on opportunities related to the nonprofit mission of the organization. What are some clues that may be used to detect if an opportunity exists? Two legal scholars of nonprofit enterprises suggest four ways in which this may be done.[28] They include:

1. The existence of excess capacity that can be rented as meeting, athletic and living facilities; i.e., the church hall being rented for weddings, meetings and concerts. (In Chapter 12 we shall describe these as joint or common cost activities.)

2. The existence of a special and favorable relationship with the public; i.e., being able to conduct sales of books, refreshments, clothing and other articles to members.

3. The ownership of property rights covering royalties, real estate, art, copyright, trademarks, name of the organization, mailing lists; i.e., real estate can be rented, copyright and patents can be leased to a manufacturer and mailing lists can be sold.

4. The existence of special expertise in the organization, such as experts who can write books that can be sold and whose skills can be hired.

To these categories we many add another: the existence of cost advantages. Nonprofits have cost advantages due to their ability to use volunteer workers and privilege to use the U.S. mail at substantially reduced rates. For example, a letter that would cost 22 cents to a private mailer would cost a nonprofit substantially less. A skilled worker such as a lawyer who may charge hundreds of dollars per hour would, as a matter of professional ethics, work pro bono for a nonprofit. Football players through the National Football League promote contributions to the United Way. Business Volunteers for the Arts is a group of approximately 1,000 bankers, lawyers, accountants and other business managers who assist over 600 art groups in 15 cities in marketing, finance and other management services.[29]

The exploitation of any one or a combination of these factors could lead to very profitable activities. In the next chapter, we see how being able to utilize volunteers to lower costs and exploiting a special relationship with the public as evidenced by hospitals selling tickets, a golf tournament can turn a handsome profit for both the private sector and nonprofit participants in the joint venture.

There are other examples of exploitation of these factors. There are hospitals renting space to physicians, running parking lots, physical fitness centers, giving lessons in yoga, gift shops, refreshment outlets and charging fees to profit. As one nonprofit veterinary clinic discovered, the quickest way for a nonprofit to run a profitable business is to charge a fee for some of the services it provides. Because the fee was based on a percentage markup on its costs, the fee not only covered costs but contributed to profits. The University College at the University of Maryland serves tens of thousands of students without a penny from the state (although it is a state institution) by charging a fee. In all these cases, annual profits can be plowed back into institutional growth and into advancing the mission of the nonprofit.

There are other illustrations. *Audubon,* a magazine owned by the National Audubon Society, *National Geographic* owned by the National Geographic Society, the *Smithsonian* owned by the Smithsonian Institute are magazines that earn millions of dollars a year in profits. This is done in part by having a special relationship with the public, including a large membership that purchases the magazines, and through lower postal rates for mailing the magazines;[30] and as we see in a later chapter in the case of the American College of Physicians, magazines owned by nonprofits are not forbidden from selling advertising space at a profit.

According to one observer, magazine production has been so profitable for nonprofits that when the Minneapolis Star & Tribune Company could not turn a good profit on *Harper's* magazine, it turned it over to two nonprofits.[31]

This book has made reference to a number of other profitable activities carried on by nonprofits. These include the operation of barber and beauty shops, the conducting of certain banking functions, the manufacture of toys, the running of parking lots, the rental of space, and the selling of art work and advertising space. The opportunities are limitless.

Some surprises also take place. A hospital in Prince Georges County, Maryland, turned in a respectable profit when its operations were turned over to a nonprofit corporation. A nonprofit hospital in Washington, D.C. eradicated its deficit by taking on a more business-type management.

GIFTS AND CONTRIBUTIONS AS SOURCES OF FINANCE

All business firms begin by individuals or firms making an investment. All nonprofit corporations begin by foundations, individuals, government or firms making a gift or contribution. Unlike for-profit firms which rely on sales as their principal source of revenues, nonprofits rely principally on gifts, contributions and support from their membership. Gifts and contributions are important to nonprofits—even those that generate considerable business income. This is not simply by tradition, but by law. Generally, as we see later, the law requires that nonprofits demonstrate a relatively high level of support from the public or from their membership. Their principal source of revenues cannot be profits from the sale of goods and services.

Ironically, the more successful a nonprofit is in doing business, the more it may have to demonstrate public and membership support. This is true, as shown in later chapters, particularly when the business income is unrelated to the mission of the organization. Consequently, business income cannot be considered a substitute for obtaining gifts and contributions. It is merely a way to increase the total revenues available to the nonprofit to carry out its mission.

Many books on fund raising focus on public and human relations techniques that work. Sophisticated fund raising goes well beyond that. A major motive for giving is to obtain tax benefits. Even when this is not the motive, the tax consequences are always taken into account by the large or smart donor.

Thus, it is said that the Howard Hughes Medical Institute was created by Howard Hughes to avoid cancellation of a profitable contract made by the Air Force to the Hughes Aircraft Company and to avoid paying taxes. The gift of the stocks of the aircraft company provided Hughes with a huge tax deduction, impressed his workers which lowered their discontent with him, and impressed the public and the Defense Department which had threatened to cancel his contract. The defense work was now being done by a company that was owned by a nonprofit and the profits would go to serve public welfare. In 1986 the nonprofit sold the Hughes Aircraft company to General Motors for $5.2 billion dollars, making the Hughes Medical Institute the single largest private foundation in the country, surpassing the Ford Foundation.[32]

The tax benefit reduces the cost of the gift to the donor. A person in the 30 percent bracket giving property worth $100,000 to a qualified nonprofit obtains a deduction worth $33,333 from the federal government. A person in the 20 percent bracket gets a deduction worth $20,000 for the same gift. With the first person, the gift of $100,000 only costs $66,667; for the second person it costs $80,000. The savings to the donor is higher as the income bracket of that donor increases. This basic relationship between taxing and giving remains though tax rates are changed. It is for this reason that the lower the tax rate, the less tax incentive there is to give; that is, the less that can be deducted and therefore the more the true cost of the gift to the donor. In Chapter 10, we shall cite some studies that support this conclusion.

Competent management must have a working knowledge of the tax laws as they apply to giving. It is the ability to work with these laws that enhances the chances of getting large commitments. Some basic points must be appreciated to be successful. These are mentioned below and discussed later.

All gifts and contributions are not deductible. Whether or not a gift is deductible and how much is deductible depends upon the item given, to whom it is given, the form in which it is given and by whom it is given. Gifts of free rent and gifts of labor (volunteering) are never deductible.

Certain gifts may lead to a deduction but only at a point in the distant future. This is particularly true when the donor wishes to retain some rights or obtain some benefits from the property, or to have someone or entity other than a charity benefit from the good. An example of this is one who makes a gift of a large portfolio of securities but wants to share in the income from it. If a deal to satisfy the donor's conditions cannot be worked out, the potential gift may be lost. Such a deal to offer a present deduction can be arranged through the proper creation of a trust.

Gifts such as art work require that a qualified professional appraisal be made of the value of the gift. Overevaluation of property can lead to penalties. While the penalty may typically fall on the donor, complicity on the part of the nonprofit will not be tolerated. This abuse was, and probably still is, common. Art work, automobiles, clothing, even bibles are commonly over evaluated. One of the best known examples of overevaluation was a scheme to acquire bibles at a low price and then appreciate their value as gifts. This is not allowed.

Some gifts are shams; others are incomplete and really are promisory notes that the nonprofit may never collect. For example, it is reported that many of the pledges made to Hands Across America were never collected. Suffice it to say here that bad checks are not uncommon; neither are proposals for gifts in which the potential donor proposes to retain control.

Some goods are not worth accepting because they lead to the assumption of large liabilities, taxable income, and large operating costs that the nonprofit may not be able to meet. Real estate is an example. Sometimes it is worth accepting such gifts and operating them under an umbrella that limits the liabilities or exposure of the nonprofit to losses. Creating a separate business or an associated nonprofit is sometimes a workable strategy. By isolating the gift under a separate corporate umbrella, the nonprofit shields itself.

Giving and receiving are subject to federal and state laws. Recall that the primary purpose for permitting tax exemption to nonprofits is to encourage their work and to encourage citizens to give to them. The purpose of the laws that limit giving and receiving is to defend against the abuse of this exemption. The laws that limit giving generally limit the percent of income an individual or corporation may give in any one year. These are federal laws. The laws that limit receiving and generally limit fund-raising behavior are state laws. It is not uncommon that a nonprofit would obtain 20 percent of the proceeds from a fund-raising activity with the remaining 80 percent going to the firm contracted to run the activity. Detractors of this type of law argue that this ratio is not unreasonable because of the cost of some fund-raisers, because what constitutes "cost" is often arbitrarily determined, and because it limits freedom of expression; that is, it rules out those fund-raising events that are very expensive or which are being conducted, not for immediate revenues, but for public relations purposes.

The state of Maryland enacted such a law in 1976 after a religious group was convicted of misuse of funds. The law limited administrative expenses for fund raising to 25 percent. The law provided that the Secretary of the State of Maryland could waiver the 25 percent at his or her discretion. It also provided that certain expenses such as feasibility studies, planning and counseling for fund raising would be excluded in calculating the 25 percent limit.

On June 26, 1984, in *Secretary of State of Maryland* v. *Joseph H. Munson Co. Inc.,* the Supreme Court of the United States in a 5 to 4 decision held that the law is unconstitutional on its face. In the majority's view, the Maryland law could not distinguish between those organizations that had legitimately high administrative costs in pursuit of their First Amendment rights and those that did not. The imprecision of the Maryland law, according to the majority of the Court, meant that its application always risked the supression of constitutional rights. Whether other state laws placing limitations on fund raising are consequently unconstitutional will depend upon the individual state law.

In addition, some state laws require registration of the nonprofit organization and disclosure of its financial information before any fund raising may be permitted. This fund raising may include collection in churches. This type of regulation stems not only from actual abuse but from the lack of public information on some of these organizations. Accordingly, the National Conference of Commissions on Uniform State Laws and the American Bar Association recommended that charitable trusts be required to register and give annual accounting to the Attorney General of each state.[33]

Appendix 3.1 is a chart of state regulations covering the solicitation by nonprofit organizations. Note that in states such as Michigan, Nevada and Nebraska there are no limitations on the amount that may be paid for the administrative costs of soliciting. In Maryland there are presently no limits. Other states such as Tennessee, Connecticut and Massachusets maintain such limits. In states such as Washington, Virginia and Wisconsin, the solicitor must reveal to the donor what percentage of the donation goes to charity and what percentage goes to the fund-raisers. In addition, in many states there is a bond that is required prior to solicitation. In the state of Minnesota this bond is $20,000. In New York and New Jersey, it is $10,000. A bond is a security to protect the public against various types of financial misdeeds on the part of the solicitor organization.

Sophisticated fund raising requires knowledge of the statistics of giving. Who gives how much to what causes? The figures from the Conference Board and the American Association of Fund-Raising Counsel are revealing. In 1984 (Table 3.1) individuals accounted for 83 percent of the dollars contributed to

TABLE 3.1   Sources of Contributions, 1964, 1974, 1984
(in billions of dollars)

	1964		1974		1984	
	Dollars	Percent	Dollars	Percent	Dollars	Percent
Corporations	0.73	5.3	1.20	4.4	3.45	4.6
Foundations	0.83	6.1	2.11	7.8	4.36	5.9
Bequests	0.95	6.9	2.07	7.7	4.89	6.6
Individuals	11.19	81.7	21.60	80.1	61.55	82.9
Total	13.70	100.0	26.98	100.0	74.25	100.0

Source: Calculated from American Association of Fund-Raising Counsel, *Giving* (New York: American Association of Fund-Raising Counsel, 1985), pp. 42–43.

charity. Foundations accounted for 6 percent, bequests (deathtime gifts from individuals) accounted for 7 percent, and corporations accounted for just less than 5 percent of all gifts. Notice that the proportion coming from foundations is relatively small and declining, and the proportion coming from individuals (including bequests) has consistently been nearly 90 percent and rising. Also note in Table 3.2 that in the past ten years, corporations and individuals have increased their giving almost equally (285 to 287 percent) well exceeding the growth in giving by foundations. These numbers suggest that the most productive strategies for raising funds for most nonprofits will not be through foundations, but by appealing to individuals and corporations. This is the reason that this book emphasizes market and individual-oriented techniques (1) through the operation in the market economy, (2) through the understanding of the corporate and individual motives for giving, and (3) through the application of sophisticated techniques to accommodate large gifts from individuals and greater corporate involvement.

TABLE 3.2   Growth Rates in Giving by Source
(in percent)

	1964–1984 (20 years)	1974–1984 (10 years)
Corporation	473	287
Foundations	525	207
Bequests	515	236
Individuals	550	285
Total	542	275

Source: Calculated from American Association of Fund-Raising Counsel, *Giving* (New York: American Association of Fund-Raising Counsel, 1985), p. 42.

CONTRIBUTIONS BY CORPORATIONS

Table 3.3 shows that corporations give less than 2 percent of their pretax net income (profits before taxes) to charities. This figure was 1.76 percent in 1982, declining to 1.46 in 1984. This figure is well below the 20 percent of taxable income limit set by law on the amount corporations may give, implying that there is substantial room for more giving by corporations. For this reason, we also discuss corporate giving and joint productive relationships between businesses and nonprofits.

TABLE 3.3   Corporate Contributions, 1970–1984

	Contributions	Pretax Net Income (billions)	Percent of Pretax Net Income
1970	$ .797	$ 75.4	1.05
1971	.865	86.6	0.99
1972	1.009	100.6	1.00
1973	1.174	125.6	0.93
1974	1.200	136.7	0.87
1975	1.202	132.1	0.90
1976	1.487	166.3	0.89
1977	1.791	194.7	0.92
1978	2.084	229.1	0.91
1979	2.288	252.7	0.91
1980	2.600	234.6	1.01
1981	2.950	227.0	1.14
1982	2.950[1]	174.2	1.69
1983	3.100[1]	205.3	1.51
1984	3.45	237.5	1.46

[1]CFAE estimate

SOURCE: American Association of Fund-Raising Counsel, *Giving* (New York: American Association of Fund-Raising Counsel, 1985), p. 34.

TABLE 3.4 15 Largest Company-Sponsored Foundations by Total Giving (all dollar figures expressed in thousands)

Name	State	Total Giving	Gifts Received	Assets	Fiscal Date
Atlantic Richfield Foundation	CA	$35,839	$32,184	$ 11,896	12/31/84
General Motors Foundation	MI	31,442	30	123,278	12/31/84
Exxon Education Foundation	NY	27,361	32,484	60,014	12/31/83
Amoco Foundation	IL	19,380	26,109	75,804	12/31/84
AT&T Foundation	NY	16,132	0	86,336	12/31/84
Mobil Foundation	NY	14,484	18,022	19,736	12/31/84
General Electric Foundation	CT	14,226	21,710	53,578	12/31/83
Shell Companies Foundation	TX	13,895	10,089	47,610	12/31/83
Proctor & Gamble Fund	OH	11,559	16,000	14,935	6/30/83
Dayton Hudson Foundation	MN	11,019	12,381	9,112	1/31/85
Ford Motor Foundation	MI	9,931	20,028	47,579	12/31/84
Alcoa Foundation	PA	9,409	0	168,000	12/31/84
Xerox Foundation	CT	9,400	0	9,100	12/31/84
Bank America Foundation	CA	9,185	0	10,537	12/31/84
Ætna Life & Casualty Foundation	CT	9,127	20,000	17,983	12/31/83

Source: Loren Renz and Patricia Read (eds.), *The Foundation Directory*, 10th ed. (New York City: Foundation Center, 1985), p. xix.

TABLE 3.5

Comparison of Charitable Contributions Expenditures—Matched Cases, 1984 and 1983
322 Companies Reporting in Both Years (millions of dollars)

| | 1984 | | | | | | 1983 | | | | | |
| | Foundation Program | | Direct Giving Program | | Total | | Foundation Program | | Direct Giving Program | | Total | |
	Sum	Percent	Sum	Percent	Sum	Percent	Sum	Percent	Sum	Percent	Sum	Percent
Cash	$528.1	99.7%	$517.3	63.3%	$1,045.4	77.6%	$448.4	99.8%	$481.4	81.1%	$927.6	89.2%
Securities	.5	0.1	6.0	0.7	6.5	0.5	*	0.0	3.2	0.5	3.2	0.3
Product	.4	0.1	137.8	16.9	138.2	10.3	0	0.0	55.5	9.4	55.5	5.3
Property and equipment	.6	0.1	155.7	19.1	156.3	11.6	.6	0.1	53.3	9.0	53.9	5.2
Total a	$529.6	100.0%	$816.8	100.0%	$1,346.4	100.0%	$449.1	100.0%	$593.4	100.0%	$1,040.3	100.0%

* Less than $.1 million.
aDetails may not add to totals due to rounding.

Source: Linda Cardillo Platzer, *Annual Survey of Corporate Contributions*, 1986 ed. (New York: The Conference Board, 1986) p. 2.

Not only do corporations give out of their pretax income, but many corporations have foundations which may act with varying degrees of independence from the corporate body itself.[34] Giving by company-sponsored foundations rose by 53 percent from 1979 to 1981 and by 20 percent from 1981 to 1983.[35] Table 3.4 shows the 15 largest company-sponsored foundations in the United States.

Table 3.5 shows how a group of 322 companies and their foundations made contributions over a two-year period from 1983 to 1984. This is a matched sample in the sense that the same companies are examined in both years. We see that total giving rose between 1983 to 1984 from $1,040.3 million to $1,346.4 million or nearly 30 percent.

In both years, corporate foundations made contributions almost exclusively in cash. This is not so of the companies themselves. In 1984, only 63.3 percent of their contributions were in the form of cash. This was down markedly from 1983 when it was 81.1 percent. On the other hand, there has been a sharp rise in the giving of products, property and equipment. Favorable depreciation rates which permit a company to rapidly write off the cost of equipment, rapid technological change which makes equipment quickly obsolete, and aggressive marketing which introduces a large potential market to the products of corporations such as the giving of computer equipment to schools, all contribute to this shift.

How are these contributions by the companies and their foundations distributed among potential recipients? Figure 3.1 shows that education is number one with 38.9 percent of contribution dollars, followed closely by health and human services with 27.7 percent in 1984, which is only slightly different from what it was in 1983.

Within the corporate sector there are distinct patterns. While education is the area most favored, it only receives 30 percent of the contributions from life and health insurance companies as shown in Table 3.6. Urban and civic organizations and the United Fund are favored over health and safety among these companies. And while these companies have less equipment and hardware to give, they do donate staff.

And the 1985 annual report of the Standard Oil Company shows the following distributions: 45 percent education, 24 percent health, human services and civic activities, 8 percent urban planning and economic development, 7 percent culture and the arts, 3 percent energy and natural resources and 12 percent other.

CONTRIBUTIONS BY INDIVIDUALS

Table 3.7 shows that individuals contribute about 2 percent of their incomes, well below the 50 percent of adjusted gross income maximum permitted by law, implying considerable room for further growth and penetration. Table 3.8 shows that persons with adjusted gross incomes ranging from $20,000 to $75,000 ac-

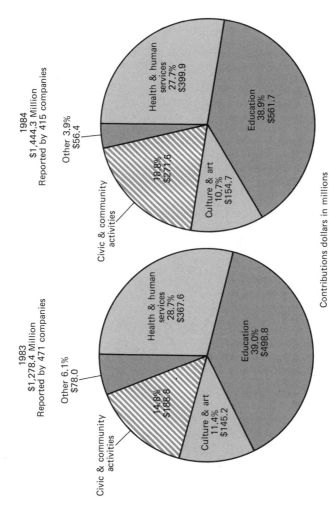

1983
$1,278.4 Million
Reported by 471 companies

Civic & community
activities

Other 6.1%
$78.0

Health & human
services
28.7%
$367.6

14.8%
$188.8

Culture & art
11.4%
$145.2

Education
39.0%
$498.8

1984
$1,444.3 Million
Reported by 415 companies

Civic & community
activities

Other 3.9%
$56.4

Health & human
services
27.7%
$399.9

18.8%
$271.6

Culture & art
10.7%
$154.7

Education
38.9%
$561.7

Contributions dollars in millions

Figure 3.1 Linda Cardillo Platzer, *Annual Survey of Corporate Contributions*, 1986 ed. (New York: The Conference Board of 1986) p. 19.

TABLE 3.6 Annual Contributions in Millions of Dollars by Insurance
Companies and Annual Contributions of Employee Services by
Insurance Companies, 1980–1984

Categories*	1984	1983	1982	1981	1980
Urban/Civic Affairs	$18	$14	$13	$13	$10
United Fund	20	17	17	16	13
Health and Safety	13	11	11	8	7
Education	25	25	23	18	16
Culture	11	9	8	6	5
Other	11	7	6	3	2
Total	$98	$83	$78	$64	$53

Number of Trend Companies (154).

	1984	1983	1982	1981	1980
Number of Loaned Personnel	313	363	350	170	182
Man-hours Contributed	61,000	75,100	70,200	44,400	52,000
Number of Released-Time Personnel	12,100	12,600	13,700	5,700	8,400
Man-hours Contributed	327,800	358,800	354,800	160,700	174,800

Number of Trend Companies (153).

Source: The Record of Corporate Public Involvement, 1985 Social Report (Washington, D.C., Center for Corporate Public Involvement of the American Council of Life Insurance and Health Insurance Association of America, 1985) pp. 6, 12.

count for approximately 64 percent of the contributions,[36] but this is roughly their fair share since these people account for 61 percent of income in the U.S. On the other hand, people with adjusted gross incomes above $75,000 have only 23 percent of U.S. adjusted gross income but make 32 percent of all contributions. Put another way, over 90 percent of charitable contributions are made by people with adjusted gross incomes of $20,000 or more with those in the upper income bracket tending to contribute more than their proportionate share.

Among individuals there are distinct patterns. For example, as Table 3.9 shows, among the elderly 23 percent of their gifts are in a form other than cash. This means that management of nonprofits would do well to understand non-cash forms of appeals and the role of trusts and wills in making contributions.

And the biggest "giver" of all is government. Governments contribute to charities in a number of ways, including contracting with them for the provision of goods and services, donating surplus equipment or goods and services for their use and for their distribution, such as the distribution of cheese. Govern-

TABLE 3.7 Contributions by Individuals,
1970–1984 (billions of dollars)

	Amount (billions)	Personal Income (billions)	Percent of Income
1970...	$16.19	$ 811.1	2.00
1971...	17.64	868.4	2.03
1972...	19.37	951.4	2.04
1973...	20.53	1,065.2	1.93
1974...	21.60	1,168.6	1.85
1975...	23.53	1,265.0	1.86
1976...	26.32	1,391.2	1.89
1977...	29.55	1,540.4	1.92
1978...	32.10	1,732.7	1.85
1979...	36.59	1,951.2	1.88
1980...	40.71	2,165.3	1.88
1981...	46.42	2,429.5	1.91
1982...	48.52	2,584.6	1.88
1983...	55.13	2,744.2	2.01
1984...	61.55	3,013.2	2.04

Source: American Association of Fund-Raising
Counsel, *Giving* (New York: American Association of Fund-Raising Counsel, 1985) p. 11.

TABLE 3.8 Distribution of Adjusted Gross Income and of Contributions
by Income-Size Class, 1983

	Adjusted Gross Income	Contributions Deduction
Size Class	Percent Distribution	Percent Distribution
$1 under $5000	*	*
$5000 under $10,000	2	1
$10,000 under $15,000	5	2
$15,000 under $20,000	6	4
$20,000 under $75,000	63	61
$75,000 more	23	32

*Indicates less than 1 percent. Figures may not add up to 100 percent because of rounding errors.

Note: Data for taxable income distribution and the distribution of contributions by income-size class for the year 1983 can be obtained from Susan Hosletter and Dan Holik, "Individual Income Tax Returns, Preliminary Data, 1983, in *Statistics of Income Bulletin* No. 1136, (Washington, D.C.: Internal Revenue Service) Vol. 4, No. 3, Winter 1984–85, pp. 19–30.

Source: Calculated from Internal Revenue Service Data reported in American Association of Fund-Raising Counsel, *1984 Annual Report* (New York; New York, American Association of Fund-Raising Counsel, 1984), p. 13.

TABLE 3.9 Contributions by Individuals 65 Years of Age or Over, 1981

Source of Adjusted Gross Income	Contributions Deduction					
	Total		Cash Contributions		Other than Cash Contributions	
	Number of Returns	Amount	Number of Returns	Amount	Number of Returns	Amount
	(33)	(34)	(35)	(36)	(37)	(38)
Total	2,715,876	5,748,782	2,704,478	4,423,912	648,729	1,529,643
Under $5,000	47,440	33,788	45,611	33,238	4,458	11,534
$5,000 under $10,000	352,400	277,773	350,273	269,020	85,788	10,742
$10,000 under $15,000	411,390	453,510	410,040	420,245	66,196	21,508
$15,000 under $20,000	355,382	365,485	355,364	340,557	66,599	24,339
$20,000 under $25,000	297,434	359,091	296,961	337,658	59,858	27,267
$25,000 under $30,000	227,310	273,337	227,310	250,635	69,441	23,534
$30,000 under $40,000	357,602	474,326	355,807	412,831	109,302	55,364
$40,000 under $50,000	224,816	458,120	224,020	374,730	57,855	67,850
$50,000 under $75,000	234,442	541,426	233,657	456,320	65,821	72,488
$75,000 under $100,000	82,740	302,144	81,447	214,479	23,331	72,921
$100,000 under $200,000	90,920	638,991	90,437	488,495	28,599	213,227
$200,000 under $500,000	27,966	882,840	27,614	383,776	10,758	330,636
$500,000 under $1,000,000 . . .	4,273	325,260	4,198	182,205	1,985	190,098
$1,000,000 or more	1,770	580,703	1,719	279,504	940	406,134

Source: Dan Holik and John Kozielec, "Taxpayers Age 65 or Over, 1977–81," Internal Revenue Service, Statistics of Income Bulletin, No. 1136, Summer 1984, pp. 1–16.

ment also underwrites donations. The cost to the federal government in terms of foregone revenues from taxation due to charitable deductions is estimated by the U.S. Treasury as $13.2 billion per year in 1983 and rising. The cost to state and local governments is incalculable. Not only are contributions deducted from state and local government taxes, but the nonprofits may pay no taxes on contributions received and they typically pay no sales or property taxes. According to the State Board of Equalization and Assessment of the State of New York, one third of the property in the state was totally or partially exempt from taxation under the nonprofit provisions of the law. The exemption shielded property with a total value of $121.6 billion from taxation.

The loss of federal, state and local revenues due to the tax-favored treatment of nonprofits has continuously caused governments at all levels to try to find ways to impose tax liabilities on nonprofits. For this reason, the tax discussion in Chapter 1 and this chapter are good references.

Sophisticated fund raising requires a good working knowledge of certain financial instruments and how they may apply to specific conditions facing potential donors. Basically, large sums are donated because the representative of the nonprofit was able to strike a deal. That is, he or she was able to accommodate the desires of a potential donor with the needs and desires of the organization. This often means more than begging. It means being professionally competent to arrive at a financially sound recommendation. Many nonprofits have made great strides once they realized this fact. Here are excerpts from a personal letter from the director of development at Mankato State University. It not only reveals the tremendous growth in their endowment, but shows the kinds of instruments used to achieve that growth:

Endowments

Planned gifts designated for the MSU Foundation Endowment Fund principal grew to $175,000 between 1958 and 1982—a period of 24 years. Today, four years later, the principal is over $700,000 with an additional $1.7 million pledged through will, life insurance, annuity or trust. The beauty of an endowment gift is that the principal will never be spent. The earnings achieve the donor's purpose year after year. An endowment to education, therefore, is an investment. . .a gift that keeps on giving. Today, there are 115 individual endowments as part of the MSU Foundation Endowment Fund.

Funding an Endowment

Careful planning needs to be given to the methods of funding an endowment to obtain maximum tax benefits. In addition to cash, assets such as land and buildings, stock, letter stock, copyrights, oil rights or individual fractional interest may be used to fund an endowment. An endowment may also be established by bequest through will or life insurance. It is even possible to establish a trust or annuity, retain lifetime income for retirement and receive tax benefits today. (Excerpts from letter to Herrington J. Bryce from Bob E. Golberg, CERF Director of Development/Planned Giving, Mankato State University April 9, 1986.)

While nonprofits rely on gifts and contributions, the degree of this reliance varies. There are some nonprofits that rely more heavily on related business income. Others really use gifts and contributions to offset large, legally acceptable business and investment income that may not be related at all to their missions. These organizations are not being deceptive. They understand that contributions alone are not sufficient to give them a sound financial base from which they may expand their charitable missions. The use of business income is, however, tricky and therefore a considerable part of this book is dedicated to understanding the role and integration of such income in the support structure of nonprofit organizations.

COMBINED FEDERAL CAMPAIGN

There is a separate fund-raising campaign that is worth noting. The Combined Federal Campaign is the only authorized charitable solicitation that can take place in the federal workplace.[37] Its objectives are (1) to give to those organizations which lessen the burden of government in meeting the needs of human health and welfare, (2) to provide a convenient channel through which federal public servants may contribute without disrupting the work place, and (3) to avoid the appearance that federal assistance is being given for lobbying and political advocacy.

To be eligible to participate in the campaign a nonprofit must be organized as a 501(c)(3) and operated for rendering human services or financing organizations that render human services in the areas of:

1. health
2. education and training
3. health research
4. education and training for the handicapped
5. treatment and rehabilitation for criminals, drug addicts, victims of family abuse, juvenile delinquents and persons of social adjustment needs
6. relief to victims of crime, war, casualty, famine, natural disasters, and other catastrophies and emergencies
7. neighborhood services for the needy including shelter, recreation, transportation, job training and the delivery of meals
8. legal aid to the poor and needy but not with the objective of defending a cause or protesting one
9. family protection through maternity, child care, counseling and guidance
10. relief to needy children through adoption
11. relief to the elderly
12. assistance to the members of the armed forces and civil service, foreign service, intelligence and public health service

13. assistance to members of federal agencies who have exceptional needs as a result of geographic isolation, injury in the line of duty, or other exceptional circumstances

14. lessening the burdens of government in respect to any of the foregoing.

With the regulations of April 4, 1986, a nonprofit may participate in the fund-raising campaign if it meets the previous conditions. It may participate as part of an affiliated group; that is, several nonprofits that join together for the purpose of raising funds such as the United Way. Or it may be a nonaffiliated local group, such as one that is permitted to participate in a local campaign as a separate entity. To do this, it must meet all of the listed standards and have a strong presence in the local community with specific facilities such as transportation, shelter, scholarship, training, feeding, institutionalization, and so forth that are available to the community.

Table 3.10 shows that since 1965, the campaign has raised $1,165,542,420 for the participating charities. Note, however, that after a healthy rise in contributions between 1983 to 1984, the total contributions for 1985 are expected to rise by less than half as much. Table 3.11 shows how these funds are allocated: 48 percent to agencies affiliated with the United Way, 20 percent to agencies affiliated with the National Voluntary Health Agencies, each of the other categories gets less than 10 percent.

AN OVERVIEW OF CHAPTERS 2 AND 3: SUMMARY AND CONCLUSIONS

This chapter and the previous one have presented certain basic ideas that undergird the remaining chapters of this book. The nonprofit is incorrectly seen as a purely voluntary, charitable or noncorporate form of organization. It is an economic organization or institution that has the advancement of public or community welfare as its mission. As such, it utilizes society's scarce resources and must compete for them. It pays for these resources and produces goods and services of value to society. Often it sells these products and services in competition with businesses operating for profit. In a later chapter we show that the nonprofit may even own these other businesses, ranging from department stores to hotels to fishing fleets.

The view of a nonprofit as a productive rather than a consuming unit places a whole different perspective on these organizations. It means, as we show in the next chapter, that they can raise money in ways other than pleading for gifts and contributions. They can take their rightful place in the economic system.

The view of a nonprofit as a productive unit is not taken lightly by those who compute the gross national product (GNP) of the United States. The output of the nonprofit sector is imputed and included in the determination of the total output of the country.

TABLE 3.10 Combined Federal Campaign Historical Statistics

Distribution of Total Receipts
(and percentage change from prior year)

	United Way		Natl Vol Hlth Agencies		Intl Service Agencies		Amer Red Cross		Natl Svc Agencies		Loc Nonaffil Agencies		Write-Ins	TOTAL	
1984	66,790,728	1.7%	27,532,234	10.7%	11,206,791	22.8%	305,502	−11.5%	9,980,921	19.9%	3,233,524	68.4%	3,620,376	122,670,076	11.25%
1983	65,681,437	5.1%	24,864,489	10.4%	9,129,179	22.9%	345,016	−11.8%	8,327,834	18.2%	1,920,681	46.0%		110,268,636	8.97%
1982	62,500,491	−4.3%	22,514,014	17.4%	7,430,822	1.7%	391,170	−17.9%	7,043,622	305.8%	1,315,199	37.4%		101,195,318	6.57%
1981	65,297,189	9.8%	19,184,125	12.4%	7,306,957	20.5%	476,322	−24.5%	1,735,556	199.1%	956,871	72.4%		94,957,020	8.26%
1980	59,480,299	−1.4%	17,074,904	5.2%	6,063,373	7.6%	631,260	0.9%	580,336	0.0%	554,895	0.0%		87,712,716	5.89%
1979	60,306,856	2.1%	16,231,136	−8.1%	5,636,104	1.2%	625,741	−6.2%						82,833,617	−0.21%
1978	59,074,434	5.2%	17,660,107	2.7%	5,571,631	4.5%	666,887	26.7%						83,006,726	4.39%
1977	56,140,434	11.3%	17,194,810	13.3%	5,332,629	10.2%	526,263	3.4%						79,516,049	11.69%
1976	50,451,887	8.1%	15,177,010	13.3%	4,837,847	9.1%	509,064	30.0%						71,192,475	8.11%
1975	46,650,439	6.2%	13,391,406	10.2%	4,436,185	6.1%	391,508	−20.0%						65,851,564	8.17%
1974	43,921,499	10.7%	12,147,906	15.7%	4,180,833	12.4%	489,168	22.8%						60,878,006	10.53%
1973	39,673,640	7.6%	10,501,025	8.0%	3,719,853	4.9%	398,285	−7.4%						55,077,890	7.50%
1972	36,887,261	12.5%	9,722,148	21.9%	3,546,334	13.5%	430,154	89.0%						51,234,426	11.60%
1971	32,801,979	23.0%	7,975,167	24.0%	3,123,336	21.5%	227,628	209.2%						45,909,421	27.87%
1970	26,672,476	8.5%	6,431,053	8.4%	2,570,808	8.2%	73,617	−3.2%						35,903,959	8.11%
1969	24,582,965	12.9%	5,930,442	12.7%	2,376,374	13.1%	76,034	−51.4%						33,210,610	13.02%
1968	21,769,108	19.4%	5,261,087	18.8%	2,101,773	19.9%	156,494	27.8%						29,385,213	19.80%
1967	18,224,885	13.8%	4,427,990	5.7%	1,752,588	8.6%	122,481	27.8%						24,527,944	11.73%
1966	16,018,210		4,190,790		1,613,714		95,830							21,953,452	21.63%
1965														18,049,436	40.16%
1964														12,877,942	
											GRAND TOTAL			1,165,542,420	

Supplied by Kent Bailey, Office of Personnel Management, Washington, D.C.

TABLE 3.11   Distribution of Combined Federal Campaign
Contributions by Recipient Agencies

Percentage Share of Total Receipts

	UW	MVHA	ISA	ARC	MSA	LMA	W-I	TOTAL
1984	54.4%	22.4%	9.1%	0.2%	8.1%	2.6%	3.0%	100.0%
1983	59.6%	22.5%	8.3%	0.3%	7.6%	1.7%	0.0%	100.0%
1982	61.8%	22.2%	7.3%	0.4%	7.0%	1.3%	0.0%	100.0%
1981	68.8%	20.2%	7.7%	0.5%	1.8%	1.0%	0.0%	100.0%
1980	67.8%	19.5%	6.9%	0.7%	0.7%	0.6%	0.0%	96.2%
1979	72.8%	19.6%	6.8%	0.8%	0.0%	0.0%	0.0%	100.0%
1978	71.2%	21.3%	6.7%	0.8%	0.0%	0.0%	0.0%	100.0%
1977	70.6%	21.6%	6.7%	0.7%	0.0%	0.0%	0.0%	99.6%
1976	70.9%	21.3%	6.8%	0.7%	0.0%	0.0%	0.0%	99.7%
1975	70.8%	20.3%	6.7%	0.6%	0.0%	0.0%	0.0%	98.5%
1974	72.1%	20.0%	6.9%	0.8%	0.0%	0.0%	0.0%	99.8%
1973	72.0%	19.1%	6.8%	0.7%	0.0%	0.0%	0.0%	98.6%
1972	72.0%	19.0%	6.9%	0.8%	0.0%	0.0%	0.0%	98.7%
1971	71.4%	17.4%	6.8%	0.5%	0.0%	0.0%	0.0%	96.1%
1970	74.3%	17.9%	7.2%	0.2%	0.0%	0.0%	0.0%	99.6%
1969	74.0%	17.9%	7.2%	0.2%	0.0%	0.0%	0.0%	99.3%
1968	74.1%	17.9%	7.2%	0.5%	0.0%	0.0%	0.0%	99.7%
1967	74.3%	18.1%	7.1%	0.5%	0.0%	0.0%	0.0%	100.0%
1966	73.0%	19.1%	7.4%	0.4%	0.0%	0.0%	0.0%	99.8%
1965								

Supplied by Kent Bailey, Office of Personnel Management Washington, D.C.

In carrying out its mission, a nonprofit can run a business and make a profit but the profit has to be incidental to other sources of revenues and support. This does not mean, however, that the profit must be small. There is no law that puts an absolute limit on the profits that a nonprofit may make. Thus, in dollar terms, the profits might be quite large. What the law does require is that the making of the profit is not the objective of the organization and, as we see in a later chapter, that the profits be balanced by gifts and contributions as a way of demonstrating public support. Thus, it is the proportion, not the absolute amount of profits, that matters. Accordingly, the more money a nonprofit makes from conducting business, the more it is likely to have to raise through gifts, contributions and other forms of support. As we shall see in later chapters, however, income from business may sometimes be included among these latter forms of support.

In keeping with its mission to advance public rather than individual welfare, no profits, income or other assets of the nonprofit can be distributed to individuals as owners, for to distribute any of these to individuals would be to advance private rather than public welfare. Let us elaborate on this private benefit or private inurement as it is sometimes called. As one legal scholar points out, this means that the nonprofit cannot be used as an instrument to pay dividends, excessive compensation, unusually generous benefits or privileges including lunches or loans, or pay unusually high fees or rentals to the founders, the management or their relatives and associates.[38]

Further, while legally a corporation, the nonprofit is different from a for-profit corporation. For-profits are organized by individuals to advance their own private welfare. These individuals are the owners of the corporation and as owners, they have legal claims to the income and assets of the corporation. The owners can and do receive dividends. On the other hand, no individual, not even the founder or primary sponsor, owns a nonprofit or can claim its assets or income.

Claims can, of course, be made by creditors in the case of the bankruptcy of the organization. But these creditors cannot bring about an involuntary closure of a nonprofit through claims of bankruptcy. From a financial point of view, a nonprofit has both advantages and limitations but the scope of its authority to engaging in financial transactions—including the running of business—is wide. These are governed by state and federal laws. States create nonprofits and empower them. The federal government accepts the creation of the state and determines whether the nonprofit is worthy of the society's resources through tax exemption. The managers of the nonprofit determine whether they will survive.

NOTES

1. For a review of the literature on this subject, see John P. Persons, John J. Osborn, Jr. and Charles F. Feldman, "Criteria for Exemption under Section 501(c)(3)," *Research Papers: Commission on Philanthrophy and Public Needs* (Washington, D.C.: U.S. Treasury, 1979), vol. 4, pp. 1909–2075.

2. Ibid.

3. Revenue Ruling 74–587, 1974–2 Cumulative Bulletin 162 and Revenue Ruling 81–284, 1981–2, Cumulative Bulletin 230.

4. General Consul's Memorandum 39047, 1/2/83.

5. Revenue Ruling 76–94, 1976–1 Cumulative Bulletin 171.

6. Revenue Ruling 81–62, 1981–1 Cumulative Bulletin 355.

7. Fraternal Medical Services Incorporated v. Commissioner, Tax Court Memorandum, 84, 644, (12-20-84).

8. *Black's Dictionary of Law,* 5th ed. (St. Paul, Minnesota: West Publishing Company, 1979), p. 212.

9. Fraternal Medical Specialist Services, Inc. v. Commissioner, Tax Court Memorandum, 84, 644, (12-20-84).

10. Church in Boston v. Commissioner, 71 Tax Court Memo 102, 106 (1978).

11. Better Business Bureau v. United States, 326 U.S. 279 (34 after 5) (1945). This is a seminal case.

12. Trinidad v. Sagrada Orden, 263 U.S. 578, 581, 44 S. Ct. 204, 205, 68 L.Ed. 458 (1924).

13. Revenue Ruling, 73-104, 1973-1 Cumulative Bulletin.

14. The American College of Physicians v. the United States, Appeal No. 84-715, September 17, 1984.

15. Revenue Ruling 73-105, 1973-1 Cumulative Bulletin 264. See Alan J. Yanowitz and Elizabeth A. Purcell, "IRS's Recent Approaches to Retail Sales by Exempt Organizations: Analyzing Standards," *The Journal of Taxation,* 59, no. 4, (October 1983), 250-255 for a comparison.

16. See Persons et al., *Research Papers,* for history and citations of Congressional debate.

    At least one economist argues that the law is unfair because it tends to encourage nonprofits to stick to related businesses. The consequence of this is that those for-profit industries that are most likely to be a related business for nonprofits must contend with competition from nonprofits while other sectors less likely to be a related business do not face the same intervention and competition from nonprofits. Competition is healthy for the economy. Susan Rose-Ackerman, "Unfair Competition and Corporate Income Taxation," *Stanford Law Review,* 34, no. 36 (1982), 1017-39.

17. Piety Inc. v. Commissioner, 82 T.C. No. 16, 1/26/84.

18. Church of Scientology of California v. Commissioner U.S. Tax Court Docket. 3352-78.

19. Society of Costa Rica Collectors, T.C.M. 1984-648, 12/13/84.

20. Annual salaries and benefits data for foundations can be obtained from the Council of Foundations and from the Society of Association Executives, both of Washington, D.C.

21. Alan Pifer, *Philanthrophy in an Age of Transition* (New York: The Foundation Center, 1984) p. 23.

22. Technically, one could make a gift to a for-profit corporation but this is not a normal source of revenues for such corporations.

23. "Seven Other Ways Nonprofits Can Boost Their Income," *Institutional Investor,* VI, no. 8 (August 1972), 73.

24. Ibid.

25. Barnaby J. Feder, "The Peril of Counting on Federal Funds," *The New York Times,* Sunday, April 6, 1986, Section F, p. 23.

26. William Meyers, "The Nonprofit: Drop the 'Non'," *The New York Times,* November 24, 1985, Section 1, p. 8.

27. Small Business Administration, *Unfair Competition by Nonprofit Organizations with Small Business: An Issue for the 1980s* (Washington, D.C.: U.S. Small Business Administration, 1983).

28. Thomas A. Troyer and Robert A. Boisture, "Charities and the Fiscal Crisis: Creative Approaches to Income Production," New York University Thirteenth Conference on Charitable Organizations, (New York University, 1983), chapter 4, pp. 1-31.

29. "Business Volunteers for Arts Help Balance Theater Community Books," *The New York Times,* Sunday, March 30, 1986, p. 46.

30. William Baldwin, "Those Nonprofit Profits," *Forbes,* September 1, 1980, p. 98.

31. Ibid.

32. Joel Brinkley, "The Richest Foundation," *The New York Times Magazine,* March 30, 1986, pp. 32–39.

33. *Uniform Laws Annotated, Business and Finance Law,* master ed. (St. Paul, Minnesota: West Publishing, 1978), pp. 745–747 and the *1985 Supplement Pamphlet to the Uniform Law Annotated* (St. Paul, Minnesota: West Publishing, 1985), p. 431.

34. See summary of various research projects on this topic by Edwin B. Knauft, Joseph Galaskiewicz, Michael Useem, and Stephen Kutner in *Report, Program on Nonprofit Organizations, Institution for Social and Policy Studies,* Yale University, no. 5 (Fall 1985), p. 6.

35. Loren Renz and Patricia Read, eds., *The Foundation Directory,* 10th ed. (New York City: Foundation Center, 1985), p. xix.

36. Adjusted gross income (AGI) is a taxpayer's total income minus certain exclusions such as workmen's compensation, interest earnings on municipal bonds, individual retirement account contributions, and death proceeds from life insurance.

37. Office of Personnel Management, Solicitation of Federal Civilian and Uniformed Services Personnel for Contributions to Private Voluntary Organizations: Final Rule, Federal Register 5 CFR Part 950, Friday, April 4, 1986.

38. Bruce R. Hopkins, *The Law of Tax-Exempt Organizations,* 4th ed. (New York: Ronald Press, John Wiley & Sons, 1984), pp. 209–28.

SUGGESTED READINGS

HOPKINS, BRUCE R. *The Law of Tax-Exempt Organizations,* 4th ed. (New York: Ronald Press, John Wiley & Sons, 1984).

NIELSEN, RICHARD, "Strategic Piggybacking Self-subsidization Strategy for Nonprofit Institutions," *Loan Management Review* Summer 1982, Vol. 23, No. 4, pp. 65–69.

State Laws Regulating Charitable Solicitations
(As of December 1, 1985)

State	Charitable Organizations						Fund-Raising Counsel	
	Registration or Licensing	Regulatory Agency	Cost Limitations	Annual Financial Reporting Requirements	Monetary Exemption Ceiling	Charitable Solicitation Disclosure	Registration or Licensing	Bonding Requirement
Arkansas	Registration	Secretary of State Trademarks Department Little Rock, Arkansas 72201 501-371-3622	None	By March 31 or within 90 days after close of fiscal or calendar year ★	$1,000 (if all soliciting done by volunteers)	Solicitors must disclose minimum percentage of gross income received by the the charity	Registration	$5,000
California	Registration	Registry of Charitable Trust P.O. Box 13447 Sacramento, CA 95813 916-445-2021	None	Annual Financial Reporting Requirements are due at the same time as 990, four and one-half months after the end of the accounting period. Report due May 15. If gross revenue or assets exceed $25,000 during the year the organization must file	None	"Sale for charitable purpose card" must be shown prior to any solicitation	None	None
Connecticut	Registration	Public Charities Unit %Attorney General 30 Trinity St. Hartford, CT 06106 203-566-5836	25% to 50% depending on total raised	In form described by the Department within 5 months of close of fiscal year and must be audited by an independent	$5,000 (if all soliciting done by volunteers)	Solicitor must disclose true name, that he is a professional solicitor, and, if working for a professional solicitor, the name of	Registration	$10,000

				accountant if public support exceeds $100,000 ★		the firm. If soliciting on behalf of a charity, but not wholly for a charitable purpose, must disclose percentage of money raised toward the non-charitable purpose	Licensing	None
District of Columbia	Licensing	Department of Consumer & Regulatory Affairs 614 H St., N.W. Washington, DC 20001 202-727-7086	None	Within 30 days after the end of a licensing period and 30 days after a demand by the mayor (formerly the commissioner) ★	$1,500 (if all soliciting done by volunteers)	Solicitors must present solicitation information card to prospective donors. Card is issued by Department of Consumer and Regulatory Affairs	Licensing	None
Florida	Registration (Names of all fund-raising employees must be registered)	Department of State Division of Licensing The Capitol Tallahassee, FL 32301 904-488-5381	None	With annual registration process on forms audited by an independent public accountant if in excess of $100,000. A review audit can be used if between $50,000 and $100,000. ★	$10,000 (if all soliciting done by volunteers)	Organizations must furnish authorization to solicitors which must be exhibited on request	Licensing (Statute refers only to professional solicitors)	$10,000
Georgia	Registration	Secretary of State Office of Special Services 2 Martin Luther King Dr. Atlanta, GA 30334 404-656-2861	30% of administrative fund-raising unless exemption is given	Within 90 days after close of fiscal or calendar year. (Quarterly Reports required in first year of operation. Report must be verified by independent certified accountant if over $50,000.) ★	$15,000 if costs are below 30%	Organizations must furnish donor with name of solicitor and purpose for which solicitation is being made	Registration	$10,000 60% of total income of PFR for preceding year, whichever is...

State	Registration or Licensing	Regulatory Agency	Cost Limitations	Annual Financial Reporting Requirements	Monetary Exemption Ceiling	Charitable Solicitation Disclosure	Registration or Licensing	Bonding Requirement
Hawaii	Registration	Department of Commerce & Consumer Affairs P.O. Box 40 Honolulu, HW 96810 808-548-4740	None	With registration statement	$4,000 (if all soliciting is done by volunteers)	Solicitors must furnish authorization on request	Licensing	$5,000
Indiana	None	Consumer Protection Div. Attorney General 219 State House Indianapolis, Ind. 46204 317-232-6233	None	None	None	Paid solicitors must disclose percent of contribution going to charity	Registration	None
Illinois	Registration Regligious organizations are also required to register.	Attorney General State of Illinois 100 West Randolph 12th fl. Chicago, IL 60601 312-917-2595	At least 75% of gross receipts must be used for charitable purposes and not more than 25% for the cost of unordered merchandise	Within six months after end of fiscal or calendar year ★	$4,000 (if all soliciting is done by volunteers	None	Registration	$5,000
Kansas	Registration	Attorney General Judicial Center Topeka, KA 66612 913-296-3751	At least 75% of gross receipts must be used for charitable purposes and not more than 25% for the cost of unordered merchandise	Appropriate form pursuant to the Kansas Statues Annotated Sec. 17–7500 et. seq. as part of registration	$5,000 (if all soliciting is done by volunteers	None	Registration	$5,000
Kentucky	None	Attorney General Division of Consumer Protection	None	None	None	None	Registration with	None

State	Registration	Reporting	Financial Report / Audit	Disclosure	Bonding	Bond Required	Agency / Contact
	Registration					$10,000	Attorney General, Division of Consumer Protection, Frankfort, KY 40601, 502-564-6607
Maine	Registration	See disclosure	If more than $30,000 raised, within six months after close of fiscal year. Must be audited by independent public accountant ★	No professional fundraiser or solicitor shall solicit funds for a charitable purpose without full disclosure to the prospective donor the estimated cost of solicitation where less than 70% of amount donated will be expended for the specific charitable purpose	$10,000 (if all soliciting is done by volunteers)		Attorney General, Augusta, ME 04330, 207-289-3661
Maryland	Registration	None	Most recent completed fiscal year. If in excess of $100,000 an audit is required by an independent certified public accountant according to the standards of accounting and financial reporting of voluntary health and welfare oranizations ★	Paid solicitor must disclose his name and that he has been engaged by the charity to raise funds; the name of the organization and the purpose for which contribution is solicited; the percent of donations received by the solicitor, percentage which may be deducted for income tax purposes; upon request a copy of organizations financial statement is available.	$25,000 (if solicitation is not done by professional solicitor. Effective July 1, 1986)	None	Secretary of State, State House, Annapolis, MD 21404, 301-269-3425

State	Registration or Licensing	Regulatory Agency	Cost Limitations	Annual Financial Reporting Requirements	Monetary Exemption Ceiling	Charitable Solicitation Disclosure	Registration or Licensing	Bonding Requirement
Massachusetts	Licensing	Attorney General Division of Public Charities	15% to a professional solicitor; 50% overall solicitation expense; unless higher is proven to be in public interest	On or before June 1 or before 60 days following a fiscal year ending in April or May on prescribed forms organizations receiving over $100,000 annually must file audited financial statement ★	None	Solicitors must exhibit authorization on request	Licensing	$10,000
Michigan	Licensing	Attorney General Charitable Trust Section 670 Law Building Lansing, MI 48913 517-373-1152	None	Within approximately 6 months of end of fiscal year. Where income from public support is $50,000 or more a certified audit is required ★	$8,000 (if all soliciting is done by volunteers and annual report is given to contributions)	None	Licensing	$10,000
Minnesota	Registration	Dept. of Commerce Registration and Licensing Division 500 Metro Square St. Paul, MN 55101 612-296-6324	Expenses of over 30% for administration, general and fund-raising costs is presumed to be unreasonable.	File annual report, financial statement, and copy of IRS 990. (If 990 meets all requirements of financial statement, it can be filed in place of financial statement.) ★	$10,000 (if all soliciting is done by volunteers)	Solicitation card must be shown prior to solicitation)	Licensing	up to $20,000
Nebraska	Certificate granted on basis of letter	Secretary of State Lincoln, NE 68509 402-471-2554	None	Can file IRS 990 in lieu of auditor's report ★	None	Solicitor must carry and show certificate and issue receipts	None	None

State	... of approval obtained from county attorney of home-office county					for donations of of more than $2		
Nevada	None	Attorney General Carson City, NE 89701 702-885-4170	None	By July 1 with Secretary of State ★	None	None	None	None
New Hampshire	Licensing	Secretary of State Charitable Trust Concord, NH 03301 603-271-4314	85% must be applied to a charitable purpose	When requested by the director of the division ★	None	None	None	None
New Jersey	Registration	Charities Registration Sec. 1100 Raymond Blvd. Newark, NJ 07102 201-648-4002	15% to professional fund-raiser and professional solicitor 50% for mail solicitation via un-ordered merchandise	Within 6 months after close of fiscal or calendar year ★	$10,000 (if all fund raising is done by volunteers)	For telephone Solicitations must disclose name and address of organization; state amount as a percentage that will be given to organization; if not tax exempt status, that must be disclosed; must disclose percent that can be deducted as charitable contribution	Registration	$10,000
New Mexico	Registration	Office of the Attorney General Charitable Organization Registry P.O. Drawer 1508 Santa Fe, NM 87504-1508 505-827-6910	None	Within 75 days of the close of the fiscal year. Accompanied by IRS 990.	$2,500	Organization must disclose upon request the percentage of funds solicited spent on fund-raising costs	None	None

State	Registration or Licensing	Regulalatory Agency	Cost Limitations	Annual Financial Reporting Requirements	Monetary Exemption Ceiling	Charitable Solicitation Disclosure	Registration or Licensing	Bonding Requirement
New York	Registration	Office of Charities Registration Department of State Albany, NY 12231 518-474-3720	None	Within 90 days after the close of its fiscal year. If in excess of $50,000 for preceding year, report must be accompanied by an opinion signed by an independent public accountant ★	$10,000 (if all fund raising is done by volunteers)	None	Registration	$5,000
North Carolina	Registration	Department of Human Resources Raleigh, NC 27605 919-733-4510	None	With application for registration. CPA Audited Reports are required if more than $250,000 in support and revenue is received. If under $100,000 a report by an independent public accountant is accepted ★	$10,000 (if all soliciting is done by volunteers)	Percent of fund raising expenses and the purpose of the organization must be given in writing upon request	Registration	$10,000
North Dakota	Licensing	Secretary of State Bismarck, ND 58505 701-224-2901	35% re-solicitation of fund-raising expenses	Within 60 days after the close of the fiscal or calendar year.	None	None	Registration	None
Ohio	Registration	Attorney General Columbus, OH 43215 614-466-3180	None	By March 31 if on a calendar year; if on a fiscal year 90 days of	$500	None	Registration	$5,000

close of fiscal year ★

State		Contact	Limits	Financial report		Disclosure		
Oklahoma	Registration	Revenue Processing Division of Oklahoma Tax Commission 2501 Lincoln Blvd. Oklahoma City, OK 73194-0005 405-521-2617	Payments to professional fund-raisers or solicitors limited to 10% of totals raised	Within 90 days of the fiscal or calendar year	$10,000	Receipts must be given contributions over $2	Registration	$2,500
Oregon	Registration	Attorney General Portland, OR 97201 503-229-5278	25% for solicitation, 50% overall, unless higher authorized	Within 4 months and 15 days of close of calendar or fiscal year ★	$5,000	Solicitor must disclose name of fund-raising firm, name of the organization for which he is soliciting and the percentage of proceeds beneficiary will receive	None	None
Pennsylvania	Registration	Commission on Charitable Organizations Dept. of State Harrisburg, PA 17120 717-783-1720	35% re-solicitation & fund-raising expenses (including payment to professional solicitor and fund-raiser) (postage is not considered a fund-raising expense) 15% to professional solicitor, unless higher authorized	Organizations receiving less than $15,000 can file signed and notarized short form; over $15,000 and under $50,000 have to accept a review by a registered, independent of organization, public accountant; over $50,000 must have a complete audit ★	None	Solicitor must produce authorization on request	Registration	$10,000

State	Registration or Licensing	Regulalatory Agency	Cost Limitations	Annual Financial Reporting Requirements	Monetary Exemption Ceiling	Charitable Solicitation Disclosure	Registration or Licensing	Bonding Requirement
Rhode Island	Registration	Department of Business Regulations Providence, RI 02903 401-277-3049	50% re-solicitation of fund-raising expenses, 25% to professional solicitor, unless higher authorized	Within 90 days after end of fiscal year audited by an independent certified accountant. Organizations receiving less than $100,000 do not require an audit ★	$3,000 (if all soliciting is done by volunteers)	Identification card must be presented for each solicitation and must contain name and address or organization; purpose for which contribution is solicited; tax exempt status; percentage which may be deducted for income tax purposes.	Registration	$10,000
South Carolina	Registration	Secretary of State Columbia, SC 29211 803-758-2244	Reasonable percentage to professional solicitor	Within six months of the close of the fiscal year ★	$2,000 (for SC organizations only)	Solicitor must produce authorization on request	Registration	$5,000
Tennessee	Registration	Secretary of State James K. Polk Bldg. Suite 500 Nashville, TN 37219 615-741-2555	25% for fund-raising costs; 15% to professional solicitor, unless higher authorized	Submitted as part of annual registration process, independent public accountant audit required for over $10,000 in annual contributions ★	$5,000	None	Registration	$10,000
Virginia	Registration	Director of Consumer Affairs Richmond, VA 23219 804-786-1343	See disclosure	Submitted as part of annual registration process ★	$5,000 (if all soliciting is done by volunteers)	Donors must be told minimum percent of donation which will be received by organization for its own use if less than	Registration	$20,000

State	Registration	Office / Address	Bond	Exemption Amount	Annual Report	Disclosure Requirements		Registration Fee
Washington	Registration	Charities Division Office of the Secretary of State Olympia, WA 98504 206-754-1920	None	$10,000 (if all soliciting is done by volunteers)	Must be filed upon request of Attorney General or county prosecutor. If financial information is requested, will accept Federal 990 Form	70% of total donation. Solicitors must produce authorization on request and furnish receipts for contributions of $5 or more		Registration $5,000
West Virginia	Registration	Secretary of State Capitol Bldg. Charleston, VW 25305 304-345-4000	None	$7,500 (if all soliciting is done by volunteers)	Financial Report must accompany annual registration statement and if in excess of $50,000 required to have an audit by an independent public accountant ★	Solicitor must identify himself, the organization; the purpose of the solicitation and name the orgnization which will receive contributions. Must disclose upon request the percentage of donations applied to fund-raising costs.	None	Registration $10,000
Wisconsin	Registration	Department of Regulation & Licensing P.O. Box 8935 Madison, WI 53708 608-266-0829	None	$3,000	Within 6 months of the close of the fiscal or calendar year ★	Donor must be told the percentage of contribution that will go to charity		Registration $5,000

★ Indicates States will accept Federal 990 Form in Lieu of Legislatively Mandated Annual Report

American Association of Fund-Raising Counsel, Inc. 25 West 43 Street, New York, N.Y. 10036 (212) 354-5799

FOUR

Inherent Opportunities
for Nonprofits
In the Market Economy

All economic institutions, including nonprofits, function within the context of the economy in which they exist. The success of their performance depends partly on how clearly their managements understand how the economy functions to generate new opportunities for nonprofits. This chapter shows how new income prospects are generated by the economy and gives examples of how they may be captured by a well-managed nonprofit. These opportunities include joint ventures and partnerhips with for-profit firms. For-profit and nonprofit corporations are not natural enemies or antagonists.

ECONOMIC PURPOSE OF NONPROFITS

Attempting to find a theoretical foundation for the laws on nonprofits, legal scholars have turned to economic arguments. One argument is that nonprofits exist because of "contract failures."[1] This means that there are a number of situations where the purchaser is uncertain of the quality of product or service that a for-profit producer would provide. The producer is seen to be motivated by profits and not necessarily by what is in the best interest of the public. Under these conditions, some contracts with a for-profit firm would fail. In these cases, a nonprofit is said to be superior to a for-profit producer because it has no profit motive, just the single mission or purpose of improving the welfare of the public.

This view is sometimes seen as too narrow. Thus, another legal scholar takes the view that the economic role of a nonprofit is that there are times when it is in the best interest of the customers to own the producers.[2] This view rests on the idea that customers often find among themselves a mutual or common interest that cannot be appropriately satisfied by the market. In such a case, through a nonprofit mode they can join together to produce the product or service themselves. Thus, in the case of a day care center, a group of working mothers may join together to create a cooperative center responding to their specific needs and desires for the kinds of services they wish for their children. In the normal operation of the market, they cannot control the production process; they can merely choose among alternative offerings—none of which may be what they really wanted.

Even the view of nonprofits as collectives or voluntary associations to exercise individual beliefs or expressions is consistent with economic theory.[3] The economic theory of groups or collectivity argues that people come together in groups or collectives because of interdependencies, or what is known as externalities. An externality in economics means that the action of one person affects another person. For example, a thousand persons of the same religious belief may not only find greater religious satisfaction by worshiping together, but they would find it cheaper to build a house of worship in which they all worship together rather than for each to build his or her own house of worship.

As a matter of fact, an article appearing in the *Foundation News* suggested that the world of nonprofits be viewed as an economic world of competitive institutions and that to the extent that some nonprofits view themselves as competitors to each other, the better each would be.[4]

The upshot of these other views is that not only is there justification for viewing the nonprofit as an economic institution, but there is justification for viewing nonprofits as a group of players in a mixed economy. As we shall see, traditional economic theory as well as current practices by the IRS and the courts are supportive.

The reasons for articulating the role that nonprofits play in the economy are more than theoretical. One reason is that nonprofits do play a central role in the market economy. The National Association of Security Dealers (NASD) regulates security dealers and brokers and carries the most uptodate and complete price quotations on the over-the-counter stock exchange. It is a nonprofit. A second reason is that the market economy generates endless opportunities to nonprofits. To understand what we mean by this, let us take a look at recent history.

THE LESSONS OF RECENT HISTORY

The recent history of nonprofits, beginning about 1980, was marked by a high inflation rate that was unprecedented, a recession that was the deepest since the Great Depression, and drastic cuts in federal, state and local government support of nonprofits at the very same time that the demand for the goods and services of nonprofits rose sharply. This was due not only to the natural increase resulting from the economic crisis, but because of a call by President

Ronald Reagan for nonprofits to assume the responsibilities no longer being carried out by government. A difficult but worthy plea.

Many nonprofits collapsed. Others began to realize the wisdom and necessity for shifting from the purely nonprofit mode toward greater self-sufficiency. Nonprofits were in tight competition for a limited amount of resources. Many nonprofit managers lost their jobs, as they could not adapt to the new world of competition, efficiency in management, the shift in public sentiment and decline in resources.[5]

Where will the new money opportunities for nonprofits arise? The most fertile source is the operation and growth of the profit sector. We begin with the obvious in stating there are basically three sectors in the economic system: for-profit, nonprofit, and public.

The public sector relies upon the private sector. It is the latter that produces the goods and services, creates income and makes the profits that are taxed as corporate and personal income taxes—the major source of revenues of the public sector. One of the ways in which the public sector uses its revenues from taxation is to support nonprofits through contracts and grants.

The support that nonprofits get from nongovernmental sources comes from individuals and firms. Individuals can make gifts and contributions because they earn an income from the for-profit sector that pays its own workers and supplies the revenues that government uses to pay its workers. These workers, both in the public and private sectors, make contributions and gifts to the nonprofit sector.

The gifts and contributions made by firms to nonprofits come from their income or profits. Hence, whether the support comes from the public sector or individuals or directly from profit makers, the ultimate source is exactly the same: the for-profit firm.

The reliance on the for-profit sector goes beyond support. It extends to opportunties created by the way for-profit firms operate. They are also created by the limited effectiveness of government action. The ability to detect the new opportunities for nonprofits outside of the purely charitable sphere requires the ability to appreciate two trends: (1) the growth of for-profit firms, and (2) the limited effectiveness of government action. To do this requires an understanding of how the for-profit market operates.

NONPROFIT OPPORTUNITIES GENERATED BY THE MARKET ECONOMY

The market system internally generates and satisfies many needs. Often, however, capacity and efficiency considerations mean that for-profit firms cannot fully satisfy all market needs even though there is no lack of ability to pay on the part of those whose needs must be satisfied. Economic growth creates a demand for sudden increases in capacity, information, and other resources often existing in the nonprofit sector. To fully appreciate this, let us look at the economic behavior of each of the major actors in the market economy. We begin each section by specific real-world examples, then we present the basic theory, and show how other opportunities may be generated to the discerning management of nonprofits.

Consumers

There are several real-world examples of nonprofits intervening in the market process to assist consumers. A nonprofit group was given tax exemption as a charity because it gave education on personal financial management to low-income households.[6] Another nonprofit was similarly classified because it provided guidance and information to low-income households on building their own home.[7] Both of these are examples of nonprofits providing information and education to benefit the community.

How does the economy operate to provide these types of opportunities for nonprofits to assist consumers? A consumer can buy a good only if he or she has an income. The good will be bought only if its price does not exceed the dollar value the consumer places on it. The money used to make purchases is the earnings of the consumer as a worker.

Consumers are free to choose how to spend the income they earn as workers. Low-income consumers buy fewer luxuries, more low-priced or inferior goods, but spend just about the same proportion of their income as higher income persons do on necessities such as food, soap and shelter.

As do other commodities, soap comes in numerous sizes, shapes, brand names, scents and chemical compositions. Each of these characteristics is represented in the price. Similarly, cars come under different brand names, with different characteristics and are all reflected in differences in price. Yet, one car can be substituted for another. They all provide transportation, some more comfortably than others. The same thing holds for soap. All can be used for cleaning, but one gives a more favorable scent than the other.

Hence, if the price of one brand of car or soap rises, consumers who want basic transportation or cleanliness would buy more of the less expensive brand if it has maintained comparable quality. They will behave in this way as long as they are aware of the prices, and the brands they want are available. In short, consumer choice depends upon information as well as income, prices, and the availability of substitutes and complements.

Thus, as the for-profit sector grows, producing goods which are substitutes for each other, or complements to each other, and some of which are unrelated to each other, the opportunities for nonprofits are also increased. The home computer industry is an example. As for-profit firms produce more models that are really varying degrees of substitutes, there is also a rise in the demand for complements (software) which are also varying degrees of substitutes for each other. This has spawned countless opportunities for nonprofits to provide the computer-related complements of information and education.

Education and training even for a fee (as many educational institutions charge) are acceptable functions of nonprofits. Education is defined, for tax-exempt purposes, as instruction, information, and training that benefit an individual and the community.[8] It should be obvious from the theoretical framework as described that the economy generates an endless number of these opportunities.

Producers

There are several real-world examples of nonprofits assisting producers and this can occur even on a small scale. One example is an organization that was awarded tax exemption for marketing the cooking and sewing of low-income women. On a larger scale is the organization that does research on color science and technology[9] or the society that was formed to do scientific research on air conditioning and ventilating.[10] On even a larger scale are the universities that conduct research that benefits producers and is often paid for by them. In a later section of this chapter we show various types of relationships between for-profit and nonprofit firms.

What is the basis of these opportunities? To maximize their profits, producers create the mix of goods consumers want at the lowest cost possible by using the best technology and workers available and by selling the goods at the highest price consumers will pay.

Research to develop technology requires specialized skills. Research and development are acceptable functions of nonprofits as long as the results are made public. A very high percentage of the research and development that eventually leads to commercial applications is done at universities and other nonprofit laboratories. This is in fields including space, crop development and land conservation, medicine and medical procedures, and marketing. Thus, the growth of the profit sector creates a demand for the talents and specialties in the nonprofit sector and trained by it. Nonprofits can provide the input necessary to sustain growth.

Workers

There are numerous real-world examples of nonprofits assisting workers. Thus, an organization that provided a registry of available nurses was given tax exemption because the registry was seen as assisting the community to find nurses, rather than the nurses to find jobs.[11] The registry was not viewed as self-promotion of the nurses, in which case it would not have been exempt, but as information to the public. Also, an organization formed to transport low-income workers to jobs due to inadequate transportation was also granted exemption.[12] An organization formed to give career counseling and to distribute educational publications was also granted exemption even though it charged a fee.[13] Day care centers are granted exemptions if nearly all of the child care service is provided to enable parents to work and if the service is available to the general public.

What are the generic factors that give rise to opportunities to assist workers? An individual in the market economy acting freely and rationally would choose the occupation for which he or she is best suited because this would improve the chances of maximizing income and minimizing the unpleasantness of work. Once in that occupation, the person would seek to work for the highest paying producer. And, naturally, the higher the pay, the greater the willingness to work.

This economic behavior of workers depends on a number of factors: having adequate information about occupations and employment, having access to training and to jobs, being compensated according to productivity, having information and access to leisure and being able to make a rational judgment between leisure and work. Meeting these training, informational, search and employment needs are acceptable functions of nonprofits.

This is precisely what job training schools do. They train and help in job search. Some nonprofits aid older workers, the disabled, veterans, women and the disadvantaged in career development and in finding jobs. In this regard, they work to help expand the for-profit sector and to improve its efficiency by training and placing workers. Not only do nonprofits train the input necessary for growth but they can assist in matching input availability (supply) with demand.

Investors

There are real-world examples of nonprofits assisting investors. Two examples were given in the previous chapter—both of organizations making loans for business purposes. We show in later sections several nonprofits working hand in hand with for-profit corporations.

Economic growth cannot occur without new net investment in plant and equipment. As economic growth occurs, it stimulates more investment as investors begin to expect acceptable rates of return on their investments. Producers must borrow to invest because the initial cost of most projects is large. They will borrow only if the expected rate of return on their investments equals or exceeds the rate of interest they have to pay for borrowed funds. It makes no sense, for example, to borrow at 15 percent and get only a 5 percent return on the investments made.

Nonprofits do have a growing opportunity to affect investment decisions. Economic development corporations and community development corporations are nonprofits capable of operating in this sphere. They can make investments that are beneficial to the community but which for-profit firms will not make because the project is too risky or the rate of return too low.

In addition, these nonprofit corporations can lower the cost to the for-profit firm by putting up seed money, making loans at below market rates, packaging and preparing land, and giving technical assistance. By lowering costs, these actions increase the profitability of the project and make it more attractive to private investors.

Savers

Investment dollars come from the savings of workers. To get more savings for investment, consumers must be encouraged to save by having safe vehicles for saving and earning high rates of interest. Encouraging saving through the education of consumers is an acceptable function of nonprofits. Thus, the organization that assisted low-income households to improve their money management was granted tax exemption.[14]

By referring again to Table 2.1, we see that there are types of savings institutions that are nonprofits although they are not classified under Section 501(c)(3) which is our principal concern. They are nevertheless worth noting. Pension trusts have billions of dollars in assets and are nonprofit organizations. Deposits to these trusts are regular, predictable, and dependable. Withdrawals from these trusts are orderly and extend over many years. Therefore, pension trusts are a primary source of dollars for long-term investment. Mutual insurance companies and credit unions are also examples of nonprofits operating to stimulate saving and to provide loans.

These discussions indicate that within the market structure itself there are potential opportunities for nonprofits to assist (1) consumers, (2) workers, (3) producers, (4) investors, and (5) savers. In a growing economy, these opportunities increase, not decrease. Many of these opportunities exist in the shaded area in Figure 4.1. In this area, nonprofits and for-profit firms may be competitors or collaborators, such as joint partners in research, information dissemination or community development.

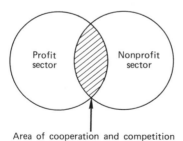

Area of cooperation and competition

Figure 4.1 Interaction of Profit and Nonprofit Sectors. Source: Author.

The Conference Board is a business information service providing assistance to senior executives on management, business, public policy and economic issues. The National Urban Coalition and the National Center for Neighborhood Enterprise share information with community groups about business creation.

The latter even helps to create neighborhood business. The Booker T. Washington Foundation assists minority businessmen in penetrating certain markets. The National Council for Urban Economic Development works with officials of local governments in improving the business environment of their local communities. The Greater Philadelphia First Corporation is a coalition of a wide range of business and community organizations focusing on cooperative approaches to urban development. All of these are 501(c)(3) organizations.

The competition even within the shaded area is limited. It often means that the for-profit and nonprofit corporations divide a market for the same product or service. Constrained by their need to make a profit, the for-profit firms would almost automatically focus on the more profitable segment of the market while the nonprofit able to rely on gifts and contributions as supplementary support and being constrained by IRS rules to demonstrate that they are not just another commercial firm but are catering to a clientele that such firms do not reach, will focus on the less profitable segment. Witness the difference between privately owned (for-profit) hospitals and community hospitals. Notice also that this does not necessarily mean economic disaster for the nonprofit. Some nonprofit hospitals do very well compared to for-profit ones.[15]

NONPROFIT OPPORTUNITIES GENERATED BY MARKET FAILURES

Externalities are created by the operation of the market. Economists use the term "externalities" to denote the effect that one entity's or person's market behavior has on others.[16] In a market economy, each person or entity acts in a manner to meet his or her economic objectives with only limited regard for its effects on others; that is, the market fails to control the impact that individuals or firms have on society. The existence of these externalities creates a demand for nonprofits.

External Diseconomies of Consumption

The use of automobiles (emitting carbon dioxide, making noise, requiring the conversion of open space to roads and highways), flying (noise and air pollution from airplanes), smoking, and the abuse of alcohol and other drugs are said to result in external diseconomies of consumption because they have deleterious effects on persons other than the user. When external diseconomies of consumption exist, the obvious reaction is to curtail the negative effects.

Government can impose laws and regulations and may even tax the purchase of the commodity with the hope that the higher price will discourage consumption. Under certain conditions, such as designating no-smoking areas in public places and in airplanes, the intervention by the public sector may only be partly effective. Experience has shown that public sector actions are not sufficient and often ineffectual. Producers and consumers of products that have strong external diseconomies are usually successful in resisting any truly impeding law or tax not only by virtue of their political power, but by calling upon constitutional protection of their rights.

Because there are usually no profits to be made in restricting consumption resulting in external diseconomies, for-profit firms are usually not attracted to such activities. On the contrary, there are often more profits to be made in the production and sale of commodities and services such as cigarettes, alcohol and drugs than in curtailing their use.

If the government taxing, law and rule-making powers have limited effect, and if the profits to be made in curtailing consumption are also limited even though curtailing consumption is socially desirable, a natural opportunity then arises for nonprofit organizations. Examples of these are nonprofits using their education and training authority to educate people about the dangers of smoking and drugs, and the organization that received tax-exempt status because it provided funds to owners of cats who could not afford the cost of having the pets spayed or neutered.[17]

The tasks before the management of the nonprofit when external diseconomies of consumption exist are (1) to identify the aspect of the external diseconomy to which the organization can properly address itself, (2) arrive at an appropriate strategy for dealing with it, and (3) use the social merit argument as well as the merits of the organization to justify public and sometimes industry financial support.[18]

External Economies of Consumption

These exist when the consumption by any one person of a good or service has a positive effect on others. Vaccinations against communicable diseases benefit both the client and others with whom he or she may come in contact. Many health and educational programs fall into this category; for example, an organization formed to give counseling in employment, citizenship, language, medical information and housing to immigrants is of this type. The more the immigrants partake of these offerings, the easier their adjustment, the lower the need for social assistance and the possibilities of infractions against the law. Consequently, the entire community is better off.[19]

Returning to the case of inoculations, profits to be made by inoculating individuals are limited by their ability to pay, their awareness of danger and their willingness or ability to make themselves available for shots. Because it is to the advantage of society to have as many persons as possible inoculated, and because for-profit firms are limited by their need to earn a profit, some needs will remain unmet. One possibility is for the public sector to directly answer those unmet needs. Another is for the public sector to subsidize both for-profit firms and nonprofits so that the unmet needs would be addressed. A third possibility is for the nonprofit to meet those needs by relying on below market rate fees, using gifts and contributions to make up the difference. Through its normal operation, the economy generates and leaves unanswered a number of consumption externalities or "spillovers," as they are sometimes called, for which fees can be charged by a nonprofit provider.

External Diseconomies of Production

These occur when the production process results in negative effects on others. Smoke emission from a plant and chemical and industrial wastes dumped in waterways are examples. Economic growth, if only by increasing the rate at which facilities are used, generates diseconomies of production.

One reason external diseconomies of production persist is that they bring down the cost of production to the producer. It is cheaper to dump waste in rivers than to properly dispose of them. In short, producers have limited incentive to curtail external diseconomies of production. When such incentive exists, it often is brought about by external forces.

One external force is the government. It can impose fines, taxes and jail sentences. Another source is for-profit firms that produce substitutes or use substitute methods of production. The production of substitutes is not enough, as can be seen in the different grades of gasoline. Moreover, the initial force for bringing about change is often a nonprofit movement as in the fields of environment and energy.

Often there are no profits to be made by discovering these diseconomies, monitoring and reporting them, or even creating solutions to them. Hence, an organization that is not constrained by profit considerations must often come to the fore. The environment movement, from monitoring to the development of alternative energy sources, in large measure represents reactions to external diseconomies of production. Thus, when external diseconomies of production exist a need for nonprofit organizations to reduce them arises. The nonprofit does not have to be in a confrontal position. There are many industry-supported nonprofits that regulate their members. The challenge before the nonprofit management is, again, to answer the three-part question: (1) what is the specific feature of the diseconomy that the nonprofit is capable of addressing, (2) what is the best strategy, and (3) what are the merits upon which funds can be obtained? A specific example of a nonprofit organization that has received tax exemption to meet this challenge is one that was formed to inform the public about the destruction of the environment due to solid waste disposal and which obtained revenues by collecting and selling solid waste for recycling.[20]

External Economies of Production

These arise when the production process creates benefits to persons outside of the firm. These are benefits that the firm is incapable of harnessing and selling. Hence, it has very little incentive to produce them at any level greater than what is incidental to its normal production even though society may benefit from more. As in the case of the consumer, the government could try subsidizing the firm to induce it to do more, but this is expensive. A less expensive way is often to increase the intervention of a nonprofit organization.

As an example, grocery stores always experience spoilage or the need to reduce the price of inventory such as baked goods after they have been on the shelf for some time. A nonprofit, viewing this is an opportunity, entered into an agreement whereby these day-old or damaged foods are distributed by the nonprofit to the poor. Here, what would ordinarily have been a loss is converted to an external economy of production and a social gain. The management of this nonprofit knew: (1) where an external economy of production existed or could be created from a potential loss, (2) how the nonprofit and its clients could benefit from it, and (3) how it could raise the very modest support needed. The goods were obtained free and volunteers were used to collect and distribute them. This activity attracted clients to the organization, many of whom purchased commodities received as gifts and sold at bargain prices in its thrift shop, thereby generating revenues.

PURE PUBLIC GOODS AND NONPROFITS

Even though they might be of inestimable value, pure public goods are not produced by for-profit firms because the principal characteristics of a pure public good is that once it is provided, no one can be excluded from its enjoyment. Clean air is an example. Once the air is clean, anyone who lives or visits the vicinity can enjoy it. Because there is no way to exclude anyone, everyone will enjoy it regardless of whether or not he or she is charged or pays a price. Who will voluntarily pay a price for something that can be gotten without paying?

A corollary characteristic of pure public goods is that they are usually not divisible. It is not possible to split them up into units that can be distributed one to an individual. Who will pay for a commodity that cannot be owned?

Another corollary of a pure public good is that the consumption by any one individual of that good does not diminish the consumption by any other person. When one person breathes fresh air, that does not diminish the amount available to any other person. As a result, there is no bidding because the good does not run out.

These features mean that pricing of public goods by a for-profit firm is impossible. How can a profit be made on a good that no one is willing to pay a price for? How can a profit be made on a good if ownership cannot be sold— who will buy it? How can a profit be made if no buyers will bid? Since the pure public good cannot be sold, a profit cannot be made and for-profit firms will not produce them.

Yet, there is a cost to producing pure public goods. Clean air is maintained at a cost. Who pays? Generally, the government pays through imposing compulsory taxes and by contracting with or subsidizing for-profit or nonprofit organizations to do the work. Public goods such as clean air are appropriate functions of nonprofits.

Associations are one type of nonprofits that produce pure public goods. Associations of employees, employers, counties, cities are all examples of nonprofits providing public goods. To understand this, one only has to appreciate the fact that once a union wins benefits for workers, those benefits can be enjoyed by workers in the trade regardless of whether or not they are members of the union. When the American Medical Association fights for and wins a legislative position favorable to doctors, all doctors potentially benefit whether or not they are members of the association.

Associations also provide some private goods. Thus, they can charge a fee for the association's magazine because the magazine is not a public good. As is increasingly the case, members who do not pay a special fee for the magazine will not get it. The magazine is divisible so that many, many subscribers may be served—each with an individual copy. On the other hand, the representative effort of the association is a pure public good. No actual or eligible member of the association can be excluded from the representative benefits. Accordingly, associations commonly place a price on some of their activities such as seminars and journals which are private goods but not on their representative efforts which are public goods.

Other examples of nonprofits providing public goods include an organization of physicians which oversees the quality of health care in a particular community.[21] The same is true of an organization created to do improvements on municipally owned property.[22] An organization created to preserve lakes for public recreation is also an example.[23]

In general, public goods offer opportunities for nonprofits because for-profit firms have no price incentive to produce such goods. A price cannot be charged. In this sphere, nonprofits have an advantage because they can charge a general membership fee and also seek additional support in the form of gifts and contributions as ways of paying for the public good.

NONPROFIT FINANCING OF PUBLIC GOODS AND RESPONSES TO EXTERNALITIES

Why, it may be asked, would nonprofits be able to find profitable opportunities in externalities and public goods when for-profit firms cannot? The answer is that nonprofits can rely on combined support from individuals, firms and government and a below market price to cover costs and produce a surplus. Private firms must rely only on market price.

Does it make sense to speak of reliance on support when such support—at least from the government—is becoming less reliable? This only means that nonprofits must increasingly diversify their revenue base, which is the purpose of this book.

Why would an individual give to a nonprofit that produces a public good or responds to an externality when neither may be particularly profitable? Because "giving" is only limitedly related to economic considerations. Moreover, an activity might have too low a return to attract a particular investor. Yet, that investor could reap significantly high tax savings by making a contribution to a nonprofit that would make the investment.

NONECONOMIC CONSEQUENCES OF MARKET BEHAVIOR AND OPPORTUNITIES FOR NONPROFITS

As the market system functions, it produces a number of noneconomic consequences. One is inequity. The market system pays people only if they work. Pay is determined by the value of the contribution of the worker to the value of the final product. Some individuals are unable to work for reasons of disability or age. In a strict market economy only those who work are able to consume because only they will have income with which to make purchases. Moreover, in a strict market economy, people who are less productive than others would not only be paid less than others but may very well be paid below the amount necessary to afford a socially acceptable minimum standard of living. Thus, poverty is consistent with a market economy. There are both working and nonworking poor.

The consequence of this is that many persons are not able to afford even basic necessities. The most efficient market economy distributes income according to productivity, not according to need. A producer cannot pay according to need. A producer can only pay according to the value of the product the worker produces, since this is the only source of revenues for the producer. For-profit firms do not get gifts and contributions.

But equity and the needs of individuals cannot be ignored in any humane society. Because revenues place a limit on what firms can pay, a need arises for an entity that is not limited by its earnings. Nonprofits are not so limited. They have other sources of support—gifts and contributions. Therefore, nonprofits are well suited for dealing with issues of equity.

Admittedly, the dimension of the equity problem may be too large for the nonprofit sector alone or for any one specialty within the nonprofit sector. This is why the following subject of understanding complex problems is important.

SOCIALLY COMPLEX PROBLEMS AND THE NEED FOR NONPROFITS

Whether opportunities appear within or outside the perimeters of the market system, they are likely to present themselves as complex problems. In the view of Professor H. Rittle, complex does not mean difficult. A complex problem is one that is (1) subject to many definitions, (2) with each definition requiring a unique set of solutions, (3) with each solution creating its own set of side problems, and (4) with each of these side problems (like the original problem) subject to many definitions and solutions and so on in a circular fashion.

Poverty is a complex problem. It has many facets including health, education, nutrition, employment, legal, and cultural. Each aspect presents a set of specialized challenges; that is, the legal questions are different to the medical and nutritional factors. Each set of specialized solutions represents a role for a special type of nonprofit. Having undertaken the challenges of one solution, a new set of problems arises. For example, setting up a health clinic does not solve the problem of getting people to attend and creates the need for a link between their social and health needs.

Moreover, the very definition of poverty is temporal and spatial; that is, the poverty level for an urban family of four is different to that of a similar family in a rural area. The poverty threshold changes every year and the cash definiton of poverty is different to the cash-plus-assistance-received definition.

The point is that a truly complex problem creates a wide range of interrelated needs with each set of needs requiring a different specialty and with each specialty requiring an organization with a specialized mission. All complex problems are not purely charitable, but even noncharitable complex problems create the need for nonprofits.

The production and use of automobiles, nuclear plants, and a residential development are truly complex problems and create a need for nonprofits partly because of the externalities as we discussed them, and partly because of the creation of pure public goods. An automobile is a private good that creates external diseconomies of consumption through gas emission and reckless driving. It also gives rise to public goods such as the creation of anti-drunk driving nonprofits. Complex problems, obviously, are also related to the operation and growth of the economy.

Imaginative management of nonprofits requires the ability to detect the existence of a complex problem, to systematically dissect it and to identify the aspects of the complex problem that the organization can adequately address.

OPPORTUNITIES FOR PROFITABLE COOPERATION BETWEEN NONPROFIT AND FOR-PROFIT CORPORATIONS

In the previous section, we show how nonprofits may intervene in the market process to carry out their charitable missions while at the same time earning revenues. To do this, it is not necessary and often is not advisable for the nonprofit to go it alone or to try to compete with for-profit firms. This section demonstrates several levels of cooperation that can benefit both the for-profit firms and the nonprofits. Buy why would these firms have any incentive to cooperate with each other?

Every successful partnership requires the interlocking of interests among the parties involved. Chapter 3 makes it clear that a nonprofit may make a profit, but it must be used to carry out the charitable purpose of the organization. This means that the dominant motive is public welfare, not private profits. However, for-profit firms are driven by the profit motive, not public welfare.

The successful partnership combines the interests of the nonprofit as an economic institution that needs revenues to serve its clients with that of for-profit firms that need markets from which to derive a profit. The market is composed of the clients and potential clients of the nonprofits. Thus, by serving the clients or mission of the nonprofit, revenues are generated for both the for-profit and nonprofit partners.

What makes these arrangements possible is that neither the for-profit nor nonprofit organizations disagree about the need for revenues. Both are interested in containing costs and in a good public image, and both are economic institutions but neither maximizes profits. Herbert Simon, a Noble prize winner, noted that firms engage in "satisfying" rather than in maximizing profits.[24] By this he means that for-profit managers try to accommodate a number of competing constituencies both within and outside the firm and that this attempt to satisfy rarely leads to maximum performance. A recent study confirms this. See the insert on the next page.

For any partnership to succeed, all parties must contribute something. What the nonprofits contribute is their advantage in meeting certain needs that the regular commercial market cannot profitably satisfy. This advantage derives basically from the following:

1. Nonprofits can sell a product or service at a lower price than for-profit firms can because nonprofits can subsidize their lower price by gifts and contributions.

2. Nonprofits often have a built-in clientele not only from their membership but from the fact that the relationship that people develop with these organizations is rarely based upon the quality of product or services they produce for sale or the price at which they sell them. If this were not so, candies and cookies could not be sold at such high prices and nonprofits could not charge such outrageous prices for chicken dinners.

3. Nonprofits are in a better position to lower costs of production by using volunteers, by obtaining plant and equipment as gifts, by lower postage rates, and by not having to pay taxes under certain very circumscribed conditions even when they run a business for profit. In this book we describe how this is done.

4. Nonprofits such as research organizations often hold licenses or patents which can be used by for-profit firms to produce a product or service while providing the nonprofits with revenues in the form of royalties.

For-profits have no such advantages but they can deduct the interest they pay on debt from their taxes, they can subtract depreciation in calculating their taxes, and prior to the 1986 tax reform, they could take an investment tax credit on the equipment they buy. An investment tax credit varied from 6 to 10 per-

☐   Contrary to popular belief, companies do not put maximum profit before all else. In practice, no absolute or eternal financial priorities exist; they change as the economic and competitive environments change.

☐   Mature companies assign priorities to multiple financial goals based on the relative power of the economic constituencies represented by these individual goals – whether capital or product markets or the market for human resources.

☐   Companies do not have an inalienable right to "dream the impossible dream" and set any goal. From the moment a company decides to enter a particular segment of the product or capital market, its competition imposes limits and sets conditions on the goals it can realistically attain.

☐   Managing a company's financial goals system is an unending process in which competing and conflicting priorities must be balanced. At any point, the system is potentially unstable because of the changing corporate environment and shifts in power and influence among constituencies.

☐   A company's internal capital market must continuously try to reconcile the demand for and supply of funds. It imposes an impersonal and objective discipline on the conflicting goals that affect the flow of funds and requires that those driving demand balance with those driving supply. An executive cannot change any goal without considering the impact on all others.

☐   Most managers find it difficult to understand and accept the entire goals system. Although financial goals appear objective and precise, they are in fact relative, changeable, and unstable. Moreover, subordinate managers normally see them from the limited perspective of their immediate responsibilities. Even top executives, tending to be more disposed to one constituency as against another, have difficulty accepting this system as a legitimate political compromise among these competing and conflicting priorities.

Gordon Donaldson, "Financial Goals and Strategic Consequences," *Harvard Business Review,* (May–June 1985), pp. 57–66. Reprinted by permission of the *Harvard Business Review,* copyright 1985 by the President and Fellows of Harvard College; all rights reserved.

cent of the purchase of old or new equipment which may be deducted from their taxes. Nonprofits cannot use these tax credits unless they run a for-profit business that pays taxes. The net effect of tax breaks like interest, depreciation and investment tax credit is to reduce costs and to increase the after-tax rate of return on their investments. In addition, for-profit firms can contribute expertise and capital.

For-profit firms can contribute marketing skills, logistical and transportation capacity to move a product or service across the globe, technological and production capacity and expertise, and capital. By exploiting the main differences between these two sectors, there are endless opportunities for cooperation between for-profit firms and nonprofits. Let us take a look at three levels of cooperative efforts. Chapter 8 discusses a matrix that helps managers decide when cooperation is advisable. The insert on the next page discusses the ingredients of a good cooperative venture.

Transactions

On the transactional level, a for-profit and nonprofit merely engage in a transaction that is mutually beneficial. A nonprofit may use its fund-raising advantage to construct a building. It can then sell that building to a for-profit firm and rent space within the same building. The deal involves the nonprofit getting a low rent, getting back the capital it invested in the building and an additional amount of money representing a gain from the sale. The for-profit buyer gets rental income from the building from the nonprofit and other tenants. The taxes on the rental income are reduced by the deduction for interest, depreciation and investment tax credit, when it applies.[25] If the depreciation is sufficiently high to represent a paper loss for tax purposes, the for-profit investor is also able to shelter income from other sources from taxes. Both parties gain by utilizing their comparative advantages. These sale-leaseback arrangements are profitable for both parties when appropriately structured.

Joint Ventures

On this level, the for-profit and nonprofit organizations work cooperatively toward a common goal. They do not, however, form a separate legal organization. They merely work together. One study identifies five types of joint ventures between universities and corporations. These include (1) research done at universities but sponsored by corporations, (2) corporate use of licenses and patents owned by universities to produce goods for commercial sales and for which the universities get royalty payments, (3) consulting agreements between the corporation and the university faculties for which the university charges a fee, (4) the sharing of laboratory space and facilities between the university and the corporation, and (5) the ownership by universities of either the majority or minority share of a for-profit corporation.[26]

The Westchester Golf classics are examples of joint ventures between nonprofit groups and private firms in a fund-raising event. The Manufacturers Hanover Trust Co., one of the largest banks in the United States, makes packages of tickets available to its corporate customers who use them to entertain clients. Fourteen hospitals also sell tickets and keep the revenues from their ticket sales. The hospitals also get a portion of the tournament proceeds including revenues from amateur golfers who pay up to $3,000 per person to play against the pros. Television pays tens of millions of dollars ($13.2 million in 1984) to carry the classics. To keep costs down, more than 1,500 volunteer workers are used.[27]

Joint ventures are also possible among nonprofits. Hospitals are increasingly entering into joint ventures with nonprofit (or for-profit) corporations

---

To survive, a corporation must make a profit and pay a return to its shareholders. A university on the other hand, searches for knowledge and educates, but it must also pay its bills.

A corporation, to protect and enhance its profitability, must initially shelter the achievements of its research by keeping them out of the public domain. But a university must lay open to the entire world the results of its research as soon as possible in order to fulfill its mission of expanding human knowledge.

And a corporation must choose its research projects carefully and pursue those which may have some possibility of a commercial return. A university has more flexibility to pursue basic knowledge and understanding for its own sake.

So look at what we have:
—profit versus non-profit;
—secrecy versus publicity; and
—basic research versus product development.

They're really — I think you must admit — completely opposite poles. But each also has things from which the other can benefit; new knowledge that can meet a need in the market, on the one hand; profits that can be invested in more research, on the other.

A good example of a long-running, mutually-beneficial relationship is a partnership we formed five years ago with the University of Utah.

Under the terms of this agreement, Abbott is the principle sponsor of a unit where clinical trials are performed on new drugs. This agreement is structured to allow the university to do contract work for other organizations when the unit is not fully occupied with Abbott projects.

Both sides are winners. Abbott is able to perform clinical trials at a lower cost, while the university gains both revenue and a valuable teaching facility.

In addition to the willingness to make a long-term commitment, look at the company's flexibility regarding the types of agreements it enters into. Stay away from companies which dictate "it shall be this way and no other." Too many good ideas have been killed that way.

Flexibility is one of the basic concepts with which our research agreements are negotiated.

We have had more than 150 contracts for research and development in diagnostics alone. No two are alike. These contracts cut across a broad spectrum and include:
—arrangements for consultants, adjunct facilities and clinical test sites;

—full-blown joint ventures; and
—simple contracts to commercialize.

In many cases, we have a direct relationship with the researcher, as well as the institution involved.

In addition to flexibility, find a company that is technology-driven.

In making this determination, look for things like:
—a high percentage of revenues and profits from products less than five years old;
—a short product life-cycle as a result of continuing innovation;
—and look for solid year-to-year increases in R&D spending.

Also, review the company's historical commitment to technology and its record of commercializing ideas that came from outside the company. Does the company have a "Not Invented Here" attitude?

Besides this historical commitment, be sure to examine the company's record of innovation in diverse areas. Ideally, it should include high levels of both basic discovery and applied development.

Another crucial element is an organization's ability to move quickly. I want to stress that this doesn't necessarily mean that a small company is best — large ones can move in an entrepreneurial fashion, too.

In addition to possessing speed, flexibility and a historical commitment to technology, the company you chose should simply be good at the "nuts and bolts" of business.

Closely analyze the organizational structure of your prospective partner. Support functions such as marketing, distribution and customer service should be fully developed. These functions may not seem glamorous, but they are absolutely essential and cannot be built overnight. I don't want to sound like I am taking a jab at start-up firms, but a few dozen people simply can't do the job in today's global marketplace. Make sure your industrial partner has the resources — both human and financial — to do your technology justice.

As I said earlier, I can't supply a lot of hard and fast rules to apply in choosing a corporate partner. There is no single litmus test you can apply.

The most important task is to somehow look inside an organization to determine its success in innovating. Some companies talk a lot about managing innovation, but have little to show for it.

Jack W. Schuler, "The University-Industry Partnership: A Marriage of Heaven and Hell," speech delivered to the Society of University Patent Administrators, and appearing in Vital Speeches of the Day, 52, no. 12, 4/1/86, 358–369. Schuler is Executive VP, Abbott Laboratories.

owned by physicians. For example, physicians may form firms to collect the fees for services the doctors performed in the hospitals.

Partnerships

One form of working jointly is through a partnership arrangement. In such an arrangement, the nonprofit enters into an agreement with one or more non-profit partners to create a separate legal organization to carry out a trade or business. The partnership is not, however, simply an agreement to work together such as a joint venture. It is a legal organization with its own identity and staff.

The partnership has one or more general partners. These are organizations or persons who are fully liable for the losses of the business and who manage it cooperatively. General partners also decide how to distribute the earnings and tax benefits among themselves and how to share the responsibility for coming up with the capital required to get the business going. Unlike a general partnership, in a limited partnership the partners cannot participate in the management and are not liable for any losses beyond the amount of money each has invested. If the limited partner invests $1,000,000, it cannot be held liable for any amounts over $1,000,000. In contrast, the general partner's liability may go beyond the investment. For example, a general partner who puts up $1,000,000 is liable for more than that amount if the business is sued or if creditors demand to be paid. One way to protect against this limitless liability is for the general partner to be insured.

This description of a partnership arrangement reveals some of the concerns that the IRS and the courts have about partnership involvements by nonprofits. Their strongest position is in being general partners because they can influence the management. But a general partnership also exposes the nonprofit to limitless losses. Moreover, the motive of the for-profit partner is distinctly different and sometimes in conflict with the assumed motive of the nonprofit. The former seeks profits for private individuals as its primary purpose for engaging in the partnership while the latter seeks profits as a means of financing a charitable activity. In the latter case, the profits are only incidental to the charitable goal. Thus, there is an inherent conflict between the two goals. Accordingly, when the facts and circumstances of the partnership arrangement are such that they jeopardize the requirements of a nonprofit organization, the IRS will deny or revoke the tax-exempt status of the organization.

Let us proceed to look at some accepted partnership arrangements in housing and neighborhood development. In one case, a nonprofit and a for-profit firm entered into a partnership to construct and operate a housing project exclusively for the handicapped and the elderly. The nonprofit is responsible for marketing and renting units, lease enforcement, supervising repairs and maintenance, and conducting social programs for the tenants. In ruling favorably on this arrangement, the IRS noted that providing housing for the handicapped and the elderly is a defined charitable goal and is consistent with the charitable purpose of the nonprofit in question. It also noted that there were sufficient safeguards to protect the nonprofit because one for-profit general partner had pledged to cover all operating deficits for a specific period of time. The risk of unlimited liability was reduced by the existence of other for-profit general partners who had agreed to share it, and the mortgages were insured by the federal government in case of default by the project.[28]

Joint ventures have also been used in the arts. In *Plumstead Theatre Society* v. *Commissioner*, the court ruled in favor of a partnership between a theater that clearly operated as a nonprofit and private individual investors who put up $100,000 in return for a sizable percentage of the profits the theater was expected to make.[29] The court ruled that the theater was not controlled by the private investors, was not required to pay them for losses, and did not depart from its tax-exempt purpose of promoting new and experimental productions and its involvement in the community.

Similarly, the court has ruled in favor of joint ventures in the field of medicine. It ruled that a nonprofit hospital that entered into a joint venture to construct and manage rental office space to its affiliated physicians had not violated its tax-exempt status. The hospital was paid a management fee, its proportionate share of the profits, was protected against losses and could provide better service to patients by having the doctors around.[30]

It is not simply the activity that counts. The courts and the IRS have also denied or revoked the tax-exempt status of nonprofits entering into joint ventures in housing, the arts, medicine, and so on. These factors matter: (1) that the organization does not depart from its charitable purpose or subvert it to the profit motive of the for-profit partner, (2) that the organization does remain free from the control of the for-profit partners, (3) that the assets of the organization are not exposed to covering the liabilities of the venture and its private partners, (4) that a significant portion of the activity be dedicated to the charitable purpose of the organization, and (5) that there is a demonstrable advantage to the nonprofit in having a for-profit partner.

Basically, the IRS uses a two-part test to determine the acceptability of an investment partnership to qualify under Section 501(c) (3). First, it must be demonstrated that the organization is legitimately serving a charitable purpose. The housing need of the elderly, for example, is a charitable purpose. But if a housing partnership provides only a token proportion of its housing units to the elderly, this would not qualify.

Second, while recognizing that in a partnership the nonprofit will have some legitimate economic and fiduciary relationship to its partners whose motives are strictly profits, the partnership agreement should insulate the organization from obligations that serve to maximize the profits of its for-profit partners or that causes the organization to veer from its charitable purpose. Thus, an arrangement where the nonprofit is placed at risk of guaranteeing profits or covering the losses of the for-profit partners is not acceptable. Neither is it acceptable that the for-profit partners would receive a disproportionate share of the profits or losses, that the nonprofit will sell assets such as land and equipment or rent space or make loans to the partnership at below market rates or that the profits to either the nonprofit or for-profit partners be excessive. Finally, the IRS looks skeptically on partnerships between the founders and managers of a nonprofit and the nonprofit organization they are supposed to be managing.[31]

THE MARKET ACTIVITIES AND THE THREAT TO NONPROFIT STATUS

In Chapter 3 and in this chapter we give examples of nonprofits operating within the market economy and making a legal profit. In Chapter 3, we discussed some sharp differences between the for-profit firm and the nonprofit. To keep things in perspective, it would be wise to remember that the nonprofit exists to carry out a welfare mission and the profits are incidental to the discharging of that mission.

Thus, in *Copyright Clearance Center* v. *Commissioner* the court said:[32]

> Although an organization might be engaged in a single activity, such activity may be directed toward multiple purposes, both exempt and nonexempt. But, in the case of multiple purposes, it must be kept in mind that qualification for exemption depends upon whether the entity in question is organized and operated "exclusively" for one or more of the exempt purposes in the statute.

The court went on to state that there is no stringent definition of the word "exclusive" and that it may also be interpreted as meaning "primary." Which ever word is used, the legal interpretation is equivalent to mean substantial. Thus, the nonprofit may be said to exist exclusively for a tax-exempt purpose if it has no substantial activity that is nonexempt; that is, the commercial activities that are undertaken cannot be a substantial part of the activities of the nonprofit. Chapters 5 and 6 elaborate more on these points.

SUMMARY AND CONCLUSIONS

In most societies, the economy is a dominant sector. By understanding how it operates, nonprofit managers are able to detect new opportunities. These opportunities derive partly from the imperfections of the market—the inability of the economy to fully satisfy important needs of the public or community.

One set of these opportunities exists within the market structure itself. These relate to the needs of consumers, producers, investors, workers, and savers. Another set of needs relates to effects that are somewhat external to the market. These are indirect effects that emanate from how the market operates. Another set of effects emanates from the fact that the market is incapable of addressing them. These are public goods and equity.

Being able to identify specific opportunities within these broad sets of functions means that the nonprofit can benefit from the dynamic growth of the economy in ways that go beyond seeking gifts and contributions. They can identify a niche that is a natural concomitant of a dynamic economy, and they can go beyond their purely welfare missions into new spheres that are not only profitable but that are consistent with the mission of nonprofits. The next chapter shows how strategic planning may be used to detect promising opportunities.

NOTES

1. Henry B. Hansmann, "Reforming Nonprofit Corporation Law," *University of Pennsylvania Law Review*, 129, no. 3 (January 1981), 397-623.

2. Ira Mark Ellman, "Another Theory of Nonprofit Corporation," *Michigan Law Review*, 80, no. 5 (April 1982), 999-1050.

3. See Tibor Scitovsky, "The Place of Economic Welfare in Human Welfare," *Quarterly Review of Economics and Business*, 13, no. 3 (Autumn 1973), 7-19; M. V. Pauly, "Cores and Clubs," *Public Choice*, 9, (Fall 1970), 53-55; and Y. K. Ng, "The Economic Theory of Clubs: Pareto Optimality Conditions," *Economica,* 40, no. 159 (August 1973), 291-98, Martin McGuire, "Private Good Clubs and Public Good Clubs: Economic Models of Group Formation" *Swedish Journal of Economics* Vol. 74, 1972, pp 84-99.

4. Philip S. Broughton, "The Economic Function of Foundations," *Foundation News,* 5, no. 5 (September 1964), 1-4.

5. The plight of nonprofits during this period is chronicled in many newspaper and journal articles. See for example, Neal R. Pierce and Erin MacLellan, "Nonprofit Groups Are Trying to Learn How to Cope with Federal Budget Cuts," *National Journal*, 13 (August 22, 1981), 1510-13.

6. Revenue Ruling 69-144, 1969-2 Cumulative Bulletin 115.

7. Revenue Ruling 67-138, 1967-1, Cumulative Bulletin 129.

8. Reg. Section 1.501(c) (3)-1(d) (3).

9. Munsell Color Foundation, Inc. v. U.S. (DC, Md; 1973), 33 AFTR2d 74-339.

10. Revenue Ruling 71-506, 1971-2 Cumulative Bulletin 233.

11. Revenue Ruling 55-656, 1955-2 Cumulative Bulletin 262.

12. Revenue Ruling 78-69, 1978-1 Cumulative Bulletin 156.

13. Revenue Ruling 68-71, 1968-1 Cumulative Bulletin 249.

14. Revenue Ruling 69-441, 1969-2 Cumulative Bulletin 115.

15. See Carson W. Bays, "Why Most Private Hospitals Are Nonprofit," *Journal of Policy Analysis and Management,* 2, no. 3 (1983) 366-81, and H. David Sherman, "Interpreting Hospital Performance with Financial Analysis," *The Accounting Review*, Vol. 61, No. 3, July 1986, pp. 526-550.

16. Other terms for externalities are indirect effect, neighborhood effect, and spillover.

17. Revenue Ruling 74–194, 1974–1 Cumulative Bulletin 129.

18. Of course, a fee could also be charged. More will be said about fees in Chapters 6 and 9.

19. Revenue Ruling 76–205, 1976 Cumulative Bulletin 154.

20. Revenue Ruling 76–204, 1976–1 Cumulative Bulletin 152.

21. Virginia Professional Standards Review Foundation 79–1, United States Tax Court No. 9167.

22. Revenue Ruling 54–296, 1954–2 Cumulative Bulletin 59.

23. Revenue Ruling 70–186, 1970–1 Cumulative Bulletin 128.

24. Herbert A. Simon, "Theories of Decision Making in Economics," *American Economic Review,* XLIX, no. 3 (June 1959), 253–83 and *Models of Man* (New York: John Wiley & Sons, Inc., 1957), Chapter 14.

25. The Deficit Reduction Act of 1984 placed some limitations on these transactions. The limitations are largely on the private partner. See David Warren, "Leases and Service Contracts with Tax-Exempt Entities after the DRA," *The Tax Advisor,* (April 1985), pp. 230–34.

26. Kendyl K. Monroe, "Collaboration Between Tax-Exempt Research Organizations and Commercial Enterprises—Federal Income Tax Limitations," *TAXES—The Tax Magazine*, 62, no. 5, (May 1984) 297–316.

27. Brenton Wellino, "The Westchester Classics: Big Bucks and Good Works," *Business Week*, June 10, 1985, p. 79.

28. General Counsel Memorandum 39005 and Alan J. Yanowitz, "Using the Investment Partnership as a Charitable Activity: A Means/Ends Analysis, *The Journal of Taxation,* 60, no. 4, (April 1984) 214–18.

29. Plumstead Theatre Society v. Commissioner, 74 Tax Court 1324, 1980.

30. IRS Letter Ruling 8201072.

31. For a discussion of these principles, see Michael Schell, "The Participation of Charities in Limited Partnerships," *Yale Law Review,* 93 (1984), 1330–63, and Louise A. Howells, "Community Development Under Section 501(c) (3) of the Internal Revenue Code: The Charity in Economic Development," *TAXES—The Tax Magazine,* 62, no. 2 (February 1984), 83–93.

32. Copyright Clearance Center v. Commissioner, T.C., 793–810, (1982).

SUGGESTED READINGS

Douglas, James, *Why Charity*? (Beverly Hills: Sage Publications, 1983).

Independent Sector, Working Papers: Spring, First Research Forum Since Filer Commission Report (Washington, D.C.: 1983).

James, Estelle and Susan Rose-Ackerman, "The Nonprofit Enterprise in Market Economies," PONPO Working Paper No. 95 and ISPS Working Paper No. 2095, Yale University, 1986.

Kramer, Ralph M., *Voluntary Agencies in the Welfare State,* (Berkeley, California: University of California Press, 1981).

ROSE-ACKERMAN, SUSAN, "Unfair Competition and Corporate Income Taxation", *Stanford Law Review,* 34, no. 5 (May 1982), 1017–39.

WEISBORD, BURTON A., *The Voluntary Nonprofit Sector* (Lexington, D.C. Heath, 1977).

WHITE, MICHELLE J., ed., *Nonprofit Firms in a Three Sector Economy* (Washington, D.C., The Urban Institute, 1981).

YOUNG, DENNIS, *If Not for Profit, For What* (Lexington, Massachusetts: Lexington Books, 1983).

FIVE

Strategic Planning To Identify Opportunities and To Determine Management Strategies

Within the market economy and aside from their strictly eleemosynary functions, nonprofit organizations may find money opportunities by concentrating on externalities generated by economic growth, public goods not produced by for-profit firms, and on functions internal to and essential to the market but for which there is insufficient market capacity. All of these represent unmet needs. The success of a nonprofit in identifying specific unmet needs and implementing successful strategies to capture money opportunities will to a large extent depend upon careful planning.

Strategic planning is a process used by for-profit firms and astute nonprofits to make the adjustments necessary to meet both the opportunities and the challenges of the future. This process cannot be blindly applied because there are significant differences between for-profit and nonprofit organizations. Therefore, this author has developed diagrams and specific discussions of differences that should be of concern to the nonprofit manager and suggests specific ways for dealing with them in the search by nonprofits for new opportunities.

STRATEGIC PLANNING IN PERSPECTIVE

In 1887 a priest, a rabbi, and two ministers founded the first United Way to meet the need of coordinating local services and to conduct a single fund-raising campaign for 22 agencies. They recognized a noncommercial need that continues to exist today.

The mission of the United Ways of America is "To increase the organized capacity of people to care for one another." This mission is consistent with

---

Strategic Planning Conference

A Strategic Planning Conference in March at Airlie, Virginia, brought together the key leadership of USO—volunteers and staff—for a frank exchange of views and information.

Stateside and overseas conference participants analyzed USO's internal and external environments. Out of these discussions, six major themes emerged:

1. Clarify and improve the relationship between various components of USO.

2. Clarify USO's mission and purpose internally, and effectively articulate them to the public.

3. Establish effective liaison, communication, and coordination of programs with the military worldwide.

4. Improve the professional development for USO staff and volunteers worldwide.

5. Design and implement resource development strategies.

6. Establish direction, priorities, and standards for worldwide USO program delivery.

A report on the Airlie strategic planning conference was presented to the Board of Governors. Following Airlie, the President of USO appointed a Long Range Planning Committee, chaired by Paula Unruh, member of the USO Board of Governors, and the six-member committee began charting the organization's future directions drawing on the Board of Governor's political, corporate, and military expertise.

For the first time in nearly a decade, USO had a chairman and a president. The president of one of the nation's leading corporations— Dennis P. Long of Anheuser-Busch, Inc. in St. Louis, Missouri—was elected chairman. And, General George S. Blanchard, USA (Ret.) former commander in chief of the U.S. Army, Europe, was elected president.

The new leadership represents a strong statement of private and military support for the men and women in the armed forces and their families through USO.

Michael E. Menster, "Strategic Planning Conference" *America's Spirit: Annual Report of the USO,* 1980, p. 5.

the definition of organizations defined under Section 501(c)(3) of the code. It is also broad enough to encompass the missions of individual United Way Agencies throughout the country.

The strategies of the United Way includes community involvement of all segments of the community, a single campaign to raise funds, and a flexible distribution of funds. These strategies do not lead to substantial commercial activities.

The programs of the United Ways of America include some 400 information and referral services that link people in need with those with resources; a management assistance program that offers consultation, training, and in-

> Fiscal year 1985 has been an exciting year of accomplishment and progress for Children's Hospital National Medical Center. In this report you will learn about our expanded Trauma Service programs; our reestablished Gastroenterology/Nutrition Department; the new faculty practice plan, Faculty Associates Inc.; and our improved financial performance. All our efforts and accomplishments cannot be chronicled in a report such as this. What was accomplished was a team effort and was done with an eye to the future.
>
> The most exciting and challenging accomplishment this past year was the beginning of the process to form a Strategic Plan. By examining exactly where we are, we hope to direct our future to further prosperity and continued growth as the preeminent pediatric facility in the mid-Atlantic region and in the nation. We've talked with physicians within and outside the hospital, with community leaders and with our employees. Listening to as many voices as possible, we should have the Strategic Plan formulated and ready to guide us into the future by the spring of 1986.
>
> By taking a long, hard look at ourselves, we can plan a future built on the strengths of our past and the opportunities of the future. One result is certain: Children's Hospital will continue to do what it has done for the last 115 years—provide the best quality care for kids and their families.

Bruce M. Perry, Children's Hospital Medical Center, Annual Report, 1985, p. 4.

formation sharing; a volunteer leadership development program to enhance the managerial and financial leadership of volunteers; a program that puts those who wish to make gifts of property in touch with those who have a specific need for the type of property to be given; and a national fund-raising campaign, the proceeds of which are distributed to other nonprofits. Each of these programs meets a specific objective consistent with the mission of the United Ways of America.

The United Ways of America cooperates with the National Football League Charities and with numerous employers and employee associations in reaching its goal. The United Way competes with other combined fund-raising groups. On occasion, it has worked along side of these groups in specific fund-raising efforts.

STRATEGIC PLANNING: PURPOSES AND APPROACHES

Strategic planning is a process through which a nonprofit organization may:

1. identify needs
2. define its mission

3. evaluate its capabilities
4. assess its external environment
5. set objectives
6. select strategies
7. design programs
8. determine a budget
9. evaluate performance

At each step in the strategic planning process, it is possible to use the most sophisticated techniques in research, group dynamics, logic, argumentation, program planning and evaluation. These techniques are discussed in standard texts.[1]

The purpose of this chapter is to show how this process may be applied to nonprofit organizations. The chapter highlights certain concepts upon which nonprofit managers should focus.

The reader will observe the strategic planning process that is briefly outlined begins with an identification of a need consistent with the mission of the nonprofit. Through a deductive process, it then proceeds to reduce the need to a manageable form for the nonprofit. Only then can realistic programs be designed. Because needs are not constant over time and programs are never perfectly designed or implemented, allowance must be made for evaluation and adjustments.

Figure 5.1 shows an outline of a strategic planning process that reflects this orientation. The process begins with the identification of societal needs which may relate to equity, increasing the efficiency of the market by assisting consumers, or one of the other roles identified for nonprofits in Chapter 4.

Once these needs have been identified, those that are most closely related to the mission of the nonprofit organization as stated in its charter or organizing document should be given priority because, as we see in the next chapter, nonprofits are required by law to adhere to the mission under which they were chartered and for which they were given tax exemption.

Because most social needs are complex and stretch well beyond the resources of any one organization, it is important for each nonprofit to identify a specific gap that it may be able to fill. This gap becomes the focus of the planning process. It is the organization's target, for it is the difference between what is being done to meet the need and what is necessary to fully address it. The gap is a measure of an unmet need.

Having identified a gap and an unmet need consistent with its mission, the nonprofit must now assess its ability to successfully fill a portion of that gap. This leads to an assessment of the internal weaknesses and strengths of the organization. Does it have the necessary management experience or capacity to fill all or a portion of the gap? What aspect of the gap is it best suited to fill?

Likewise, it is necessary to assess the external environment. What opportunities are presented to the organization so that it may successfully fill the gap

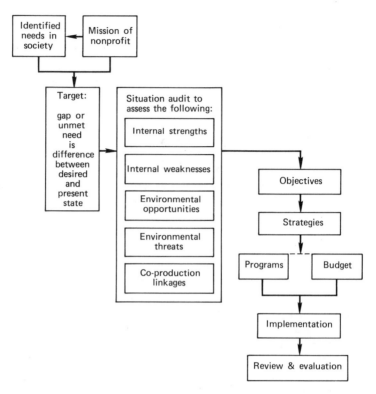

Figure 5.1   A Strategic Planning Process. Source: Author.

it has identified and targeted? What are the external obstacles or threats the organization will face once it has attempted to fill the gap? Are there other organizations operating in the same area of unmet need and specifically in the gap targeted by the nonprofit? Is there room for one more nonprofit? Are there licensing laws or political and locational factors that would impede the nonprofit's attempt to fill the gap?

Next, the organization must take into account the interaction between itself and a number of external forces. This is particularly important in nonprofit organizations because much of what they do depends upon co-production. Co-production, to be discussed later in this chapter, means that the organization's success or failure in supplying a good or service depends upon the participation of others—including the clients—in the production process. Therefore, the nonprofit must be certain about its co-producers as well as the linkage or interaction that brings all factors together to make the production process successful.

An example of this is education. For a school to rank high in the educational performance of its students depends upon the quality of the faculty, the facilities, parental support, and the quality and dedication of the students. The students are more than passive clients. They are critical to the production of high scores, for if all the other factors were present and the students were of low intellectual capability or uninspired, high scores would not be possible.

Another example is the resolution of crime. Students of police performance have discovered that the ability of the police to respond quickly and to resolve crimes depends heavily on the nature and speed of response and cooperation of the victims. The victims, by virtue of their cooperation with the police, are co-producers of police performance.

After taking these steps, the organization is now prepared to state its objectives. Objectives are statements of intent to meet specified unmet needs or to fill specified gaps. Objectives are meaningful if they reflect the internal and external constraints (opportunities, weaknesses and threats) to the organization. This is why it is best to state objectives only after the gap is clearly analyzed and identified and after a complete assessment of the organization's capacity and environment including the strength of linkages among co-producers has been made.

Once the objectives have been specified, the strategic planning process may proceed to develop strategies. Strategies are statements of how the objectives will be accomplished. They are statements of mode or direction. How will the unmet needs be met? Strategies should be broadly stated to provide room for imagination, flexibility and realism in the design of programs.

Programs activate strategies. Programs are clusters of action that, when implemented in the mode or direction specified by the strategy, enable the organization to meet its objectives.

Programs are of two types. Action programs are clusters of interrelated activities. Program design is an art well beyond the subject matter of this book. However, assuming that the staff of the nonprofit has designed a set of programs, choices must be made because resources are limited. To choose wisely among the various possible programs, the nonprofit must set certain criteria such as the costs of the programs, the benefits to be derived from each, and the feasibility and desirability of each. The challenge for the nonprofit is to select the "best" program. We show later in the chapter a simple technique for making this choice.

Once the preferred programs are chosen, strategic planning moves toward implementation. The length of the implementation process depends upon the type of program, but it also depends upon decisions concerning the availability of resources, the duration of unmet needs as targeted by the nonprofit and the effectiveness of the programs. Accordingly, implementation should be accompanied by continuous monitoring and periodic reviews and evaluations. Through this process, the need for adjustments can be detected and the adjustments can be made before resources are wasted.

With the foregoing outline, a manager ought to be able to employ a strategic planning process that is useful. More sophisticated processes do require technical assistance and more research on need assessment, program planning and evaluation and on the subject matter (the gap or unmet need) of the planning process. Whether sophisticated or not, for the nonprofit manager, some basic concepts deserve further elaboration. One is the selection of strategic options because this is what decision making is all about. A second essential concept is co-production because this is central to the operation of most nonprofits. A third basic concept is the life cycle of needs because their fulfillment is the ultimate mission of nonprofits. We discuss each in turn.

STRATEGIC OPTIONS: PROFITS VERSUS MISSION

Before an option is selected, it must be compared with other options along a number of dimensions simultaneously. One dimension is nonmonetary: Is the option feasible, desirable, and consistent with the mission of the organization? As we see in the next chapter, veering from its mission can have dire legal and tax consequences on a nonprofit.

Another dimension along which options should be compared is monetary: Do the monetary benefits exceed the monetary costs; and if so, by how much? This does not mean that the managers always have precise measurements of the benefits, costs, feasibility or other criteria. It means only that they are able to make some reasonable judgment such as, "we believe that the benefits are five times the costs."

But the fact that the benefits may exceed costs is not enough upon which to make a decision. Often monetary considerations conflict with mission and manageability or feasibiity of an option. To appreciate this, let us consider a case where a nonprofit has five options for tending to an unmet need.

Assume that the five, A through B, have the following benefit-to-cost ratios: $A = 5$, $B = 4$, $C = 3$, $D = 2$, $E = 1$ and $F = 0.1$ meaning, for example, that in A, the benefits are five times the costs; in D benefits are only twice the costs. Is A to be chosen over D? To answer this, see Figure 5.2 which shows these options as they fall on a graph that simultaneously considers the feasibility and desirability of the options.

Option A has the highest benefit-cost ratio and, according to Figure 5.2, is very feasible but not desirable. Many options are economically sound but do not comport with the organization's image or value system; moreover, some options not only lead to tax consequences for nonprofits but may even cost them their tax-exempt status.

On the other extreme, while D has the third lowest benefit-cost ratio, it is more desirable and feasible than A. D is superior to A. Although C's benefit-cost ratio is only average, it is more desirable than A. C ranks second to D.

F is both the most feasible and desirable option. However, F has a benefit cost ratio less than 1. Its cost exceed its benefits.

Option B is desirable, and has the second highest benefit-cost ratio but the organization is incapable of implementing it. E is infeasible, undesirable,

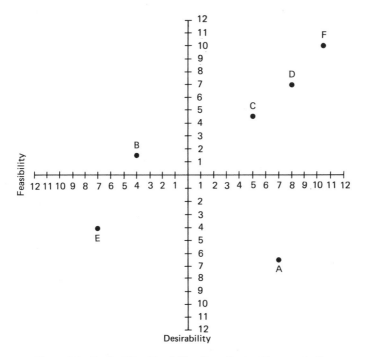

Figure 5.2 Desirability-Feasibility Coordinates. Source: Author.

and its benefits just match costs. This leaves options C and D. Both may be chosen because they may be complementawry—pursuing one enhances the success of the other. A secondary school could use a primary feeder school.

Both C and D may be chosen if the are independent of each other because this reduces the risk of failure. This is a diversification of options. Both may be chosen because together they will share costs. Finally, both may be chosen even if they are contradictory because the selection of options is often based on political considerations; that is, "pacifying," "satisficing" the opposition or compromising between opposing but legitimate viewpoints.

The lesson for this exercise is that the choice of options is rarely based on the simple calculations of costs and benefits and that sometimes the attractiveness of choices may be influenced by other considerations. This does not mean, as is usually implied, that nonprofits should not be motivated in their decisions by dollar costs and benefits and should not try to maximize the difference between the two so that dollar benefits far outweigh costs. It merely means that often such programs are not within the realm of feasibility or desirability of the organization from the point of view of its mission. One way to overcome this obstacle is by the creation of an unrelated business (the subject to Chapter 7) or allied nonprofits (the subject of Chapter 6).

STRATEGIC OPTIONS: COMPETITORS
AND COOPERATORS

One important factor in the selection of options is the role of other organizations. The choice of options is influenced by other organizations whether they are competitors or allies of the nonprofit. How do other organizations influence the choice of options?

Zero-sum Games among Competitors

While nonprofit managers may not be aware of it, often they are more exposed to competitors than for-profit firms. The capital requirements, technology, licensing and regulations that affect the rate of entry of new firms in the for-profit market do not exist to the same extent in the nonprofit sector.[2] In many ways, entry of new competitors into the nonprofit market is relatively easy to accomplish. Nonprofits cannot stop the entry of new competitors and the laws are often not so stringent as to be prohibitive to new organizations.

Aside from the rate of entry of new organizations (both private and nonprofit) over which a nonprofit may have no legal control, there is the issue of how to compete with an actual or potential competitor once entry has occurred. The basic question is: What will be the reaction of a competitor if the nonprofit should pursue a particular strategy? Suppose, for example, nonprofit A decides to target a specific income group to give drug counseling. Will nonprofit B, in order to justify its funding, intensify its efforts to give drug counseling to the same group? Will it choose a narrower group such as teenagers? Would it focus on specific neighborhoods, or drugs, or sex? Notice that each of these counterstrategies of B chips away at the overall clientele of nonprofit B. If the size of the drug population in the community is relatively fixed, say 1,000 people, A can only increase its clients of drug abusers by reducing the number available to B and vice versa; if A chooses a strategy, any counterstrategy of B that is successful will reduce the extent to which A will increase its clientele.

This is known as a zero-sum game because the overall size of the market is fixed, so that one group can only grow at the expense of the other. This is captured in Figure 5.3 which is called a payoff matrix. The rows show the strategies, 1 through 6, that A may choose. The columns show the strategies available to B. The number in each cell is the percentage of the market that A will gain when it chooses a specific strategy that is countered by B's choice of one of its six strategies. The number of cells depends upon the number of strategies available. Obviously, the greater the number of strategies under consideration, the greater the number of cells. For this example we assume that each nonprofit has six options.

Accordingly, if A chooses strategy 1, it will gain 90 percent of the market if B chooses strategy 2; but only 5 percent if B also chooses its strategy 1. If A chooses strategy 3 and B chooses 1, A gets 94 percent of the market; but

Strategies of Nonprofit B

		1	2	3	4	5	6
Strategies of Nonprofit A	1	5	90	48	39	19	27
	2	7	38	75	1	33	79
	3	94	4	88	19	42	39
	4	67	85	22	50	80	0
	5	57	8	37	40	0	10
	6	53	0	69	29	50	40

Figure 5.3 Payoff Matrix of Nonprofits in Highly Competitive Zero-Sum Market. Source: Author.

if B counters with 2, A only gains 4 percent. Likewise, if A chooses 6 and B counters with 2, A gains nothing; but if B chooses 3, A gets 69 percent.

The central utility of payoff matrices is that they discipline strategy choices so that managers take into account the consequence of counterstrategies by competitors. Hence, the choice of policies 1 through 6 by A will partly depend upon what strategy, 1 through 6, it expects B to be most likely to pursue either in response to its own pressures or because of the threat posed by A. Hence, A will not choose 5 if it believes that B will also undertake 5. In the drug example, A will not focus on teenagers if B has a competitive advantage working with teenagers, strategy 5. If, however, A felt that B will counter with 4, A may still pursue 5 and split the market somewhat evenly. A may choose to deal with teenagers if it believes that B will shift its focus to alcoholism.

Nonprofits may have a cooperative relationship so that if A and B undertake supporting strategies they could expand the market for both of them. Suppose that A and B are nonprofits with a mission to eradicate smoking. Suppose that the total number of smokers is 50,000 but A only reaches 5,000 and B only 10,000. There are 35,000 more persons to be reached. A and B may decide to cooperate in advertising, in seminars, or by each specializing in a particular subgroup of the 35,000. The situation is depicted in Figure 5.4.

We see that if A chooses strategy 7 and B, 3 they are relegated to the small inner circle; that is, the market share of both is small. But if A chooses 4 and B 1, the frontier is expanded and both organizations increase their range. They can reach the entire market if A chooses 1 and B chooses 7. If in a moment of noncooperation A should choose 7 and B chooses 1, then both are hurt relative to where they were when A had chosen 1 and B 7.

Fortunately for nonprofits, they are not constrained as for-profits firms are through rigid application of law prohibiting collusion in cooperating to expand markets. Therefore, nonprofits may openly cooperate. By cooperating they can reach the outer boundaries of their market. Thus, nonprofit A may decide to focus on teenage smokers if it has a particular advantage in working with youth, and B may focus on adults if this is where its comparative advan-

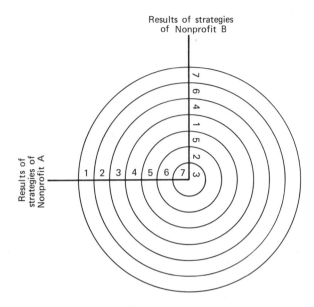

Figure 5.4   Schematic of Nonzero Sum Game among Cooperative Nonprofits. Source: Author.

tage lies. Moreover, they may agree among themselves to share the market without one ever having to fear intrusion by the other.

Under certain conditions, the nonprofits may face a "prisoner's dilemma." Suppose nonprofit A and B could benefit by doing nothing once A is at 7 and B is at 1 because they have expanded their market to its maximum. It could occur, as it often does, that both A and B become suspicious of each other so that A believes that B will change its strategy. B may rationally choose to do so because it believes it can exist without A, can outdo A, or because there are pressures for it to shift course. B may harbor the same suspicions about A. Being suspicious, they both act. The consequence of this is that they are both worse off.[3] Any combination of policies other than A taking 7 and B taking 1 is inferior.

The prisoner's dilemma does not have to be so extreme. It is also possible for events to occur in this sequence: A chooses 2 and B chooses 6. Suspicion and discontent arise between the two. A decides to move to 1. What is the probability that B, without knowing that A was going to move to 1 would counter by moving to 7? The probability is small. The chances are that B's countermove would be something other than 7 (if all choices are randomly chosen). The consequence is that both would be worse off.

Co-production: Working With Clients and Community

Strategic planning is of particular applicability to nonprofit organizations because it is a method that promotes participation and focuses on a mission.

As we see in the next chapter, a nonprofit, unlike a for-profit, must justify its existence and tax-exempt status by demonstrating public support and participation and by adhering closely to its mission. Strategic planning begins with the identification of unmet needs and moves to the articulation of a mission, strategies and programs. Throughout the strategic planning process, a wide level of participation by the public as well as the leadership and staff of the nonprofit is encouraged and easily accommodated by making them part of the strategic planning group. This group is set up in a manner so that the pros and cons are discussed.[4]

One aspect of participation common to many nonprofits is co-production. Figure 5.5 shows interaction when co-production is absent. A private or public foundation, for example, may provide funding for a nonprofit to produce a newsletter, poetry, a play, painting—products that the nonprofit can produce without direct involvement of clients in the creative process. A newsletter can be produced without its readers writing, printing or distributing the articles.

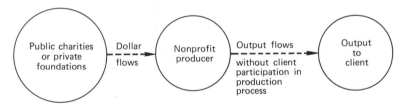

Figure 5.5 A Schematic of a Simple Production Relationship in the Nonprofit Sector. Source: Author.

Contrast this simple process with Figure 5.6 which is a depiction of an actual co-production process involving a nonprofit. It is a description of the National Urban Policy Roundtable funded by the Charles F. Kettering Foundation and coordinated by the Academy for Contemporary Problems (ACP).[5] The mission of the Roundtable was to produce policy analyses and recommendations for federal, state, and local governments and the private sector. It did this by involving scholars, federal, state, local and private leaders in a steering committee and in a roundtable. Working papers were prepared, published and disseminated. Many of the products of the Roundtable were utilized in the annual report of the President of the United States to the U.S. Congress, and by the associations of state and local governments which were represented on the governing board of the Academy, the steering committee of the Roundtable, and whose members were frequently a target group of clients. Figure 5.6 traces the complex co-production relationship.

1. The Charles F. Kettering Foundation, a private operating foundation, finances a project. But, as we see in the next chapter, the law requires that such foundations directly participate in many of their projects. It is not sufficient to send a check, it is necessary that their assets and staff be directly involved.

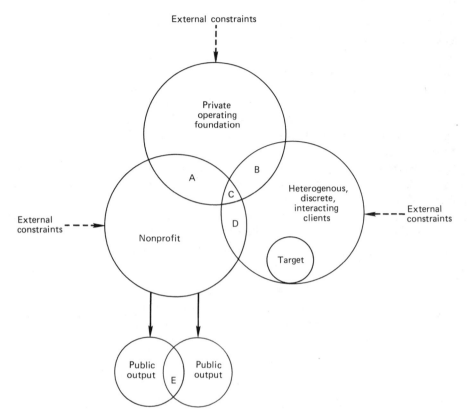

Figure 5.6   A Schematic of Complex Co-Production in the Nonprofit Sector. Source: Author.

The consequence of this is intersection A that shows both the private operating foundation and the nonprofit (ACP) as co-producers.

2. In order to insure the policy relevance of the project as well as public participation, both the nonprofit and the private operating foundation encouraged the participation of the clients which in this case were the public, publicly elected and appointed officials, and private sector leaders.

Because the clients were persons from different sectors (public, private, and community) and different groups within each sector (bankers, builders, governors, state legislators, mayors, citizens), these groups are referred to as heterogenous, discrete and interacting. Indeed, these groups could also be described as atomistic because they were independent of each other. They sometimes cooperated, and at times had radically divergent and antagonistic positions on the same issues. No issue was equally relevant to all groups. Consequently, for each issue, a prime target group was identified.

3. The co-production process also involves direct relationships that the client group may have with the private foundation, either as a group or as individual constituencies within the group. This is represented by intersection B. Such relationships while not directly involving the ACP, the nonprofit, their influences were always indirectly felt. For one thing, the co-production activity had to be so defined that it did not infringe on other relationships between the private operating foundation and the clients. In effect, this partly defined the boundaries of the ACP and circumscribed the scope of activity of the Roundtable.

4. Similarly, the clients may have direct relationships with the nonprofit outside of the direct co-production relationship. This is represented by intersection D. In the case of the Roundtable, many members of the client group were also members of the board of directors of the ACP and were conducting other joint programs among themselves and with the ACP.

5. Intersection C is the core of the co-production activity. It is the interaction among the client, the private operating foundation and the nonprofit. In the case of the Roundtable, the ACP, the nonprofit, is the principal producer; the private foundation is both the funding source and a co-producer and the clients are both consumers and co-producers.

6. As a result of this interaction, a final product, E, is obtained. The final product, the production and dissemination of the policy documents, is not unrelated to other products being produced by the ACP. This is often the case, since one activity of an organization draws upon and contributes to other activities in the organization. Note that by the very nature of nonprofits, the products even though targeted to a specific population, may have positive external effects very much as described in Chapter 4. Indeed, as discussed in that chapter, that is precisely one reason for nonprofits.

A factor that makes co-production difficult is that the actual interaction among all parties, C, may represent a small part of the activities of any one of the organizations. Yet it brings the central producer, the nonprofit, under the influence not only of its external constraints, but those of all co-producers. One example is worth noting. The Roundtable produced a study listing the cities with greatest potential for fiscal default. One of the cities was vitally related to the client group and the private foundation. The morning the study was released, the city announced its intentions to offer a new issue of municipal bonds. Although not required to rescind its results, the nonprofit, as coordinator of the ACP, not just the Roundtable, expended a significant amount of energy explaining its results and the timing of its release. The actions of the Roundtable, though honoring its own constraints for objectivity, affected the external constraints of a key member of its client group to raise badly needed capital at favorable lending rates, and involved the entire corporate body of the ACP of which the Roundtable was only a part.

LIFE CYCLE OF NEEDS: TIME TO CHANGE

The level of need that a nonprofit addresses can be expected to change over time. It may increase or decrease at a rapid, slow or constant rate. Some needs may remain constant for a long period of time while others may be fleeting. It is important that strategic planning for the nonprofit reflect how the needs it plans to address will change over time. The ability to answer these questions, even in general terms, helps the organization to avert disaster. Imagine investing in meeting an "unmet need" when the need has already fulfilled or failing to prepare properly for a need that is rapidly escalating. Indeed, the plight of many nonprofits stems from their inability or unwillingness to track the decline in public ranking of the need to which the organization was dedicated or a change in the true level or intensity of the need.

Consequently, it is useful to know the approximate life cycle of the need being addressed by the nonprofit. This involves two separate questions. How long will the need last and how will it change over time? Figure 5.7 shows some possibilities. It is possible that once the program is launched, the need for it declines uninterruptedly. The pattern of decline may be as in line (a) in the first panel or like lines (b) or (c). The decline in (a) begins rapidly and then flattens out so that a very low level of need is maintained until the end of the planning period which, in this example, is the twelfth year of the program.

Alternatively, the decline could be steady but rapid as in line (b) or steady but slower as in line (c). These are not simply geometric expressions. The point is that how rapidly a need disappears has an important bearing on how the organization should plan for it. A nonprofit should not go into debt or assume an obligation for more than five years if the need is likely to have a life cycle such as depicted in line (b). Its commitment would outlive the problem. On the other hand, if the life cycle is like (a), a long-term commitment up to 10 years can be made and the organization can gradually extricate itself year by year from such commitments.

Alternatively, the need could be an increasing one over time. Here too the life-cycle pattern is significant. The increase could be at an increasing rate such as line (d), a constant rate such as (e) or a decreasing rate such as (f). If (d) is the line that is applicable, then the organization must plan to rapidly increase its capacity over time. This can place great strain on the internal factors that may now become the major constraints. If however, the life cycle is as depicted in lines (f) or (e), the strain would be less.

Another possibility is that the life cycle is as shown in the third panel, indicating that it remains constant for the planning period. The dot in line (g) indicates that the life of the need expires at the end of one year, which ever year the need arises. In this case, the need is anticipated to occur in five years and will expire in that year. The dot indicates that during the year, it may be at only one level which is represented by a dot. Is this unlikely? Many of the local activities for the 1984 Olympics in Los Angeles were precisely of this nature. Activities celebrating the Bicentennial of the birth of the United States of

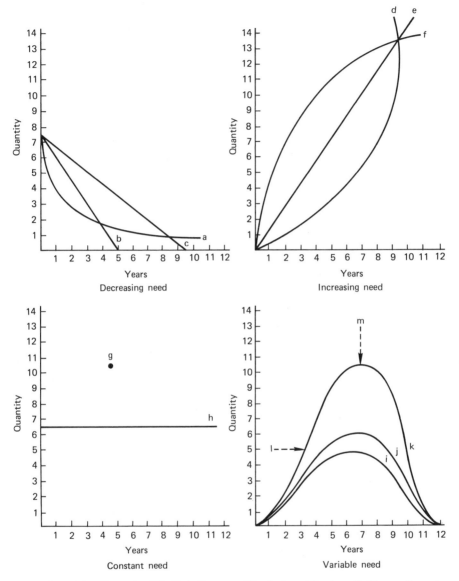

Figure 5.7   Alternative Life-Cycle Patterns of Products and Services of a Nonprofit.
Source: Author.

America were also of this type. They started and ended. They had a known and predictable short life. A profit was made partly because management knew the life cycle of events.

A constant pattern is represented also in line (h). In this case, the need remains fairly constant over the planning period. Planning for schools in a community that is relatively stable is an example. The need for additional facilities may remain stable for a long period of time until affected by dramatic population changes.

The need may be one that varies over time. This is reflected in the patterns shown in the fourth panel. The need may rise rapidly at first up to point (l) and then increase at a slower rate eventually reaching a peak (m) and thereafter decline. The need may reach its peak very rapidly as in line (k) or less rapidly as in lines (i) or (j) and be more prolonged as in the case of (i) which gives the lowest peak but the most sustained one lasting roughly two years as opposed to one year in (k). The organization would then have to plan its capacity so that it would meet the rapid and short peak as in (k) or the slow rise but prolonged peak such as in (i). Can you give examples? Natural disasters?

Being able to spot the turning points such as (l) and (m) is important in the ability of the organization to quickly and efficiently adjust to changing needs. It is possible, for example, that once the peak has been reached, the nonprofit would begin planning to shift its resources toward meeting new and emerging needs perhaps even in the same general field. A drug abuse center could begin shifting its attention from LSD to PCP, from marijuana to crack.

It is not likely that any nonprofit or for-profit firm will know the exact rate at which the need for its services or products changes. But as economists who estimate demand over time know, it is infinitely better to make plans based on rational expectations of how needs will change over time than to have such changes occur unexpectedly. If the change is a rapid rise in need, the nonprofit will be unable to meet the escalation and consequently opens the door for dissatisfaction and the entry of new competitors that will quickly displace the existing nonprofit. If the change is a rapid decline, then the nonprofit will find itself having invested scarce resources to meet a need that no longer exists at the levels it once did.

SUMMARY AND CONCLUSIONS

This chapter has examined strategic planning as a process that can be used by managers of nonprofit organizations to identify unmet needs, assess the ability of their organizations to meet those needs given both internal and external constraints, to develop strategies and programs and to make necessary evaluations and adjustments.

Strategic planning, though commonly used in the for-profit sector, must be amended for application to the nonprofit world. This chapter focuses on the necessity to recognize the central role of co-production, the selection of options that reflect internal and external constraints, and the recognition that each need has a life cycle. Failure to anticipate this cycle can lead to futile effort and the fatality of nonprofits.

NOTES

1. See the references following in this chapter.
2. This does not ignore the fact that many sectors in the nonprofit world have barriers to entry. Schools, hospitals, and day care centers are some examples.
3. Recall that each of these circles represents a maximum frontier. Each represents a point superior to the preceding circle and can only be reached by the combination of policies indicated. The situation is analogous to production frontiers in economic theory of production; those frontiers are technically circles.

   The "prisoner's dilemma" is usually presented in a matrix. The intent in this paper is not to present a discussion of the dilemma, but to use the principle to demonstrate how possibility frontiers; i.e., market size and share can be affected by that principle. Thus, the major purpose of the discussion is an application of the principle rather than a theoretical discussion of it.
4. See the references, in particular, the works by Mason and Mitroff. The reader should also see Young for real examples of nonprofits wrestling with decision making.
5. The Academy for Contemporary Problems, now the Academy for State and Local Governments, was owned and operated on behalf of the Council of State and Local Governments, International City Management Association, National Association of Counties, National Conference of State Legislatures, National League of Cities, and the U.S. Conference of Mayors.

SUGGESTED READINGS

ANTHONY, P. WILLIAM, "Effective Strategic Planning in Nonprofit Organizations," *The Nonprofit World Report*, 2, no. 4 (July–August 1984), 12–16.

deSMIT, J. and RADE, N. L., "Rational and Non-Rational Planning," *Long-Range Planning*, 13, no. 2, 1980 82–101.

KOTLER, PHILIP, *Marketing for Nonprofit Organizations* (Englewood Cliffs, NJ: Prentice-Hall, Inc. 1982).

MASON, RICHARD O. and MITROFF, IAN I., *Challenging Strategic Planning Assumptions* (New York: John Wiley, 1981).

———, *1980 Census: Policymaking Amid Turbulence* (Lexington, Massachusetts: Lexington Books, 1983).

DALE D. MCCONKLEY, *MBO for Nonprofit Organizations* (New York: Amacom, 1975).

NUTT, P. C. "A Strategic Planning Network for Nonprofit Organizations," *Strategic Management Journal*, 5, no. 1 (February–March 1984), 57–76.

Public Management Institute, *The Effective Nonprofit Executive Handbook*, (Washington, D.C.: Public Management Institute, 1982).

RITTLE, HORST, "Systems Analysis of the First and Second Generations" and "Structure and Usefulness of Planning Information Systems," in Pierre LaConte, J. Gibson, and A. Rapport, eds., *Human Energy Factors in Urban Planning* (New York: Martinus Nijhoff Publishers, 1982), pp. 35–52 and 53–64.

YOUNG, DENNIS, *Casebook of Management for Nonprofit Organizations*, (New York: Haworth Press, 1985).

WALKER, J. MALCOLM, "Limits of Strategic Management in Voluntary Organizations," *Journal of Voluntary Action Research*, 12, no. 3, (July–September 1983), 39–55.

WORTMAN, MAX JR., "A Radical Shift from Bureaucracy to Strategic Management in Voluntary Organizations," *Journal of Voluntary Action Research*, 10, no. 3 (January–March 1983), 62–81.

SIX

Corporate Structure of Non-profits and the Legal Limitations on Operational and Financing Strategies

All nonprofit organizations are classified.[1] Some organizations are private foundations others are private operating foundations. Others, known as public charities, include organizations directly serving the public welfare and those that simply exist for the funding of nonprofits that directly serve the public. There are several reasons why it is important to understand these specific organizations. Each has a different set of legal constraints on how it may operate financially. A misunderstandings of these constraints can lead either to overly restrictive managerial policies or managerial policies that lead either to penalties or to the loss of tax-exempt status.

CORPORATE AND FINANCIAL SIGNIFICANCE OF 501(c)(3) STATUS

As stated in Chapter 2, nonprofit corporations are creations of the laws of individual states. A nonprofit becomes exempt from taxation when it is given a 501(c)(3) status by the Internal Revenue Service. (See Figure 6.1.) To qualify under Section 501(c)(3) of the *IRS Code,* the organization must contain in its charter the stipulation that none of the income or assets will be distributed to individuals and if the organization is dissolved, its income and assets will be distributed to a similarly qualified organization or to the state. Note that this stipulation is required both for state recognition and for IRS exemption. Where it is not required by the state, it is nevertheless required by the IRS. These are not duplicate requirements.

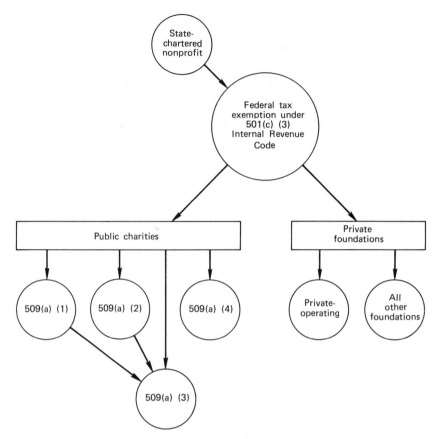

Figure 6.1 Transformation of Organization by Tax-Exempt Status under Section 501(c)(3). Source: Author.

The organizing document, the charter or deed, must also state that the nonprofit exists exclusively for one or more of the following purposes: charitable, religious, educational, scientific, literary, testing for public safety, fostering national or international amateur sports competition (excepting the provision of athletic facilities or equipment), or the prevention of cruelty to children or animals.[2] These are the only missions that would allow an organization to qualify under Section 501(c)(3).

Finally, the organizing document must say that the nonprofit will not use a substantial part of its energies or resources for lobbying. Under no condition may 501(c)(3)s be involved in campaigns of candidates for political office. This rule cannot be evaded by setting up a separate account for endorsing or supporting candidates. In short, while some lobbying is permitted, no involvement in a political campaign is tolerated of a 501(c)(3) organization.[3] Violations lead to loss of tax exemption.

A nonprofit that meets the conditions as discussed may qualify to be exempt from taxes under Section 501(c)(3) but only a few nonprofits automatically qualify for tax-exempt status. Except for churches and their affiliates, public nonprofits with gross annual receipts of less than $5,000 and public nonprofits that are chapters of an exempt public foundation, all other nonprofits must apply and meet certain specific tests before they will become exempt.

To be exempt under 501(c)(3) a nonprofit must prove that it is publicly supported and must also pass three tests: organizational, asset, and political. The organizational test determines if the purpose of the nonprofit coincides with the purposes permitted under Section 501(c)(3). The purpose must be one or more of the following: charitable, religious, educational, scientific, literary, testing for public safety, fostering national or international amateur sports competition (excepting the provision of athletic facilities or equipment), or the prevention of cruelty to children or animals.

Because all of these functions could be done for profit, it is necessary to demonstrate that the nonprofit organization intends to carry them out in a noncommercial mode. To demonstrate that the mode is charitable is sufficient to distinguish a for-profit from a nonprofit providing the same service; for example, a community clinic from a private clinic. One definition of the word "charitable" is that the beneficiaries are a class of needy people whose needs are not otherwise met in the marketplace.[4]

To qualify under Section 501(c)(3), a nonprofit must also pass an asset test. To pass, the organizing document must prohibit the nonprofit from distributing any of its assets or income to individuals. Further, the organization may not be used for the personal benefit of the founders, supporters, managers, their relatives or personal or business associates. Moreover, if the nonprofit is terminated the assets will be distributed to a qualified public charity or to the state or local government for charitable purposes and not to any individual.

Finally, to qualify under Section 501(c)(3), a political test must be passed. The organizing document must forbid the nonprofit from participating in any political campaign on behalf of a candidate. Participation is meant to include the preparation and distribution of literature. This test does not prohibit voter education but because such an activity can be broadly interpreted, it is wise to seek specific exemption through an IRS letter ruling if such an activity is contemplated.

Public Charities: Financial and Legal Limits

Once a nonprofit has won classification under Section 501(c)(3), it must, by law, be classified as shown in Figure 6.1. It must either be classified as a private foundation or a public charity. Public charities enjoy several privileges. Contributions to them receive the most favorable tax treatment in the sense that contributions are deductible by the donors.[5] They do not have to pay an excise tax on their investment income.[6] Unless they fall into the special category, noted as 509(a)(3), they do not have to make annual distributions of their assets to other charities the way private foundations do.

Sections 509(a)(1) Organizations

Section 509(a)(1) organizations are nonprofits that are classified as public charities and are known as publicly supported organizations because their common characteristic is that they are supported by the general public. The characteristics required to be classified under this section are given in Section 170(b)(1)(A) of the *Internal Revenue Code.*

The types of organizations that are exempt under Section 170(b)(1)(A) are shown in Table 6.1. These are generally the public charities that provide direct services to the community, but also defined under Subtitle v are state and local government agencies. The Constitution of the United States is based on the principle that the federal government is the creation of the state and not vice versa. Therefore, the purpose of Subtitle v is not to create states; its principal purpose is to provide for gifts and contributions to be made to state and local government agencies and be deductible by the donors. Thus, we can make contributions to reduce the deficit of a jurisdiction, including the federal deficit and deduct that amount. Also, when in a recent case an official of the government of the District of Columbia was accused of accepting payments for travel from a private contractor, the Board of Ethics of the District of Columbia concluded that this was a contribution to the district rather than to the official and therefore was not a bribe.

TABLE 6.1 Nonprofits Described Under Section 170 of the Internal Revenue Code

Section 170(b)(1)(A)	Type of Nonprofit Described
i	churches
ii	educational institutions
iii	hospitals and medical research
iv	agencies that support government schools
v	government units that receive gifts for public purposes
vi	publicly supported charities
vii	certain private foundations
viii	509(a)(2) and (a)(3) organizations

Source: The author

Also note that Subtitle vii includes private foundations and private operating foundations. This is to accommodate a special type of private foundation such as a pooled trust where the individual donors can dictate which charities should be the beneficiaries of their gifts, and be assured of periodic accounting about the gifts made in their names by the trust and the trust investment performance. Subtitle viii refers to two other sections to be described later in this chapter.

Subtitle vi refers to public supported charities—a broad category. This encompasses most of the organizations that we know as public charities and nonprofit organizations. Take a look at Figure 6.2 in the upper right hand corner. We see that Martha's Table is a public charity a 501(c)(3) as defined under 509(a)(1) and 170(b)(1)(A)(vi). Martha's Table runs a soup kitchen, a thrift shop, and educational programs for poor children.

Internal Revenue Service District Director	Department of the Treasury
Date Aug. 20, 1980	Foundation Status Classification: *509(a) (1) & 170(b) (1) (A) (vi) Advance Ruling Period Ends

Martha's Table
3318 Volta Place, N.W.
Washington, D.C. 20007

Dear Applicant:

Based on information supplied, and assuming your operations will be as stated in your application for recognition of exemption, we have determined you are exempt from Federal income tax under section 501(c) (3) of the Internal Revenue Code.

Figure 6.2   Reprinted with permission of Matha's Table, Washington, D.C.

Similarly, in Figure 6.3 we see that the Joint Center for Political Studies, a public policy organization, has a similar status. The IRS specifies it is not a private foundation. Both organizations may accept donations which are deductible by the donors. Neither is subject to the restrictive rules of private foundations. Their missions are distinctly different although both fall under the same broad category. However, importantly, both must demonstrate public support. Both are public charities.

Proof of public support for 509(a)(1) organizations comes in the form of passing two tests: the one-third support test or the 10 percent support and facts and circumstances test. How do these work?

To demonstrate that it "normally" has public support through the one-third test, a nonprofit must show that over the preceding four years, one-third of its support came from the government or the general public or a combination of the two. This is not simple. The words, "support," "normal," and "public" are specifically defined.

Support includes gifts, contributions, membership fees (excluding the portion that is an assessment for special services), net income from unrelated businesses, gross investment income, revenues from taxes levied by the government for the benefit of the nonprofit, and the value of facilities furnished by the government free of charge if those facilities are usually rented or sold.

There are many aspects of support that deserve to be highlighted. Note that support refers to income from unrelated business rather than to related

Internal Revenue Service
District Director

Department of the Treasury

Date: 31 Jul 1979

Our Letter Dated:
June 14, 1976

Person to Contact:
F. Buchanan

Contact Telephone Number:
(301) 962-4773

The Joint Center for Political Studies, Inc.
c/o Walter Slocombe, Esquire
1101 17th Street, NW
Washington, DC   20036

This modifies our letter of the above date in which we stated that you would be treated as an organization which is not a private foundation until the expiration of your advance ruling period.

Based on the information you submitted, we have determined that you are not a private foundation within the meaning of section 509(a) of the Internal Revenue Code, because you are an organization of the type described in section _____*_____ . Your exempt status under section 501(c) (3) of the code is still in effect.

Grantors and contributors may rely on this determination until the Internal Revenue Service publishes notice to the contrary. However, a grantor or a contributor may not rely on this determination if he or she was in part responsible for, or was aware of, the act or failure to act that resulted in your loss of section _____*_____ status, or acquired knowledge that the Internal Revenue Service had given notice that you would be removed from classification as a section _____*_____ organization.

Because this letter could help resolve any questions about your private foundation status, please keep it in your permanent records.

If you have any questions, please contact the person whose name and telephone number are shown above.
* 509(a) (1) & 170(b) (1) (A) (vi).

Sincerely yours,

Gerald G. Portney

Gerald G. Portney
District Director

31 Hopkins Plaza, Baltimore, Md. 21201   Letter 1050 (DO) (7-77)

Figure 6.3 Reprinted with permission of the Joint Center for Political Studies, Washington, D.C.

business.[7] This means that a nonprofit cannot include in its calculation of support any revenues it receives from an activity for which it is tax exempt if the payment benefits the payor. To illustrate, a nonprofit exempt as a day care center cannot include as support fees from parents for caring for their children. These payments benefit the payors and are in conjunction with the tax-exempt purpose of the day care center. If the day care center owns a fast food restaurant, an unrelated business catering to the general public, the net income from this business may be included in the calculation of support. If the parents made a contribution for assisting children (other than their own) who are members of the general public, this would be support. If the parents contributed anything such as services that are not deductible contributions, they will not be included in the calculation of support.

Also membership dues qualify as support only after adjustment is made for the portion of the dues that is a payment for services such as a magazine. It is only the portion that is for the general support of the organization that counts.

Facilities received by the organization from the government cannot be included as support unless the government usually charges for the use of these facilities or sells them.

By "public" is meant governmental units and the general population. A gift or contribution from a community trust, itself a tax-exempt nonprofit, is a contribution from the public if these trusts receive their funds primarily from contributions from the general public and are based on public participation. Earnings from an endowment created by public funds is also considered a public contribution. Obviously, contributions from individual persons and entities are also public. It is the concentration of contributions in a few that creates the problem.

The word "normally" also has a precise meaning indicating experience over the preceding four years. The classification of the nonprofit is determined for a current and the next year based on the performance of the organization over the four preceding years. It is publicly supported in years 1985 and 1986 if it passes the public support test in 1981 to 1984. It is publicly supported in 1986 and 1987 if it passes the test for the period 1982 to 1985, and so on. A nonprofit can have its classification changed depending upon how it performed over the preceding four years. Since a classification is not given in perpetuity, a publicly supported organization will lose that favored status when it can no longer prove public support.

For a nonprofit to be classified as a public charity under 509(a)(1) as defined in Section 170(b)(1)(A) by proving it has public support, it must demonstrate that a minimum portion of its total support, as previously defined, is from the general public. One test requires that at least one-third of such support must come from the general public (government and people from the community at large). Alternatively, the nonprofit may show that at least 10 percent of its support comes from the general public but that the facts and circumstances surrounding the operation of the organization prove that it encourages and involves public participation.

The nonprofit cannot meet either test by merely getting a few large contributions from individuals. Let us demonstrate the test. Based on the definition of support given earlier, assume that nonprofit A has investment income (interest and dividends) of $100,000, contributions from its community chest of $40,000, and from Mr. W for $50,000, Mrs. Y for $10,000 and Mr. Q for $1,000. Its total support is $201,000. According to the rule, one-third ($67,000) of the total support must be from the general public. Note, however, that $101,000, about half of the amount coming from the public, came from one source, Mr. W who contributes $50,000. To defeat this ploy, the rules state that no individual's contribution may be included to an extent that it exceeds 2 percent of the total support (in this case, 2 percent of $201,000 or $4,020). Thus, the contributions of Mr. X and Mrs. Y are valued for calculation purposes at $4,020 each, or a total of $8,040. When this $8,040 is added to the $1,000, and the $40,000 from the community chest, the sum, $49,040, is less than the required $67,000, so the organization fails the one-third support test.

The nonprofit would have made the one-third support test if instead of two large individual contributions by Mr. X and Mrs. Y, it had at least 15 small contributions of no more than $4,020 each.[8] Again, the purpose is to avoid defeat of the intent of the law that public support be demonstrated.

Should a nonprofit fail the one-third support test, it may try under the 10 percent and facts and circumstances test. To do this, the nonprofit must show that at least 10 percent of its support is normally (as defined) obtained from government and public sources, and that there is a continuous effort to attract public support, for example, through fund-raising drives.

In the preceding example, the 10 percent of the total support of $201,000, would be $20,100. Since public support is calculated to be $49,040, the 10 percent test is met. But with the lowered requirement of a minimum of 10 percent, the IRS looks deeper into the facts and circumstances surrounding the sources of support of the nonprofit. These tests are more subjective. One focus is on the source of the other 90 percent. Is there some reasonable way to say that the amount came indirectly from the public? For example, is it the earnings on an endowment created by the public? If so, the nonprofit wins or maintains classification as a public charity. In the example just given, the bulk of the support came from investment income. If the interest and dividends are from the investment of funds in a publicly created endowment, the organization will pass but not if the investment income is from a gift from a single individual.

But the IRS may focus on the 10 percent rather than on the 90 percent. If this came from one or two individuals, the lack of public support may be implied. Because the test is subjective, we cannot be sure how the given example will be interpreted. But observe that the 10 percent came from only four sources: the community chest, Mrs. Y, Mr. Q and Mr. W. The nonprofit would probably have failed this test without the inclusion of the community chest.[9]

Other considerations in the facts and circumstances test are even more subjective. In one approach the IRS looks into the composition of the governing board of the nonprofit. If the board is a cross section of the community including elected or appointed public officials, the IRS is likely to conclude that there is evidence of public support.

Public support is also said to exist if the nonprofit makes its facilities and membership open to the public, conducts programs for the public, and is heavily dependent on a public foundation such as the United Way for support.

Section 509(a)(2) Organizations

The 509(a)(2) and (a)(1) organizations are similar. Both are publicly supported organizations. The key difference is that 509(a)(2) includes income from related businesses as support and the 509(a)(1) includes instead income from unrelated business. The (a)(2)s have clients who can pay for services and therefore their business income is heavily program-related and is considered support. Universities and museums are examples. The (a)(1)s have clients who cannot pay or provide services for which charges are not reasonable. They depend more heavily on gifts and contributions. All income streams are available to both groups; it is a matter of weight.

In addition, a 509(a)(2) is subject to two tests. The first puts a limit on income from unrelated business and from gross investments. Specifically, such organizations should not normally derive more than one-third of their support from the sum of investment income and the portion of the taxable income from unrelated business that exceeds the amount they paid in taxes on such income. Section 509(a)(1) organizations are not subject to such limitations.

Second, these 509(a)(2) organizations must show that more than one-third of their support comes from gifts, contributions, membership fees and program-related businesses. The effect of this is to require an emphasis on the public support of the program and to de-emphasize the ability of the organization to gain support through shrewd investments.

Section 509(a)(2) organizations are not conceptually different from 509(a)(1)s. They are alternatives to each other based upon the way their public support test is calculated. Most organizations that would satisfy one would satisfy the other.

Diversification and Choice between Sections 509(a)(1) and (a)(2)

A comparison of the requirements of 509(a)(1) and (a)(2) classifications reveals that it is not simply the source of support that counts but the composition or structure of support as well. Diversification of funding sources is always wise because it reduces the risk of financial failure. But, as we shall see, diversification has an important implication for how a nonprofit is classified. Furthermore, because one classification tends to favor certain types of support while other types of support are favored by the other classification, it does not necessarily follow that the favored combinations would lead predictably to either one or the other classification—a Section 509(a)(1) or (a)(2).

In referring to Figure 6.4, suppose nonprofit A expected to have a large investment income and a large unrelated business income (cell 1). Since both of these are included as support in the calculations for 509(a)(1) status, we may at first conclude that such a status is what nonprofit A should seek. The problem is that this combination only increases the size of support. The rule requires

		Type of business	
		Unrelated	Related
Other income	Investment income	1	2
	Gifts, grants contributions membership fees	3	4

Figure 6.4 Hypothetical Major Sources of Funding of Public Charities. Source: Author.

that one-third of the support be public. Thus, the larger the amount associated with cell 1, the greater the amount that has to be obtained from the general public in order for the nonprofit to meet either the one-third or the 10 percent support test.

If the organization's fund-raising strategy is represented by cell 1, electing to be a 509(a)(2) may not be the answer either. This is so because the rules stated earlier limit that combination to no more than one-third of the total support. Thus, the higher the amount represented in cell 1, the greater the amount of public support (the other two-thirds) that will be needed to meet the requirements to be a 509(a)(2).

Consider cell 4. The rules suggest that a nonprofit that emphasizes gifts and grants and related business as sources of income may be better off selecting Section 509(a)(2) because those two sources of funding are favorably treated. Indeed, the rules would be satisfied if all the funds came from this combination. Suppose, however, 60 percent of the funds fell in cell 4. Then the nonprofit may fail to qualify as 509(a)(2) if more than one-third of the remaining 40 percent falls in cell 1. This is so because a second rule, as described earlier, says that no more than one-third of the support may be a combination of unrelated business income and gross investment income. Again, it is the composition of support that counts.

All the cells present problems of the same type. The lessons are two: The classifications do not permit escape from the requirement of public support and it is the composition or structure of support rather than the individual source (unless all the funds come exclusively from public sources) that matters. Good management should pay attention to diversification to avoid risk of financial failure and also to meet and maintain the classification requirements.

COMPARISON OF 509(a)(1) AND (a)(2) ORGANIZATIONS

Both the 509(a)(1) and (a)(2) organizations must demonstrate public support and in this sense they are both publicly supported nonprofits. Both must have a mission to advance public welfare and both may conduct related and unrelated businesses. The basic difference is that the (a)(2) organizations are financed more by business income, particularly related business income, than are the 509(a)(1) organizations. Museums such as the Colonial Williamsburg Foundation cited in Chapter 1 are good examples because their support is heavily weighted in the direction of fees, subscription revenues for magazines, sales of related art products, and other business income and is less dependent upon contributions by individuals or foundations. The backbone of 509(a)(2) organizations is that they are good businesses conducting a public service and generating a substantial amount of their support through sales.

On the other hand, 509(a)(1) organizations cannot rely as heavily on their selling of their goods and services as a means of demonstrating public support. They rely more on gifts and contributions including contributions from foundations and may supplement these through conducting a business.

Section 509(a)(3) Organizations

Section 509(a)(3) organizations are nonprofits that exist to support and aid publicly supported nonprofits [(Sections (509)(a)(1) and (a)(2)]. Basically, these supporting organizations, as they are called, could not technically exist without publicly supported organizations. Yet, they are not chapters. They have their own organizing documents as corporations or trusts and must obtain their own tax-exempt status. The basis upon which the IRS confers that status upon them, however, is that their sole mission will be to support an existing publicly supported organization.

A nonprofit may obtain tax-exempt status as a public charity under Section 509(a)(3) if it is (1) operated, supervised, or controlled by, (2) supervised or controlled in connection with, or (3) operated in connection with a nonprofit that has public charity status as a 509(a)(1) or (a)(2) organization. These concepts provide subtle but important degrees of independence as far as daily management is concerned. In all cases, however, the supporting organization exists to assist the publicly supported organization. Thus in Figure 6.1 the 509(a)(3) is shown as an independently chartered and exempted organization but subordinate to the 509(a)(1) and (a)(2).

By "operated, supervised, or controlled" is meant that the management and the governing body of the nonprofit is elected or appointed by the governing body of the parent public foundation. They might elect and appoint themselves. Thus, the supporting organization is a subsidiary to the parent. The organizing document of 509(a)(3) organizations falling into this category must limit the activities of these organizations to carrying out missions on behalf of the parent organization and furthering the cause of the parent. Thus, it is not enough for a 509(a)(3) organization to serve the same clients as its parents, but it must do so because it is furthering the mission of the parent.

One restriction that is placed on these nonprofits "operated, supervised, or controlled" by a parent 509(a)(1) of (a)(2) is that it cannot be under the influence of a disqualified person other than the manager. For instance, Carlos creates a foundation that gets 509(a)(3) status by being a subsidiary to Carlos's church. Carlos is a disqualified person with respect to the foundation he has created which means that he is barred from having a business relationship with it. His church cannot circumvent this proscription by making him a member of the board of directors of the church with responsibility over the foundation he created.

The term "supervised or controlled in connection with" has very much the same meaning as "operated, supervised or controlled by" except that instead of the governing body being elected and appointed by the parent organization, the very same persons who form the governing body of the one also form a similar body for the other. This assures subservience—the objective of the law.

By "operated in connection with" is meant that (1) the organization exists in support of the publicly supported organization, (2) is integrally a part of its activities, (3) is guided constantly and regularly by it, (4) conducts only missions which advance its cause, and (5) is not influenced by a disqualified person.

Obviously, the subservience of one nonprofit to another may be stifling but there are advantages. A supporting foundation such as a 509(a)(3) may operate a business, conduct specialized research and technical assistance services, and may shield the publicly supported organization from risks and liabilities. While managers of the supporting organizations may complain, the fact is that these organizations could not exist without being subservient. These organizations are often called community foundations or community trusts.

These nonprofits are not permitted to accumulate funds but must distribute them to their parent organizations. There might be an exception to this rule if it can be demonstrated that the 509(a)(3) has some special advantage over its parent organization in conducting some activity. The Cleveland Foundation, the New York Community Trust, and the San Francisco Foundation are three of the largest community foundations in the country and they support local activities.

Section 509(a)(4) Organizations

Section 509(a)(4) organizations will not be discussed in this book because they are highly specialized in testing consumer products for safety. While serving this important function, they do not fall into the general category of the public foundations discussed.

PRIVATE FOUNDATIONS: FINANCIAL AND LEGAL LIMITS

Let us turn now to a discussion of private foundations. A good understanding of these foundations is desirable for several reasons. First, they are the primary source of foundation funding that public charities receive. There are some 28,000 such foundations giving well over \$4 billion dollars a year to public charities. One out of every \$10 contributed to nonprofits comes from private foundations.[10] Appeals to private foundations have a better chance when there is a clear understanding of the framework in which these foundations operate. Second, while private foundations include the Howard Hughes, Ford, the Robert Wood Johnson, Andrew Mellon, Rockefeller, MacArthur, and Pew which are among the seven largest in terms of assets, all public charities—all nonprofits classified as 501(c)(3) organizations—are potentially private foundations.

The private foundation status is given to any nonprofit under 501(c)(3) failing to meet the strict requirements as stipulated for 509(a)(1) or (a)(2) organizations. The organization may fail this test upon making its application for 501(c)(3) status. Notice that the Joint Center in the example given earlier did not fail the test and therefore was classified as a public charity as other public policy and research organizations are.

The letter to the Joint Center is instructive for other reasons. Note that it makes reference to a provisional classification. The IRS initially classifies an organization that qualifies as a 501(c)(3) as a public charity on a provisional basis pending evidence of how it actually operates and is financed. Thus, if an organization violates the rules concerning financing and operation, it can lose its tax-exempt status. When that happens, the IRS publishes the name of the organization among those that have lost its status. This information appears regularly in the IRS publication known as the *Revenue Bulletin.* A principal purpose of the announcement is to notify potential donors that they can no longer make contributions to this organization and take the deduction accorded a public charity which is 50 percent of adjusted gross income. They must take the lower limit (30 percent of adjusted gross income) accorded a private foundation. That is what the IRS is referring to in paragraph three of the letter. Moreover, it is saying that those individuals who are responsible for an organization's losing its cherished public charity classification cannot be protected by claiming ignorance.

Once the organization has lost its public charity classification, it then becomes a private foundation and is subject to all of the stringent rules that apply to such foundations. These rules are discussed later in this chapter.

Finally, the letter states that the Joint Center for Political Studies is in good standing and may use this letter to assure the public (including potential donors) that it is a public charity—not a private foundation—and therefore, by implication, their contributions will qualify for the maximum deduction of 50 percent of adjusted gross income. We discuss these limits in Chapter 10.

Another reason for our discussion of private foundations is that any public charity that is operating an endowment is operating a private foundation. Endowments and trusts are subject to the same rules as private foundations. Each separate trust and each separate endowment operated by a university, hospital, museum, or any other nonprofit is technically a private foundation and subject to those rules to be described in this chapter.

Except for the fact that private foundations are not publicly supported, they are also nonprofits with a public welfare or charitable mission. They too must qualify under Section 501(c)(3) of the Internal Revenue Code (IRC) and are also economic institutions with a public or community welfare mission.

If private foundations are 501(c)(3) organizations, why are they treated so differently from other public charities? The special treatment is to safeguard against abuse. Since these organizations are not subject to public involvement and because many of them are created by private individuals or their families for personal as well as altruistic reasons, the rules are intended to insure that these funds are used for public rather than private benefits.

PRIVATE NONOPERATING FOUNDATIONS: FINANCIAL AND LEGAL LIMITS

Contributions to private nonoperating foundations (hereafter referred to as private foundations) are less favorably treated than public charities.[11] These foundations are subject to a 2 percent tax on their investment income, and they are subject to an excise tax on their failure to distribute income. Moreover, there are a host of penalties that can be imposed both on the foundation and its management. The central objective of the regulations and restrictions on these foundations is to prevent their use for the advancement of private and political aims of their founders and contributors or the business or personal associates of these persons.

Disqualified Persons

The key to understanding this thrust is the term "disqualified person." A disqualified person is a person or entity that is barred from having a business relationship with a private foundation. One such persons are substantial contributors to the private foundation. A substantial contributor is a person or entity that gives a total of $5,000 or more if this amounts to 2 percent of all the contributions received by the foundation since its beginning. But the law does not stop here.

The spouse, children, parents and grandchildren of a substantial contributor are also substantial contributors even if they did not contribute a penny. Based on the legal principle of attribution, the theory is that such close relatives are subject to the control and influence of the contributor. In the eyes of the law they are all one. Oddly, brothers and sisters are excluded from the taint of attribution.

Attribution also extends to businesses in which the substantial contributor owns 20 percent or more of the voting stocks. And if the business is a substantial contributor so is the owner. Attribution runs both ways.

Management or anyone who has authority to set policies is also a disqualified person. The attribution rule also applies to the family of the managers of the nonprofit and their businesses to disqualify them from engaging in business transactions with the organization.

Government officials are also disqualified persons. This includes elected as well as appointed officials and at every level of government and in every branch whether judicial, legislative, or executive. Again, the attribution rule can be applied. Government officials are included among disqualified persons to preclude the use of the private foundation to influence these officials. The conditions under which government officials may receive benefits from private foundations are generally restricted to nonmonetary awards, annuities associated with employee programs during periods that the government official previously worked for the foundation, reimbursement for travel cost if the purpose of the travel was consistent with the tax-exempt purpose of the private foundation, and payment in anticipation of employing the government official if such payment is made within 90 days of termination from government service.

Self-Dealing

Direct or indirect business transactions between the private foundation and disqualified persons can lead to penalties imposed by the IRS for self-dealing. What kinds of transactions lead to charges of self-dealing? Hiring, loans, the sale and purchase of assets, the paying of excessive compensation or reimbursement of expenses, the providing of facilities to disqualified persons, and the leasing of space by a disqualified person to the private foundation are all subject to charges of self-dealing.

There are some exceptions worth noting. A lease by a disqualified person to a private foundation is not self-dealing if there are no rental fees involved. Self-dealing is not incurred if the transaction is for less than $5,000 in one year or if the transaction is generally favorable to the organization. The basic way to avoid issues of self-dealing when a disqualified person must be engaged in a business transaction of any type is to be sure that the transaction is ordinary for such a private foundation, is necessary to discharge its duties, the good or service could not otherwise have been provided more favorably by dealing with a qualified person, and that the private foundation was appreciably the net beneficiary of the transaction.

A penalty for self-dealing may be imposed upon the self-dealer as well as the management if it can be shown that the management participated in the action or could reasonably be expected to have known about it, did not try to stop it, engaged in it, or remained silent. The penalty to the self-dealer can rise to 200 percent of the value of the transaction. For the manager, the penalty can rise to 50 percent of that amount.

While these penalties are imposed by the IRS, an individual may bring civil charges. A son of the founder of the McArthur Foundation brought charges against the members of the board (persons disqualified because of their management status) for self-dealing. The basis of the charge was an alleged overcompensation assumed to be extraordinarily large and unusual for board members of such a private foundation. The charges have since been dropped.

Distribution of Income

Unlike public foundations, private foundations are required to distribute their income annually. Three types of distribution meet the qualification. The private foundation may distribute funds for paying expenses and for making grants to public foundations for conducting those activities for which the private foundation is tax exempt. A second type of distribution that qualifies are set asides to purchase assets to be used in the tax-exempt purpose if those set asides are absolutely necessary (as they are in a building program) and if the funds will be used within 60 months. Set asides or accumulations must be approved by the IRS. A third type of qualifying distribution is the amount spent to purchase assets to be used by the private foundation in its tax-exempt mission or other charitable purpose. These latter amounts, unlike the set asides, do not have to receive prior IRS approval.

The actual dollar amount that a private foundation must distribute is technically determined. Basically, it is substantially all (although 85 percent is acceptable) of the greater of either its minimum investment return or its adjusted net income. Its minimum investment return is the fair market value of its assets not used for tax-exempt purposes minus the debt associated with those assets multiplied by 5 percent. Its adjusted net income is all income including those from unrelated businesses minus the expenses associated with producing that income.

Private foundations must have good accountants and appraisers because the failure to distribute the correct amount can lead to stiff penalties starting at 15 percent of the amount that should be distributed and rising to 100 percent if the distribution is not made in the time allotted for correction. Fortunately, unlike the self-dealing tax, this tax does not fall on the management but on the private foundation itself. When in doubt, an overpayment is often preferable since any such amounts may be carried over the next five years.

Jeopardy of Investments

Private foundations and their managers are prohibited from making investments that would jeopardize the financial well-being of the organization. Included among the prohibited actions are certain investment strategies such as buying puts and calls, warrants, buying stocks on margin, selling short, and trading in commodity futures or in futures markets in general. This poses a problem of interpretation since some of these actions, such as buying a put, are viewed in some investment quarters as defensive and conservative in the sense that they may put a limit on losses. Interpretation of the motives for certain transactions is subjective, based upon the investment intent and strategy, the frequency with which they are used, and so on. States may restrict the type of securities or the companies whose securities may be bought.

Certain investment risks are acceptable and encouraged if they are program related. Offering loans to individuals deemed to be among the least preferred risks by a commercial lender is acceptable as long as the making of such loans is within the tax-exempt mission of the nonprofit. Recall the loans to minority and rural businesses referred to in Chapter 4.

If this rule is violated, a 5 percent tax is imposed on the foundation and another 5 percent on the manager who is aware of or participates in the investment decision. In a case such as this, the finance or investment committee of the board of directors, the president, the investment officers of the organization all could be held responsible.

Excess Business Holdings

There is a limit on the business holding of a private foundation. No more than 20 percent of the voting stock or interest of a single business may be owned by a private foundation and all of its disqualified persons combined. Some types of businesses are unaffected by this rule. These are program-related businesses and businesses that make their income through dividends, royalties, rents, interest, or so-called passive income, rather than by sale of goods and services.

A private foundation cannot own a sole proprietorship unless gotten by bequest or prior to 1969. The reader should not confuse a sole proprietorship with sole ownership of a corporation or unrelated business as previously described. The term "sole proprietorship" simply means that the business is unincorporated and that the nonprofit would be totally liable for any failures of the business. If sole proprietorships were allowed, all of the assets of the foun-

The Altman chain was offered for sale earlier this year to comply with Federal and state regulations restricting the business activities of private foundations.

The foundation was created by Benjamin Altman shortly before his death in 1913 and under his will, received virtually all stock in the company. However the Federal Tax Reform Act of 1969 required the foundation to divest "excess" business holdings — about 50 percent of its stock — or face heavy penalties.

The sale of the chain also was pressed by the State Attorney General's office, which wanted to maximize the money made available for local charities. It maintained that the management of the store in today's competitive retail market was not aggressive enough to provide adequate resources for the foundation.

Kathleen Teltsch, "Stores' Sale Is Bonanza for Altman Foundation," *The New York Times,* Sunday, October 20, 1985, p. 52. Reprinted by permission.

dation would be exposed to claims by creditors of the business. A large claim against the business that it could not meet by itself would lead to claims against the assets of the foundation.

Should this rule be broken, the penalty is 5 percent of the value of the excess holdings. This penalty is imposed on the foundation, not the management. The penalty could rise to 200 percent if left uncorrected in the time allotted.

Prohibited Expenditures

Some expenditures by private foundations such as those aimed at influencing legislation lead to tax penalties. Legislation includes any action by a legislative body at any level of government. School boards, commissions, and authorites such as housing or economic on any level are considered administrative rather than legislative bodies and therefore expenditures to influence them are not prohibited. In addition, expert testimony in response to a written request by a legislative body or nonpartisan studies made public are not construed to be attempts to influence legislation and are not prohibited.

Expenditures to influence the outcome of any election are prohibited. Such expenditures include producing or distributing supporting literature or paying campaign workers or providing facilities for campaigns. Critically, any expenditure such as voter registration is also prohibited if it is centered in a specific geographical area.

This prohibition is not violated if the private foundation makes a contribution to (1) an organization that is exempt under 501(c)(3), (2) if the activities of that receiving organization are nonpartisan and are conducted over more than one election period, and in at least five states, (3) the organization spends most (at least 85 percent) of its income on the tax-exempt purposes for which it is organized, (4) 85 percent of its support is from the public (government units and the general public), and (5) the contributions from the private foundation are not used solely for a specific election or geographic area.

The prohibition against political activities has given way in recent years to the development of a new strategy. Supporters of political candidates form a nonprofit group under 501(c)(3)—not to support the candidate but to do research and disseminate information on subjects close to the heart of the potential candidate and even to support the potential candidate's travel to speak (not campaign) on these subjects. These foundations may even give money to public charities. Under this guise, the organization does not become involved in politics because its activities are deemed to be educational.

There are several advantages to going this route. (1) The contributions to a nonprofit are deductible and do not suffer the same limitations on giving as do contributions to a political campaign. (2) The nonprofit organization has several cost advantages including the lower postal rate. (3) Gifts to foundations are not subject to public disclosure as are contributions to political campaigns. (4) Many persons who may not otherwise contribute to a candidate may contribute to a foundation. (5) It gives the unannounced candidate a platform and a way of being identified with an issue in a nonpartisan light. (6) It becomes a source of information and dissemination of information with which the potential candidate can be identified, (7) The foundation may support foundation-related speaking engagements for the candidate that, simultaneously, coincide with the issues with which the candidate seeks identity and in the communities in which the candidate needs exposure.

Another category of prohibited expenditures is grants to individuals. Here the intent is to be certain that grants to individuals are intended to assist them in meeting some measurable objective such as writing a book, earning a degree, is a bona fide prize or award, is nondiscriminatory (that is, not targeted as a payoff or bribe), or aims at improving skills.

Expenditures to carry out missions that are not religious, scientific, charitable, or to foster those activities that permit an organization to qualify under 501(c)(3) as discussed earlier are also prohibited.

Finally, private foundations may not make grants to organizations other than those 509(a)(1), (a)(2) and (a)(3) previously discussed unless the foundation takes responsibility for how these funds are used by the donee. This means being sure the funds are used only for the purposes for which they are given, keeping proper and thorough records, and reporting expenditures to the IRS.

Violation of these rules against prohibited expenditures leads to a 10 percent tax based on the amount involved on both the foundation and its management. An additional tax of 100 percent may be imposed on the foundation and 50 percent on the manager if they fail to correct the situation during the allotted time.

Investment Income

Finally, private foundations must pay a 2 percent tax on net investment income. Net investment income is the total of all income including rents, royalties, dividends, interest, and business income plus net capital gains. From this amount is subtracted all ordinary and necessary expenses for producing that income. These include management fees, depreciation, rents, supplies, and the like. Capital losses are deductible only to the extent of capital gains. For example, if the private foundation had $2,000 in capital losses and $4,000 in capital gains, its net capital gain is $2,000 and that becomes part of its net investment income. If, however, it had $2,000 in losses and no gains it would not deduct anything as a capital loss in deriving its net investment income.

PRIVATE OPERATING FOUNDATIONS: FINANCIAL AND LEGAL LIMITS

The private operating foundation is a special type of private foundation. It is subject to all the rules governing private nonoperating foundations except contributions to it are treated as favorably as those to public foundations. Operating foundations may receive gifts from private foundations under circumstances previously described and an operating foundation may own up to 85 percent of the voting interests, not just a combined 20 percent, of a single business that need not be of the special type mentioned earlier. Operating foundations are not subject to the excise tax on undistributed income.

The major distinction of private operating foundations is that they conduct and implement programs. They operate in ways other than the disbursement of funds. The rules that govern these organizations are intended to insure this distinction. Foundations like the Howard Hughes Foundation, The Getty Museum described in the insert on pg. 155, and the Twentieth Century Fund are operating foundations carrying on major research activities.

The Income Test

For a private nonoperating foundation to qualify as an operating foundation, it must pass an income test. This test requires that the foundation spend at least 85 percent of its adjusted net income or minimum investment income, whichever is lower, on activities for which it received tax exemption and in which it is a direct participant.[12] Making a grant to a nonprofit that has a similar mission is not enough, but assigning its staff to work with that nonprofit or using its facilities is. Thus, many on the staff of the Howard Hughes Foundation do their research on university campuses. In short, the private operating foundation must do more than contribute money. It must directly participate through staff or facilities or a combination of the two.

Asset, Endowment and Support Tests

In addition to the income test, a private operating foundation must meet one of three other tests: asset, endowment or support. The asset test is designed to detect how much of the facilities or other assets of the foundation are being used directly in activities for which it received exemption. At least 65 percent of the assets of the private foundation must be used directly in the meeting of its tax-exempt mission. If the organization chooses, it may satisfy this condition by running a program-related business using 65 percent of its assets to do so. Or it may control a for-profit corporation by owning 80 percent of all its voting stocks, and 80 percent of all other types of stocks issued by the corporation—if all (or 85 percent) of the assets of the corporation are devoted to the same types of activities for which the organization received its exemption.

As an alternative to the asset test, the private operating foundation may elect to demonstrate that its grants are aimed at advancing its charitable cause. This is the essence of the endowment test. The basic requirement is that two-thirds of the minimum investment return is expended on qualifying distributions as defined earlier: expenses for conducting the tax-exempt mission, authorized set asides, and expenses for acquiring assets to conduct the mission.

Instead of the asset or endowment test, a private foundation seeking to be an operating foundation may elect to pass the support test. Notice that this

LOS ANGELES—The world's most feared art museum is an easy drive from Hollywood. Take Sunset Boulevard to Malibu and turn right at the ocean. There, above the beach, among the hillside houses, is the villa-in-a-garden that J. Paul Getty dreamed. The style of his building is touchingly eccentric, part Pompeii-preposterous, part Cecil B. De Mille. They ought to make a movie here, a suspenseful big-bucks thriller, a California fantasy. The story of the Getty, the museum and its offshoots, is a story that's got everything—precious objects, private jets, a gray and cunning millionaire, jealousy and fear.

Stuck there in the suburbs, open only by appointment, Getty's red-roofed villa would be of small concern to the world's great museums—were they not so frightened of its cash.

• The J. Paul Getty Trust, which runs the art museum, has $2.17 billion craftily invested.

• The trust has so much money that the *least* that it can spend, by law, is $1.77 million every week.

• The Getty is so rich that, if it desired, it could crush its competition and forever dominate the international art market. In fiscal 1983, it spent $85,431,706 expanding its collections of art and books.

• The trust has so much money that if it does as well this year as it has been doing, it will earn $434 million in 1984. If the law allowed, it could easily support the Metropolitan Museum (whose fiscal 1983 operating funds were $43.7 million), the National Gallery ($40.9 million), the Smithsonian's museums ($33 million), as well as all the programs of the National Endowment for the Arts ($143.8 million in fiscal 1983). And even if it paid those bills—while holding back enough to counteract the drain of 5 percent inflation—it would still have more than $50 million to lavish on itself.

On Feb. 13, the trust sold Texaco 9,320,340 shares of Getty Oil stock for $128 each. While that $1.19 billion sale enriched the trust's endowment, treasurer Joseph Kearns says its other liquid assets—worth an additional $1 billion—"have generated a return of more than 20 percent compounded for the past two years." The trust's net income is subject to a 2 percent federal excise tax.

The Getty must spend millions. It doesn't have a choice. It is obliged, by law, to disperse a minimum of 4.25 percent of its appreciated assets three years out of four. And unlike the $3.4 billion Ford Foundation—the only one that's bigger—it does not dispense grants. It is an "operating foundation," and under U.S. law, at least 85 percent of the money it spends must be on programs that it runs.

Paul Richard, "Museum of the Big Bucks," *The Washington Post,* Friday, April 13, 1984, p. B1.

test is elective, unlike public charities. This can be done by showing that 85 percent of the support of the foundation comes from the broad public and governmental units, from more than five tax-exempt foundations, or that no more than 25 percent of its support is normally (as defined earlier) received from any one tax-exempt organization, or that not more than 50 percent of its support is normally received from gross investment income.

One of the problems with public charities that deal with private operating foundations is that the latter constantly interferes. This, as we see, is because of legal requirements to be directly involved. Private nonoperating and public foundations (to the extent that the latter makes grants) are not similarly constrained.

A Mirror Image of the Rules

One of the rules that we discussed in this chapter requires both the private operating and nonoperating foundations to make regular qualified distributions. These rules are more stringent on the latter than on the former. However, public foundations are not required to make such distributions although they may. Hence, one of the effects of the distribution requirement is that it defines the role of the different types of foundations. This is one of the side effects of the rules we have discussed.

SUMMARY AND CONCLUSIONS

Section 501(c)(3) permits more than one choice of tax-exempt status. The differences among these choices are to be found in the rules that not only define the types of foundation but also limit the types of actions they may take. The principal objectives of these rules are (1) to protect the income and assets of the foundations from the personal use of the founders, donors and management and their associates, (2) to restrict the use of these income and assets to the missions previously selected by each nonprofit and to which it is legally committed in its charter, and (3) to assure some degree of responsiveness to the general public as participants but surely as beneficiaries of the income and assets of the nonprofit. Herein lies the significant difference between a nonprofit and a for-profit corporation. Section 501(c)(3) provides alternative ways of satisfying these concerns.

The rules impact on the financing activities of the nonprofit. Business, investment income, gifts, grants, contributions, membership fees, and government aid are all accepted sources of finance. They do not all have equal weight in fulfilling the requirements of demonstrating public support. Because the demonstration of such support is critical, particularly to public charities, good management will aways be alert not only to the sources of financial assistance but to the relative weight of each kind of support in the entire financing effort. It is not simply the amount of money raised that is important, but from what sources and in what relative amounts.

APPENDIX 6: INTERNAL REVENUE SERVICE EXAMPLES OF ARTICLES OF INCORPORATION OF NONPROFIT TAX-EXEMPT CORPORATIONS

In this chapter we discussed the nonprofit as a corporation. In Chapter 2, we noted that as a corporation, the nonprofit is a creation of the state. However, in order to receive the benefits of tax exemption, the articles of incorporation must meet a federal standard. Rarely are these in conflict. The federal standard is focused on avoiding the distribution of assets or earnings of the corporation to individuals or the use of the nonprofit corporation for the personal power of a donor or his or her relatives or business associates. On p. 158 we illustrate what should be contained in the charter.

If the reader is interested in the restrictions of the nonprofit when it takes the form of a trust, Chapter 11 and the appendix of that chapter should be read.

NOTES

1. *The Internal Revenue Code, 1954* as amended in 1969, created these categories. See the two IRS publications listed in the following Suggested Readings.

2. The charter is to be distinguished from the bylaws. The charter is a legal document analogous to a birth certificate. While the bylaws outline how the organization is to function, the charter states the purpose. The purpose of the organization, regardless of its bylaws, must coincide with the missions included under Section 501(c)(3).

3. Public charity (as defined later) may choose to get a specific dollar and percentage limitation rather than "substantial," and to have lobbying expenditures distinguished from grass-roots expenditures. Lobbying expenditures are aimed to influence legislation while grass-roots expenditures are aimed at influencing the general public. When the percentage limitation is used, a violation consists of spending 150 percent of the permitted amount. The permitted amount is based on a percentage of the tax-exempt expenditures. Grass-roots expenditures are limited to 25 percent of the expenditures permitted on lobbying. Violation means that the organization loses its status as a 501(c)(3) and becomes a 501(c)(4)—a civic league or local association of employees or a welfare organization. Contributions to them are not tax deductible.

4. See discussion of the word "charitable" in Chapter 2.

5. The differences in the treatment of gifts and contributions will be discussed in Chapter 10.

6. This is discussed later in this chapter.

7. See Chapter 7 for a discussion.

8. Strategies for handling large gifts are discussed in Chapters 10 and 11.

9. We are assuming that the community trust is a publicly supported organization. Trusts must also pass public support tests. More is said about community trusts in this chapter.

10. Margaret Riley, "Private Foundation Information Returns, 1982" in *Statistics of Income Bulletin,* 5, no. 2, Fall 1985, (Washington, D.C.: U.S. Government Printing Office, 1985), 1–28.

11. See discussion in Chapter 10.

12. Note that the income test for private operating foundations requires the lesser of the adjusted net income or minimum investment income. The distribution requirement for private foundations requires the greater of the two be distributed.

Articles of Incorporation of

The undersigned, a majority of whom are citizens of the United States, desiring to form a Non-Profit Corporation under the Non-Profit Corporation Law of ——, do hereby certify:

First: The name of the Corporation shall be ——.

Second: The place in this state where the principal office of the Corporation is to be located is the City of ——, —— County.

Third: Said corporation is organized exclusively for charitable, religious, educational, and scientific purposes, including, for such purposes, the making of distributions to organizations that qualify as exempt organizations under section 501(c)(3) of the Internal Revenue Code of 1954 (or the corresponding provision of any future United States Internal Revenue Law).

Fourth: The names and addresses of the persons who are the initial trustees of the corporation are as follows:

Name   Address

Fifth: No part of the net earnings of the corporation shall inure to the benefit of, or be distributable to its members, trustees, officers, or other private persons, except that the corporation shall be authorized and empowered to pay reasonable compensation for services rendered and to make payments and distributions in furtherance of the purposes set forth in Article Third hereof. No substantial part of the activities of the corporation shall be the carrying on of propaganda, or otherwise attempting to influence legislation, and the corporation shall not participate in, or intervene in (including the publishing or distribution of statements) any political campaign on behalf of any candidate for public office. Notwithstanding any other provision of these articles, the corporation shall not carry on any other activities not permitted to be carried on (a) by a corporation exempt from federal income tax under section 501(c)(3) of the Internal Revenue Code of 1954 (or the corresponding provision of any future United States Internal Revenue Law) or (b) by a corporation, contributions to which are deductible under section 170(c)(2) of the Internal Revenue Code of 1954 (or the corresponding provision of any future United States Internal Revenue Law).

[If reference to federal law in articles of incorporation imposes a limitation that is invalid in your state, as in California, you may wish to substitute the following for the last sentence of the preceding paragraph: "Notwithstanding any other provision of these articles, this corporation shall not, except to an insubstantial degree, engage in any activities or exercise any powers that are not in furtherance of the purposes of this corporation."]

Sixth: Upon the dissolution of the corporation, the Board of Trustees shall, after paying or making provision for the payment of all of the liabilities of the corporation, dispose of all of the assets of the corporation exclusively for the purposes of the corporation in such manner, or to such organization or organizations organized and operated exclusively for charitable, educational, religious, or scientific purposes as shall at the time qualify as an exempt organization or organizations under section 501(c)(3) of the Internal Revenue Code of 1954 (or the corresponding provision of any future United States Internal Revenue Law), as the Board of Trustees shall determine. Any such assets not so disposed of shall be disposed of by the Court of Common Pleas of the county in which the principal office of the corporation is then located, exclusively for such purposes or to such organization or organizations, as said Court shall determine, which are organized and operated exclusively for such purposes.

In witness whereof, we have hereunto subscribed our names this — day of —— 19—.

Articles of Incorporation. Source: Internal Revenue Service, Tax-Exempt Status for Your Organization, Publication 557, rev. January 1982, (Washington, D.C.: U.S. Government Printing Office, 1982), p. 10.

SUGGESTED READINGS

GODFREY, HOWARD, *Handbook on Tax-Exempt Organizations* (Englewood Cliffs, New Jersey: Prentice-Hall, Inc., 1983).

OLECK, HOWARD L., *Nonprofit Corporations Organizations and Associations,* 4th ed. (Englewood Cliffs, New Jersey: Prentice-Hall, Inc., 1980).

TREUSCH, PAUL E. and NORMAN A. SUGARMAN, *Tax-Exempt Charitable Organizations,* 2nd. ed. (Philadelphia: American Law Institute, American Bar Association, Committee on Continuing Professional Education, 1983).

Internal Revenue Service, Department of the Treasury, *Tax-Exempt Status for Your Organization,* Publication 557, Revised February 1984, (Washington, D.C.: U.S. Government Printing Office, 1984).

_____ *Tax Information for Private Foundations and Foundation Managers,* Publication 578, Revised October 1981, (Washington, D.C.: U.S. Government Printing Office, 1981).

```
┌─────────────────────┐
│       SEVEN          │
└─────────────────────┘
         │
┌─────────────────────────────────────────┐
│                                           │
│   Financing Through the                   │
│   Operation of a Business                 │
│                                           │
│                                           │
└─────────────────────────────────────────┘
```

This chapter discusses both related and unrelated businesses. It shows how these businesses may be integrated into a simple or conglomerate structure. Nonprofit businesses enable the organization to perform its community or public welfare mission by providing a stream of income over which the nonprofit has total control.

An unrelated business is one which is not integrally related to the mission of the organization. Its principal purpose is to generate income. As stated in Chapter 3, income generated from an unrelated business is taxed. However, income from an unrelated business is classified as support and enables the organization to qualify for public charity status.

A related business is one that is integrally a part of the mission of the organization. That is, the income it generates is directly a result of the organization's conducting its community or public welfare mission. The income from this kind of business is not taxed at all.

DEFINITION OF RELATED AND UNRELATED NONPROFIT BUSINESSES

An unrelated business is a trade or business regularly conducted by a nonprofit for the purpose of making a profit. The unrelated business makes little or no substantive or programmatic contribution to the exempt mission of the organization. Its primary contribution is money. A program-related business, on the other hand, is directly and integrally related to the programmatic and substantive goals of the nonprofit. Thus, program-related business would be carried on even if it were not profitable. An unrelated business is pursued because it is profitable.

There are three keys to determining if an activity is an unrelated business. First, it is a trade or a business conducted to generate a profit.

Second, an unrelated business is a regular activity, not a one-time or occasional event. It is regular if it is conducted by the nonprofit with the same frequency as would a for-profit firm. A one-time bake sale is not an unrelated business. Regularity does not mean everyday. It means the frequency that is customary among for-profit firms in the same trade or business.

Third, an unrelated business is not substantially related to the tax-exempt mission of the nonprofit. It may raise money but is not programmatically integral to the tax-exempt mission. Some examples will help clarify this point.

A halfway house organized to provide room, board, therapy, and counseling for persons discharged from alcoholic treatment centers also operates a furniture shop to provide full time employment for its residents. The profits are applied to the operating costs of the halfway house. The income from this venture is not unrelated trade or business income.

An exempt organization, organized and operated for the prevention of cruelty to animals, receives income from providing pet boarding and grooming services for the general public. This is income from an unrelated trade or business.

An exempt organization whose purpose is to provide for the welfare of young people rents rooms primarily to people under age 25. This income is not considered unrelated business income since the source of the income flow is substantially related to the purpose constituting the basis for the organization's exemption.

A hospital with exempt status operates a gift shop patronized by patients, visitors making purchases for patients, and employees and medical staff. It also operates a parking lot for patients and visitors only. Both of these activities are substantially related to the hospital's exempt purpose and do not constitute unrelated trades or businesses.

These four examples offered by the IRS illustrate the differences between a program-related business and an unrelated business. The former is an extension of or part of the tax-exempt function of the organization. The latter is not.

The same activity can be either a related or unrelated business depending upon how it is handled. See the insert below. Wittenbach and Gallagher show how to make an activity a related business and thereby tax-exempt.

A service run exclusively for members of an organization or completely provided voluntarily by them is a related business. But the same services provided by the same nonprofit for the public or by paid employees would be an unrelated business.

A service such as a laundry or store operated exclusively for the membership of a tax-exempt organization is not an unrelated business. The sale of a product of a program-related business across state lines yields income from an unrelated business.

Income generated by tax-exempt organizations

Income-producing activity	Tax planning strategy
1. Sales of merchandise	Establish a connection between the items sold and the organization's exempt purposes. Including descriptive literature with the sale can, in some cases, provide the requisite link.
2. Provision of services	Avoid narrowly defining the entity's exempt purpose in organizational documents.
3. Royalty arrangements	Avoid entering into a partnership or joint venture arrangement with the licensee.
4. Leasing of facilities	Make only the facilities available to the lessee. Do not provide services.
5. Broadcasting rights	Like football, other school events presented off-campus that generate revenue should be defended as nontaxable in that the performance is made available to a broader audience.
6. Sale of an organization's mailing list or directory to its members	List the members in a noncommercial format, without advertising, and with all members listed in a similar fashion.

An income-producing activity of an exempt organization will be subject to tax under Sec. 511 if the activity is an unrelated trade or business that is regularly carried on. As most of the rulings and cases summarized in this article suggest, the most troublesome issue is the determination of whether the income-producing activity is substantially related to the organization's tax-exempt purposes.

Nonetheless, with careful planning, an exempt organization may be able to avoid tax. Included in the table, at left, are a few planning techniques that should not be overlooked.

If the classification of the activity as a regularly carried on unrelated trade or business cannot be avoided, it does not necessarily mean that such an activity should be terminated. After all, the organization will still be able to retain its after-tax dollars. However, care must be exercised to make certain that such activities do not become so extensive that the organization stands to lose its tax-exempt status.

James L. Wittenbach and Lawrence G. Gallagher, "The Tax Implications to Exempt Organizations of Six Income-Producing Activities," *The Tax Adviser* (March 1985), pp. 170–83.

Services only for or by members, that sell donated property, that do not engage in interstate commerce, trade shows that are educational, and the rental or sale of mailing labels to other nonprofits are also related businesses. The latter two were added in the 1986 tax law.

EXCESS PROFITS: A DISTINCTION BETWEEN RELATED AND UNRELATED INCOME

An IRS regulation announced in *The Internal Revenue Bulletin,* April 28, 1986, No. 1986–17, page 9, is instructive. The case is that of a large metropolitan hospital that provides services such as data processing, food service and purchasing services to other hospitals. The IRS rules that the earnings would be related income if all of three conditions hold: (1) the hospitals purchasing the service has a maximum capacity for inpatients of 100 persons; (2) the service, if performed by the recipient hospital, would have been a normal service for it; (3) the fee in excess of actual cost is not more than one and one-half times the average rates of interest on public debt obligations issued by the Federal Hospital Insurance Trust Fund.

If all of the above conditions do not hold, then the earnings are unrelated business income and taxed. This case not only shows the thin line between related and unrelated business income, but that while an absolute dollar level of profits is not stipulated, any profit above a normal rate of return is likely to be considered unrelated business income.

INTEGRATION OF BUSINESS OPERATIONS INTO A CONGLOMERATE STRUCTURE

Figure 7.1 shows a possible configuration of for-profit unrelated businesses and nonprofit entities in conglomerate structure of a nonprofit corporation under Section 501(c)(3). A nonprofit that is a public charity as defined by Section 509(a)(1) or (a)(2) may not only have its internal departments within its corporate corpus but may also house both unrelated and program-related businesses.

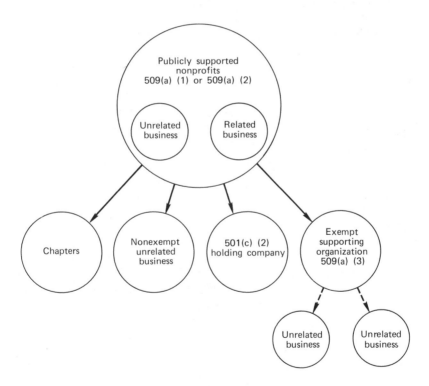

Figure 7.1 Structure of nonprofit corporation or conglomerate. Source: Author.

In addition, the 509(a)(1) or (a)(2) may also have chapters. These are not separate entities having their own tax-exempt status; rather they fall under the umbrella of the parent organization. The 509(a)(1)s and (a)(2)s may also have 509(a)(3) organizations as subsidiaries or corporations wholly beholden to them. Unlike chapters, these are independently chartered and tax-exempt organizations whose existence relies on their relationship with a publicly supported organization. Furthermore, it is acceptable that these 509(a)(3)s run both program-related and unrelated businesses.

The 509(a)(1) or (a)(2) may also run an unrelated business outside of its immediate corporate corpus. For example, an organization may advertise in its journal. The advertisement is an unrelated business, but the articles comprise a related business. This is best done within the corporate structure of most nonprofits. On the other hand, the same nonprofit may be part or sole owner of an apartment building or hotel. This is best done outside of the immediate corporate structure of the organization.

Note that it does not matter if the unrelated business is within the corpus of the organization or if it is a separate corporation owned or controlled by the nonprofit. In either case, they pay taxes. What does matter is that as independent entities, a corporation outside of the structure of the nonprofit shields the latter from liability, provides for separate management, can raise its own capital, shields the nonprofit from unwanted publicity, and provides for the participation of individuals as owners and profit-makers.

Figure 7.1 also shows that the 509(a)(1) or (a)(2) may also own a holding company. This company may be exempt or nonexempt. If exempt, it merely serves as a holder of title of property consistent with the tax-exempt function of the parent organization and reports its taxes in combination with the parent. As a nonexempt organization it may hold title to other properties and report its taxes as a separate corporation. Hence, a nonprofit could, as a holding company, hold title to all its real estate.

Viewing the complete Figure 7.1 and imagining all of the subordinate circles that could be drawn, it is obvious that an imaginative nonprofit could easily create a conglomerate. Some have, as evidenced by the conglomerate of the Unification Church described in the insert on p. 165.[2] Such conglomerations are perfectly legal.

Now that we have juxtaposed both a for-profit and a nonprofit, it is worth remembering that the significant difference between the two is that the income and assets of a nonprofit cannot be distributed to individuals as they can be in the for-profit sector. Indeed, individuals are the owners of such corporations. Their ownership is evidenced by stock certificates. The reward they obtain for such investment is in the appreciation of the value of their stocks and in the payment of dividends. While an owner like other shareholders, nonprofits are given better tax treatment on their dividends than other shareholders. As we shall discuss, nonprofits may pay no taxes whatsoever on dividends received. Other taxpayers may at best exclude a portion, paying taxes on the remainder.

❦

Founded by Moon in South Korea in 1954, the Unification Church has grown into a multinational conglomerate of business, political and cultural organizations. Causa International, a church-financed political group headed by Moon deputy Bo Hi Pak, has spent millions of dollars in recent years on anticommunist lobbying in Latin America and the United States.

The diversity of church businesses is enormous: the church has invested more than $60 million in Uruguay in recent years, buying the country's largest luxury hotel, its fourth-largest bank, a publishing company and large tracts of farm land.

It owns four South Korean manufacturing companies, including a ginseng tea company, a titanium firm and a machine-tool and weapons manufacturer, that had estimated total assets of $198 million last year, according to figures published in the Maeil Economic Daily newspaper in Seoul. It also operates tuna fleets and fish-processing plants in Gloucester, Mass., Norfolk and Alaska and owns newspapers in Montevideo, Cyprus, Tokyo, New York and Washington.

In the Washington area alone, besides The Times, the church owns a downtown construction firm, Monumental Construction and Moulding Co.; an Alexandria television production firm, Tele-Color Studio, and a number of McLean-based companies, including Unification Church International (UCI), which was incorporated in 1977 by Pak, and has been described by federal investigators as the ultimate church holding company in the United States.

UCI owns One Up Enterprises, which in turn owns News World Communications, which in turn owns The Washington Times, according to interviews with former church members and corporate records on file in the District and in Fairfax County.

Another McLean-based UCI subsidiary, U.S. Foods Corp., collects $497,310 a year from the D.C. government for office space it rents to the Department of Human Services and other city agencies at 605 G St. NW, according to city records.

John Burgess and Michael Isikoff, ''Moon's Japanese Profits Bolster Efforts in U.S.,'' *The Washington Post,* September 16, 1984, p. A20.

Organization of an Unrelated Business

In the for-profit world, businesses are organized as corporations, sole proprietorships, or partnerships. Joint ventures may be undertaken between two or more organizations on a specific project. A trust could also be created to hold and exercise the rights of ownership of those who own a business organization.[3] Except for sole proprietorships, these organizations are adaptable to an unrelated business owned and operated by a nonprofit.

A common way of organizing an unrelated business is as a corporation. A corporation, unlike a partnership or a sole proprietorship, is an independent legal and tax entity. Liabilities for failure and error of the corporation do not extend to its owner as with partnerships and proprietorships. Corporations have centralized management and do not have to share management decisions with all owners as with general partnerships. Unlike proprietorships, corporations can raise capital by selling shares of stocks. A partnership may do so by selling partnership interests but such interests rarely have as wide a market as a corporation's stocks. Unlike a general partnership, a corporation does not have to be dissolved in the case of withdrawal of an owner. It has a perpetual life of its own and ownership can be easily transferred from one person to another. A corporation is easier and safer than other forms of business organizations. Most importantly, even if the nonprofit organized its business as a partnership, it would be taxed as a corporation.

A nonprofit may choose to be a minority, majority, or even sole owner of a for-profit corporation. Its minority ownership may be insignificantly small or significantly large, but a critical concept of ownership is control. A nonprofit is said to be the controlling owner of a corporation if it owns at least 80 percent of its voting stocks and 80 percent of all other stocks. How a nonprofit is treated for tax purposes depends not on whether it is a minority or a majority stockholder but whether it is the controlling organization. In the case of nonstock corporations which nonprofits are, control means controlling 80 percent or more of the board of directors or trustees.

The way the unrelated business is treated depends upon the form of business organization. If it is a corporation or partnership, it will face the same tax rate as other corporations.[4] It will also be subject to a minimum tax.[5]

BENEFITS, CONSEQUENCES, AND OPPORTUNITIES OF UNRELATED BUSINESSES

Obviously, the single most important reason for running an unrelated business is because it is profitable. There is no overriding charitable purpose. The income from these enterprises not only finances the activities of the nonprofit but also satisfies the requirement of demonstrating public support. The reader should recall our earlier discussion of the role of unrelated business in defining support and in determining whether or not a nonprofit can demonstrate that it is publicly supported.

Yet another perspective is worth noting. Let's go back to the principles in Chapter 6. Nonprofit A, which receives $100,000 in investment income, $40,000 from a community chest, $50,000 from Mr. W, $10,000 from Ms. Y, and $1,000 from Mr. Q would fail the one-third support test. Now, assume that it had an unrelated business with a net income of $400,000. Now, its total support is $601,000. One-third of this is $200,333. Each individual donor's contribution is not valued at more than 2 percent of the total support, or $40,066. This means that instead of being valued at $4,020, Mrs. Y's contribution is now valued at its full $10,000 and Mr. W's at $40,060. Now add the contributions of the community chest, $40,000, Mr. W at $40,066, Mrs. Y at $10,000 and Mr. Q at $1,000. The sum is $91,000 and the organization fails the one-third test and passes the 10 percent test as before. However, there is a subtle difference. Since each individual's contribution can receive a higher true value closer to the actual contribution made by the donor, the organization may be able to pursue a strategy concentrated more toward larger contributions than it could otherwise have done and still demonstrate public support.

Another benefit of an unrelated business other than support is that it enables the organization to carry out some of its programs by subsidizing them. The advertising in a magazine published by a nonprofit for its members subsidizes the magazine. The advertising may be an unrelated business if it is unrelated to the mission of the organization. A pharmacy catering to the general public but located in a hospital is an unrelated business, although without the pharmacy the hospital could not provide its services as well. Tours unrelated to the tax-exempt mission of the organization that are conducted by a nonprofit for its members and others are unrelated businesses but they help to maintain contact and cohesion and provide a basis for future fund-raising.

An unrelated business can also extend the social involvement of a nonprofit while making a profit. An unrelated business can make deductible contributions to tax-exempt organizations as long as they are not given to its nonprofit parent and it can make such contributions up to 5 percent of its taxable income. If this limit is exceeded, it can deduct the excess over a five-year period.[6]

An unrelated business can also be used to hire disadvantaged workers and receive a tax credit for doing so, thereby reducing the tax liability of the unrelated business. The credit also means that the full wages of the worker are not paid by the business but shared with the federal government.

Consequences of Unrelated Businesses

The consequences of running a program-related or unrelated business are significant. A related business is not taxed; an unrelated business is.

For 509(a)(1) organizations, unrelated businesses are considered to be support, whereas related businesses are not. For 509(a)(2) organizations, unrelated business has a limit to the extent to which it is included in support while unrelated business income is generally included fully. Unrelated businesses take the nonprofit beyond its tax-exempt purpose, related businesses by definition do not.

On a smaller though significant scale, however, development of the District's commercial center and the rebuilding of the old burned-out corridors have been shaped by nonprofit entrepreneurs, primarily churches and institutions of higher education. Driven by different motives, these groups have contributed substantially, nevertheless, to the economic growth of the District.

George Washington University's role as a real estate developer is a prime example. Frequently referred to pejoratively as "Real Estate U," the university has become a developer and owner of commercial real estate properties over the past 17 years. Although not considered a major competitor of for-profit commercial real estate developers, the university, nonetheless, has assumed a prominent role in the development of prime office space bordering its campus in Foggy Bottom.

Although sensitive to criticism of its acquisition and development of property for nonacademic purposes, GWU continues to add to its land bank. Unlike other major developers who are driven by the profit motive, the university, according to officials, is guided by a desire to maintain the integrity of its urban campus.

In the early 1950s, "it became apparent [to university officials] that people had started to build west of 16th Street and that they would move west to Rock Creek Park and wash away property in their path," said Charles E. Diehl, GWU's vice president and treasurer.

The university "started off with 2,000 to 4,000 square feet, and now we have about 4 million square feet of land" in 19 blocks, Diehl noted.

This massive development program, he added, has enabled the university to achieve many of its academic goals. "One building builds another. Since 1968, we have built 2.5 million square feet of academic space."

Much of the academic space was built with federal funds as well as the money that GWU has made as a developer. In addition to buying buildings, aggressive land acquisition and development has enabled GWU to provide resources for its on-campus constituency and to play a significant role in the economic growth of the District.

The university paid $2.8 million in real estate taxes last year on five commercial buildings with net rentable space of 1.7 million square feet.

"We were able to get land off the back of the university and put it in use and create a resource for the city in taxes," Diehl said.

Equally important, he added, the transactions "don't penalize the university's constituency. We don't have to ask students coming here to pay for that land."

Neither does the university want to be compared with Robin Hood, he added, by charging affluent patients in its hospital exorbitant fees to compensate for the inability of the poor to pay full medical expenses.

"We put out pretty close to $10 million a year in uncompensated medical expenses, and only through our real estate assets can we afford to do that," Diehl said.

Although its role in a major downtown office project is not as extensive as that of George Washington University, one of the District's oldest and most prominent black churches is a limited partner with a major developer. In a joint venture headed by Boston Properties, Metropolitan AME Church will own 5 percent of 1615 M St. NW when the project is completed.

Described by Boston Properties Senior Vice President Robert E. Burke as "a real model of public- and private-sector partnership," the 1615 M St. project will link the historic Sumner School and nearby Magruder School to a new nine-story office building. Developers of the $30 million project, which is being built on District-owned land, agreed to restore the Sumner School building as a museum and archival center for the school system.

Rudolph A. Pyatt, Jr., "Nonprofit Groups Join Building Boom." Source: *The Washington Post*, (Washington Business), April 29, 1985, pp. 32–33.

A nonprofit may simultaneously run both related and unrelated businesses. The accounting must be kept separate and time of employees or use of facilities must be properly allocated if they are shared by both types of businesses.

Opportunities for Unrelated Businesses

Virtually any legal trade or business may be conducted as an unrelated business by a nonprofit.

A substantial opportunity for the development of unrelated businesses arises from the concept of externalities as described in Chapter 4. In carrying out their tax-exempt functions, there are "external economies of production" that the nonprofit may harness into a profitable business. There is a whole class of unrelated businesses resulting from exploiting opportunities arising from the discharge of tax-exempt missions. These businesses rise from a tax-exempt organization using its position, process, good will or reputation to make money in a way that is not directly related to its tax-exempt mission. The IRS gives the following example.

An exempt scientific organization enjoys an excellent reputation in the field of biological research. It exploits this reputation regularly by selling endorsements of various items of laboratory equipment to manufacturers. The endorsement of laboratory equipment does not contribute importantly to the accomplishment of any purpose for which exemption is granted to the organization. Accordingly, the income from the sale of endorsements is gross income from an unrelated business.

Capturing the benefits of carrying out its mission is also evidenced by the opportunity nonprofits have to make dual use of plant and equipment. The same plant or equipment that it uses for conducting its tax-exempt mission can also be used to produce unrelated business income. The university stadium may be used for professional football. When this is done, the nonprofit must separate the two types of income and expenses for reporting purposes.

Still another example common to nonprofits is the use of their publications to generate income. This can be done by selling advertising space. See the next insert. The income from the advertising can be unrelated income.

Furthermore, the publication's income and costs are divided into portions so that if the readership portion (its tax-exempt purpose) is operating at a loss, all additional costs above that loss level may be deducted from the advertising portion (its unrelated business) as long as such a deduction does not result in the unrelated business showing a loss for tax purposes. In short, the cost of serving the readership may provide a tax deduction to the unrelated business.[7]

There are several variations to this example. The basic rule is that if an unrelated business exploits the activities of a related business, the losses from the latter may be deducted from the former if such a deduction does not lead the unrelated business to report a loss. In short, the IRS is willing to reduce the taxes of the unrelated business but not eliminate them. Two effects occur:

> There is no merit to the Government's argument that Congress and the Treasury intended to establish a blanket rule requiring the taxation of income from all commercial advertising by tax-exempt professional journals without a specific analysis of the circumstances. There is no support for such a rule in the regulations or in the legislative history of the Internal Revenue Code.

Supreme Court of the United States, United States vs. American College of Physicians, No. 84-1737, April 22, 1986, p. 2.

The tax-exempt mission is subsidized by the unrelated business and the tax liability of the latter is reduced by the losses of the former.

A CASE STUDY OF A BUSINESS OWNED BY NONPROFITS

This case is excerpted by permission from an article written by Garis F. Distelhorst, "When Associations Become Entrepreneurs," and, appears in *Association Management*, February, 1985, pp. 109–11. Copyright © by The American Association Executives, Washington, D.C., all rights reserved. It is about the National Association of College Stores (NACS) in Oberlin, Ohio.

> As the largest association serving college and university bookstores, 61-year-old NACS provides traditional services such as education and training programs, a variety of publications, research, trade shows, and marketing aids to 2,600 member stores and 1,000 associate members who are publishers and suppliers.
>
> These programs are carried out by 25 full-time employees, within the confines of a $3 million-plus annual budget. Yet NACS does possess one distinguishing characteristic as an association: NACSCORP is a for-profit subsidiary. Member stores use it to order books, calendars, and computer software, to participate in a magazine subscription program, and to sign up for the Graduate Career Network, a computerized resume referral service.

The author continues:

> . . .NACSCORP has a budget nearly four times that of NACS, it employs up to 75 staff members, and leases some 55,000 square feet of office and warehouse space from NACS. Income for 1984 is expected to top $12 million—three times the sales volume of just five years ago and nearly 240 times that for NACSCORP'S first year of operation in 1960.

According to the author, the idea behind NACSCORP is that:

> The association would purchase books in large quantities at discount prices, then resell them to member stores at near cost and use the small profit to cover the

association's expenses. . .NACSCORP developed a full-time staff and added paper-bound trade books, mass market books, and calendars to its offerings. It assumed control of the association's student magazine subscription fulfillment program and has recently begun marketing computer software and supplies—all targeted specifically at the college market.

NACSCORP is actually a large department of NACS, with an executive who provides day-to-day management of a small professional staff. . . . Although NACSCORP appears as a department on the NACS organization chart, it does have an independent board of directors. Appointed by the president of NACS, this board establishes the overall policy for the subsidiary and is composed of individuals with strong business backgrounds, both within and outside the college-store field. Directors are appointed for three-year terms and report only to the NACS board of trustees, which acts as shareholder for the association's 2,600 members. The NACS board of trustees does not set policy or give direction to the NACSCORP board. It turns over to the NACSCORP board all responsibility for the subsidiary, with one very important exception: the hiring or firing of the president—the title that I hold concurrent with that of executive director of NACS. . .

Thus, the subsidiary operates as a profit-making, shareholder-owned company, although the customers are also shareholders and members of NACS, the 'parent' institution.

Buying, warehousing, and reselling quality paperbound books, calendars, and computer software for the college market accounts for 95 percent of NACSCORP's dollar volume. This activity is promoted as a major service to association members.

The magazine-subscription program is very profitable. . .It features student-rate magazine subscriptions offered by magazine publishers through college stores. NACSCORP has arrangements with *Time* and *Newsweek* to distribute subscription cards in bulk to member college stores and then to collect from students who take advantage of the special rates.

NACSCORP receives 10 percent to 15 percent of the subscription price in return for its involvement, while the college store that distributes the card receives $4 to $5 per subscription.

NACSCORP is in partnership with Publishers Clearinghouse, the largest magazine-fulfillment agency in the world, and provides most of the same services as it does for the *Time* and *Newsweek*. . .programs, plus some marketing and promotion. . .Member stores receive a 25-percent commission and NACSCORP a 10-percent commission on paid subscriptions. The total amount in commissions paid to member stores and to NACSCORP is well in excess of $1 million.

In addition, NACSCORP sponsors the Graduate Career Network. . .(It) allows graduating college seniors to place their resumes on a national database service. . .used by major corporations and other employers.

NACSCORP has also, from time to time, engaged in other for-profit ventures, such as the distribution of Student Value Packs—a collection of samples from a number of consumer-goods manufacturers. . .

The private subsidiary not only provides useful services to NACS members, but benefits the association in other ways as well.

First, NACSCORP's top-flight management personnel bring a critically important perspective to all NACS activities. In addition, NACSCORP pays NACS more than $50,000 per year in rent, plus a share of all utilities and services.

Because it is a for-profit corporation, NACSCORP can take advantage of many attractive tax law provisions. For instance, all major equipment, such as copiers or collators used by either NACSCORP or NACS, is owned by NACSCORP. NACS then pays a fee for the use of the equipment, while NACSCORP takes advantage of depreciation and investment tax credits for its property.

NACS also uses NACSCORP's sophisticated computer system for all its membership records, inventory control, general ledger, annual meeting exhibit management, annual meeting registration, and regional meeting registration. . .

The subsidiary also enhances communication with members. During a recent one-month period, more than 1,000 members called NACSCORP to place orders for books or software. . .How many associations can boast that 40 percent of their members are in telephone contact every month?

Beyond these immediate benefits, we now have a thriving corporation in place that could be used if we need to move other association activities into for-profit status. As the data network we are establishing begins to generate access fees, it will probably need to become a tax-paying entity. With NACSCORP already in place, that could be accomplished merely by developing a separate accounting system.

Our experience demonstrates that associations should consider a tax-paying, for-profit subsidiary if they are engaged in, or plan to become engaged in, commercial activities that could threaten their tax-exempt status.

The tax implications are obvious. Instead of being tax exempt and only paying taxes on unrelated business income, the subsidiary must pay taxes on all its net income, just like any other corporation. For this reason, you should not move any association activities into a subsidiary if the activities are tax exempt or support the organization's claim to tax-exempt status.

. . .With sales approaching $12 million and a gross margin of just over 16 percent, there is no room for error in managing NACSCORP. . .if you are running a successful business, you will probably want to plow almost all of the profits back into the business, so dividends to the parent association should not be a high priority—at least in the beginning.

Another consideration is how much time you can give to running another operation. . .you must not neglect the parent organization.

. . .You will find the opportunity to allocate a number of expenses between the association and the subsidiary, such as basic costs for telephone, rent, building maintenance, support departments, and utilities. The sharing of expenses is obviously a potential benefit to the association, but this is also an area that can cause real difficulty with the IRS. Your allocations should be justifiable and approved by both the association's board and the governing group of the subsidiary corporation.

Subsidiaries, after all, are a small but growing part of association life. Why not be a pioneer on this new frontier?

TAX TREATMENT OF UNRELATED BUSINESS INCOME

Some unrelated business incomes are not taxed. Royalties, rents, interests, dividends, and annuities, so-called passive income, are generally not considered unrelated incomes and therefore are not taxed. But there are important exceptions to this rule.

Dividends are not taxed unless they are received from property subject to debt. This means that a rich source of income for nonprofits are dividends from controlled corporations or profit-making subsidiaries.

There are certain guidelines that may help in setting up these subsidiaries so that the dividends from them will not be taxable to the nonprofit. These guidelines are:

1. While the parent (nonprofit organization) may appoint the board of the subsidiary for-profit corporation, the majority of the members of the board of directors, the employees, and the officers of the for-profit must not be related to or be agents of the nonprofit organization.

2. The parent organization must not participate in the daily activities of the for-profit firm.

3. Any business transaction between the subsidiary and the parent nonprofit organization must conform to strict business principles similar to those governing two organizations that are independent of each other.

4. The subsidiary must be organized for the purpose of conducting a legitimate business which is truly unrelated to the business of the nonprofit organization. Its purpose must be to make a profit through a trade or business unrelated to the mission of the nonprofit parent.

Under the above conditions, expressed in the General Counsel Memorandum 39326, the dividends received by the nonprofit from its for-profit subsidiary are received tax free. The for-profit subsidiary, however, is subject to all taxes of normal corporations.

Interest earnings, royalties, and rents are taxable to the nonprofit if they are payments from an organization that the nonprofit controls whether or not the organization is itself tax exempt or a for-profit firm. These revenues, like dividends, are also taxable if they are derived from a debt-financed property.

Capital gains from selling property are not subject to tax as unrelated business income unless the property was part of an inventory, acquired by debt, or is sold as an ordinary practice in a trade or business. This again puts a nonprofit corporation in a superior position to most owners of property, including stocks.

The use of property that is contiguous to other property owned by a tax-exempt organization even for an unrelated business purpose may escape being treated as unrelated business if there is a clear intent to use that property within the subsequent ten years for a tax-exempt purpose. The IRS must be convinced of this intent every five years. Churches have fifteen years to use the property to generate income without being taxed.

Some types of activities receive favorable treatment. Income from bingo is not taxed if for-profit firms within the local jurisdiction are barred from holding bingo games to make a profit. If they are permitted, then the nonprofit must pay a tax. The idea is to avoid placing the for-profit firm at a disadvantage.

Income derived by agricultural groups from growing and selling crops contiguously to a retirement home is specifically excluded as unrelated business income if the income provides less than 75 percent of the cost of running the retirement home. Income earned by religious organizations using a federal license is excluded if that income is used for charitable purposes and the prices charged are neither significantly higher nor lower than commercial prices. Research conducted for the United States government, its instrumentalities or agencies, or any other level of domestic government is not considered an unrelated business. Further, fundamental research is not an unrelated business and organizations such as hospitals and educational institutions are not subject to unrelated business tax on the income derived from research whether it be fundamental or applied.[8]

Property Subject to Debt

Certain properties owned by a nonprofit may be subject to acquisition indebtedness. All earnings derived from such properties are considered unrelated income and subject to tax. Acquisition debt is any debt (1) incurred to acquire or improve a property, (2) was incurred in anticipation of the acquisition or improvement, or (3) was incurred because of the acquisition or improvement. For example, if a nonprofit incurred a debt to acquire or improve a property, that is an acquisition debt. If the nonprofit purchases a property or is given a property that is subject to a mortgage, that is acquisition indebtedness even though the organization may not be responsible for paying off the mortgage. Or, if after acquiring a property that might be free of debt, the nonprofit enters into debt directly linked to its decision to purchase the property, that is also acquisition indebtedness. In all these cases, the property is said to be debt financed.

Again, the consequence of acquisition indebtedness is that income derived from the property as interest, rent, royalty, dividends, or capital appreciation is unrelated business income and taxed. It does not matter if the income is recurrent or nonrecurrent. If during the taxable year the property is subject to debt, all income that it yields during that year is unrelated business income.

There are some modifications to this seemingly harsh rule. One very important one is that property obtained upon death (bequest and devise) is not considered subject to debt for ten years after its acquisition if (1) the donor held the property for at least five years, (2) the debt is at least five years old, and (3) the nonprofit did not agree to be responsible for the debt.

Another exception to the general rule occurs when the entire property (at least 85 percent) is used for a tax-exempt purpose by the organization itself or by an organization that it controls.

Finally, rents from personal property, earnings from thrift shops, and property used in research are not considered debt-financed property and, therefore, are not subject to tax as unrelated business income. Concern should center on rents and proceeds from the sale of real estate, income and proceeds from the ownership and sale of securities, and proceeds from the sale of personal property (as opposed to rents from such property).

The Complexity of Rental Income

Income from renting real estate has the feature of showing how easy it is for a nonprofit to operate an unrelated business even when it does not intend to do so.[9] It should also alert nonprofit managers to the questions that should be raised before accepting real estate as a gift.

As stated earlier, generally income from the rental of real estate is not unrelated income. However, if the rental is from a property subject to acquisition indebtedness, then all rental income derived from that property is unrelated business income and is so taxed.

If the rental income is from a related organization carrying out its exempt mission, it is not treated as debt financed even if the property is acquired by debt. Yet, the income can be taxed if the organization is controlled by the nonprofit because all rents from a controlled organization are taxed regardless of whether or not the organization that pays it is tax-exempt.

Rental from real estate is also subject to unrelated business income tax if the use of the space is coupled with a service, such as room service in a hotel. Further, if the rental income is combined with a rental fee for the use of personal property such as equipment, the entire income would be subject to tax if the personal property part of the rental exceeds 50 percent. If it is less than 10 percent, the entire rental is exempt.

If the rental is from an organization that is controlled by the nonprofit, the rental income is unrelated business income regardless of whether the organization that pays is a for-profit or a nonprofit.

If the space is used for both tax-exempt as well for-profit activities, the amount of the rental must be allocated between the two uses and taxes paid on the part that is for-profit in origin.

If the rentals are from a tax-exempt related organization and it is used for research or for a thrift shop, it is not treated as debt financed and not subject to unrelated business tax as such. However, it could be considered unrelated business income if the organization paying is controlled by the nonprofit landlord.

If the parent organization uses a debt-financed property (in which case it does not pay rent itself) exclusively for research or thrift shop, income derived from that property is not unrelated business income.

If the property was gotten through a bequest or devise and was held by the donor for at least five years, and the debt is at least five years old and the nonprofit does not agree to assume it, then it is not immediately treated as unrelated business income. There is a ten-year grace period.

There are infinite combinations of these confounding examples. Some of the key questions that must be raised are: Is it debt financed? Is it to be leased along with personal property and, if so, what will be the percentage of the total rental that could be deemed to be derived from the real estate portion of the package? How was the real estate acquired? For what purpose will it be used and by whom?

A Simplified View

There are three main sources of unrelated business income: A. unrelated business activities, B. debt-acquired property, and C. controlled organizations. Some general rules follow.

Source A.   All revenues from unrelated business activities are taxable to the nonprofit unless the revenues are dividends, interest, royalties, and annuities. Revenues from sales, for example, are taxed.

Source B.   All revenues from debt-financed properties are taxed as unrelated business income unless they are already being taxed under Source A or arise from a tax-exempt mission.

Source C.   All rents, interests, royalties, annuities, and other payments (excluding dividends) to the controlling organization from its subordinates are taxed regardless of whether the subordinate is tax exempt or not.

SUMMARY AND CONCLUSIONS

This chapter has contrasted program-related and unrelated businesses and showed how they both fit into the corporate structure of a nonprofit to make it a virtual conglomerate. Unrelated businesses are conducted purely for profit. More importantly, nonprofits receive favored tax treatment on their unrelated business income. Opportunities for deriving unrelated business income are available to most nonprofits. They may arise simply from discharging their tax-exempt mission.

NOTES

1. See discussion of this point in Chapter 6.
2. The reader will recall that the Rev. Sun Myung Moon was not incarcerated for charges against his businesses but against him. The businesses have not been shown to be illegal.

3. In Chapter 11 the use of trusts is discussed as it relates to giving.
4. The choice is between being taxed as a trust or as a corporation. In this chapter we presume that the organization is a corporation.
5. The minimum tax limits the extent to which the organization may use accelerated depreciation, capital gains, depletion, and amortization to reduce their taxes.
6. Other corporations have similar carryover provisions, but may deduct 10 percent of their taxable income. As Chapter 1 points out, the average contribution for all corporations is less than 2 percent of the corporation's taxable income.
7. There are special rules governing advertising, and the manager may wish to go over them more carefully than is possible here. For example, circulation costs and revenues must be distinguished from advertising costs and revenues; membership fee must be allocated, and so on.
8. Fundamental research is distinguished from applied or commercial research. The latter is done for assisting others to be profitable and the results need not be published within a reasonable time.
9. More is said about this in Chapter 7.

SUGGESTED READINGS

BROWN, PETER C. & Associates, *In Search of Cash Cows* (Minneapolis: The Twin Cities Regenerative Funding Project, 1983).

CAGNON, CHARLES, *Business Ventures of Citizens Groups* (Northern Rockies Action Group, 1982).

Center for Urban Economic Development, *Business Spinoffs* (Chicago: University of Illinois, Chicago Circle, 1982).

CRIMMINS, JAMES C. and MARY KEIL, *Enterprise in the Nonprofit Sector* (Washington, D.C.: Partners for Livable Places, and New York: The Rockefeller Brothers Fund, 1983).

DUNCAN, WILLIAM A., *Looking at Income-Generating Business for Small Nonprofit Organizations* (Washington, D.C.: Center for Community Change, 1982).

FIRSTENBERG, PAUL B., *Managing for Profit in the Nonprofit World* (New York: The Foundation Center, 1986).

HANSMANN, HENRY B., "The Role of Nonprofit Enterprise," *The Yale Law Journal,* April 1980, p. 838.

EIGHT

Investing the Dollars of Nonprofit Organizations in a Business

This chapter deals with the questions that the management of a nonprofit should ask in contemplating an investment decision whether that decision is to enter into a business or to continue one. Chapter 14 emphasizes the investment of cash balances.

Prepared in a socratic format, the objective of this chapter is to come as close as possible to actual questions the management should ask. The questions are followed by answers or the accepted procedures for working out an answer. The questions are:

1. How will the investment affect the tax-exempt status of the organization?
2. How should a business be acquired?
3. Should the business be related or unrelated?
4. Should the business be incorporated as a for-profit corporation?
5. Where does the money come from to acquire the business?
6. Is the business profitable?
7. Is profitability enough?
8. What will the investment cost?
9. Will the expected benefits exceed the costs?
10. Can the benefit/cost ratio be calculated?
11. When will the organization recapture its investment?
12. What are the risks?
13. What will it take to break even?

14. What can be done with the earnings of the business?
15. How will entry into the business be made?
16. How is cash managed?
17. Can the decision now be made?

HOW WILL THE INVESTMENT AFFECT THE TAX-EXEMPT STATUS OF THE ORGANIZATION?

If this is not the first question to be asked, it surely is the last. As we saw in Chapter 3, 4, 6, and 7 while investment in a business is not barred and is encouraged by the law, income from such investments can seriously affect the tax-exempt status of the nonprofit. The issue in every case is the proportion of revenues of the nonprofit that comes from a business or from investments. The proportion that is permitted without serious consequences on the tax-exempt status depends upon the section of the *Internal Revenue Code* under which the organization falls.

The impact is not always negative. A private operating foundation can meet the asset test, for example, if at least 65 percent of its assets are stocks of a corporation that it controls (that is, it owns at least 80 percent of the corporation's voting and other stocks) and if at least 85 percent of the assets of that corporation are devoted to the tax-exempt purpose of the private operating foundation or to a related business. Also, income from businesses is considered to be part of the support justifying classification of a nonprofit as public foundation, for example, under Sections 509(a)(1) or (a)(2). In short, the answer to this question depends upon the tax-exempt classification of the nonprofit and the balance between business income and other types of support such as gifts and contributions. But in no case is business or investment income barred and in no case is there a limit on the number of dollars that can be earned.

HOW SHOULD A BUSINESS BE ACQUIRED?

Ownership or control of a business can be acquired as a gift, by purchase, or by starting it up from scratch. All three of these involve investment decisions. With a gift, the management has to take into account the tax consequences and costs of operating the business, its development, and ultimate disposition. Recall, for example, that a business that is acquired through debt even if it is a gift produces taxable income from activities closely related to the tax-exempt mission of the nonprofit.

In starting up a business from scratch, the management has to incorporate, register, certify, and obtain licenses where these are required, hire employees, locate and acquire plant or office space, invest in inventory, establish lines of credit, establish relationships with suppliers and distributors, develop a market and a clientele, and work hard to establish credibility and name recognition.

These are expensive and time-consuming activities. Each involves a risk and each delays the flow of revenues into the coffers of the nonprofit.

An alternative is to buy an existing business. In that case, the nonprofit purchaser avoids the difficulties and risks of starting from scratch. The seller of the business will include those start-up costs in the selling price as part of what is known as "good will."

If the business is to be bought, the nonprofit may use one of two approaches. It may buy the stocks of the business if it is a corporation, or it may buy the individual assets—plant, equipment, and land. This second approach has the advantage that the purchaser does not have to assume the liabilities of the business that are not related specifically to the assets that it is purchasing. For example, if a nonprofit buys all of the machines in a business and all of the plants, it has to consider only the liabilities (debt) that relate directly to those assets bought.

However, this approach to buying a business does have its disadvantages. First, all of the assets have to be individually valued and the seller may be reluctant to finalize the sale if there are assets that the nonprofit does not want to buy. It is easier and often less expensive to sell the entire enterprise. Second, the nonprofit purchaser does not get the benefit of having a fully operating business in place; that is, one with a clientele, a line of suppliers, distributors, and creditors.

Hence, the option of purchasing the stocks of the corporation and thereby the entire corporation is often used. Buying the entire corporation, however, means assuming all its assets and liabilities. The advantage of this approach for a nonprofit is that it gets a running start by acquiring an operating business. Starting from scratch is best accomplished when the business is related without requiring large investments of capital and when the necessary skills are closely allied to those the nonprofit has or cultivates in satisfying its tax-exempt mission.

SHOULD THE BUSINESS BE RELATED OR UNRELATED?

To begin with, we recognize that this choice is subject to the legal definitions as discussed earlier. Whether a business is related or not is a legal question based on the facts; when in doubt a private letter ruling as decribed in Chapter 1 should be obtained. Further, it is evident that when capacity and capital are scare there is less risk in conducting a related business. Such a business also provides for tax-exempt income and this income flows directly from the business into the organization.

An unrelated business can be equally simple given that its key difference from a related business is that it is unrelated to the tax-exempt mission of the nonprofit. "Unrelated" has nothing to do with capacity, capital, or complexity that characterizes the enterprise.

SHOULD THE BUSINESS BE SEPARATELY INCORPORATED?

The income from an unincorporated business flows directly to the nonprofit. When, however, a risky and complex business is being contemplated, it might be best to incorporate it to separate it from the nonprofit. Such action shields the nonprofit from the liabilities and risks of the business. If the business fails, the nonprofit is not in jeopardy. It is not necessary that the new corporation be a for-profit firm. A nonprofit that qualifies under Section 509(a)(3) as discussed in Chapter 6 may conduct a related or unrelated business to benefit its parent nonprofit. It may make a profit but the profit must be used to support the parent organization and its tax-exempt mission. Unrelated income of these corporations is taxable; related income is not.

If a for-profit corporation is acquired, its income is taxable at the level of the for-profit.[1] Dividends to the nonprofit may be received tax free. By creating a separate corporation to do its business rather than doing it itself, the nonprofit interrupts the direct flow of income from the business activity into its coffers. This is because the created corporation must have a board of directors who decide on the dividends the corporation will pay to the nonprofit owner.

The absence of a direct flow is not necessarily a meaningful disadvantage compared to a direct flow of revenues from the business to the nonprofit when the business is unincorporated. First, corporate board members with a sympathetic ear to the nonprofit can be chosen, although their first responsibility is to the corporation. Second, even if dividends are lower than the revenues in a direct flow, they are likely to be more steady. In a direct flow, the receipts of the nonprofit go up and down reflecting the net revenues of the business each year. However, dividends can be declared in dollar terms (so many dollars per year) rather than as a proportion of earnings. And dividends can be paid out of past earnings retained by the corporation. Financial planning is easier when flows are steady and reasonably predictable year to year.

WHERE DOES THE MONEY COME FROM TO ACQUIRE THE BUSINESS?

One deterrent to the purchase of a business is the lack of initial capital but there are a number of imaginative financing techniques that can be used, including a special fund-raising campaign. Also, a so-called leverage-buy out can be arranged. When this is done, the assets of the business are used to make the sale by securing a loan for the purchase. A second approach is to use an installment sale which may require little or no down payment. The seller receives an annual payment that is comprised of three parts: (1) a return of the capital invested in the company, (2) capital gains or the amount the business increased in value over the seller's basis (initial investment plus improvements and minus depreciation), and (3) interest on the outstanding portion of the payments. An installment sale is attractive to the seller because it constitutes a regular annual payment, the portion that is a return of the capital is not taxable. The return of the owner's investment is not taxable.

In some cases, a business reorganization plan may be used to acquire the enterprise. In this case, the owners give up their common stocks in the business to the nonprofits for preferred stocks that the nonprofit would create and issue in the business. These latter stocks have preference over common stocks in receiving dividends and in protection if the business goes bankrupt. This exchange gives the seller an annual income (the dividends) and gives the buyer (the nonprofit) control. It also gets all the capital gains resulting from a future sale of its common stocks. It retains the expertise of the business owner who will remain interested in the future of the business because the payment of dividends depends upon it. Moreover, if the exchange is prepared properly, the seller will not have to pay taxes on the gains received in the swap of stocks at the time that the swap is made, but will be taxed at a future time if and when the preferred stocks are sold.

IS THE BUSINESS PROFITABLE?

The answer is for whom, when, and how much. Imaginative entrepreneurs have been able to turn losing enterprises around and new businesses often experience losses.

Immediate high levels of profitability might not be a good reason for buying a business. In a market economy, high levels of profitability may be only temporary because they tend to attract other investors. The more investors there are the lower the amount of profits each receives; the large profit eventually disappears.[2]

Similarly, low levels of profits are not necessarily permanent. Profits can be low because of bad management, high costs, and limited markets—all of which can be reversed. Profits can also be affected by the method used to value inventory. In a period of rising costs, a method that values the inventory of a business at the current market price deflates profits. This is because all goods would appear to cost more than they actually did when the business bought or produced the goods sold. A method that values inventory at the original, lower cost inflates the true levels of profits.

Moreover, the earnings of a corporation may be affected by extraordinary nonrecurrent factors. The sale of a piece of land or a plant may result in an extraordinary loss or gain. Such losses and gains are not derived from the operation of the business and will tell us nothing about whether the business is being operated profitably. Also, we must distinguish between after-tax and before-tax earnings of the business.

To illustrate, the gross profit is the difference between the revenues from sales and the cost of the goods sold. Remember that the cost of goods sold is partly determined by the value of those goods in inventory. This gross profit, however, is not the complete story. When other operating costs such as labor, utilities, and insurance are deducted, income before taxes is derived. If the corporation is running an unrelated business, taxes must be paid. Only after these factors are taken into account do we get net income from operations.

In certain years, the corporation may have extraordinary gains or losses due to damage, the sale of assets such as plants and equipment, and so on. The gains must be added and the losses must be subtracted to income from operations to calculate the net income of the corporation. Hence, in evaluating the income performance of a corporation, its own or one that it wishes to buy, the management ought to focus on income from operations. What the business will have to offer the nonprofit barring an extraordinary event is net income from operations—specifically, income from operations minus expenses after taxes.

IS PROFITABILITY ENOUGH?

Looking at the income from operations (after taxes if the business is unrelated and pays taxes) of the business in only one year will not suffice. Any one year may be an aberration. Moreover, the nonprofit is interested in the flow of income during the years in which it will remain invested in the business. Based upon the information in the income statements over several years and an analysis of future operations and markets through a strategic planning exercise, let us assume the nonprofit may reasonably expect to receive $100,000 per year for the next ten years. Will it be worth the investment of the nonprofit's money? Remember the nonprofit is not a gambler, and it handles money in public trust for a public purpose. While income is necessary, is it worth the investment of public money?

A good manager faced with this question will quickly consider the fact that the same investment could be placed in a United States Treasury bond without risk but with ultimate safety and a good rate of return. Why put it in a business and take the risk? Obviously, this will be done only if the expected rate of return from the business is higher than the Treasury bond and if the rate is also sufficiently high to compensate the nonprofit for the risk it will be taking. The manager will then say that the investment must yield a rate of return that is higher than the opportunity cost (the amount it will give up by not investing in the Teasury bond) plus a premium for the risk. Thus, in general the investment is worth it only if it compensates the nonprofit for the opportunity cost plus any risk premium. If the rate is not that high, the manager might as well invest in U.S. Treasury bonds because profitability is not enough. The investment must also give a favorable rate of return.

The rate of return in any single year of an investment is calculated by dividing the amount of earnings after taxes from that investment by the amount of investment made. Obviously, the significance of this ratio is that it gives a measure of how much each dollar that the nonprofit owner has tied up in the business earns for the organization.

Incidentally, this is one reason why perfectly healthy and profitable businesses are often available for sale. It is not because they are unprofitable but the rate of return might be too low to justify the investment by a particular investor. Again, an advantage for nonprofits is they do not have to compete for investors' dollars by constantly offering higher rates of return than their competitors. They have no individual investors to satisfy. For-profit corporations do, so they often will sell a perfectly profitable subsidiary or operation to seek higher rates of return elsewhere.

WHAT WILL THE INVESTMENT COST?

Sometimes the nonprofit will be a price taker. This means that it faces a price that it must pay because it is not in a position to negotiate or to influence the price in any way. Such is the case when the nonprofit purchases stocks or bonds on the stock market. In other cases, such as real estate, the nonprofit is in a position to negotiate a price and can determine what a reasonable price will be by comparing the market price for similar properties in the surrounding area. In yet other cases, a reasonable price may be ascertained by looking at the performance of the business over the past (usually a minimum of five years).

In still other cases, it is possible to ascertain a reasonable price by looking at the book value of the enterprise. The book value is roughly the owner's equity in the business—the net amount the owner of the business has in it—the assets minus the liabilities. But the asking price by the seller will rarely equal the book value. It would invariably be higher because the book value does not reflect valuable intangibles such as an existing clientele, lines of credit, or a good name. This additional amount, over and above the book value, is called goodwill. The asking price will be the book value plus the good will.[3] Whether or not the seller will get the asking price depends upon the ability of the nonprofit to negotiate. This ability is enhanced if the nonprofit has an independent professional appraisal made of the business. At the end of this negotiating process, the seller will set an asking price. This is what it will cost the nonprofit to buy the business.

WILL THE EXPECTED BENEFITS EXCEED THE COSTS?

One of the disciplines learned from Chapters 3 and 7 is that when a nonprofit enters into an investment or an unrelated business, its main purpose is to earn money. There is no other reason regardless of the rhetoric to the contrary. Business is business and the main benefits are measurable in dollars. If at this point the honor of earning a dollar cannot be accepted by the board of the nonprofit, it should drop the idea of making an investment for it will fail.

From a strictly financial perspective, both benefits and costs are measurable in terms of dollars. The benefits are the dollars that are expected to flow into the coffers of the nonprofit over the years it remains invested in the enterprise. The costs are the dollars it has to lay out today in order to acquire the investment.

Obviously, the nonprofit should not invest in the business if the amount of money it has to lay out initially is higher than the amount of benefits it expects to receive over the entire life of the business. But note that the initial investment has to be paid with today's dollars. The benefits will flow over several years and while a flow into perpetuity may be desired, given inflation, every dollar that is received several years in the future is worth less than the dollar paid today. What is the future flow of benefits worth today? Is it less than, equal to, or greater than the cost that must be met to acquire and operate the business?

To answer this question, we must discount the future flow of benefits by a factor which reflects the rate at which inflation will lower the value of the dollar over time. This discount rate may also reflect the risk that is involved in the investment; for example, we may take the rate paid on Treasury bonds and add a premium to reflect the risk. In this way we arrive at a discount rate—the rate at which we discount the flow of future earnings from the business to find out what those earnings are worth in today's dollars. This discounted future earnings is called the present value of the expected flow of benefits.

Naturally, if the present value of benefits exceeds the costs of the investment or business, then the investment makes economic sense. If it is less than the cost, the investment makes no economic sense. If it is equal to the costs, the investment is marginal, but still worthwhile. Sometimes the present value of the benefits and the costs are expressed in the benefit/cost ratio. A ratio greater than 1 indicates that the benefits exceed the costs; a ratio of less than 1 implies the reverse; a ratio of 1 indicates that the costs and benefits are equal.

CAN THE BENEFIT/COST RATIO BE CALCULATED?

In principle, yes. To illustrate, let us assume that the seller's asking price after negotiation is $700,000 and the independent professional appraiser agrees with this figure. Let us also assume that we may expect $100,000 per year to flow into the coffers of the nonprofit if it should undertake this investment and that it intends to remain invested in this business for 30 years. Is it worth $100,000 per year for 30 years given an initial cost of $700,000? The answer depends upon the discount rate which reflects how risky the investment is compared to a safe one paying high rates such as the Treasury bond. It also depends upon the expected rate of inflation which will erode the dollar over time. Suppose we decide that after taking all these factors into account, we should discount the future earnings by 15 percent which is not unusual during periods of high expected inflation. What is the present value of the benefits?[4]

To answer this question, we refer to Table 8.1 and note the number 6.566 in the cell that corresponds to 30 years and 15 percent. If we multiply $100,000 (the annual expected return) by 6.566, we get $656,600 which is the present value of that $100,000 expected over 30 years when discounted at 15 percent. Because this amount of $656,600 is the benefit and the asking price, the cost, is $700,000, the investment is not acceptable to this nonprofit.

TABLE 8.1 Present Value of an Annuity of $1 a Year

INTEREST

Years	1	2	4	6	8	10	12	14	15	16	18	20	22	24	25	26	28	30
1	0.990	0.980	0.962	0.943	0.926	0.909	0.893	0.877	0.870	0.862	0.847	0.833	0.820	0.806	0.800	0.794	0.781	0.769
2	1.970	1.942	1.886	1.833	1.783	1.736	1.690	1.647	1.626	1.605	1.566	1.528	1.492	1.457	1.440	1.424	1.392	1.361
3	2.941	2.884	2.775	2.673	2.577	2.487	2.402	2.322	2.283	2.246	2.174	2.106	2.042	1.981	1.952	1.923	1.868	1.816
4	3.902	3.808	3.630	3.465	3.312	3.170	3.037	2.914	2.855	2.798	2.690	2.589	2.494	2.404	2.362	2.320	2.241	2.166
5	4.853	4.713	4.452	4.212	3.993	3.791	3.605	3.433	3.352	3.274	3.127	2.991	2.864	2.745	2.689	2.635	2.532	2.436
6	5.795	5.601	5.242	4.917	4.623	4.355	4.111	3.889	3.784	3.685	3.498	3.326	3.167	3.020	2.951	2.885	2.759	2.643
7	6.728	6.472	6.002	5.582	5.206	4.868	4.564	4.288	4.160	4.039	3.812	3.605	3.416	3.242	3.161	3.083	2.937	2.802
8	7.652	7.325	6.733	6.210	5.747	5.335	4.968	4.639	4.487	4.344	4.078	3.817	3.619	3.421	3.329	3.241	3.076	2.925
9	8.566	8.162	7.435	6.802	6.247	5.759	5.328	4.946	4.772	4.607	4.303	4.031	3.786	3.566	3.463	3.366	3.184	3.019
10	9.471	8.983	8.111	7.360	6.710	6.145	5.630	5.216	5.019	4.833	4.494	4.192	3.923	3.682	3.571	3.465	3.269	3.092
11	10.368	9.787	8.760	7.887	7.139	6.495	5.937	5.453	5.234	5.029	4.656	4.327	4.035	3.776	3.656	3.544	3.335	3.147
12	11.255	10.575	9.385	8.384	7.536	6.814	6.194	5.660	5.421	5.197	4.793	4.439	4.127	3.851	3.725	3.606	3.387	3.190
13	12.134	11.543	9.986	8.853	7.904	7.103	6.424	5.842	5.583	5.342	4.910	4.533	4.203	3.912	3.780	3.656	3.427	3.223
14	13.004	12.106	10.563	9.295	8.244	7.367	6.628	6.002	5.724	5.468	5.008	4.611	4.265	3.962	3.824	3.695	3.459	3.249
15	13.865	12.849	11.118	9.712	8.559	7.606	6.811	6.142	5.847	5.575	5.092	4.675	4.315	4.001	3.859	3.726	3.483	3.268
16	14.718	13.578	11.652	10.106	8.851	7.824	6.974	6.265	5.954	5.669	5.162	4.730	4.357	4.033	3.887	3.751	3.503	3.283
17	15.562	14.292	12.166	10.477	9.122	8.022	7.120	6.373	6.047	5.749	5.222	4.775	4.391	4.059	3.910	3.771	3.518	3.295
18	16.398	14.992	12.659	10.828	9.372	8.201	7.250	6.467	6.128	5.818	5.273	4.812	4.419	4.080	3.928	3.786	3.529	3.304
19	17.226	15.678	13.134	11.158	9.604	8.365	7.366	6.550	6.198	5.877	5.316	4.844	4.442	4.097	3.942	3.799	3.539	3.331
20	18.046	16.351	13.590	11.470	9.818	8.514	7.469	6.623	6.259	5.929	5.353	4.870	4.460	4.110	3.954	3.808	3.546	3.316
21	18.857	17.011	14.029	11.764	10.017	8.649	7.562	6.687	6.312	5.973	5.384	4.891	4.476	4.121	3.963	3.816	3.551	3.320
22	19.660	17.658	14.451	12.042	10.201	8.772	7.645	6.743	6.359	6.011	5.410	4.909	4.488	4.130	3.970	3.822	3.556	3.323
23	20.456	18.292	14.857	12.303	10.371	8.883	7.718	6.792	6.399	6.044	5.432	4.925	4.499	4.137	3.976	3.827	3.559	3.325
24	21.243	18.914	15.247	12.550	10.529	8.985	7.784	6.835	6.434	6.073	5.451	4.937	4.507	4.143	3.981	3.831	3.562	3.327
25	22.023	19.523	15.622	12.783	10.675	9.077	7.843	6.873	6.464	6.097	5.467	4.948	4.514	4.147	3.985	3.834	3.564	3.329
26	22.795	20.121	15.983	13.003	10.810	9.161	7.896	6.906	6.491	6.118	5.480	4.956	4.520	4.151	3.988	3.837	3.566	3.330
27	23.560	20.707	16.330	13.211	10.935	9.237	7.943	6.935	6.514	6.136	5.492	4.964	4.524	4.154	3.990	3.839	3.567	3.331
28	24.316	21.281	16.663	13.406	11.051	9.307	7.984	6.961	6.534	6.152	5.502	4.970	4.528	4.157	3.992	3.840	3.568	3.331
29	25.066	21.844	16.984	13.591	11.158	9.370	8.022	6.983	6.551	6.166	5.510	4.975	4.531	4.159	3.994	3.841	3.569	3.332
30	25.808	22.396	17.292	13.765	11.258	9.427	8.055	7.003	6.566	6.177	5.517	4.979	4.534	4.160	3.995	3.842	3.569	3.332

Suppose, however, the investment were less risky or that we expected a lower rate of inflation so that our future earnings would not be eroded. In that case, we may use a discount rate of 10 percent which is not uncommon when inflation is not rampant and investments are not very risky. By referring to Table 8.1, we note that at 10 percent for 30 years, the number is 9.427. We multiply $100,000 by 9.427 and get $942,700. In this example, the benefits ($942,700) exceed the costs ($700,000). A good deal!

Try the same example, discounting at 14 percent. Here the present value of the benefits is $700,300 compared to a cost of $700,000. We are at the margin where benefits and costs are about equal and the benefit/cost ratio would be approximately 1. What would you do? It is these marginal cases that are most challenging.

WHEN WILL THE ORGANIZATION RECAPTURE ITS INVESTMENT?

The benefit/cost ratio and methods of discounting future earnings to determine whether the rate of return on the investment is acceptable are based on the assumption that the nonprofit will remain invested usually for a long period of time or for the expected life of the investment. Some investments such as in automobiles may have a life of no more than three to seven years, while others such as a building may have a useful life exceeding 30 years. Given the pressures on funds, the need to be prudent, and the need to satisfy a board, the management of the nonprofit may ask another question: How long will it take to get our money out of the investment? Technically, how long is the payback period? For an inexperienced or shy manager or for an organization that takes a conservative approach to investment, it might be ideal to invest only in business projects in which the payback period is short.

It is easy to determine the approximate length of the payback period. Merely divide the investment to be made (the cost or initial outlay) by the amount that can be expected to flow into the coffers of the nonprofit annually. This is the approximate period of time that it would take to retrieve the investment. Notice, however, that these are projections. There is no certainty. Notice also that a low payback period implies a high rate of return on the investment and recall that high rates are associated with risks. They are the rewards for taking high risks in the market economy.

WHAT ARE THE RISKS?

Every investment is subject to risk. One type of risk is that the investment will go sour and another is that the earnings from the investment may be eroded by high rates of inflation. A third risk is that the investment may be illiquid, meaning that it cannot be converted to dollars easily without a severe penalty.

Another risk may be that the investment is not marketable. Which risk is most important depends upon the type of investment. For example, investing in certificate of deposits holds very little risk of total loss of investment compared to investments in hot go-go stocks. And while stocks are easily marketable, the risk is high because they can fall in price dramatically. Risks have to be compensated for and the compensation is the rate of return. Would you invest in a high-risk venture if you did not believe that it offered fantastic gains? No, and neither would anybody else. Rational investing is the art involving matching risks with returns. Would you keep your money in an extremely risky investment for a long period of time? No, that is why your organization may want to look at a short payback period when risks are high.

The ultimate risk for a nonprofit is that it would lose its tax-exempt status. This risk cannot be numerically taken into account by increasing the discount rate. It and other qualitative risks must be evaluated as in Figure 5.2. This risk can only be evaluated by understanding Chapters 1–7.

Holding idle cash balances is not a way to avoid taking risks. Cash invites theft and mishandling. Uninvested cash erodes in value due to inflation. Holding cash is an opportunity cost—the loss of earnings that the nonprofit organization could use.

WHAT WILL IT TAKE TO BREAK EVEN?

Part of judging the suitability of an investment is knowing what is required to break even. It is not enough to know that the recovery period for one's investment may be short or long or that the rate of return might be high enough to compensate for the risk. It might also be important to be able to judge the amount of effort that it might take to at least break even. This means to be able to cover the full cost of operation so that the organization is not dipping into its own pocket or into general support in order to sustain the business. The business is at least supporting itself.

An approximation of a break-even point can be calculated and shown graphically. Recall that the break-even point for a product occurs at the level where the revenues from sales are just enough to cover all costs of producing the product. This is like saying that the difference between the revenues and costs is zero or that revenues equal costs. Graphically, this occurs at point A in Figure 8.1. Above this point, total revenues exceed total costs and the business is profitable. Below that point the reverse is true and the business is operating at a loss.

Notice that point A is the intersection of total revenue amount of $7,000 and a total quantity of output of 600. Thus, the break-even point is said to be reached when the business is producing 600 copies of books at a total cost of $7,000. Total revenues equal total costs.

Total revenues is the quantity sold multiplied by the price at which each unit is sold. Total cost is the number produced times the cost of producing each

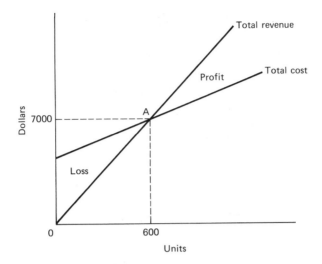

Figure 8.1 Break-even point. Source: Author.

unit. In the appendix to this chapter, we demonstrate that once the break-even point is known, it is simple to answer a question that should be significant to every nonprofit owner of a business: How much must be produced to meet a target rate of earnings flowing from the business into the nonprofit?

WHAT CAN BE DONE WITH THE EARNINGS OF THE BUSINESS?

To this point, we have been selfish. We see the after-tax earnings of the business as being the property of the nonprofit owner of the business to carry out its mission. This is technically accurate and should be the primary motive. However, the earnings of a business may be used to make further investment—increasing the capacity of the nonprofit to self-finance.

HOW WILL ENTRY INTO THE BUSINESS BE MADE?

Charles Berry and Edward Roberts recently developed a typological approach to answering this question.[5] While their examples pertain to for-profit firms, with some modification, they can apply to nonprofits as well. Figure 8.2 is a slightly modified version of the original. A discussion of five cells is sufficient for our purposes.

The idea is that when an organization chooses to enter into a new business venture, it should begin with an assessment of its familiarity with the market for the goods and services to be produced by the new venture and with its technical competence to produce the goods or services. When the organization is total-

Market Factors		Technologies or Services Embodied in the Product	
New Unfamiliar	Joint Ventures	Venture Capital or Venture Nurturing or Educational Acquisitions	Venture Capital or Venture Nurturing or Educational Acquisitions
New Familiar	Internal Market Developments or Acquisitions (or Joint Ventures)	Internal Ventures or Acquisitions or Licensing	Venture Capital or Venture Nurturing or Educational Acquisitions
Base	Internal Base Developments (or Acquisitions)	Internal Product Developments or Acquisitions or Licensing	"New Style" Joint Ventures
	Base	New Familiar	New Unfamiliar

Technologies or Services Embodied in the Product

Figure 8.2 Optimum entry strategies. Souce: Charles A. Berry and Edward B. Roberts, "Entering New Businesses: Selecting Strategies for Success," *Sloan Management Review,* 26, no. 3 (Spring 1985), 13. Reprinted by permission of the Sloan Management Review Association. All rights reserved.

ly unfamiliar with the technology and the market (cell C), it would be very risky for the organization to go it alone or even to be a working partner in the business. Wiser strategies would be to invest money in the business (venture capital), or acquire the business but keep its present technical staff to run it (educational acquisition). Cells B and F represent the same type of situation. The organization is unfamiliar with the technology and only slightly understands the market. These are risky and depend upon the learning curve.

Alternatively, the nonprofit may find itself attracted to a business in which it is already involved in both the market and the technology. It has a base in both (cell G). In that case, it would be sensible for the nonprofit to consider going it alone and building internally or by acquiring additional productive resources even if this meant purchasing the business of a competitor.

Another possibility is that the nonprofit may have a base either in the market or in the technology but not both (cells A and I). Joint ventures make sense here. The nonprofit enters into an agreement with another organization which takes responsibility for either the technology or market, whichever it does best, and the nonprofit takes responsibility for whichever it does best. Notice that what makes a joint venture practicable is that each party has what the other needs to be successful. A joint venture is frequently attractive in business deals because each party maintains its own corporate identity. They merely choose to work together on a specific project. To protect themselves, they might form a whole new corporation or partnership simply for the purpose of carrying out that one business deal.

The nonprofit may be attracted to a business opportunity in an area in which it has familiarity both about the market and the technology. While the market and technology are familiar, the business would be risky because the nonprofit had never been actively involved in it (cell E). For protection, the nonprofit may form a separate group or corporation (internal venture) to engage in the business. Or, it may acquire an outside firm through purchase that is already in the business. It could also enter the business by acquiring all rights or a license and lease them to a firm that can actually do the production. Owning a copyright or a patent right amounts to pursuing this type of strategy.

In yet another scenario, the nonprofit may have a good sound footing in the technology, but has never marketed the product, although it has some familiarity with what the market is like. In this case (cell D) the nonprofit may wish to develop an internal marketing department, or it might acquire a firm that specializes in that kind of marketing, or it may establish a joint venture with such a firm to take advantage of its expertise.

In cell H the organization is solidly grounded in the market, but the technology is new. Here, the possibilities for internal development of the technology may be considered, although this may be expensive and risky. Better alternatives may be to acquire a firm that is already producing the product or by controlling the license of such a production. A joint venture may also be possible here with the nonprofit doing the marketing, and the for-profit providing the products. This is precisely what happens when books, insurance, travel plans and the like are offered through associations. They are actually doing the marketing of a product or service produced by a for-profit firm.

HOW IS CASH MANAGED?

One of the most important aspects of investment decision making is cash management. This is necessary whether the cash is being raised for a major project, to enter into business or if it is excess cash arising from normal operations. We shall visit cash management again in Chapter 14.

The management of every nonprofit ought to examine the monthly accounting books of the organization to see how much money flows in, how much flows out, and the difference between the two. If there is a net cash inflow, then it ought to be invested. If there is a net outflow, (1) a line of credit ought to be obtained so that the organization can readily pay its bills, (2) the payment schedule may be modified so that the cash inflow and outflow are better sychronized, (3) income collection may be accelerated, and (4) new sources of income should be established.

What should be done with the excess cash depends upon the liquidity preference of the organization. This is analogous to asking how quickly must it have the cash back. In today's market even an organization that chooses to remain very liquid can earn interest on its cash. Incidentally, as we saw in Chapter 7, as long as the nonprofit does not control the institution paying the interest, the interest earned can be tax exempt.

There are a number of readily available financial instruments that can meet the needs of liquidity and reasonable safety of principal that are easily obtained. One is a checking account that pays interest. Such accounts, commonly known as NOW (for negotiable order of withdrawal) accounts are readily available. They require very small balances to open and to maintain. Another variation of the same idea are money market accounts. All these accounts pay variable interest, meaning that interest fluctuates depending upon the current prime rate or rate paid on U.S. Treasury obligations. They require small balances, and checks can be drawn. In none of these is the organization's money tied up.

Certificates of deposits, also readily available, are less liquid. They can be bought with a maturity period of a minimum of three months. Certificates of much longer maturity are also available at higher rates of interest. CDs, as they are called, can be bought with fixed or variable rates. They also can be bought for relatively little money and are generally backed by the insurance of the bank or thrift institution, although in recent months we have seen a loss of confidence in state-level insurance and a preference for federal insurance.[6] Large CDs ($100,000 or more) may be negotiable, meaning there is a market where, in the event the nonprofit needs the cash before maturity, it can sell the CD at its going market price and get all of the interest earned up to that point. Smaller CDs are not negotiable. Redeeming them before maturity leads to a penalty, usually the loss of three months interest.

Aside from CDs, the nonprofit may also consider repurchase agreements. These have short maturities of approximately three months. With REPOs, as they are called, the nonprofit purchases an agreement with an institution. The agreement states that for the nonprofit's cash, the institution will turn over a security, usually a U.S. Treasury obligation. At the end of the holding period, the institution buys back the security. The nonprofit not only gets its cash back but interest as well. Although REPOs are not insured, they are perfectly safe if the security used is a U.S. Treasury obligation.

All of these strategies require the nonprofit to come up with the exact amount of cash because purchases are at par. That is, if the CD is for a $1,000, the nonprofit must come up with $1,000. This is not the case with U.S. Treasury obligations. These are sold at discounts, meaning that a $10,000 obligation can be bought with less than $10,000 cash. This discount represents the interest rate. When the security is redeemed, $10,000 is received. These securities are obviously the least risky.

U.S. Treasury obligations come in the form of bills, notes, and bonds. Bills are bought at a discount and mature in 91 to 360 days. Treasury bonds can be redeemed after 60 days and now carry variable rates with a guaranteed floor below which the rates will not fall. Their normal maturity period is nine to 10 years.

Municipal bonds, another security, are riskier than U.S. Treasury securities, and are available. Unless the nonprofit is borrowing to buy—in which case all earnings from those borrowed funds are taxable (as discussed in Chapter 6)—there is no particular advantage to buying government securities other than their low risks. These securities normally pay a lower rate of return than nongovernmental securities.

In short, the nonprofit manager has a wide choice of ways to invest the money of the organization. The ownership of a business is not the only route. Even if it is, and certainly it ought to be seriously considered, the funds that are being accumulated to acquire a business can be invested in the interim. What the manager has to weigh is liquidity, safety, and rate of return just as if the decision were to own a business.

Beyond these relatively safe investments, there are stocks and bonds from corporations. Bonds are evidence that the corporation has borrowed money from the nonprofit. In the case of bankruptcy, holders of bonds would be taken care of before stockholders. Bonds may be attractive for their interest rates, but default (the failure to be able to pay interest) is not unknown. Therefore, bonds of a high quality, A to AAA, should be the only ones bought by nonprofit managers.[7]

Stocks are the most risky of all of these securities. Prices are volatile. In case of bankruptcy, the holders of common stocks are the last to be considered. The holders of preferred stocks are considered after bondholders and other creditors. Preferred stockholders purchase these instruments because they pay good dividends and because they may experience rises in their prices. But preferred stocks, like bonds, are subject to swings in price depending upon the interest rate. When the interest rate rises, the price that these securities can command falls. When the interest rate falls, prices increase.

A nonprofit can participate in these markets for corporate securities without exposing itself to the full magnitude of the volatility of any one stock. The nonprofit can do this through mutual funds. Mutual funds are investment companies that buy the stocks and bonds of many corporations and jurisdictions. By so doing, the portfolio of the mutual fund is diversified. Hence, it is less likely to be affected by the movements in any one company or one sector of the economy unless it is a specialized fund investing principally in that sector. Moreover, with mutual funds, the daily investment decisions are made by professionals whose incentive to do well comes from the fact that their commissions are tied to performance.

Some nonprofits may choose to have an arrangement with an institution such as a bank, insurance company, or stock brokerage to manage its investment funds. This is not unusual but should be done only when the funds to be managed are extremely large. Moreover, in this case, it may be prudent to divide up the investment portfolio among more than one investment advisor so that each competes knowing that his or her share will go to the other if performance is unsatisfactory.

CAN THE DECISION NOW BE MADE?

No. The management of a nonprofit has a fiduciary relationship over the money in the nonprofit. In a sense, the management must make investment decisions usually with a social conscience and often governed by the "prudent man's rule" stating, in effect, that overly risky investments are to be avoided. Further, the charter and bylaws of the organization may designate what types of investments the nonprofit may legally make. State laws may limit the type of investments nonprofits may make and there might be restrictions in the agreements under which trusts, endowments, and gifts were made.

Furthermore, no good manager attempts any sizable or meaningful investment without consulting a lawyer, an accountant, and the investment or financial committees of the nonprofit. Once all of this has been done, the decision can be made.

SUMMARY AND CONCLUSIONS

This chapter has sought to answer the question: Given the discussions in Chapter 1 to 7, what are the guidelines for action? The chapter addresses the chain of questions that will arise in making an investment decision. Whether in the for-profit or nonprofit sector, investment decisions are influenced primarily by the expected rate of return and the extent to which benefits exceed costs as measured in dollars. But there are other questions that should influence the decision. These include the payback period and the ability to finance the purchase without unduly mortgaging the future of the organization. It should be remembered that while there are no explicitly stringent rules on investment decisions of public charities, there are on private foundations as discussed in Chapter 6.

Indeed, there may be legal, social, and organizational considerations that prohibit a nonprofit from investing in certain types of enterprises. But such constraints may also apply to for-profit firms though less frequently and less stringently.

Managers of nonprofits should always consider the short-term or interim investment of cash which provides a lucrative source of income. We shall return to this theme in Chapter 14. The menu of investments from which to choose is large; there is an opportunity for every nonprofit. Skillful cash management means varying maturities such that funds can be earning interest until such time as they are needed. When in doubt, as a general rule it would be wiser to take a shorter maturity even though the interest earned may be lower. This is so due to the penalties that are associated with early withdrawals. There are enough short-term instruments so that even if a shorter period than required was taken, the money can be reinvested in an instrument that pays interest daily.

If a longer term than necessary was chosen, the instrument may be used as a collateral for a short-term loan. Sometimes this has to be weighed over redeeming the instrument and paying the penalty. The point is that profitable cash-management strategies are available to all organizations.

One of the advantages that nonprofits have over for-profit firms is that the former do not have to seek the highest rate of return within its permissible scope of investments. It has no investor-owners to whom it must appeal. This permits the nonprofit organization to seek high rates of return because it can take atypically high risks to the extent that these prove prudent within the mission of the organization. And, it can also take extremely low risks reflecting low rates of return because the success or failure of such organizations or their ability to attract and keep investors is not related to their rates of return. Typically, however, what nonprofits do in program related investments is take high risks and accept low rates of return; for example, investing in low-income neighborhoods. They can do this only because these risks are underwritten by gifts and contributions as discussed in the next chapter.

APPENDIX 8: BREAK-EVEN POINT

Recall that point A in Figure 8.1 represents the break-even point where the total revenues from a business owned by the nonprofit equals the total costs. Total revenues (TR) is nothing more than the unit revenue (or average revenue brought in by a unit of product or service sold; that is, the price of that unit) multiplied by the number of units sold. If we sold 200 apples and the average price received per apple was 25 cents, the total revenues (TR) would be equal to the unit revenue (UR) or price multiplied by the quantity (Q) sold.

Total cost (TC) is composed of three parts. First, there is the total fixed cost (TFC) which is the cost to the business for simply existing. It does not vary with the amount of production. Whether the business produces or not it has to pay contractual costs such as rent and mortgages. The bankers and landlord charge for space and once the organization signs that contract, it pays for the space regardless of how much it uses it. The cost is fixed.

Other costs are variable. They vary with the amount produced. The amount of materials and supplies used and the number of hours per worker vary with the production level. The greater the production, the more is the total variable cost *(TVC)*. Total variable costs can therefore be divided into two parts: the quantity produced *(Q)* and the cost per unit produced *(UC)*. Together, *TFC + TVC* make up total production cost *(TC)*.

Accordingly, the break-even point is where:

$$(TR) = (TC)$$

or,

$$(UR) \times (Q) = (UC) \times (Q) + TFC$$

if we divide both sides by *Q* and simplified we get,

$$(UR) = TFC/Q + (UC)$$

solving for *Q* we get,

$$Q = TFC/UR - UC.$$

This tells us that the break-even point is equal to the total fixed cost divided by the difference between the unit revenue and the unit cost. This difference *(UR − UC)* is called the unit contribution, or the contribution margin.

Suppose that the nonprofit has a need for $50,000. It decides that this must come from the operation of its business. This business has a fixed cost of $10,000 and a unit contribution of $2.00; that is, the difference between the average price or unit price and the average or unit cost of the item it sells is $2.00. Each unit sold contributes $2.00 to the total operating income of the business. By applying the following formula, it is possible to ascertain the minimum amount of units the business must produce and sell. The formula is:

$$(Qr) = TFC + DI/UR - UC.$$

Qr is the quantity required to meet the income target of the organization ($50,000)

TFC is the total cost.

DI is desired income or income target.

UR − UC is the unit contribution.

Accordingly,

$$Qr = \$10,000 + \$50,000/2.$$

The answer is that 30,000 units must be bought and sold to meet the organization's income target of $50,000.

NOTES

1. Nonprofits cannot be shareholders in Subchapter S corporations which are corporations with special tax advantages. We are therefore referring to a regular corporation.

2. Economic or normal profits is the percentage, over full cost, that represents a return to capital when the capital market is in equilibrium; that is, when no lender wishes to shift funds to some other user. For-profit firms in highly competitive markets that are new and developing often use a price that is so low that potential competitors are kept out because they would not be able to make a profit or pay the interest on the funds they would have to borrow to enter the business. Contrary to popular opinion, a for-profit firm does not always charge the highest price possible.

3. Good will is the amount paid for assets that is above the value of the asset. Good will reflects a number of intangibles such as the existence of a clientele, good location, and a good reputation. A seller of a business that has a large clientele would ask more for that business than if the business had no clients at all.

4. When we refer to benefits and present value in this section, we are talking about a net concept. The expected operating costs each year are deducted from the expected operating revenues and we find the present value of this net. In the income statement, it is represented by the income or revenues from operation.

5. Charles A. Berry and Edward B. Roberts, "Entering New Businesses," *Sloan Management Review*, 26, no. 3 (Spring 1985), 3–15.

6. Recent experience with some thrift institutions in such states as Ohio and Maryland show that even in so-called safe institutions, investors may not have access to their funds. The governors in these two states, fearing a run on these institutions, placed a limit on the amount that savers could withdraw. This proves that there is no investment including the holding of cash that is without risk. Holding cash takes on risks of theft, decrease in value due to inflation, and loss of earnings.

7. Bond ratings can be obtained from a rating service. The highest rating is Aaa or AAA. There is no prudent reason for nonprofits to be dealing in B and C rated bonds, as these represent very high risks. We shall discuss ratings more fully in a later chapter of this book.

NINE

Benefit Structures
for Attracting
and Retaining Employees
and Minimizing Costs

The financial success of an organization depends upon its ability to contain costs. A major cost factor is the hiring of competent workers. The most rapidly growing part of this factor is the cost of employee benefits. The purpose of this chapter is to describe the types of benefits available to attract and retain competent employees in nonprofit organizations. Properly structured, the costs of these benefits can be contained and tax advantages can be enjoyed by the employees. Thus,

> *Benefits*
>
> Over the last few years there has been a dramatic change in benefits administration due to tax and legal constraints, as well as the "run-away" costs of health and liability insurance. As staff, we took the necessary steps to find alternative ways of containing, if not reducing, some of these spiraling costs. We are exploring the impact of new ways of administering these programs to serve our employees better. The Council has improved its coverage in the areas of basic hospitalization, surgical-medical, major medical and disability insurance. We have also added a Dental Program, for all staff, to the total benefits package.
> In this Triennium the NCCC Pension Plan has undergone numerous changes to enhance the benefits our employees will receive upon their retirement from the Council.

"Benefits" Source Triennial Report, National Council of the Churches of Christ in the U.S.A., 1982–84, p. 59.

One very important benefit is coverage of both the organization and the management including the directors against liability suits. Such suits are now commonplace as virtually all states and courts no longer hold nonprofits immune from suit.

Further, this chapter discusses the legal permission that nonprofits have to construct profit-sharing plans and the recommended components of such plans. The chapter also discusses other benefits including life, disability, medical and hospitalization insurance, and retirement and pension plans. It shows how retirement and pension plans can be integrated with social security to reduce costs. Prior to January 1, 1984, nonprofits could elect not to be covered by social security, but now they must make contributions for employees earning $100 or more in a year. Because of the compulsory participation in social security, the wise manager of a nonprofit should know how such participation may be integrated into a benefit package to keep costs down and benefits at a desirable level. This is important because benefits are the most rapidly rising costs and, therefore, a key to understanding the management and financing of nonprofits.

DISABILITY INCOME INSURANCE

We must distinguish between disability income insurance and workmen's compensation. The latter is required by law and covers employees for injury sustained on the job regardless of who is at fault. The premiums are paid exclusively by the employer and are based upon the type of work done, the occupational composition of the work force, and the past history with respect to the number and seriousness of past claims.

Disability income insurance is not compulsory. It covers disability whether or not it resulted from work-related activities. One of its purposes is to protect the nonprofit against the cost of paying both the salaries of an incapacitated worker and a replacement. It also assures the worker of continued income during periods of incapacitation. The insurance company pays the incapacitated worker while the nonprofit pays the replacement.

Because disability income insurance is not compulsory, the nonprofit may elect self-insurance by having written contractual agreement with its employees to continue the payment of salary to a worker when incapacitated. Unless this is a written plan, all payments received by the worker during periods of incapacity may be fully taxable.[1]

An alternative to self-insurance is for the organization to purchase a disability insurance policy, particularly for its key employees. An insurance policy may be for long-term or short-term disability. A short-term disability policy will cover the worker for approximately five months if the worker is unable to conduct normal functions. A long-term policy may cover the worker usually up to age 65, the expected time of retirement.

A critical difference between long-term and short-term policies is in the definition of disability. Commonly, the short-term definition of disability is the incapacity of the worker to perform normal occupational functions. The long-term definition is most often the incapacity of the worker to perform any occupational function whatsoever given his or her age, work and educational experiences. Since these are often subjectively interpreted, a long-term claim could be denied on the grounds that the person can do some renumerative work.

In structuring a disability income plan, the nonprofit management may begin by considering the option of not providing it for any employee or only for its key or executive employees. While this may seem inexpensive, it may make it difficult to employ certain people. Second, the nonprofit may consider the option of self-insurance which may be less expensive, depending upon the number of employees who have claims and the length of time for which each incident is covered. Self-insurance should only be undertaken if a detailed plan can be written defining disability, what constitutes a new or a continued claim, how many claims each employee may make in a period, what constitutes a benefit period, and so on.

A third option is to provide only a short-run or only a long-run policy. Providing only a long-run policy means that the employee would normally have to wait five months before receiving a check from the insurance company, but during this time the nonprofit may continue full or partial salary payments to the employee.

An alternative is to purchase a short-run policy that has a waiting period. This is a period that the employee must wait before receiving the first check. The policy would most likely cover the employee for five months after the waiting period. At the end of this period, social security begins payment if the employee is elegible. Social security disability income payments are long term (up to age 65). Yet another alternative is to provide no short-term coverage and wait until social security payments begin in the sixth month of disability.

It is necessary to understand the rules of social security disability if it is to be integrated into the benefit package of a nonprofit. Elegibility depends upon the age of the worker when disability occurred and the number of quarters of credits earned prior to the disability. For example, to be eligible a worker 31 years of age or more must have five years (20 quarters) of coverage in the ten years prior to the disability.[2] Workers who become disabled before their 24th birthday, need only 1 1/2 years (six quarters) of credit to be eligible.

The disability must have lasted or be expected to last at least 12 months, be permanent, or result in death. In addition, the worker must be unable to work at any job regardless of age, work experience and education. Fitness to work is determined by a state agency physician, not by the private physician of the employee. Moreover, the employee must enroll in a state vocational rehabilitation program.

Regardless of which option the nonprofit chooses, it should be aware that other segments of the benefit package may have a disability component. Pension plans and life insurance policies usually provide some disability protection. However, it might not be enough to rely on this simply because it is usually incidental. For example, the most common disability provision in a life insurance policy merely pays the premium on the policy so that it does not lapse. And the most common disability provision in a pension plan is to permit early retirement.

LIFE INSURANCE

Death benefit payments are not compulsory. A nonprofit may or may not choose to make a token gift to the family of a deceased worker.[3] A nonprofit which chooses to be competitive for good workers would also choose the more common alternative which is to purchase life insurance policies on its workers.

A life insurance policy may be purchased by the nonprofit to protect itself. When a key employee dies, there is work interruption, the need to have an audit, and to recruit and train a replacement. A policy bought and owned by the nonprofit on the life of its key employee or on the position held by such a person, would upon the death of the incumbent, provide proceeds that can be used to defray these expenses.

In addition, life insurance may be bought to protect the dependents of the deceased employee against the total loss of income. The life insurance contract may be of one or two broad types: (1) permanent insurance or (2) term insurance. There may also be an individual or group policy.

A permanent insurance policy is one that does not have to be renewed or converted. It lasts as long as the premiums are paid and the premiums are usually the same year after year. These policies are expensive. On the other hand, a term policy lasts only for a specifically predesignated term, one, five, ten or fifteen years and after the predesignated term the policy must be renewed for another term, usually at a higher premium. By prior agreement with the insurance company, it is possible to convert a term policy to a permanent one.

A disadvantage to the worker of a permanent policy is that the part of the premium that is in excess of what the premium would have been on a term policy is taxable to the worker as income. Therefore, the permanent policy tends to be more expensive to the organization and leads to taxable income on the part of the employee. Yet, many employees may prefer a permanent policy because even with the tax, it is less expensive for the worker to have the organization buy the policy than for the worker to do so. In some instances, a permanent policy for key employees may be an incentive to attract such persons to the organization.

Because of its simplicity and lower costs, the group term policy is best suited for the work force of the nonprofit. The term of the insurance is usually one year. This makes sense because people enter and leave the employ of the organization every year.

The nonprofit may also elect group or individual policies. Group policies are less expensive and often superior in their coverage. They are less expensive because certain administrative costs decline on the average as the group gets larger. Most importantly, group policies protect the insurance company against adverse selection. This refers to the inclination of individuals who are most adversely exposed to the possibilities of death to be the most eager to select life insurance coverage. If only such persons were covered, the insurance company could find itself continuously paying claims. But the larger the group, the more high-risk workers would be balanced by low-risk workers, and therefore the lower the premium the company will charge because the number of claims will be relatively lower.

For important legal purposes, a "large" group is one with ten or more members. For groups of that size, the nonprofit management may exclude certain classes of workers from coverage. A class may be excluded if it is based on such broad definitions as occupational classification, salary, full or part-time employment or union status. The class must be defined to avoid individual selection or exclusion. Individuals may be selected or excluded, because of their membership in a class within the larger work force of the nonprofit, not because of individual characteristics.

There are important flexibilities with group policies. Upon retirement or separation, the policies may be converted to an individual policy. This conversion is normally possible regardless of the reason for separation including the demise of the organization.[4] Group policies may have a waiver of premium rider which waives premiums if the worker becomes permanently disabled. Hence, disability would not cause the policy to lapse.

The nonprofit is free to choose a policy that would give death benefits that exceed $50,000. For tax purposes, however, the maximum benefit is $50,000. Any policy that offers a benefit in excess of this amount would create taxable income to the employee. The tax will be levied on the premium paid for the amount in excess of $50,000. Here again, some executives will gladly pay that tax since any comparable policy bought on the open market is likely to be more expensive even after considering the tax. Of course, the tax can be avoided altogether. If the policy on the life of the employee has a death benefit that exceeds $50,000 and the policy is donated and owned by a nonprofit as a charitable gift, then the excess premiums are not taxable.

Even though a group policy, the policy is owned by the individual employee. Thus, the employee is free to name beneficiaries, change them, or even use the policy as collateral for a loan. If the policy is a permanent policy, not only could it be used as collateral for a loan, but it would also have a loan value. That is, there is a periodic accumulation (called the cash or surrender value) that could be borrowed. Term policies (unless of 15 years or more) have no such value and, therefore, can at best be used only as collateral.

Upon the death of the employee, the beneficiaries may choose one of several settlement options. They may choose to receive the benefits in a lump sum, or over a specific number of payments, or a specific amount per payment; they may guarantee a minimum number or amount of payments; they may take interest, leaving only the principal to another beneficiary; or payments may be made for the life of the beneficiary and terminate upon that beneficiary's death.

Each of these has important tax and financial implications. For example, a lump sum leads to no taxes to the beneficiary. An interest only leads to a $1,000 annual deduction if the beneficiary is a spouse but a tax on everything above the $1,000. Periodic payments are partially taxed. What is important is when organizations increasingly offer financial advice as one of their benefits, there is an awareness of the income, gift and estate taxes associated with various death benefit options.

With compulsory participation in social security, a nonprofit manager may find it wise to consider survivorship benefits in determining the percentage of the employee's income the nonprofit would wish to replace through its own insurance. Here again it is important to consider the social security eligibility criteria. Upon the death of a worker, dependent children receive survivorship benefits if the worker was covered by social security for 1 1/2 years or six quarters before death. The surviving spouse is eligible for benefits if caring for a disabled child or one under 16 years of age or if the spouse is eligible for benefits based on the earnings of the deceased.[5]

There may be a probationary period before an employee is covered for life insurance and employees may also be required to contribute to the premiums. A probationary period often makes sense since it would give benefits to an employee who has made at least a minimal commitment to the organization, even though it could be a hindrance to recruiting workers. Employee contributions are particularly useful if the employee wishes to have the policy cover the life of a dependent or spouse. However, requiring a contribution on the part of the employee to cover his or her own life is a disincentive.[6]

ACCIDENTAL DEATH AND DISMEMBERMENT

A nonprofit may wish to protect its employees who travel or are exposed to risk of injury and death due to accidental causes. Insurance can be bought to protect against losses due to accidental death and dismemberment. This coverage may be bought separately or as part of the life or health insurance policies.

To some extent, accidental death represents a duplication of coverage. Dismemberment is a real fear in some occupations but not in others; moreover, the disability coverage may well offer sufficient compensation. The death benefit may be covered under the life insurance policy. If it is not, perhaps it should be. Is it any more expensive to die from an accident than to die from natural causes? Why seek a higher or independent coverage for accidents? These are policy questions that should be asked before entering into an independent contract for accidental death and dismemberment coverage.

The conditions under which the beneficiaries or insured may collect under accidental death policies are strict. Death must usually occur within a specific period of time, perhaps 90 days after the accident. Moreover, death must be due exclusively to the accident and not attributed to or the result of another cause.[7] Further, death resulting from certain types of accidents may be excluded from coverage.

MEDICAL AND HOSPITALIZATION INSURANCE

Medical and hospitalization costs have been rising dramatically—faster than the rate of inflation. Health and medical benefits are intended to protect the employee against these costs. This protection may be provided through regular commercial insurance, Blue Cross/Blue Shield, or through a health maintenance organization (HMO). These three differ in operation and are competitors.

Medical and hospitalization insurance policies differ by company and there may be several different alternative policies from which the nonprofit organization may choose. The most simple and perhaps least expensive insurance plan is the basic plan. The principal characteristic of basic plans is that they emphasize hospital-related benefits. Such plans cover hospital services, some emergency costs, and basic surgical fees. Basic plans may differ from company to company and one company may have more than one alternative.

Under the basic plan, hospital room and board are covered. The payments may be for a specified amount per day up to some maximum dollar amount or number of days. Other hospital charges such as medicine, drugs, and X-rays are usually paid as a percentage of the benefits being paid for the room and board. Surgical fees may be paid according to a schedule or according to what is usual, customary and reasonable for similar surgical services in the geographic area.

Major medical insurance policies cover a larger number of medical events, pay a higher maximum, and are more expensive than basic plans. Major medical protects against catastrophic illnesses. A major plan may be a supplement to a basic plan so that it covers illnesses excluded by the basic plan or picks up payments when the basic plan reaches its limits. In this latter case, there may be a deductible before the major plan kicks in. Alternatively, the major plan may be independent of the basic plan or may incorporate it into a comprehensive plan. Again, major plans differ among and within companies. The law does not regulate what is included.

Because of the breadth of coverage of major plans, the insurance companies impose cost-sharing devices. One such device is the deductible and another is the co-insurance. A deductible requires the employee to pay the first dollars on a claim, often the first $50 or $100. When the claim exceeds the deductible, the company may share the cost further by paying only a specified percentage of the amount in excess of the deductible, usually 80 percent of that amount.

The remaining 20 percent of the claim is paid by the employee. Above the level of co-insurance, the company may pay 100 percent of the claim up to some maximum.

The insurance company may limit its exposure even further. It may limit the amount it would pay to an employee or a family either per calendar year or per policy year, per medical event, or for all events combined. Similarly, deductibles may be per person, per family, per policy period, and so on. All of this is in addition to an overall maximum limit over the life of the employee. Hence, a policy could read that it is limited to $100,000 per calendar year per employee and $400,000 over the life of that person. At this limit the company reserves the right to terminate the policy.

In the same way that the insurance company may wish to limit its exposure, so too should the worker. Therefore, it is wise to seek out a policy that has a stop-loss feature. This means that beyond a certain cost, the insurance company takes over 100 percent of payments up to its maximum limit.

In considering medical insurance, the choice is between a basic or a major plan or a combination of the two either with the major supplementing the basic (which means that the first dollars of payment come from the basic) or a comprehensive plan which contains both the features of a basic and a major plan.

Comprehensive and major plans are expensive. The cost can be lowered if the nonprofit accepts a higher level of co-insurance and deductible and by making the plan contributory (meaning that the employees pay part of the premium if only for their dependents). Other cost-saving devices include the nonprofit recommending to employees the use of hospitals and physicians who are competent but lower priced and by excluding some routine visits from coverage. The trade-off with cost-saving devices might be the postponement of preventive care.

Partly because of the growth of two-worker families, there is the increased likelihood that each spouse would have independent coverage under the same or different employer plans. This duplication of coverage is costly and wasteful. The rules and practices of health insurance companies require that benefits be coordinated. This means that workers or their dependents can collect from only one policy at a time. While a dependent child must first collect from the father's policy, a child of divorced parents may also have to collect first from the father's policy. The rules of coordination of benefits includes considerations of divorce, separation, length of coverage, sex of spouse, and so on. In a nutshell, they simply remove the possibility of collecting from more than one company at the same time and for the same cause.

A closely related principle is the indemnity principle. This says that the insured cannot collect more than the cost of the health and medical service. When this principle is considered with the principle of coordination of benefits, it becomes clear that there is no way to recover from being overinsured as far as medical and health insurance are concerned. The premium is wasted.

Blue Cross and Blue Shield

Blue Cross and Blue Shield are nonprofit corporations although tax reform to take place in 1986 will alter this nonprofit status.[8] They compete with for-profit insurance companies. They are examples of nonprofits operating within the market sphere. As corporations, Blue Cross and Blue Shield are creations of individual states. These organizations differ in coverage, cost and charter from state to state.

Blue Cross is made up of cooperating hospitals within a state and Blue Shield of cooperating physicians. They are separate organizations although they may share facilities and cooperate and offer their coverage as a unit; hence, the familiar term, Blue Cross/Blue Shield.

Being nonprofits and tax exempt, neither organization pays taxes on premiums. Again, this is slated to be changed with the new tax law. Insurance companies do. Because there are several other elements that determine cost, the tax difference is usually not enough to distinguish between the premium level of an insurance company and of Blue Cross/Blue Shield.

Blue Cross makes benefit payments directly to the hospital while insurance companies reimburse the employee. Blue Cross may have a closer relationship with cooperating hospitals and Blue Shield a closer relationship with physicians than do insurance companies. But the same hospitals and physicians that accept payments from Blue Cross/Blue Shield accept payments from patients covered by insurance policies.

Insurance companies offer a wider range of products (including pensions, life and disability insurance) which make up a complete benefit package. Therefore, it is possible to construct a benefit package with one insurance company, but not with Blue Cross or Blue Shield. Finally, both Blue Cross and Blue Shield and individual insurance companies offer options in the design of health and medical benefit contracts with each option being differently priced with different coverage.

Health Maintenance Organizations

Unlike insurance companies and Blue Cross/Blue Shield, health maintenance organizations (HMOs) are direct providers of health and medical services. The employee gets a wide range of services such as hospital care, outpatient X-ray and laboratory services, physical examinations, eye examinations, routine gynecological examinations, and maternity care—all at no extra cost other than the initial capitation fee. Many HMOs are also nonprofit.

Often there is no deductible and no co-insurance, although there may be a co-payment for prescription drugs. Two misunderstandings about HMOs should not influence decisions about them. There is the possibility of 24-hour service even if the person is away from the service district of the HMO in which membership is held. Some HMOs may also require that the enrollee pick up some costs. There are exclusions covering such things as cosmetic surgery, some organ transplants, dental care and custodial services.

Because most of the services are provided without extra charge, HMOs are less inclined to prescribe unnecessary treatment and hospitalization. They must absorb all costs. On the other hand, because the enrollees have prepaid for all services, they may be less reluctant to use them and are therefore able to catch potential problems early when treatment is likely to be more successful and least expensive.

As of October 1, 1984, the United States Department of Health and Human Services reported that there were some 220 federally qualified HMOs— ones having federal certification based partly on their offer of a required minimum amount of service. When a nonprofit employer is considering a health and medical benefit package, it may be required by law to offer its employees the opportunity to select a federally qualified HMO. This is so when the non-profit employer: (1) has and contributes to a health and medical benefit plan for its employees, (2) if the employer has 25 or more employees, (3) if it pays at least the minimum wage, and (4) if a federally qualified HMO in the area where the nonprofit has 25 or more employees submits a written request to be considered and if those employees are not presently served by an HMO.[9]

Recognizing that there is a threshold when an HMO option must be offered, a nonprofit employer who is below this threshold may choose among HMOs, Blue Cross/Blue Shield, or an insurance company. The choice ought to be made based upon cost to the employer and employee, the package of benefits, the competence of the selling agent, the experience of others with the quality of service. While it is possible for the nonprofit employer to create its own health and medical benefit package or self-insure, this is not recommended. The anti-discrimination laws which are intended to protect workers and to prevent management from reaping the major benefits are complicated and stiff. The law presumes that these antidiscrimination restrictions are satisfied if the insuring responsibility falls on a third party (such as the insurance company) rather than on the employer. Moreover, the organization could experience considerable drain on its resources as employees become ill.

In comparing the HMOs with other medical and health providers, a criticism that is often heard is that the employee does not have a choice of physicians. This is not altogether true. Physicians may form an HMO among themselves as independent providers. The individual may choose among these physicians and still obtain the benefits of an HMO. Such a group of physicians is referred to as an independent practice association or IPA.

RETIREMENT AND PENSIONS

The major objective of a pension plan is to provide support for the employee during retirement years. A properly designed pension plan can provide a number of additional benefits including the deferring of income taxes and the ability to withdraw cash to meet emergencies.

It is possible for a nonprofit to institute a pension plan that would cost it virtually nothing and still benefit employees. Section 403(b) was passed by Congress to give nonprofits a special vehicle. Before discussing Section 403(b) in particular, there are some basic principles about pensions that the nonprofit manager ought to know.

Pensions are of basically two types: defined benefits and defined contribution. The defined benefit plans stipulate the amount of benefits an employee will receive upon retirement. This may be a flat number of dollars, a percentage of salary earned over the years the employee worked with the nonprofit, a percentage of the employee's final pay, or an amount adjusted for the number of years of service.[10]

Because the benefits to be received upon retirement are stipulated in a defined benefit plan, the nonprofit must resolve an actuarial problem. It must determine how much it has to deposit in each of the remaining working years of the employee so that the promised amount will be available on the date the employee retires.[11] Furthermore, in order to insure that the promise will be kept, the nonprofit may have to comply with several regulations. These involve paying premiums to the Pension Guarantee Corporation to insure the plan against financial failure.

The defined contribution plan differs from the defined benefit plan because it stipulates the amount of contributions that will be made rather than the amount of benefits to be paid. The only promise that the nonprofit makes is that it will contribute a specified percentage of the employee's salary to his or her retirement account each year. The Section 403(b) plan to be discussed later is a defined contribution plan.

Defined contribution plans are usually simpler to administer. They are not as regulated by the government as are defined benefit plans and do not require annual estimates about how much the organization must contribute in order to meet its pension promises in the distant future. The only promise is to make an annual contribution of a specific percentage of the worker's base pay.

Another approach is called a target plan. This stands between a defined benefit and a defined contribution plan. In this approach the organization sets a target benefit it would like to meet upon the retirement of the worker and defines its contributions in terms of that target. Unlike the defined benefit plan, however, the organization has no legal obligation to achieve the target.

Whether a plan is defined contribution, target, or defined benefit, it may be contributory or noncontributory. A contributory plan provides for the employee to make either voluntary or mandatory contributions. The latter, which has to be set at a low enough level so that all employees may meet it without undue hardship, is simply an amount the employee is required to contribute annually in order to remain in the plan. The voluntary amount is the amount employees may, on their own volition, contribute to building up their accounts.

In a contributory plan, the organization may also make a contribution but in a noncontributory plan, only the organization makes a contribution. The employees make none. This latter approach is often seen as simpler to administer. The contributory plan, however, may have an advantage in that it could be designed to accommodate the employee's savings and individual retirement account (IRA).[12]

The contributions made to the retirement plan may be deposited into a variable or a fixed account as elected by the employee. Deposits into a variable account are used to purchase common stocks so that the rate at which the contributions grow is determined by the growth in value of the stocks.

Contributions made to the fixed account are invested in securities such as bonds and money market funds where there can be some reasonable assurance of earning no less than some specific rate. Insurance companies are willing to guarantee a rate of return for a specified period.

The employee can maintain a similar distinction between variable and fixed account earnings upon retirement. The first means that each check will reflect the earnings in the stock market; that is, some checks will be higher than others. The fixed amount means that every check will be the same.

The employees may also choose the manner in which they would like to receive payments upon retiring. The entire retirement benefit can be taken in a lump sum, in periodic payments guaranteed either in terms of the number or amount per payment, in periodic payments that terminate upon the death of the employee or continue after death to a designated survivor. All plans are required to give married employees the option of payments that continue to the surviving spouse upon the death of the retiree. The employee is not required to accept the option but if the option is rejected, the employee must supply evidence that the spouse accepts this rejection. The aim is to secure a flow of income to surviving spouses. One reason why the option may be rejected is that the periodic payments are lower than those the worker would obtain under the option that terminates payments upon the worker's death.

Each option has income and estate tax implications. The law requires that the employee be told of the consequences of choosing a lump-sum option. The entire amount of a lump-sum payment may be subject to income tax but the burden may be relieved by 10-year income averaging for older plans and persons reaching 50 years of age by January 1, 1986, and 5-year averaging after that. If this method of decreasing the tax liability is chosen, then the worker cannot exclude $100,000 of the employer's contribution when the estate tax upon the death of the employee is due. But the estate tax can be avoided by contributing the entire amount to a tax-exempt nonprofit.

While we have presented the general features of pension plans, there are specific rules that must be followed. One set of rules requires annual reporting to the employees on the developments and earnings in the plan during the year, including any pertinent changes. A second set of rules determines if the plan will be qualified for tax advantages. These rules should be appreciated by managers of nonprofits.

To review the tax benefits, if the plan qualifies, contributions to the retirement plan, and earnings of the plan are not taxed to the employee. Taxes are postponed until retirement years when the worker is supposedly in a lower income bracket. For a young worker 21 years of age, taxes could be deferred some 40 years until retirement. To be qualified for this tax benefit, the plan must conform to certain rules.

The basic rule is that the plan must not exist only for the benefit of high-salaried workers, directors, managers, trustees, and key supporters (such as disqualified persons discussed earlier). If discrimination may not occur in the determination of eligibility for participation or in the contributions to the plan, how, then, is eligibility determined?

Aliens, part-time workers, workers who come under a union agreement providing for some other source of coverage, and workers under 21 years of age can be excluded automatically from eligibility without fear of violating the rules against discrimination. The effect of this is to reduce the number of persons the organization has to cover and therefore cost.[13]

Eligibility might be immediate, or after one year of service (defined as 1,000 hours of paid employment in a 12-month period). No more than two years may elapse before the worker becomes eligible. If a two-year waiting period is used, all contributions are 100 percent vested when participation starts, according to the 1986 law. In those cases where a defined benefit plan is utilized, the employer is not required to make an employee eligible if that employee is within less than five years of the normal retirement age, which is usually 65.

The reason for putting an upper limit on the defined benefit plan is to avoid placing a financial burden on organizations. For example, if a new worker has only a short time to work before retiring, an organization would have only a short time in which to accumulate the retirement benefits to which it has obligated itself in a defined manner. The amount required, to begin paying a worker 30 percent of his or her final pay for a lifetime only after two years of service might be very large. This problem does not exist with a defined contribution plan and such plans do not carry an upper age limit for participation.

The plan must have a vesting schedule. This schedule gives the rate at which the employees acquire ownership over the employer's contributions to their retirement accounts. Note that the vesting schedule refers only to the employer's contributions. All of the employees' contributions are 100 percent vested when made. The employees cannot forfeit their contributions.

The 1986 tax law simplified the vesting schedule from three to two. One provides for 100 percent vesting of all the employer's contributions to the employee's retirement account after five years of service. The other requires vesting of 20 percent after three years, 40 percent at the end of four, 60 percent at the end of five, 80 percent at the end of six, and 100 percent at the end of seven years.[14]

An employee can lose vesting credits or eligibility if there is a break in service; that is, if the employee fails to do paid work for the organization for at least 501 hours in a 12-month period for reasons other than military and jury duty, pregnancy, vacation time or layoffs. Federal law now requires that people be given a grace period of five years before all previous credits toward vesting or eligibility be lost because of a break in service. Within the five-year period, the employee ought to be able to buy back into the system, picking up all previously earned credits and all credits that may have been accumulated during the break in service.[15]

A pension plan must be permanent unless termination is the result of business difficulties. Termination of a plan by the employer leads to 100 percent vesting of all accumulated amounts in the employees.

A Funding Agency

Once the plan has been designed and approved by the governing body, a decision has to be made about the funding agency. Who will manage the fund and service the program?

There are several alternatives. Banks, mutual funds, and insurance companies are common funding agencies of pension plans. The best advice to give a manager in selecting among these is to know the services each provides. An insurance company, for example, may have a mutual fund and may offer certain guarantees such as a guaranteed rate of return over a given time frame.

Social Security Integration

Now that nonprofits must participate in the social security system, it is wise to integrate the pension plan of the organization with that of the system. Integration of pension plans lowers the organization's costs of providing pension benefits. Basically what one does in integrating pension systems is to use the social security system as a floor. The private plan of the organization provides benefits above that floor. The actual mechanics of accomplishing this depends upon whether the plan is a defined benefit or a defined contribution plan. For each, integration is different, but the results are basically the same—using the private system to go beyond the threshold set and paid for by social security.

Because participation in the social security system was only recently required of nonprofits, workers for these organizations who are 55 years of age on January 1, 1984 or older are allowed to retire with full social security benefits with less years of credit than other workers of the same age who are covered outside of the nonprofit sector.

Section 403(b)

Section 403(b) is a special retirement plan for 501(c)(3) organizations. Only they, public schools, and certain hospitals may use this defined contribution plan. Section 403(b) permits nonprofit employers to contribute to a pension contract for their full or part-time employees.

Section 403(b) plans have several advantages. Yearly contributions by employer and employee and earnings on those contributions are not taxed until funds are withdrawn. All employees regardless of part or full-time employment and regardless of age can be made eligible.

Section 403(b) allows withdrawals prior to age 59 1/2 without penalty because of death of the worker, disability, early retirement, or medical expenses that are deductible. All other early withdrawals are subject to income tax and a 10 percent penalty.

One disadvantage of the 403(b) is that if on retiring the worker takes all his or her money in one lump sum, he or she will pay taxes on the entire amount. There is no way to average the income over ten or five years—a device used to lower taxes on lump-sum payments in some pension plans. To avoid this problem, the worker may wish to take the funds in periodic annual payments in which case part of the payments will be received free of taxes.

The nonprofit can construct a 403(b) plan for its employees at no cost to the institution and the organization need not contribute. The contributions can be made through salary reductions where employees agree to reduce their salaries by a specific amount to be used by the employer to make the contributions.[16] The employee's income for tax purposes is lowered by the amount of the contribution, meaning that this amount is not presently subject to tax. The employee can continue to make contributions until age 59 1/2—all the while sheltering income and the earnings on the accumulated amounts for taxes. Furthermore, all contributions by the employee and all of the interest earned on these amounts is immediately vested at 100 percent. It cannot be forfeited.

Unlike other retirement plans, the amount that can be contributed through a 403(b) depends upon the number of years the employee has worked for the nonprofit in question, for contributions can be made even for back years before the plan went into effect. Obviously, the greater the number of years, the greater the amount that can be contributed by the employee. There is a new statutory limit, however, of the lesser of 20 percent of income or $9,500. This amount is subject to revision by Congress in order to adjust for inflation.[17]

CAFETERIA PLANS

Cafeteria or flexible plans are increasingly considered by nonprofits as a way of packaging benefits. Cafeteria plans are based on the premise that no two employees may need exactly the same amount of each type of benefit: One employee would prefer more life insurance and less health and hospitalization. Under a cafeteria plan, the employee may make the trade-off. Each employee can create his or her own mix among the benefits included in the plan. If a cafeteria plan does not exist, all employees in a category must be treated alike.

Thus, all employees making $25,000 or all administrators would have the same amount and mix of benefits.

With a cafeteria plan, the employer places all benefits including health and life insurance, retirement plans, cash, disability or other nontaxable benefits in a package. Each employee chooses the amount and combination of desired benefits. The employee may choose between cash and nontaxable benefits.[18] As in a cafeteria, the employee chooses from a variety of offerings as much as is wanted (within permissible limits) and leaves what is not wanted.

PROFIT-SHARING PLANS

In more than one ruling, the IRS has stated that a nonprofit may have a profit-sharing plan.[19] These plans are of two major types: bonus or incentive plans or savings and retirement plans.

Basically, the bonus or incentive plans are those that compensate employees on a percentage basis which is a percentage of the revenues or cost savings of the organization. A study of one plan approved by the IRS prior to the 1986 tax law suggests that the plan should have the following properties:[20]

1. The bonus should not make the total compensation of the employee (regular salary and benefits combined) unreasonable compared with another person with similar education and experience in a similar position in a comparable nonprofit in the same geographic area.

2. The organization should not deviate from its tax-exempt mission, and benefits should not inure to private persons. Thus, an unreasonable compensation or one that is solely for the benefit of certain managers may be construed as a plan to promote their private welfare.

3. The plan should be based on some indicator that proffers benefits to others such as a bonus plan based on cost savings to patients or clients so that they too are beneficiaries.

4. The plan should be so calibrated that if the performance is not achieved, the incentive or bonus payments would not be made.

Two experts, also writing prior to the 1986 tax law, caution that the plan should also have the following properties:[21]

1. The organization's management should be omitted from the plan to remove suspicion that the plan is to serve them.

2. The plan should be established as a result of an arm's-length negotiation between the management and workers of the organization.

3. The plan should contain a statement of how it will help the organization advance its tax-exempt status.

4. There should be a limitation on how much each person can receive in a period so that no one would be unreasonably compensated.

5. There should be a formula for calculating the benefits so they would not result in increasing prices and charges to the public.

6. There should be a system of annually comparing the compensation with those in other organizations to maintain reasonableness in compensation and in the quality and quantity of services being provided.

The second type of profit-sharing plan is a savings or a retirement plan known as a 401(k) that is typically used by for-profit firms to share their profits with their employees. In view of the 1986 tax law, nonprofits need to reconfirm the availability of 401(K)s before establishing new ones. The 401(k), named after the section of the *Internal Revenue Code* in which it is described, is very similar to the 403(b) discussed earlier in this chapter. The major differences are these:[22]

1. In a 401(k), the employee may be given cash by the organization or the organization may make contributions to the employee's retirement account, thus deferring taxes on these amounts until the funds are withdrawn by the employee. In the 403(b), receiving cash is not an option.

2. These plans may provide for loans to employees. The 1986 tax law requires amortization payments of the loan at least four times a year and places a maximum outstanding balance of $50,000 at anyone time. It is repayable within five years, but longer only if the loan is used for purchasing or rehabilitating the principal residence of the employee. It also limits the deductibility of interest payments on these loans.

3. The 1986 law stiffens the nondiscrimination rules of 403(b) to match the 401(k). The purpose is to require the organization to make the plan available to low level, as well as highly compensated employees, board members and officers.

4. The 401(k) offers more investment options. The 403(b) provides for investments only in mutual funds, annuities and policies that offer incidental insurance. The 401(k) participant can invest in all of these and in common stocks and plans managed by banks.

5. Upon retirement, the 401(k) offers the opportunity to reduce taxes by spreading the income from the plan over five or ten years. The 403(b) does not.

6. The organization must vest 100 percent of the contributions in the 403(b) in the worker at the start. With the 401(k) plan, the vesting can be delayed.

7. The 403(b) gives the employee who has worked for a nonprofit for 15 years the chance to put in up to $15,000 maximum or $3,000 per year to make up for the absence of such a plan in the organization in previous years. The 401(k) does not.

Nonprofit organizations are not immune to suits.[23] Table 9.1 shows that there are at least 40 areas that are fertile for suits against directors, officers,

LIABILITY INSURANCE

ANOTHER AIR DISASTER

Seven former students of the Maharishi Mahesh Yogi are suing their ex-guru because he promised to teach them to fly, but left them sitting on the runway, flapping their knees. They're asking $9 million each. Truly, man is an interesting creature.

The deal was this, complain the earthbound litigants: In exchange for lengthy spells of meditation (and in some cases, it is charged, working for His Holiness at $25 a month), the student would become a "Master of Creation," which meant learning to fly and read minds.

Didn't work, complain the unwilling groundlubbers. They can neither fly nor think straight. "Flying," they discovered, meant hopping around with the legs folded in the lotus position. Moreover, all that time spent meditating, they say, "arrested and retarded the normal process of maturation and development," making it difficult to get a job on the stock exchange or otherwise pursue an ordinary life.

True believers will maintain that the plaintiffs are giving up too soon, that if they just stuck with it a while longer they'd soon be flying circles around Peter Pan. Skeptics, resigning themselves to the dangers of commercial air travel, will say that anyone who thinks he can be taught to fly deserves all he gets, and it is true that, for the right price, someone can be found to teach you almost anything you want to know.

But what is it, do you suppose, that makes grown-ups think they can overcome the law of gravity by shutting their eyes, crossing their legs, and putting their joints in overdrive? Two explanations come to mind. Hope springs eternal is one. The other, a commentary on the backsliding of traditional institutions, suggests that those who stand for nothing will fall for anything.

-The Washington Times, Wed., 9/11/85, p. 9

---

or trustees (management) of an organization. While Table 9.1 was developed principally for for-profit firms, they also apply to nonprofits.[24]

The nonprofit should consider protecting both itself and its management against suit. A number of court cases have established that nonprofits can be held liable even for the performance of their volunteers or workers. These suits are frequently brought under the principle of "respondeat superior."[25] This principle holds that the nonprofit participates in a master-servant relationship with its workers, that the servant (employee) was operating within the scope of his or her employment, and that an injury resulted from the negligence or will of the employee.

Table 2

Potential Claim Areas for Directors, Officers, or Trustees

(1) Acquiescence in conduct of fellow directors engaged in improper self-dealing.

(2) Acts beyond organization powers.

(3) Acts of executive committee.

(4) Approval of organization acquisition with resulting loss of organization assets.

(5) Attendance at directors' meetings and committee meetings.

(6) Conflicts of interest.

(7) Continual absence from meetings.

(8) Disclosure of material facts.

(9) Dissemination of false or misleading information.

(10) Dissent from improper or wrongful acts by board of directors or committee.

(11) Examination of all reports and documents before signing.

(12) Extension of credit where not warranted.

(13) Failure to ascertain whether extension of credit would be warranted.

(14) Failure to detect and stop embezzlement of organization funds.

(15) Failure to file annual report.

(16) Failure to inspect organization books and records in order to keep abreast of its activities.

(17) Failure to require withholding in connection with social security and income tax.

(18) Failure to record dissent from wrongful acts by board of directors whether or not dissenting director attended the meeting at which such action was taken.

(19) Failure to supervise the activities of others in a proper manner.

(20) Failure to verify facts in official documents before signing and filing them.

(21) False or misleading reports.

(22) Fraudulent conduct.

(23) Fraudulent reports, financial statements, or certificates.

(24) Ignorance of organization books and records.

(25) Inducing organization to commit breach of contract.

(26) Inducing or abetting organization in commission of torts.

(27) Inefficient administration resulting in losses.

(28) Loans from officers, directors, or trustees.

(29) Permitting organization to engage in activities prohibited by statute.

(30) Permitting organization to make improper guarantees.

(31) Permitting organization to pay bribes or make other illegal payments.

(32) Preferences at the expense of organization creditors.

(33) Sale of organization assets for unreasonably low price.

(34) Shrinking responsibility.

(35) Transactions with other companies in which officers or directors are personally interested.

(36) Unreasonable accumulations.

(37) Violations of specific provisions of articles or bylaws.

(38) Violations of state statutes.

(39) Wasting of organization assets.

(40) Willful wrongdoing.

Reprinted, with permission, from the *Journal of the American Society of CLU,* Vol. XXXIX, No. 6 (November 1985). Copyright 1985 by the American Society of CLU, 270 Bryn Mawr Avenue, Bryn Mawr, PA 19010

In protecting its management and itself from suit, an organization may purchase liability insurance or indemnification insurance. The latter reimburses the management for its expenses after a judgment is made or it reimburses the organization if the organization paid the expenses.

Liability insurance policies, unlike indemnification policies, have a "duty to defend" clause which means that the directors or officers do not have to use their funds or the organization's funds to defend themselves and then wait for reimbursement after a judgment is made. In a costly and lengthy trial this could lead to financial hardship both for the organization and for the manager.

Whether through indemnification or insurance liability coverage can be obtained on a blanket basis, covering all directors and officers rather than each individual separately. Coverage excludes a libel or slander, governmental penalties or fines, bodily injury, claims covered by other insurance, active and deliberate dishonesty, and actions leading to personal or illegal profits or gains.

If desired, it is possible to get extra coverage by buying an umbrella policy. This is an insurance policy that covers all liabilities—property and personal—beyond the amount covered by each liability policy the organization has. Thus, an umbrella policy would provide protection beyond the automobile, property, and directors, officers, and trustees policies previously described. All of these individual policies would have their limits raised by being under the umbrella policy. Thus, a policy to cover the mangers may be for $1,000,000 and the automobile policy for $200,000. An umbrella policy for $1,000,000 means that it can be used to pay any claims that exceeds the $200,000 for automobile and the $1,000,000 for directors.

SUMMARY AND CONCLUSIONS

Nonprofits must compete for competent workers. To do this they must devise benefit packages enabling them to attract and retain such workers while controlling costs. The management of nonprofit organizations must also be mindful that they are not immune to suits and must therefore seek protection.

This chapter describes various elements of a benefit package and shows how costs may be contained. It also shows that one type of feasible benefit is a profit-sharing plan. The recommended properties of such a plan are also given.

NOTES

1. Disability tax liabilities depend upon who pays the premiums and the extent to which the payments of disability income may be construed as regular salary payments. If they can be construed as regular salary payments, then they are neither exempt nor eligible for tax credit but are taxable as regular income.
2. The requirements are more lenient when the disability is blindness.
3. Death benefits for any single death that do not exceed a total of $5,000 are exempt from income taxes by the recipients.

4. The requirements for conversion may be more difficult if the separation is due to the demise of the organization.

5. Survivors who are themselves recipients of social security retirement benefits may elect between their check or the check of the deceased spouse but two checks cannot be received.

6. Consider the tax effect. When an organization pays the contribution, it is not taxable to the employee as income. However, if the employee receives the same amount as payment, not only will it be taxed as income, but the after-tax income, being smaller, will buy less insurance.

7. Basically, both the event that caused the injury and the injury itself must be accidental.

8. Blue Cross and Blue Shield are not uncommon as insurance companies that were tax-exempt. There are at least four sections of the *Internal Revenue Code* that provide for insurance-type companies to be nonprofits. While this paper discusses Blue Cross and Blue Shield as separate organizations, they do cooperate and sometimes merge.

9. See Title 13, Section 13-10 of the Public Health Service Act of 1973, and Section 42 of the Code of Federal Regulations, Part 110-801.

10. There are several variations of benefit definitions; for example, it might be the average salary earned in the final ten, five, or three years of the worker's tenure. The years may or may not have to be consecutive. There are numerous variations.

11. The factors that are placed in the actuarial equation to determine the amount that must be contributed include: the defined benefit, the annual valuation of the pension fund, the expected mortality rate, the withdrawal rate, and the expected interest earnings.

12. There are Simplified Employee's Pension plans that permit the employer to make deposits into the IRA accounts held by the employee.

13. Actually, there is a strict mathematical rule stating that 70 percent of the workers (excluding those previously mentioned) must be eligible and if only 70 percent are eligible, then 80 percent must benefit.

14. The IRS disallows vesting schedules that are too restrictive. Variations from the schedules discussed should be attempted with extreme caution.

15. An organization may give a worker a five-year period during which he or she may be away from paid employment with the organization. But at the end of that period, the worker either buys back into the system and becomes a participating employee in the plan, or all previous credits earned toward vesting or eligibility may be forfeited. Once the employee re-enters the plan, he or she may recoup one year of eligibility for every one year worked.

16. It is important that this process be understood. The plan must be the employer's, not the employee's. Even though the contributions come from the employee's pay, the transfer of funds must be made by the employer in accordance with a written agreement. The employee cannot first receive pay, and then give money to the employer to place in the fund. This would constitute constructive receipt and the contribution would be taxed as income to the employee.

17. The actual amount that can be contributed depends upon the election of one of three formulas by the employee. There was an upper limit, however, of the lesser

of 25 percent of income or $30,000. This limit has been changed to $9500 by the U.S. Congress.

18. Prior to January 1, 1985, the employee could choose among cash, nontaxable, taxable benefits and property. Now, the employee must choose between cash and nontaxable benefits.

19. Revenue Ruling 69-383, 69-2 Cummulative Bulletin 113, General Counsel Memorandum 38283, Internal Revenue Service, February 15, 1980, and prior to that General Counsel Memorandum 35638, January 28, 1974. For a brief history of the IRS position on these plans, see Edward J. Schnee and Walter A. Robbins, "Profit-Sharing Plans and Tax-Exempt Organizations—A New Benefit for All," *TAXES— The Tax Magazine*, 62, no. 4 (April 1984), 220–23.

20. See General Counsel Memorandum, 35638, Ibid.

21. Schnee and Robbins, "Profit-Sharing Plans and Tax-Exempt Organization," pp. 220–23. The 1986 updates are by the author.

22. For a comparison of 403(b) and 401(k) properties, see Labh S. Hira, "Profit-Sharing Plans for Nonprofit Entities", *TAXES—The Tax Magazine*, 62, no. 10 (October 1984), 679–83. See also Robert J. Angell and Joseph E. Johnson, "403(b) Loans: A Money Machine," *Journal of the American Society of CLU*, 39, no. 1, 1985, 56–61.

23. See Douglas J. Besharov, "Liability in Child Welfare," *Public Welfare*, (Spring 1984), pp. 28–33; Julie J. Bisceglia, "Practical Aspects of Directors' and Officers' Liability Insurance—Allocating and Advancing Legal Fees and the Duty to Defend," *UCLA Law Review*, 32, no. 3 (February 1985), 690–718; and Jeffrey D. Kahn, "Organizations' Liability for Torts of Volunteers", *University of Pennsylvania Law Review*, (1985), 1433–52.

24. Michael S. Gawel, Jagat P. Jain, and Vincent Agnello, "Directors and Officers Indemnification Insurance: What Is Being Offered?" *American Society of CLU*, 39, no. 6 (November 1985), 92–101.

25. For a review of these principles see, Jeffrey D. Kahn, "Organizations' Liability for Torts of Volunteers," pp. 1433–52.

SUGGESTED READINGS

1. ALLEN, EVERETT, JOSEPH J. MALONE, and JERRY S. ROSENBLOOM, *Pension Planning*, 5th ed. (Homewood, Illinois: Richard D. Irwin, Inc., 1984).

2. BISCEGLIA, JULIE J., "Practical Aspects of Directors' and Officers' Liability Insurance—Allocating and Advancing Legal Fees and the Duty to Defend," *UCLA Law Review*, 322, no. 3 (February 1985), 690–718.

4. GAWEL, MICHAEL, "Directors and Officers Indemnification Insurance: What Is Being Offered?" *Journal of the American Society of CLU*, 39, no. 6 (November 1985), 92–101.

5. HIRA, LABH S., "Profit-Sharing Plans for Nonprofit Entities," *TAXES—The Tax Magazine,* 62, no. 10 (October 1984), 679–84.

6. HUEBNER, S. S. and KENNETH BLACK, Jr., *Life Insurance,* 10th ed. (Englewood Cliffs, New Jersey: Prentice-Hall, Inc., 1976).

7. KAHN, JEFFREY D. "Organizations' Liability for Torts of Volunteers," *University of Pennsylvania Law Review*, 133, no. 1409, (1985), 1433–52.

8. ROSENBLOOM, JERRY S. and G. VICTOR HALLMAN, *Employee Benefit Planning* (Englewood Cliffs, New Jersey, Prentice-Hall, Inc., 1981).

9. SCHNEE, EDWARD J. and WALTER A. ROBBINS, "Profit-Sharing Plans and Tax-Exempt Organizations: A New Benefit for All," *TAXES—The Tax Magazine*, 10, no. 4 (April 1984), 221–23.

```
┌─────────────────────────┐
│          TEN            │
└─────────────────────────┘
            │
┌───────────────────────────────────┐
│                                   │
│         Fundamentals             │
│      for Increasing Gifts        │
│       and Contributions          │
│                                   │
└───────────────────────────────────┘
```

The competition for gifts and contributions is very stiff. Not only do nonprofits compete among themselves, but they must compete with other uses that both corporate and individual potential donors have for their dollars. One responsibility of financial management in an economic institution such as a nonprofit is to assist the organization to increase the amount and dollar volume of gifts and contributions. To accomplish this requires a working understanding of the motives that corporations as well as individuals have for giving, the limitations on giving, and strategies for receiving large gifts. These are the subjects of this chapter.

THE COMPETITION FOR GIFTS AND CONTRIBUTIONS

Some portion of income earned by a household or a corporation must go to pay current liabilities. For corporations and to a large extent for individuals, these are legal obligations due to be paid within a year and most within 30 days. The obligations include the payment of rent, alimony, child support, food, tuition, credit card balances, mortgage payments, payment of wages and salaries, current insurance and taxes, and notes and accounts payable. These are often contractual and legal obligations that claim a substantial part of the income of any household or firm. Therefore, these dollars are usually not available for giving.

Aside from current liabilities, both corporations and households have some discretionary use of their dollars. But a good portion of these dollars must go toward advancing the welfare or future of the household or corporation. These include saving and planning for retirement and future obligations of the family, investment in new plants or equipment, buying of furniture, buying of automobiles, repayment of long-term debt, paying of dividends to stockholders, and so on.

For most households and corporations, it is only after such household or corporate needs are met that there is a residual which can be donated. We may call this residual donatable funds. This amount is immediately competed for among the approximately one million nonprofits in existence. For the nonprofit that approaches a household or corporation, it is a marketing challenge to cause that corporation or household to view the nonprofit as more deserving than most if not all other nonprofits; or, to obtain a commitment such as a tithe so that giving to it becomes the moral equivalent of a legal obligation.

A similar litany of obligations can be developed for foundations. They too have financial obligations that must be met. They must pay for office space, equipment, workers, and sometimes taxes. Some foundations also have long-term commitments to support specific nonprofit organizations. Like individuals and corporations, they sometimes experience a decline in their income. It is only after they have met all obligations that donations can be made.

Table 10.1 shows that nearly 50 percent of all donations from all donors (individuals, corporations and foundations) go to religious groups; 14 percent goes to health groups and to hospitals; 14 percent to education; 11 percent to social services; 6 percent to arts and humanities; and 3 percent to civic groups concerned with environmental, women, neighborhood rehabilitation and similar issues. Obviously, not only is there competition or funds among these large groupings, but within each as well. Thus, civic groups compete with religious

TABLE 10.1   Recipients of Contributions, 1964, 1974, 1984
(in billions of dollars)

	1964		1974		1984	
	Dollars	%	Dollars	%	Dollars	%
Religion	6.14	44.9	11.84	43.8	35.56	47.9
Education	2.28	16.7	4.04	15.0	10.08	13.6
Social Services	1.92	14.0	3.02	11.2	8.01	10.8
Health and Hospitals	1.68	12.2	4.19	15.5	10.44	14.1
Arts and Humanities	0.44	3.2	1.20	4.4	4.64	6.2
Civic and Public	0.39	2.9	0.67	2.5	2.08	2.8
Other	0.83	6.1	2.05	7.6	3.44	4.6
Total	13.68	100.0	27.01	100.0	74.25	100.0

Source: Calculated from American Association of Fund-Raising Counsel, *Giving* (New York: American Association of Fund-Raising Counsel, 1985), p. 44–45.

groups and with other civic groups for the limited amount of funds left over after potential donors have met all other obligations. With such keen competition, an understanding of the motives and methods of giving offers an important edge and adds to the emotional reasons for giving. What are some of these motives and methods?

INDIVIDUAL AND CORPORATE MOTIVES FOR GIVING

The evidence is very strong that the ability to deduct all or some portion of a gift is a strong impetus for giving.[1] This is so because the deduction means that the cost of the gift is shared by the government. Thus, for a person in the 30 percent bracket, a gift of $3,000 means that the gift only costs that person $2,000 since income tax liability is reduced by $1,000 or one-third. A person in the 20 percent bracket who makes the same gift saves $600 from income tax so that the gift costs only $2,400. Thus, the higher the income tax bracket, the greater the savings and the less the gift costs the donor. For this reason, economists agree that tax reform lowering the income tax rates dampens the tax motive for giving and by the same token, any increase in the rate strengthens the motive.

The tax motive for giving occurs even when planning one's estate. Thus, economists have found that the ability to deduct 100 percent of all charitable deductions at death is an important reason why wealthy donors pass on property and cash to nonprofits at the time of their death.[2]

There are also nontax reasons for giving that go beyond the emotional appeal. Some people give to express thanks. Thus, alumni make gifts to their alma mater. Gifts are also made to further a mission with which the donor agrees such as donations to religious causes. Gifts are made in response to group pressures, objectives, common goals and expectations—contribution campaigns in which the office sets or is given a target. People also give simply because they are asked—street corner collections. People give to honor and to memoralize others or special events. Giving sometimes bring notoriety, influence and satisfaction. Giving is both altruistic and egotistic.

Sophisticated ways of appealing to a potential donor have been studied. Social psychologists[3] have studied the effect of "foot-in-the-door" approaches.[4] These imply that there can be increased giving if an approach that begins with a plea for a small gift is followed by a plea for a larger gift. The thinking here is that a smaller request provides an entry that can be used to get a larger gift once the organization has gotten a foot in the door.

There is also some evidence to support the "door-in-the-face" approach.[5] This approach confronts the potential donor with a very large request which one does not expect to receive, and then follows with a smaller request. Supposedly, the potential donor after rejecting the larger amount is more receptive to the smaller as a compromise. It appears that the efficacy of these approaches depends upon the length of time that passes between the first and second appeal and the probability that the same person in a family or in a corporation receives both appeals.

It has also been shown by social psychologists that "modeling" can influence giving.[6] This means that a potential donor is more likely to make a gift when there is evidence that some other person who has significance to him or her has made a similar or larger gift.

Such phrases as "even a penny" or a "generous family donation" are also considered to be stimuli for giving.[7] The former legitimatizes paltry or small gifts and the latter implies a large gift reflecting well on the family rather than on a single individual. There is even reason to believe that seeking a check is preferred to cash because persons are more accustomed to dealing with larger numbers when writing checks. The gift is, therefore, likely to be larger.[8]

When these techniques are used within a framework that maximizes the tax benefits from giving and that appreciates that most people who give had no legal, tax, or charitable advice on how to give for tax purposes,[9] and that most people give at the time a request is made rather than a long time after,[10] it is evident that a good education in the tax fundamentals of giving could enhance the productivity of fund raising.

Before turning to the fundamentals of giving, however, there are preliminaries to be discussed. Not only do households have reasons for giving, but so too do corporations. The evidence is clear that corporations are influenced by the ability to deduct their gifts.[11] However, there are also nontax reasons.

There are at least three broad nontax reasons.[12] One is the belief by many corporate leaders that they have a social responsibility to respond to the needs of the community and that this is a form of expressing corporate citizenship.[13] A second belief held by some corporate leaders is that giving is a form of a prudent investment.[14] It stimulates good will with workers, clients, and the community and improves the corporate market. A third view is that giving represents "enlightened self-interest."[15] This view states that the motive for corporate giving is a combination of corporate citizenship, prudent investment, and the desire to take a leadership role in promoting an activity to encourage others to give, permitting each donor to be identified with the success of the project to reap direct and indirect benefits from the gifts.

These motives for corporate giving are buttressed by responses of corporate leaders about why they give to specific causes. It has been shown that the two most important reasons for corporate giving are a sense of corporate citizenship and to protect and to improve the corporate business environment.[16]

As in the case of households, the method of appeal is as important as the motive. Some methods have been identified to stimulate corporate donations.[17] One method is to form a corporate group that pledges a certain percentage of their pretax net income (profits before taxes) and that challenges other corporations to do the same. A second is for the stockholders as a group to instruct the corporation to send perhaps $2 per share owned by the stockholders to a specific organization or to have it set aside for a specific nonprofit mission. A third method is to get the corporation to match employee contributions to qualified nonprofits.

All these methods must be incorporated into a good marketing scheme whether the target is made up of individual donors or corporations or combinations of the two. The marketing scheme will be more successful as more is known about the primary motives for giving—one of which is the tax deductibility of gifts.

Just as individuals and corporations have motives for giving, so too do governments and foundations. Foundations give to certain causes because this is the purpose of their being. While the government rarely gives, it contracts out government services as a means of promoting social welfare in a manner that is more efficient than if the government itself would conduct the activity. As a matter of fact, foundations and governments are similar in the sense that most of what they "give" are explicit or implicit contracts. That is to say, they typically give with the understanding that only certain activities will be conducted with their funds. Some of these are highly restrictive and are really payments for services and should not be confused with gifts. A gift is an unrequited transfer where nothing of equal value is given in return. We shall say more about this later.

DIVERSIFICATION OF GIFTS AND CONTRIBUTIONS

Reliance on any single source for gifts and contributions exposes the organization to the risk of having to terminate its activities should that one source terminate its support. It also leaves the organization open to an IRS challenge of its public charity status especially if the single donor is an individual or a corporation. In addition, it exposes the organization to the powers and preachment of the single donor. These results are likely even if there are a few donors but one is by far the single most important.

In considering its support base for gifts and contributions, the organization will benefit from an evaluation of the advantages and disadvantages of relying on gifts from individuals, corporations, foundations or the government. Table 10.2 shows these advantages and disadvantages based on the experiences of managers of nonprofit organizations. These are self-explanatory. However, recent experiences in the early 1980s with government contracting would suggest that there are disadvantages in addition to the ones listed in Table 10.2. Government contracts can be withdrawn even after the nonprofit has started to fulfill the terms of the contract and has incurred expenses in doing so. Government contractors are subject to audits which could leave them liable for returning monies to the government well after the contract has ended. There can be considerable discontinuity in government contracting as project officers change and as the political leadership changes.

TABLE 10.2   Alternative Source of Funds: Advantages
and Disadvantages

The heads of Chicago philanthropic organizations agreed generally on the following "pros" and "cons" of each source of funds.

1. INDIVIDUALS
    Advantages
        Freedom to use funds without restriction
        Donors have local identification with problem
        Involves volunteers in organization
        Contributions likely to continue in future years
        Large potential of funds available
    Disadvantages
        Great deal of effort required to cultivate; competition increasing
        Gifts are often small
        Capriciousness of some individuals

2. COMPANIES
    Advantages
        Size of gifts
        Support tends to be consistent over time
        Helps develop community understanding
    Disadvantages
        Difficult to approach; requires personal contact
        Frequent turnover of top executives

3. FOUNDATIONS
    Advantages
        Freedom from political pressure
        Competence of professional staffs
        Willingness to support unusually innovative or unpopular projects
        Ability to act quickly
    Disadvantages
        Unwillingness to support ongoing operating costs
        Occasional interference or too much supervision

4. GOVERNMENT
    Advantages
        Large amount of dollars available
        Competence of Washington personnel at upper levels
    Disadvantages
        Red tape
        Unreliability of congressional action
        Annual time horizon too short for planning
        Lack of local community and volunteer involvement
        Political pressures
        Loss of autonomy

Source: The Commission on Foundations and Private Philanthropy, *Foundations, Private Giving, and Public Policy* (Chicago: The University of Chicago Press, 1970), p. 237. Copyright © 1970. The University of Chicago Press. All rights reserved.

GOVERNMENT PROMOTION OF GIVING

Recall that a tax deduction is available to donors and this provides an incentive for their making gifts. This deduction is provided as a deliberate aim of public policy to encourage public support of certain nonprofits providing services that are socially desirable but that neither the government nor the market system can or is providing in sufficient quantity. In Chapter 4, examples of these were given. So much so is this the case, that not only does the federal government, but state and local governments as well encourage people to give. This is done by not only offering a tax deduction, but also by facilitating how gifts may be made.

Thus far we have emphasized that the federal government allows a deduction for charitable contributions. States also allow such a deduction. In addition, in 34 states as of 1985, there is a check-off system. This system allows the taxpayer to check off an amount that is to be forwarded by the state to a specific charity as designated by the taxpayer. The most common available check off is for wildlife (31 of 34 states). Other check-off possibilities include arts and child abuse prevention, covered by less than ten states as specific check-off categories. See the article by S.J. Diamond in the references at the end of this chapter.

Most of the donations made by taxpayers through this check-off method come from their designating a portion of their expected refund to a charity. Thus, the check-off method is less often used when the taxpayer is not expecting a refund.

An advantage of the check-off system is that it is simple and allows the taxpayer to make a contribution almost painlessly. To date, one disadvantage is that most of the funds tend to go to state agencies. This, however, is more a consequence of the law than of the preferences of the taxpayer. In California, for example, The California Senior's Fund in 1983 was a check-off possibility. However, only the amount of total contributions in excess of $325,000 would go to the direct provision of services.

As is true of any public policy, laws are written so that the policy will not be abused. Three court decisions highlight some of the abuses which the law holds in check. In *Venni* v. *Commissioner,* taxpayers were denied a charitable tax deduction for donations made to a church and for property transferred to the local congregations of the church.[18] The donors could not show that the congregations qualified as a tax-exempt religious group; that the donations were not intended for the personal benefits of the donors given that the donors maintained control over the gifts; or that the gifts were not made because the donors expected something in return. Similarly, in *Davis* v. *Commissioner,* the donation made by a couple to a church was not deductible because the wife maintained sole control over the accounts.[19] And in *Magin* v. *Commissioner,* the court held that the contribution made by the taxpayer was not deductible because the recipient was not qualified and because the contribution inured to the private benefit of the donor.[20]

Petitioners seek to deduct as charitable contributions certain transfers of land and money to the Kneadmore Life Community Church (KLCC). The KLCC's members occupied the land as an "intentional community where [they] could pursue common values of living in harmony with nature." The KLCC provided its members, inter alia, with rent-free accommodations and farmland, use of farm equipment and seed, and food grown in community gardens and orchards. These benefits were not provided as compensation for services performed. *Held*, petitioners' deductions denied because the KLCC was operated for a substantial nonexempt purpose and because its net earnings inured to the benefit of its members. Sec. 170(c)(2), I.R.C. 1954.

Canada v. Commissioner, 82 T.C., No. 73, June 1984, p. 973.

With these and other cases to be illustrated in mind, we can appreciate some of the constraints placed on the deduction of contributions. This knowledge helps in designing effective contribution campaigns. Let us begin with the definition of a gift.

LEGAL CHARACTERISTICS OF A GIFT

A deductible gift is an irrevocable transfer of property or cash from a qualified donor to a qualified donee for less than full consideration. The property or cash must be accepted by the donee without any retained, remainder or partial rights belonging to the donor. The donor must not maintain control or influence over the property and may not continue to receive economic benefits from it.

Cash or Property

Deductible gifts must be in the form of property or cash, not services or free rent. While services are not gifts, expenses such as unreimbursed meals or transportation costs that are necessary for providing the service may be deductible.

Likewise, free rent is not deductible. A donor would be better off to rent the space and then donate the rental to the nonprofit. Alternatively, the building might be donated.

Transfer

Deductible transfers must be voluntary, purposeful and complete. A transfer of property under duress is not a gift. A transfer that is clearly the result of a misunderstanding is also not a gift. Neither is a transfer that takes place when the donor is not mentally or legally competent a gift. A transfer made in expectation of death is not a gift if the person survives.

Typically, a transfer that is partial or incomplete is not a gift. Technically, writing a check in the name of a nonprofit is not a gift. To illustrate, Rene writes a check for $400 in the name of his favorite charity. If he holds the check or destroys it, either action nullifies giving. The situation is only slightly better if he hands the check over to a responsible officer of the nonprofit or if he mails it. Neither of these constitutes a complete gift, for Rene could have insufficient funds in the bank, he could call and cancel the check, or the bank could refuse to honor the check. Checks are conditional gifts. The gift actually takes place when the checks are honored by the bank.

A nonprofit does not have the same recourse as a for-profit when a check bounces. A check made out to a firm represents payment for a service or goods bought. It is a legal obligation. A promise of a gift constitutes no such legal obligation.

State and local laws specify how some properties are to be legally transferred. Suppose instead of $400 in cash, Rene gave the nonprofit her automobile This act by itself does not constitute a gift. He must also sign, date and complete the information required on the car title and hand the title over to the nonprofit.

Real property, land and buildings, are transferred in a similar manner. A proper title must be completed, conveyed and the transaction recorded. A person who holds stock certificates must endorse and deliver them to the nonprofit or its agents if the gift is to be complete. Gifts of United States Savings Bonds must follow rules prescribed by the federal government. These rules might require changes in registration. In some cases, the bond may have to be cashed. Gifts of art must be accompanied by gifts of their copyrights. Gifts to help low income persons pay their energy bills are deductible but the amount of the gift should be indicated as a specific part of the total paid the utility company; that is, it must be possible to distinguish the gift from the consumer's own bill.

Irrevocable

A transfer must be irrevocable to constitute a gift, meaning there is no way in which the donor may repossess the property other than by arm's-length purchase. Any transfer with the intent or with conditions to permit repossession even by purchase is not a gift.

To illustrate, suppose Jeanine makes a transfer of her car and attaches conditions to its use. Suppose she requires that the automobile be returned to her if it is abused. This is not a gift. The transfer provides conditions for revoking the "gift." In a similar vein, an option to buy is not a gift until the option is exercised.[21]

Retained Rights

There are times when a potential donor wishes to make a gift of property but also wishes to retain certain rights over it. The rights might simply be to enjoy its use. Let us couple the concept of retained rights with that of irrevocability and see the results. Shauna makes an irrevocable gift of her horse to a riding academy with the stipulation that she has use of it on Saturdays. The gift is irrevocable if there are no conditions by which she may recapture ownership of the horse. However, she has retained rights over its use. The consequence is that the gift is partial from the point of view of the IRS and therefore there is no tax deduction. It is, however, legally irretrievable. The horse belongs to the academy.

Remainder Rights

Sometimes potential donors would consider making a transfer to a nonprofit with the condition that after some event or passage of time, all or some portion of the property be returned. These are remainder rights.

To illustrate, assume that the academy needs the horse to prepare for a show. Shauna might make a transfer with the condition that the horse be returned at the end of the show. This is not a gift. She has maintained remainder interests. No deduction is allowed and the nonprofit has no more than a loan. Furthermore, she cannot deduct the rental not charged the academy, since free rents are not deductible gifts.

Present Interests

A donor may choose to make a gift at some time in the future. This is a future-interest gift which is not deductible. A gift has to be of present interest to be deductible. This means that the nonprofit must acquire immediate and full control and ownership of the property or cash without restrictions. By inference, a future-interest gift becomes deductible only at the time that full control becomes effective; that is, where the conditions of future interest no longer exist so that the future interest is now a present interest. Accordingly, an option to buy a property in five years is a future interest and not deductible until the five years has passed and the option is exercised.

There is an important exception to the present-interest rule when the gift is of real property, such as a building or house. This exception will be discussed later in the chapter. What is to be remembered is that as far as tangible personal property (property other than real estate and intangibles) is concerned, future interests are not deductible until all of the contingencies of control, either by the donor or someone related to the donor, are removed. Thus, a gift that is to go from Beverly to her son and then to a charity is not a deductible future-interest gift. But if after her son receives it, he passes it on to an unrelated person,[22] the gift at that point becomes deductible even though it has not yet reached its final destination of the nonprofit.

Exceptions to Incomplete Transfers

In general, a transfer must be complete and of present interest to be deductible. This means that the donee must acquire complete and immediate control of the gift. The donor must maintain no retained, revocable, partial, or remainder rights.

There are notable exceptions to the general rule. One exception pertains to a situation where the donor owns less than 100 percent of a property and is therefore unable to give the entire property. Under these conditions, the donor must give an undivided share of his or her total interest in a property if such a gift is to be deducted. To understand this exception, consider the following example. Shauna owns one-half of an interest in a property comprised of a stable and ten horses. Her undivided interest is one-half of the property as it is comprised. Thus, the maximum she can give and take a deduction for is one-half of the property. One-half is 100 percent of what she owns of each horse. She may give less than 100 percent but the amount she gives must be substantial and undivided, that is, the property is the stable and horses together. She cannot divide the property such that she gives some of the horses and none of the stable.[23]

A second exception to the general rule refers specifically and only to a principal residence or a farm. A person may make a future-interest gift of either of these two properties to a qualified nonprofit and get an immediate tax deduction. Accordingly, Marisa could get an immediate tax deduction on a gift of her home to her favorite nonprofit while continuing to live in it.

A third exception to the complete transfer rule relates to gifts of real property for qualified conservation purposes. Qualified conservation purposes include preservation of land area, protection of natural habitat, preservation of open space, and preservation of an historic site. The gift of the property must be accompanied by some easement that will restrict the future use of the land for any purpose other than for conservation. The donor may continue to use the property until some date in the future when it passes to the qualified organization.[24]

The other exceptions to the requirement that gifts be complete and of present interest require the use of a trust. We shall postpone discussion of these other exceptions until the next chapter.

Qualified Donor

Gifts can only be made by qualified donors who must be of age, of sound mind, and must own the property. Ownership occurs in various forms, some of which compromise or defeat the goal of giving.

The most straightforward form of ownership is called fee simple. In this case, the person owns all rights to the property by himself or herself and is free to do with it as desired. Simon buys a typewriter for cash and is the sole owner. He owns it fee simple and may do with it as he wishes.

Some properties are owned in the form of tenants for the entirety. This is a form of ownership normally used only by spouses. It means that neither party may give the property without the express consent of the other. Many homes are owned in this form and therefore no single spouse may, under normal circumstances, give the property without an affirmative approval of the other.

Other properties may be owned as tenants in common. This means that either party may make a gift, but only of that share of the property that he or she owns. When a percentage of ownership is not specified, it is assumed that each co-tenant has an equal share. This might be a little more tricky than tenants in the entirety where one-half ownership by each spouse over the entire property is presumed. In the case of tenants in common, an unequal share or only a specified piece of the property may be owned by the donor.

Property may also be owned in the form of joint tenants with the rights of survivorship. Many properties are owned in this form. It is a popular form of ownership among people who are trying to avoid probate. The objective is to be sure that upon death, the property is passed directly to a designated person. It is impossible to make gifts of property owned in this form at the time of death. Full ownership passes automatically on to the survivor.

In the states of Idaho, Washington, Nebraska, California, Arizona, Louisiana, Texas and Nevada, there is a form of ownership called community property. It is presumed that any property bought during marriage is owned on an equal basis by both spouses. The laws on the transfer of community property differ by state, but in general, a person is only free to give the one-half of the property owned.

A person may have ownership that terminates upon death, such as a life estate. This form of ownership is obviously temporary. The owner of the life estate can give only the earnings received during his or her life, but cannot give the property that yields those earnings. That property must be passed on to another beneficiary when the first dies. Furthermore, the person with the life estate is obligated to preserve the property so that it may be transferred.

For example, Marisa may own the earnings of a rental unit through bequest from her mother who stipulated that the unit should belong to Marisa's sister. Marisa can donate the earnings, but not the property. However, she cannot donate the earnings if by doing so there are no funds to repair and maintain the unit to transfer it to her sister in good condition. In the same vein, Marisa's sister cannot give the rental unit while Marisa is still alive, particularly if her giving it means that Marisa's flow of income would be terminated.[25]

Ownership may be contingent or nonvested. In these cases, ownership takes place only after some condition is fulfilled. Until those conditions are recognized as being satisfied, the "owner" has no legal power to give. A common contingency is the passage of time. If, for example, ten years must pass before ownership of the amounts in a pension account is vested, then prior to that time, the person in whose name the account appears has no power to give those funds, even though they appear in his or her name.

Acceptance

For a gift to be complete, it must be accepted by a donee. Acceptance may be affirmatively stated but it may also occur if the donee fails to properly disclaim the gift. A proper or qualified disclaimer is one that is written within nine months after receiving the property and does not tell the donee how to dispose of the property once it is returned.

A donor who makes a gift that is rejected by a donee in a qualified manner as described may nevertheless get a tax deduction if the property ends up in a nonprofit. This is so even though the transfer of property is governed by state law. Therefore, even though the property ends up with a nonprofit purely by the operation of the state law, a deduction may still be taken.

Qualified Donee

Qualified donees are domestic charities such as the ones described in Chapters 2 and 6. Also included are nonprofit cemetery companies, volunteer fire companies, war veteran organizations, states, territories and possessions. We are reminded that all nonprofits are not tax-exempt, and only tax-exempt nonprofits qualify for tax deductible contributions.

Less than Full Consideration

A key concept in defining a gift is that the transfer must be for less than full consideration. Simply, this means that the donation must exceed the value of anything the nonprofit may give the donor as an inducement or in appreciation for the gift. By way of illustration, suppose that the fair market value for Shauna's horse is $4,000. That is, the most that she could get from someone who wants to buy her horse is $4,000. If she gives it to a nonprofit and receives a check for $4,000, this is a sale; it is not a gift.

Suppose, however, that instead of a check for $4,000, the nonprofit gave her a check for $2,000. The transaction has two parts: a gift of $2,000 and a sale of $2,000. The gift is the difference between the market price and the amount received by the donor in the transfer. If Shauna had received nothing from the nonprofit, her gift would have been a full $4,000. A gift is the difference between the fair market value and the consideration or compensation received by the donor.

A gift also occurs when one pays more than the value of a service. Hence, a gift occurs when one buys a banquet or dinner ticket for more than either is worth. Paying $150 for a dinner when the dinner and entertainment are worth $50 results in a contribution of $100. The value of the service is declared by the nonprofit sponsor of the event.

Here is another illustration. A university accepted annual payments from individuals in the amount of $300 each for membership in the university's athletic scholarship program. For an additional $120, each member was permitted to purchase a season ticket to the university's home football games and to have preferred seating between the 40-yard lines. Nonmembers were not allowed to sit in this area. Some 2,000 persons were on the waiting list for membership. The IRS ruled that no part of the $300 was deductible because the right to preferred seating was of considerable monetary value to the donee. These were not gifts, but purchases of rights for value.[26]

In a similar ruling, the IRS held that a symphony that obtained $20 contributions from donors to whom it gave season memberships, the privilege of attending cocktail parties and a motion picture premiere, and reserved seats at concerts that were not otherwise available were not deductible contributions, but purchases of rights at least for value.[27]

The 1986 tax law allows full deductions for tickets bought for sporting events if the sponsors turn over the net receipts to the nonprofits and use volunteers (See page 109).

PROBLEMS OF ACCEPTING GIFTS SUBJECT TO DEBT

Many properties are bought on credit. The purchaser borrows to acquire the property so that part of the dollar value of the property represents ownership or equity; the other part is debt. Raymond owns a home subject to a mortgage. The fair market value of the home is $50,000 and the home is subject to a $30,000 mortgage, meaning that Raymond's equity is $20,000. He makes a gift of the home to his favorite nonprofit. How much has he given?

Raymond can only give that which he owns. He owns only $20,000 so that the gift is worth $20,000. But who is going to pay the bank? Suppose that the nonprofit decides to assume the mortgage. In that case, Raymond has made a gift for which he gets a tax deduction, but he now has to report income. The relieving of his $30,000 debt is income to him even though he has not received a dime. If he agrees to pay the debt, then this payment is included as part of the deductible gift.[28]

Let us assume that the debt is not paid by Raymond. The nonprofit has obtained a piece of property worth $50,000 for which it has only to pay the $30,000 of outstanding debt and over a period of years. In addition to assuming a debt it must now pay operating costs. If it rents the house, it must pay taxes since the property is subject to debt. If it tries to sell the building it may be subject to tax for the property is subject to debt.[29] If the building has declined in value, the nonprofit must support an asset with a diminishing market value. Raymond may offer to pay the mortgage. If he defaults, the nonprofit pays the bill or loses the property.

BARGAIN SALES AND LOSSES

Raymond may contemplate a different strategy. He may resort to a bargain sale. Assume that he paid $50,000 cash for the home and owns it fee simple. He has no debts and may do as he wishes with the property. Assume further that the property is in an attractive neighborhood so that rather than declining in price, it appreciated to $100,000. He may decide to give it to his favorite nonprofit through a bargain sale. Instead of the nonprofit paying $100,000, it pays $50,000. Since he receives less than full consideration, the difference between what he gets and the fair market value ($50,000) is a gift. A gift?

The bargain sale is part gift and part sale. Its effects on the donor can be devastating. It is beyond the scope of this book to illustrate all the potential results, but a simplified approach may be useful. In this example, the gift amounts to $50,000 which is one-half of the fair market value. Thus, Raymond gave away one-half of what he could have gotten had he sold the house. He must now reduce his cost by half. Thus, he is deemed to have paid only $25,000 for the house. Since he received $50,000 from the nonprofit, he is deemed to have made a gain of $25,000 on the deal and he must pay taxes on it. Bargain sales can be very cruel to donors because they can lead to taxes on gains never received. In this case, Raymond reports a gain of $25,000 even though he sold property for the amount he paid for it, and $50,000 less than its true market value. He would have been better off selling the property, paying the tax and taking a deduction for the contribution.

A bargain sale may also lead to a loss of a deduction because a bargain sale is subject first to the regular rules of gifts and sales and then to the specific rules governing bargain sales. To illustrate, suppose Raymond bought stocks a month ago for $4,000. The stocks rise to $10,000 in two months. Sale of these stocks under any circumstance would lead to an ordinary income tax on the $6,000 of gain. Suppose Raymond decides to give the stocks to his favorite nonprofit. He cannot deduct $10,000 because this is an ordinary income property. The rules say that ordinary income property is deductible at cost. Recognizing that he cannot get $10,000 worth of deductions, suppose he takes a check from the nonprofit for $4,000 to cover his cost and then gives them the stocks. Will he be able to deduct the $6,000 difference as a gift? No.

The reasoning is that his cost was $4,000 for which he got a check from the nonprofit. The stocks are ordinary income property deductible at cost. The cost is $4,000 but he was paid that amount from the nonprofit so there is nothing to deduct. He has lost $10,000 worth of stocks.

Losses

While gains may be implied and taxable even when not actually realized by a taxpayer, the converse is not true. A loss realized by making a contribution cannot be deducted. Thus, stocks that have fallen in price with potential for rising may be attractive to a nonprofit but foolish for a person to give. Losses experienced in giving cannot be deducted but losses experienced in the sale of the property can be deducted. Hence, it is often wiser for the potential donor to sell the property, deduct the loss, give the proceeds to the nonprofit, and deduct the gift of cash.

VALUE OF GIFTS

In general, the value of a gift for purposes of a tax deduction is the fair market value of the property. The fair market value is the price a knowledgeable buyer would willingly pay and an equally knowledgeable seller would willingly accept for the property on a specific date, that is, its valuation date.

An acceptable figure for the fair market value of a property is the actual price for which it is sold in the same location as the donor and donee on or about the valuation date. If actual sale prices are used, the market must not have changed radically between the date of sale and the date of the valuation of the gift. A donor cannot deduct $50,000 for a gift that has declined to $20,000 on the date it was given. The value is then $20,000.

Some properties are not easily valued. Used clothing is valued at the price it may be sold for at a thrift shop. Real estate may be valued at the price similar properties are being sold for in the same jurisdiction at the time, or it may be valued according to the expected future income stream, or at replacement cost. Some properties like collectibles require a competent appraisal. Other properties such as the stocks of a closely held corporation may be valued through an appraisal, or through a price or a formula agreed to by the owners at an earlier date and at which they would be sold to any willing buyer. Some closely held stocks may be discounted either because there is no public market for selling them or because the owner who gives them has such a large quantity that selling them depresses the price.

The point is that valuation can either be easy or highly technical. Errors in valuation that place the property at a value 150 percent higher than its true value, that reduces the tax liability of the donor by $1,000 and that the donor owned for at least five years (and therefore should presumably know its true value) will lead to the imposition of a tax penalty by the IRS to the donor.[30]

Some goods must be treated for valuation purposes as ordinary income goods. An ordinary income good is one that, when sold, the proceeds from the sale are taxed as ordinary income such as wages and salary. Examples of ordinary income goods that may be given are (1) items from the inventory of a retailer or dealer, (2) a product in the hands of its producer such as a piece of art in the hands of the artist or a machine in the hands of its manufacturer, (3) a piece of equipment or machinery used in a trade or business such as a truck in the hands of a construction company, (4) property held for investment purposes but for less than six months, such as stocks in the hands of an investor held for less than six months, and (5) some properties subject to depreciation recapture such as a real estate using a method of rapid depreciation.[31]

Ordinary income property is valued for purposes of deducting a contribution at cost rather than at fair market value. The fair market value of the property is determined technically. From this, the amount of appreciation over cost that is ordinary income is subtracted. The remainder is the value of the property for tax deduction purposes. Usually it equals cost.

Jeanine buys stocks for $1,000 and holds it for two months. The stocks appreciate to $10,000. The gain of $9,000 is short term and is subtracted from the fair market value of $10,000 in determining the amount that can be deducted as a gift. This is equal to $1,000 or the cost.

Capital gain properties are ones in which the proceeds from their sale would be taxed as capital gains. Examples of capital gain property are (1) properties held for investment purposes but for a period of greater than six months such as stocks or real estate held for more than six months, and (2) coal and timber by special treatment of the tax law. Generally, capital gain property may be deducted at fair market value. However, there are important exceptions that we shall discuss concerning appreciated property.

Before doing that, however, it would be useful to see one consequence of treating a good as a capital gain or an ordinary income good. Robert is a painter and has produced a masterpiece. The cost of supplies and equipment is $1,000. The market values the painting at $920,000. Should Robert donate that property, he would be able to deduct only $1,000, not $920,000. If he sold the property to Yvonne for $920,000 and its value rose to $1,600,000 while in her hands for a year, under the general rule she would be able to deduct its fair market value which is now $1,600,000. In her hands, held for more than six months, the property is a capital gain property.

Whether Robert or Yvonne makes the contribution may be of consequence to the nonprofit if the property is subject to debt. If it sold the painting for $2,000,000 after receiving it from Comila, it will pay taxes on the appreciation of $1,080,000. This is the difference between its cost to Yvonne ($920,000) and the sale price ($2,000,000) to the nonprofit. If it sold it after receiving it from Robert, it will pay taxes on $1,900,000 (the sale price of $2,000,000 and the cost to Robert of $1,000). In this example, the tax base for the nonprofit will be nearly $900,000 greater if it received the property from Robert. This is so because when a nonprofit accepts a gift, it simultaneously accepts the value of the gift when it was in the hands of the donor.[32]

Appreciated Property

We have introduced the concepts of ordinary income property and capital gain property.[33] While ordinary income property is valued at cost regardless of the appreciation, capital gain property is usually valued at its fair market value.

There are notable exceptions to this favored treatment of capital gain prop-, erty. If the property is tangible personal property (a property other than real estate or an intangible such as stocks) and if it is given to a public charity, private or private operating foundation to be used in any way that is not related to their tax-exempt purpose (an unrelated business), then the appreciation must be reduced by 40 percent. The 40 percent reduction also applies to any appreciated gift to a private foundation that is not an operating foundation and that does not make qualified distributions of these amounts within 16 months.

Simon makes a gift of an appreciated tangible personal property (a gold ring) to his favorite nonprofit, a secretarial school that runs a jewelry store solely for the purpose of raising money. The jewelry store is unrelated to teaching secretarial skills. Simon bought the ring for $100 and it is now worth $500. He cannot deduct $500 but must deduct $100, not $240 (60 percent of the appreciation of $400), as under the old rules (See page 240).

The reduction of the appreciation by 40 percent is also necessary if the donor wishes to exceed the usual limits on the amount of adjusted gross income that can be deducted for all charitable organizations. Before discussing limits, let's see how a gift of a highly appreciated property may lead to a sharply decreased deduction when the combination of rules governing appreciated property is applied.

Clive has owned and operated an apartment building as an investment for over six months, thereby making it a capital gain property. He bought it for $150,000. In order to use the property to shelter his income, he utilizes a method of rapid depreciation. During the period of his ownership, the building appreciated by $100,000. Because he uses a rapid method of depreciation, a part of previous depreciation must be repaid to the government. This part, as we mentioned earlier, is ordinary income and therefore must be subtracted from the appreciation. For the sake of illustration, let us assume that the amount is $20,000. If he gives the property to a private foundation which is not an operating foundation, he must reduce the remaining $80,000 of appreciation by 40 percent, leaving $48,000. If for some reason he also decides to escape the limit on personal contributions in a single year, he must further reduce the $48,000 by 40 percent, leaving $28,800. Thus, an apartment building bought for $150,000 that has appreciated to $250,000 does not provide a deduction of $250,000 if given under the circumstances described. At most, it provides a deduction of $178,800, which is a loss of $72,000 that cannot be deducted. If he had given the property before the six-month period had expired, he would have been able to depreciate only $150,000 even if it had risen to $250,000 during that time, for it would be short-run or ordinary income property.

Prior to the 1986 tax law, Clive's experience would have been as described. The new law does not allow for six-month difference, but it does allow for appreciated property, and does distinguish between ordinary property and capital gains property. As the regulations are written, the discussion in this section on value of gifts could change.

LIMITS ON GIVING

One way in which the laws are written to stem abuse of the tax deduction allowed for contributions to nonprofits is to place a limit on the amount that can be deducted each year. In this section, we discuss these limits, and in the next we discuss strategies that nonprofits may take for accepting large gifts. Certain large gifts can cause a change in the nonprofit tax status.

Foundations

Unlike individuals and corporations, the law seeks to encourage giving on the part of foundations, primarily private foundations. Public charities are often not grant making and are not required to give. These rules were discussed in Chapters 6 and 7. An example of the exercise of these rules is the B. Altman Foundation which has held the great majority of the stocks of the B. Altman stores. As a result of the excess business holding rules and pressure by the State Attorney General of New York, this foundation divested itself to increase its giving.[34]

On the other hand, there are limits to the amount of charitable gifts that an individual or corporation is permitted to deduct in any one year beginning in the year the gift was actually made. It is important to establish the year the gift is made. Let's refer back to several sections in this chapter.

Conrad signs the certificate of stocks he owns as a gift to a nonprofit. The certificate is to be delivered by an agent of the company. The gift occurs when the change in name is recorded on the books of the company. If Conrad signed the certificate on December 31, it is unlikely that the recording of the gift would have occurred in time for him to properly take a deduction in that year. The same kind of situation occurs in real estate. Recall the earlier discussion explaining that a gift must be complete.

Assuming that the date of the gift is properly established, the limits depend upon whether the donor is a corporation or an individual, the type of foundation, the purpose of the gift, and if the gift is appreciated.

Individuals

A person is permitted to deduct charitable contributions up to 50 percent of adjustable gross income if the contribution is made to a public or a private operating foundation.[35] If the contribution is to a private nonoperating foundation, the annual limit is 30 percent. The only way in which this 30 percent limit can be raised to the 50 percent level for a private nonoperating foundation is if the foundation agrees to distribute all of the donation within a period of approximately 16 months.

A limit also applies if the individual donates appreciated property. The 30 percent limit may be raised to 50 percent by reducing the appreciation by 40 percent. Audrey buys a ring that cost her $400, now valued at $1,000. To use the 50 percent limitation, the $600 appreciation is reduced by $240. The 1986 law restricts her deduction to her basis, which is the purchase price minus depreciation plus any improvements. She can deduct $400, not $760.

The 40 percent reduction also applies, as stated earlier, if the appreciated property is donated to a private nonoperating foundation or if the property is a tangible personal property used in an unrelated business.

The limit on the individual in the previous paragraphs presumes that the gift will lead to a qualified distribution on the part of the nonprofit.[36] If the gift is to be used by the organization, the limit is 20 percent of the adjusted gross income.

Trusts and Wills

One strategy for limitless giving that individuals may use is the creation of a trust which is the subject of the next chapter. A charitable trust is permitted limitless charitable contributions as long as the trust does not engage in unrelated business, unreasonable accumulation of funds, distribution of funds for noncharitable purposes, prohibited transactions, and its funds are not used against the best interest of the charitable beneficiaries. If it does any of these, it is subject to the same limitations imposed on individuals.

Another strategy to avoid the limits on individuals is to make the gift contingent upon the death of the donor through a will. These types of gifts will also be discussed in the next chapter. Through a will, a gift can be made of limitless cash or property as long as there is sufficient capital in the estate to meet the legal obligations of the deceased.

Corporations

Corporations are limited to 20 percent of their taxable income regardless of the type of foundation to which they give. Any excess over this 20 percent is deductible over five years. However, corporations are permitted to deduct up to 50 percent of the appreciation on the value of equipment used in their line of business or of their inventory if the nonprofit will use them solely for the caring of the ill, the needy and infants. The 50 percent is not permitted if the nonprofit will sell the gift once it has been received. To assure compliance with these conditions, the corporation must receive a letter from the nonprofit promising that it will comply with the no-sell restriction.

Corporations are also allowed a deduction of up to half of the appreciation on certain research property that they contribute. The donation must be made to an educational institution. The 1986 law restricts some corporate deductions of appreciated property to the firm's basis.

Corporations controlled by a nonprofit can deduct up to 5 percent of their taxable income each year if the donations are made to a nonprofit other than the ones that control them. As stated in Chapter 6, controlled corporations may also carry excess contributions forward five years.

PROBLEMS AND STRATEGIES OF LARGE GIFTS

Nonprofits do not normally see themselves as being limited to the amount that they may receive from any one source. But gifts and contributions are evidence of public support and that public charities must demonstrate a high level of public support. Intuitively, one may think that getting a large gift or contribution would be evidence of public support but this is not necessarily so.[37]

First, in calculating the one-third or 10 percent of public support described in Chapter 6, no one contribution may be included at a level that is greater than 2 percent of the entire support level. Thus, if the support level is $200,000 and Angela gave $88,000, her gift will be treated as if it were only $2,000 of the $200,000. If Emeline gave $105,000 hers would also be treated as $2,000. The effect of this is to cause the organization to fail the one-third support test because $4,000 (the 2 percent sum of the two gifts) is less than one-third of $200,000.

Second, large gifts and contributions risk making the nonprofit a private foundation and the donor a disqualified person. The rules do, however, provide some protection against this eventuality. If the large donor is not a disqualified person and is not likely to be disqualified because of death, or if the donor is unable to place any conditions or exercise control over the organization, an unusually large gift that is in response to a public appeal may be omitted in calculating public support.

An individual who makes a large gift to a nonprofit may follow one of several strategies. The excess may be deducted over five years. Or, the individual may make the gift at the time of death because there is no limit on charitable deductions made at that point. The process is discussed in Chapter 11. Or, the individual may form a private foundation or a public charity such as 509(a)(3) and make it a subsidiary to a public 509(a)(1) or (a)(2). These are some of the possibilities described in the following article first appearing in the *Washington Post* and then in a number of newspapers across the country.

MICHAEL JACKSON HAS A TAX DILEMMA
LIKE JOE LOUIS, THE MORE HE GIVES AWAY TO CHARITY
THE MORE HE HAS TO EARN

By Herrington J. Bryce

Michael Jackson's decision to donate his estimated $5 million in proceeds from his multi-city "Victory" tour is an uncommon act of charity, but it could land him in deep trouble with the Internal Revenue Service.

Wealthy as his work has made him, Jackson would do well to review the bitter experience of heavyweight champion Joe Louis. Louis donated large portions of the proceeds from his fights to his country's war effort. But the manner of his giving left him with enormous tax liabilities that ruined him financially. It took a presidential directive to absolve him of his entanglements with the tax laws.

Commonly, when celebrities perform for charity, they do so by prior agreement not to be paid. They designate organizations or institutions to receive the proceeds, or a share of them. Since no pay is received, no tax liability is created and there is no deduction.

From everything that has been printed and stated about Jackson's financial arrangements, however, his contract calls for him to be paid. From a tax standpoint, this means that it may be too late for him to declare that he is performing without compensation and intends to donate his full share to charity. His services are not deductible. And the tax rules clearly state that income once earned cannot escape taxation by shifting it to another entity, even if it is a charity.

All this means that Jackson's performances will create a sizeable tax liability. At his level, 50 cents of every dollar earned is potentially payable as federal taxes. Hence, his $5 million will create a federal tax liability of approximately $2.5 million, on top of state and local levies.

For Jackson to deduct the full $5 million in the year he donates it, he will have to earn some $10–$16 million. This is because the IRS currently limits charitable deductions to 30 percent or 50 percent of income, depending on whether the recipient is a public or private charity. So the more Jackson gives, the more he must earn in order to get the full tax deduction from his contribution in one year. Yet the more he earns, the larger his total potential tax liability will be.

If he gives the full $5 million to a *public* charity such as his church (he is a Jehovah's Witness), he has to earn only $10 million. The tax laws allow deductions to such charities of up to half an individual's income. If he fails to earn $10 million, he can still apply unused portions of his deductions to public charities to his returns during the subsequent five years.

If he donates to a *private* charity, such as a family foundation, he would only be allowed to deduct up to 30 percent of his adjusted income and would have to earn some $16 million in order to deduct the full $5 million that he plans to donate.

Because giving to a public charity has a substantial tax advantage over giving to a private charity, Jackson, faced with a huge tax liability and wanting to keep his commitment to donate his share to charity, may choose to sprinkle his gifts among a number of worthwhile public charities.

It may be too late for him to completely solve his immediate tax problem. But there is a step he could take to ease future difficulties, deal with other immediate concerns and perpetuate his goodness for many years. This is the creation of a charitable foundation.

Dispensing charity through a foundation rather than by making random personal gifts would benefit Jackson as much as it has benefited other wealthy Americans.

Even the initial disadvantages, including the possibility that all $5 million might not be deductible in one year, can be overcome by distributing the gift over several years and by making the gift while seeking tax sheltering investments to make up the difference.

Moreover, foundations help shield donors from the animosity of disappointed charity seekers. Not every applicant can be satisfied. Foundations deflect criticism and bad publicity.

Foundations can invest their resources and grow. Jackson's contributions would attract donations from others. Invested prudently, these funds could touch the lives of deserving persons for many years.

Foundations have the time and expertise to evaluate options for charity and to nurture causes to which Jackson is committed.

And a foundation must make sure that the assets and earnings are not used for purposes that do not qualify, such as the personal benefit of donors and their relatives.

Jackson won't be able to control the foundation once it is operating. But neither will he be able to control the use of his direct contributions after they are made. In setting up the foundation, he could stipulate its overall mission, choose the board of directors or trustees, and withdraw his support if he became dissatisfied with it.

This is an opportunity that should not be lost. Few blacks who have done well in entertainment or sports have been able to accumulate and preserve great wealth. Few persons white or black, in any walk of life, have created lasting philanthropic memorials to celebrate their struggle and achievement and to perpetuate their generosity. The $5 million Jackson has committed to charity gives him the rare opportunity to be an exception.

Herrington J. Bryce, "Michael Jackson Has a Tax Dilemma," *The Washington Post*, Sunday, C5 August 5, 1984.

Individuals who make large gifts should always be concerned with the possibility that the gift would be so large that it would convert the organization from a public charity to a private foundation and disqualify that individual. The way individuals may avoid such a taint is to obtain a letter from the organization assuring him or her that the gift would not have a disqualifying effect, or by making the gift as a response to a public appeal without stating any conditions of control over the gift, and by not being in a position to exercise any control over the organization. Being dead is an acceptable position for this purpose. At death large gifts do not disqualify donors under the assumption that no control can be exercised.

Nonprofits, particularly public charities since they are more vulnerable than private foundations, may take certain defensive measures when large gifts are expected:

1. They may increase the number of contributions from sources such as the government and the public that is considered public support and, therefore, this would not hinder their tax-exempt classification as a public charity.

2. They may modify their computation period to include the year of the large gift plus the four preceding years. This tends to dampen the magnitude of the large gift.

3. They may shift from attempting to qualify under 509(a)(1) to (a)(2), or vice versa, depending upon the amount obtained from investment income, unrelated business or related business sources.

4. They may exclude any extraordinary large contributions both from the calculation that gives the sum of all support and from the portion that is considered public support. This removes it from consideration in the calculation of the one-third or 10 percent test. Such exclusion is only possible, however, if the person is not disqualified and had no reason to believe that the effect of the contribution would have been to jeopardize the public charity classification of the organization.

SUMMARY AND CONCLUSIONS

Gifts and contributions are the two most common forms of support of nonprofit organizations. An underlying reason for giving is the tax deduction. Therefore, understanding the impact of taxes on donors increases the efficiency of the appeal. There are many forms of giving that expose the nonprofit to high risks once the gifts are received. Thus, it is important that the nonprofit manager understand the pitfalls of giving and receiving.

There are many appeals that are likely to fail because the contribution works to the financial and tax detriment of the potential donor. Knowledge of these pitfalls avoids resentment, waste of energy, a disservice to unwitting donors, and can be avoided by taking the steps to be discussed in the next chapter or the strategies of dealing with large contributions discussed in this chapter.

NOTES

1. The 1986 tax reform allows only taxpayers who itemize deductions to deduct charitable contributions. The literature showing a close and strong correlation between the deductibility of a gift and giving is extensive. It includes Charles T. Clotfelter, *Federal Tax Policy and Charitable Giving* (Chicago, Illinois: University of Chicago Press, 1985); Martin Feldstein and Charles Clotfelter, "Tax Incentives and Charitable Contributions in the United States," *Journal of Public Economics,*

5, (1976), 1–26; Charles T. Clotfelter and E. Eugene Steuerle, "Charitable Contributions," in Henry Aaron and Joseph Pechman, *How Taxes Effect Economic Behavior* (Washington, D.C.: The Brookings Institution, 1981); Michael Taussig, "Economic Aspects of the Personal Income Tax Treatment of Charitable Contributions," *National Tax Journal*, 20:1 (March 1967), 1–19.

2. On the relationship between taxation and the estate tax, see Thomas Barthold and Robert Plotnick, "Estate Taxation and Other Determinants of Charitable Bequests," *National Tax Journal*, 38, no. 2 (June 1984), 225–36; Michael J. Boskin, "Estate Taxation and Charitable Bequests," *Commission on Private Philanthropy and Public Need* (Washington, D.C.: U.S. Treasury, 1977), pp. 1453–83, Martin S. Feldstein, "Charitable Bequests, Estate Taxation, and Intergenerational Wealth Transfer," Ibid., pp. 1485–97.

3. For a review of the literature on this topic, see Melvin M. Mark and R. Lance Shotland, "Increasing Charitable Contributions: An Experimental Evaluation of the American Cancer Society's Recommended Solicitation Procedures," *Journal of Voluntary Action Research*, 12, no. 3 (April–June 1983), 8–21.

4. J. L. Freedman and S. C. Fraser, "Compliance Without Pressure: The Foot in the Door Technique," *Journal of Personality and Social Psychology*, 4, 1966, 195–202.

5. R. B. Cialdini, J. E. Vincent, S. K. Lewis, J. Catalan, D. Wheeler, and B. L. Darby, "Reciprocal Concessions Procedure for Inducing Compliance: The Door-in-the-Face Technique," *Journal of Personality and Social Psychology,* 31, 1975, 206–15.

6. C. Wagner and L. Wheeler, "Model, Need, and Cost Effects in Helping Behavior," *Journal of Personality and Social Psychology,* 12, 1969, 111–16; and J. H. Bryan and M. A. Test, "Models and Helping: Naturalistic Studies in Aiding Behavior," *Journal of Personality and Social Psychology,* 6, 1967, 400–407.

7. R. B. Cialdini and D. A. Schroeder, "Increasing Contributions by Legitimizing Paltry Contributions," *Journal of Personality and Social Psychology*, 34, 1976 599–604.

8. See Mark and Shotland, "Increasing Charitable Contributions." p. 11.

9. James N. Morgan, Richard F. Dye and Judith H. Hybels, "Results from Two National Surveys of Philanthrophic Activity," *Research Papers: Commission on Philanthrophy and Public Needs*, 1 (Washington, D.C.: U.S. Treasury, 1977), 157–324, especially Table 17.

10. Ibid., p. 201.

11. Charles T. Clotfelter, *Federal Tax Policy and Charitable Giving.*

12. R. Palmer Baker, Jr. and J. Edward Shillingburg, "Corporate Charitable Contributions," *Research Papers: Commission on Philanthropy and Public Needs*, 3, op. cit., 1853–1905.

13. Alfred C. Neal, "A More Rational Basis for Nonprofit Activities," *The Conference Board Record*, 5 (January 1968), 5–7.

14. Richard Eells, "A Philosophy for Corporate Giving," *The Conference Board Record*, 5 (January 1968), 14–17.

15. W. J. Baumol, "Enlightened Self-Interest and Corporate Philanthrophy," *Foundations, Private Giving and Public Policy: Report and Recommendations of the Commission on Foundations and Private Philanthropies* (Chicago, Illinois: University of Chicago Press, 1971), pp. 262–75.

16. James F. Harris and Anne Klepper, "Corporate Philanthropic Public Service Activities," *Research Papers: Commission on Philanthropy and Public Needs,* op. cit., pp. 1741–88.

17. For a review of these see Bette Ann Stead, "Corporate Giving: A Look at the Arts," *Journal of Business Ethics,* 4, no. 3 (1985), 215–22, and Frank Koch, "A Primer on Corporate Philosophy," *Business and Society Review,* 38, 1980, 48–52.

18. Venni v. Commissioner, Tax Court Memo 1984–17, 1/10/84.

19. Davis v. Commissioner, 81 Tax Court No. 49, 10/26/83.

20. Magin v. Commissioner, Tax Court Memo 1982–383, 7/7/82.

21. The value of the gift is the difference between the exercise price and the fair market value of the property at the time the option is exercised.

22. See the discussion of the attribution rule in Chapter 4.

23. A donation could not be made of the legs of the horse while the owner keeps the body. The property may be made up of a single item or many items.

24. The value of the easement is the difference between the market price before the easement and the price after the easement. The easement tends to reduce the price of the property by restricting its use and market.

25. Properites such as this are best passed on by creating a trust. As we shall see in Chapter 11, these rules are aimed at preserving the property for the person with the remainder interest.

26. Revenue Ruling 84–132, 1984–1 Cumulative Bulletin.

27. Revenue Ruling 67–246.

28. The principal on the debt is deductible as a gift, but the interest is not since the interest is otherwise deductible as other interest payments are.

29. See Chapter 6.

30. The current penalty is 30 percent of the true tax liability.

31. Depreciation is a deductible allowance for the use of capital in production of income. Excess depreciation is the difference between a constant sum taken every year and one that assumes that the rate of use of capital per year is largest in the first years.

32. It is true that most times capital gains are not taxable to nonprofits. However, this example is not unlikely if the gift is to a private foundation holding it as an investment, if the property is acquired by debt as that concept is defined in Chapter 6, and if the property is part of an inventory. Any of these could lead to the results stated.

33. Long-term capital gain property must be held for six or more months.

34. Kathleen Teltsch, "Stores' Sale is Bonanza for Altman Foundation" *The New York Times,* Sunday, October 20, 1985, p. 52.

35. Adjusted gross income is essentially all of one's income except such items as workmen's compensation, insurance proceeds, individual retirement account contributions, and certain expenses such as moving expenses.

36. This term is fully defined in Chapter 6.

37. "Large" simply means sufficient to affect the classification of the nonprofit. The number of dollars that may be large for one organization may be small for another.

REFERENCES

American Association of Fund-Raising Counsel, Inc., *Giving in U.S.A.* (New York: American Association of Fund-Raising Counsel, issues from 1978–1984).

American Institute of Certified Public Accountants, *Tax Planning Tips* (New York: AICPA, produced annually).

ANDERSEN, ARTHUR AND COMPANY, *Tax Economics of Charitable Giving*, 8th ed. (Chicago: Arthur Andersen & Co., 1982).

DIAMOND, S. J., " ' Chickadee': Bird in Hand for Charities," *Los Angeles Times*, Friday, April 5, 1985, pp. 1 and 12.

The Funding Exchange, *Gift Giving Guide* (New York: Fund Exchange, 1981).

GOLDBERG, STEPHEN, *Taxation of Charitable Giving*, (New York: Practicing Law Institute, 1973).

HOPKINS, BRUCE R., *Charitable Giving and Tax-Exempt Organizations: The Impact of the 1981 Tax Act* (New York: Wiley, 1982).

HOPKINS, BRUCE R., *Charity under Siege: Government Regulation of Fund Raising* (New York: John Wiley, 1981).

Internal Revenue Service, Department of the Treasury, Determining the Value of Donated Property, Publication 561 rev. November 1983, (Washington, D.C.: U.S. Government Printing Office, 1983).

Internal Revenue Service, Department of the Treasury, Charitable Contributions, Publication 526 rev. November 1983, (Washington, D.C.: U.S. Government Printing Office, 1983).

Internal Revenue Service, Department of the Treasury, Tax Information on Corporations, Publication 542 rev. November 1983.

Internal Revenue Service, Department of the Treasury, Federal Estate and Gift Taxes, Publication 448 rev. May 1982.

ELEVEN

Strategies for Large Gifts: Trusts, Wills, Annuities, Life Insurance and Endowments

A sophisticated money-raising campaign must do more than appeal for cash or property that the potential donor can immediately surrender. Many donors rightfully wish to make a gift of property that they are totally unwilling to surrender any time in the near future. Trusts, wills, insurance, and annuities are instruments that accommodate such desires. They permit the donor to defer the actual transfer of the gift until some future date while getting an immediate benefit either in the form of tax savings, the continued use of the property and the satisfaction of having made a charitable commitment. The nonprofit benefits because it does not take the risk that in the future the gift would not be available or that the donor might give it to some other group.

Some donors wish to give larger sums than they can presently afford. An insurance policy is one way in which a small gift may multiply itself several times. In many ways, it is one of the most intriguing forms of making a gift. The American Bar Association Endowment gets gifts from bar members by having them donate the dividends on their insurance policies to the association.[1] Such gifts involve no out-of-pocket expense to the members because the dividends are paid by the insurance company rather than the members.

This chapter is a discussion of sophisticated techniques that can be used to increase the magnitude of giving. They all involve legal and tax technicalities. No person or manager should attempt to implement any of them without very competent legal and tax advice. The reason is that while the law is permissive and encouraging of the use of these techniques, it also requires that specific rules be obeyed. This chapter has been prepared so that the manager of the nonprofit will be in a position to: (1) identify situations when one of these techniques may be appealing to a donor, (2) recognize the specific reasons why a donor may be attracted to a specific technique and what may be the reasons for being leery about it, and (3) identify the benefits to the organization, and the constraints on the organization once a specific technique is adopted. In short, the chapter aims to put the manager in a position to negotiate large and difficult gifts.

THE USES OF TRUSTS: DEFERRED, EXTENDED BENEFITS AND CASH FLOW

A trust is a legal entity created by one or more persons for the purposes of receiving, accumulating, managing and distributing wealth according to an agreement between those persons who create the trust and the trustees who manage the trust. All of this is done on behalf of one or more persons or institutions that are the beneficiaries named by those who created the trust.

The person who creates a trust is called the grantor, creator or donor. The trust may have more than one grantor and may be created by the donation of property or cash. This initial contribution is called the principal, corpus or res of the trust.

The creators select a trustee or trustees to manage the trust according to an agreement signed by the trustee and the creator. This agreement specifies the purpose of the trust, the beneficiaries, the term of the trust, and other conditions required by state law. The trust, like the corporate nonprofit, is a creation of the state.

The trustees may be the nonprofit itself, individuals who may or may not be donors, a bank or a combination of these. A bank may be the custodian or keeper of the corpus. The creator of the trust may serve as a trustee and, in some cases where the beneficiary is some person other than the creator, the creator may be the sole trustee. This is often unwise, however, because any incidence of ownership or control by the creator over a trust could lead to income as well as estate taxes falling on the creator, nullifying any possibility of a deduction since the donor may be construed not to have made a gift.[2]

Like a corporation, a trust is an independent tax and legal entity. It pays its own taxes and is responsible for its own liabilities. As an independent legal entity, a trust has legal ownership over the property entrusted to it. Its relationship to the beneficiary is said to be one of a fiduciary. This means that the obligation of the trustees is to act in ways that promote the interest of the beneficiaries. Violations of this fiduciary relationship can result in civil and criminal charges.

A trust may be simple or complex. A simple trust is one that cannot make charitable contributions, cannot distribute its corpus and must make annual distributions. Naturally, such a trust cannot be used as a vehicle to make gifts to nonprofits. A complex trust, on the other hand, may accumulate income, distribute its corpus, and make charitable donations. A simple trust is automatically converted to a complex trust once it makes a charitable donation, accumulates income, or distributes its corpus. For the purposes of giving, trusts ought to be initially designed as complex rather than simple. Arriving at this status by default or accident is poor planning.

Trusts may be revocable or irrevocable. A nonprofit that obtains a transfer in a revocable trust may have no gift at all because the transfer may be revoked. The donor will receive no tax deduction and indeed will have to pay taxes on the earnings of the trust if it is revocable. Recall from Chapter 10 that revocable transfers are not gifts. Thus, from the vantage point of nonprofits, obtaining contributions by way of trusts means using an irrevocable, complex trust.

Trusts may be created to operate during the lifetime of an individual (inter vivos) or upon death (testamentary). The rules and discussions are for the most part the same. Obviously, a revocable trust becomes irrevocable at death.[3]

Trusts as Charitable Organizations

A nonprofit can be organized as a trust rather than as a corporation. As a charitable organization, the trust must abide by the two central restrictions on corporations: the assets and income cannot be used for the benefit of individuals and when the trust is dissolved, the assets and income must be distributed to a qualified tax-exempt nonprofit. At that point, the rules of control and attribution discussed in Chapter 6 apply.

Specifically, the governing document of a trust that is a nonprofit should contain the following if it is to qualify for tax-exemption.

1. The trustees will have the power to accept and dispose of property according to the terms of the trust, but may not accept property if it requires distribution of the income or principal to organizations that are not charitable.

2. The trustees may accept additional property and distribute such property at their discretion as long as they are for charitable purposes. These distributions may be made through a nonprofit or the trustees may make such expenditures directly. But the donations of a U.S. corporation may not be used for any other purpose than one in the U.S. Further, no distribution shall inure to the benefit of individuals or may be used in political campaigns, and no substantial part may be used to influence legislation.

3. The trust will exist in perpetuity unless the trustees determine otherwise. The donor authorizes them to use the funds to create a nonprofit corporation if the trust is dissolved.

4. The trustees may amend the trust.

5. No less than two trustees are permitted.

6. The trustees have the power to invest, sell, hold, exchange, lease, or borrow any type security, and to execute contracts, to vote, to reorganize, to employ a bank and to use investment advisors.

7. The powers of trustees are exercisable only in a fiduciary capacity.

8. Any person dealing with trustees may accept their actions as representing that of the trust and need not inquire further about the representation.

9. The declaration of trust is governed by the law of the state in which the trust is created.

This last provision is worthy of additional note because it does affect the actual operation of the trust in the interpretation of some of the items previously enumerated. For example, the state may restrict the types of investments a trust may make. Generally, these restrictions are intended to prohibit risky investments or investments in the business of the trustees.

A trust that is a charitable organization is bound by the rules that cover private foundations. This is so even if the trust becomes a public charity. This means that trusts are bound by rules of self-dealing, they have to pay taxes as do private foundations, and so on. The purpose is to protect the assets and income of the trust against abuse and invasion for individual benefits. Thus, the trustees are bound not merely by the general rules of trusts and the particular stipulations of trust agreement, but by the rules of a private foundation as well.

A special example of a trust is the community trust. A community trust, unlike the community chest, is a trust normally started by one or two individuals. It may subsequently become a public trust by passing the one-third public support test, by having an organizing document stipulating the conditions mentioned before, or by passing the facts and circumstances test. A community trust may be one single entity, or it might be a composite of individual trusts. Unlike a community chest, it does not have to carry on a campaign to gain a large number of small contributions.

A trust as a nonprofit organization may be created by one or more persons. It may specifically designate one or more charitable beneficiaries and it need not receive additional donations. The task of the trustee is principally to manage the principal so that it grows and to distribute it prudently or according to the trust agreement among the stated beneficiaries. Again, once such a trust is created having only charitable beneficiaries, it immediately becomes a "charitable" trust and is subject to the rules governing private foundations.

Trusts for Future, Remainder and Partial Interests

In another vein, trusts can be used to make partial, future, and split-interest gifts (gifts that are split between a charitable and a noncharitable beneficiary). Only through a unitrust, annuity trust or pooled trust can such gifts be deductible.[4] When a trust is used to split interests between a charity and a noncharity, it may operate as a regular trust that is not subject to the special tax-exempt rules of nonprofits until such time that the interests of the noncharity are exhausted. The trust is treated as a private foundation and subject to all the stringent rules discussed in Chapter 6.

A basic characteristic of unitrusts, annuity trusts and pooled trusts is that it distinguishes between remainder interest (what is left after the occurrence of some event, usually the passage of 20 years or death) and the income interest, the annual earnings and distribution. One of these interests is kept by the donor or given to someone other than a nonprofit, and the other interest is given to the nonprofit.

In those trust arrangements where the donor or a noncharity receives the income leaving the remainder to the nonprofit, the trust is referred to as an income trust. In these cases, the charity is the remainderman; it gets what is left of the principal or corpus of the trust. The charitable lead trust is one where the nonprofit gets the income and the donor or the designated noncharitable beneficiary gets the remainder of the principal or corpus.

Essentially, then, a trust permits a donor to give a property and still enjoy it or to give it to more than one beneficiary (only one of which is a charity) and in both cases get an immediate income tax deduction. Obviously, the trust is a useful money-making tool.

Recall our discussion of incomplete or partial transfers in Chapter 10. With the exception of a primary residence or farm, transfers that are partial or of future interest do not qualify as gifts and are therefore not deductible. Without the possibility of a tax deduction, the person may prefer not to give the property. How can a tax benefit be arranged?

Moreover, there are times when the donor wishes to continue enjoying the property and would prefer to relinquish it at a time in the distant future. The nonprofit, on the other hand, is eager to obtain the property as a gift. How can a deal be arranged?

A trust can solve these types of problems. They can satisfy both the interests of the potential donor and the interests of the nonprofit. The trust can provide for a gift to be split between a beneficiary that is a charity and one that is not. It can provide for a property to be given but still enjoyed by the donor and it can do this while getting the donor an immediate tax deduction for a property not fully relinquished.

From a tax perspective, a trust does the following for the donor. It provides for an immediate deduction of the present value of the gift. It solves an estate tax problem by removing the property from the donor's estate. At the same time it allows the donor to receive some benefits from the property (even though it has been given away) or to assign some benefits to others, such as a relative or a friend.

To illustrate, Angela wishes to make a gift of $1,000,000 to a nonprofit but knows the needs of her parents. It is possible to arrange to have the money set aside to produce a steady stream of income for her parents and at the end of their lives the remainder could be donated to her favorite nonprofit.

Remainder Trusts

There are three types of remainder trusts, each of which permits the donor to make a contribution to a charity, get an immediate tax deduction on that contribution, and still get an annual income from the gift or to provide an annual income for a spouse, children or some other beneficiary that is not a charity for a period up to 20 years or for the remainder of their lives. Some or all of this income may be free from taxes. Hence, it is possible for the donor not only to get a tax deduction, but also a tax-free income for life or for the life of a beneficiary including a spouse.

At the termination of the designated period, the remainder that is left in the trust will go to the charity. The donor may even be a trustee of the trust, thus having some influence over its investment policy. The trust may even carry the donor's name.

There are three types of remainder trusts: an annuity trust, a unitrust, and a pooled income trust. Let us see how each works.

A remainder trust that is in the form of an annuity trust is one that offers the donor or some other designated beneficiary or beneficiaries the income generated by the trust. Remember the donor may designate himself or herself as a beneficiary. They receive the income for a term that cannot exceed 20 years or for the life or lives of the donor and/or one or more beneficiaries alive at the time the trust is made. Accordingly, the donor and the spouse may receive the income from the trust for their lives; or, the donor may choose to give the income from the trust to a child for a period not to exceed 20 years or for the life of the child. In short, the donor has a choice of whom and how many beneficiaries he or she may wish to give the income of the trust, and that gift can be made over the life or lives of the individual(s) or for a specific period of time called a term.

All or part of the income received by the donor or beneficiaries might be tax free. This is so if the trust is funded by the use of securities such as municipal bonds that are tax exempt. It is also the case when part of the income is a return of the original investment of the donor. This part of the original investment is not taxed. (See inserts on p. 254)

Once the annuity trust is created, however, no further contributions can be made to it. And the amount of income that will be given to each person must be at least 5 percent of the value of the assets of the trust at the time it is created. This amount must be paid to the income beneficiaries at least once a year.

As long as the trust does not invest in an unrelated business, its income is not taxed. If it does so invest, all its income, not just the portion coming from the unrelated business, is taxed. In any period, when the income of the trust exceeds that which is necessary to make the payments to the beneficiaries, a donation can be made to charity. Thus, it is possible for the charity to also

Loyal alumnus and long-time University supporter Ben Dyer (ENGR '31) recently made an important move, both for himself and for the University of Maryland Foundation. He gave a planned gift of real estate that is expected to bring more than $1 million to the University of Maryland.

The arrangement illustrates the benefits of a new gift plan offered by the University of Maryland Foundation. In the tailor-made plan for Mr. and Mrs. Dyer, their Howard County home and farm—Hickory Hill—was given in trust to the UM Foundation and subsequently sold to a third party. To facilitate the sale of the property, the Foundation was able to provide favorable financing to the buyer.

"Ben Dyer has made a wonderful gift to his University. I am pleased that the Foundation could offer exactly the right program to meet his needs," said University President John S. Toll. "The Foundation's planned gift program is designed to help our friends support the University in ways that are most beneficial to them by helping to develop estate plans that will preserve capital and enable donors to make a maximum philanthropic contribution."

The Dyers might have sold Hickory Hill outright, used the proceeds to buy their new home, and invested the remainder. But federal and state tax liabilities on a direct sale would have been substantial. Mr. Dyer had built the impressive stone house on the 225-acre farm 30 years ago and faced a sizable capital gains tax on the appreciation.

Many years ago, Mr. Dyer arranged for a bequest in his Will to leave a considerable part of his estate to the University of Maryland. By arranging a lifetime gift, he was able to accomplish that objective as well as to gain immediate benefits.

In a "bargain sale" gift arrangement made through the Foundation, Mr. and Mrs. Dyer were able to:
- Receive cash to purchase a new home and to pay moving and other expenses.
- Receive a life income from $1 million in trust funds.
- Reduce capital gains liability.
- Receive a substantial charitable income tax deduction.

The arrangement established two trust funds. Both trusts will pay income for life to the Dyers and then come to the University. Their income will be a fixed percentage of the principal in the trust funds. As the principal grows, the dollar amount of their income will increase, providing a hedge against inflation.

One of the trusts is set up so that the principal can be used, if necessary, during their lifetimes as emergency protection.

For more than a quarter of a century, Hickory Hill has been the site of the annual College of Engineering Alumni Bull Roast. Happily, the new owners have agreed to continue that wonderful tradition.

A 1931 graduate of College Park, Mr. Dyer received the Distinguished Engineering Alumnus Award in 1970. He is a charter member of the Presidents Club, a member of the M Club and the Heritage Club, and a past president of the Terrapin Club.

Source: *Milestones, The University of Maryland Foundation Newsletter,* 2, no. 3 (February 1986), p. 1.

be receiving annual donations from the trust (although this amount is not tax deductible by the donor). Moreover, part of this excess income could also go to the income beneficiaries as long as it is to cover a shortfall in the payment they received in a past year.

Because the income that the donor and other income beneficiaries receive is a fixed proportion of the value of the assets at the time the fund is created,

Trustee Ralph J. Tyser, president of Globe Distributing Company in Alexandria, VA, has used municipal bonds to fund a trust that will bring $235,000 to UM. He will receive a lifetime, tax free income, in addition to an income tax deduction.

Milestones, The University of Maryland Foundation Newsletter, 2, no. 2, (November 1985), p. 4.

they do not participate in the growth of the assets; conversely, if the value of the assets decline, they do not suffer. If the initial value of the assets is $1,000,000, 5 percent is $50,000 and $50,000 is received regardless of whether or not the value of the assets increases. If the assets decline, $50,000 is still owed and any shortfall can be made up in future years.

This brings us to an important point. No tax deduction of the gift is gotten by the donor unless there is a strong (at least 5 percent probability as calculated by special IRS tables) that the assets in the charity will not be used up so that at the end of the term or the lives of the income beneficiaries, nothing will be left for the charity.

In times past, donors would arrange the trust so that they or their relatives who held the income interests would exhaust both the income and the principal of the trust so that eventually there was nothing left for the charity. Today, this is less likely. For one, both the unitrust and annuity trust require that the amount or percentage to be paid be stated when the trust is created and that this amount be set so as not to deplete the trust. Second, trust agreements often provide that capital gains should not be distributed but added to the principal of the trust. Hence, if a trust included among its holdings a property that was worth $1,000,000 at the time it was received, if that property is later sold for $1,200,000, the $200,000 gain is added to the principal of the trust and not distributed to the person or entities holding the income interests. Third, the fiduciary rules require that the remainder interest always be protected.

Despite this fact, however, the annuity trust does pose a risk for the charity. Because the income is based on the value of the assets at the opening of the trust, some trust assets may have to be sold to keep that promise in years when the earnings of the trust are not sufficient to meet its payments to the beneficiaries and if they are unwilling to wait to make up the difference. Because of this fact, annuity trusts tend to invest in securities that maintain their value or provide a steady stream of income, at least to cover the amount the trust must pay annually to the donor or other designated beneficiaries.

Recall that the income from the annuity trust was based on a predetermined percentage or amount of the value of the assets at the time the trust was created. The unitrust is different on this point. It too is a remainder trust with all of the characteristics of an annuity trust except that the amount it pays is determined annually. That is, the trust is valued annually, and a fixed amount of that value (as determined each year), is paid to the income beneficiaries. Thus, if the value goes up, the amount they receive goes up. If the value goes down, the amount they receive declines. Thus, the unitrust trades off the possibility of greater amounts of annual income (if the assets grow) or for less income (if the assets decline). An annuity trust does just the opposite.

In addition, a unitrust provides that the donor may make annual contributions to the trust. Furthermore, unlike the annuity trust, the unitrust can protect the interest of the charity by having a clause written into the trust agreement that says that the donor or the beneficiaries are paid only from the income of the trust. This is not permitted with an annuity trust. This clause is important because it means that the assets of the trust do not have to be sold in order to meet the required annual payments to the beneficiaries.

Still a third type of remainder trust is possible. This is a pooled income trust. These trusts are particularly useful when the potential donor does not have sufficient money to justify the cost of setting up and administering a separate trust and investment agreement. How does this work?

The donor makes a gift to the charity, and gets a tax deduction for the gift. The donor can also be named or name some other person or persons as beneficiaries. Unlike an annuity or unitrust, this designation cannot be for a term or number of years; it must be for the life or lives of the individuals.

Also, unlike the unitrust or annuity trust, there is no separate identity. The trust cannot carry the name of the donor because the trust is a pool to which many donors have contributed. Their funds are all co-mingled into one trust. Furthermore, neither the donor nor any beneficiary may serve as a trustee of the trust, and the trust may not invest in tax-exempt securities. One disadvantage of this is that all of the income that the donors or their designated beneficiaries get regularly from the trust is taxable.

The amount of income the donor or beneficiaries get annually is not based on the value of the assets of the trust but on their pro rata share of the trust. Thus, a donor whose contribution makes up 10 percent of the pooled income trust will get 10 percent of the earnings it distributes.

The pooled income trust can be a good tax shelter. To illustrate, a university recently used a pooled income trust to finance the construction of athletic facilities. Being a tax-exempt organization, some of the tax benefits could not be used by the university. The IRS ruled (GCM 30976) that the depreciation expense and the investment tax credit could be passed on to the contributors of the pool. These "expenses" although they were not incurred by the donors could nevertheless be used by them to reduce their taxable incomes. Hence, the donor to a properly structured pooled income trust can get a tax deduction, a regular flow of income, and an "expense" to reduce taxable income.

Charitable Lead Trusts

With the remainder trust, the donor or a designated beneficiary got the annual income and the charity got the remainder that was left after the predesignated period. Is there a technique that might reverse this process so that the charity gets the annual income and the donor or beneficiary gets the remainder? Such an approach would provide a steady and regular annual flow of income into the coffers of the nonprofit. But what would it do for the donor? Why should he or she go along with the proposal?

The technique is called a charitable lead trust. Such a trust provides a steady flow of income to the nonprofit. This trust must also be either in an annuity form (the flow being based on a fixed amount or percentage of the value of the initial assets) or the unitrust form (based upon an annual appraisal of the value of the assets). In either case, unlike the remainder trust, the payments can be less than 5 percent.

As in the case of a remainder trust, the payments to the charity could cover the life of an individual or individuals (either coterminously or consecutively); but unlike the remainder trust, there is no limit to the number of years if the donor prefers to make the payments for a term of years rather than for the life of some person or persons.

What is the appeal to the donor? The charitable lead trust offers four distinct approaches, each with its advantages and disadvantages to the donor. In one approach, the trust is set up and the donor can take a one-time deduction for the gift. The size of this deduction is based on calculations of what the present value of the amount the charity will receive over the years will be. The way the special IRS tables for calculating this deduction works, the deduction will generally be larger the greater the amount and frequency of payments to the charity (called the payout rate) and the longer the period over which this payment is to be made (designated either in terms of years or the lives of individuals).

If this first approach is taken, part of this deduction will be recalled (recaptured) if for some reason the donor should cease to honor the trust. On the other hand, every annual payment the charity gets counts against the 50 or 30 percent individual limit for charitable contributions discussed in Chapter 10. Hence, the donor gets a large one-time deduction covering all of the years that the charity is expected to receive annual payments, but takes the risk of recapture and limits the amount of annual contributions thereafter. For most donors, the recapture possibilities are more serious than the annual limitations because few donors ever legitimately approach that annual limit.

A second approach to setting up a charitable lead trust is to forego the one-time large deduction for annual deductions. This will appeal to only a few potential donors because the law requires that if they take an annual deduction, they must also report the earnings of the trust as theirs. For most potential donors, this will put them in an adverse position because it will increase their income and therefore their tax liability.

A third approach to a charitable lead trust is to set up a trust in which the donor does not by implication or otherwise act as the owner of the trust. In this case, the donor does not have to report the earnings of the trust as his or her own, but neither can the donor take the deduction. This amounts to giving the charity an interest-free loan.

A fourth alternative way of using the charitable lead trust which is the most common is to reduce transfer (estate and gift taxes). For example, a potential donor wishes to make a gift to a charity in the form of an annual payment. The donor can be persuaded to do so by pointing to the fact that a trust can be set up such that at the end of some period, payments to the charity are ended and the remainder of the trust is turned over to a beneficiary. If the trust is well invested so that the annual income is very high and the payments to the charity are correspondingly high, these payments would constitute a deduction so large that they would wipe out the estate tax upon the death of the donor. The benefit of this is that more of the wealth of the donor would be passed on to his or her heirs rather than to the state and federal governments in the form of death, estate or inheritance taxes.

Note that to this point we have talked about the charitable lead trust as providing annual income to the charity. But it can simultaneously provide a flow of income to the donor or beneficiary. The price for doing this is that the deduction will be decreased by the amount that all noncharitable beneficiaries get. Furthermore, these latter beneficiaries can get paid only after the charity is paid, even if some of the assets of the trust must be sold to meet the obligations to the charity. The donor gets no deductions for the sale of assets to meet the obligations of the trust.

EXAMPLES OF THE APPLICATION OF TRUST CONCEPTS

We shall take a look at some illustrations of how some of the concepts concerning a trust may be applied. There are infinite variations; therefore, the wise financial officer learns to consult an expert.

Illustration 1

Myra, who is going to be 44 on April 1, 1985, transfers $100,000 to a pooled income fund, and retains a life income interest in the property. The highest rate of return experienced by the fund in the immediately preceding three years is 9.2 percent. What will be the amount of deductions that Myra can take on her income tax?

Turn to the table on page 259. The factor in the cell referring to age 44 and 9.2 percent is .12167. By multiplying the fair market value of the gift, $100,000 by .12167, we get $12,167, the amount of her deduction. If she is in the 50 percent bracket, she saves $6,083 on her income tax (50 percent of $12,167). But she will get an annual income from the trust. Suppose the trust payed her $4,000 in income the following year.

To calculate the rate of return, her net investment would be $100,000 minus the $6,083 she saved in income taxes. This is $93,917 and the rate of return on her net investment is 4 percent. Thus, she would have made a gift, gotten a deduction, and continued to get a positive rate of return for as long as she lives and as long as the pool earns money. The advantage is even greater if one recognizes that often gifts are made of appreciated property. Thus, she might have made a gift with a market value of $100,000 for which she paid substantially less. Thus, the true rate of return might well exceed 4 percent.

Note that the effects of this transaction depend upon the age of the donor; that is, the donor's life expectancy is the number of years the donor may ex-

TABLE, SINGLE LIFE, UNISEX, SHOWING THE PRESENT WORTH OF THE REMAINDER INTEREST IN PROPERTY TRANSFERRED TO A POOLED INCOME FUND HAVING THE YEARLY RATE OF RETURN SHOWN

TABLE, SINGLE LIFE, UNISEX, SHOWING THE PRESENT WORTH OF THE REMAINDER INTEREST IN PROPERTY TRANSFERRED TO A POOLED INCOME FUND HAVING THE YEARLY RATE OF RETURN SHOWN

(1) Age	(2) Yearly rate of return				
	9.2%	9.4%	9.6%	9.8%	10.0%
5	.01283	.01221	.01164	.01111	.01062
6	.01350	.01284	.01224	.01168	.01116
7	.01425	.01356	.01292	.01233	.01178
8	.01512	.01439	.01372	.01309	.01252
9	.01612	.01535	.01464	.01398	.01337
10	.01724	.01644	.01569	.01499	.01435
11	.01851	.01766	.01688	.01615	.01547
12	.01991	.01902	.01819	.01742	.01671
13	.02139	.02045	.01958	.01877	.01802
14	.02288	.02190	.02098	.02013	.01934
15	.02435	.02331	.02235	.02146	.02063
16	.02575	.02466	.02366	.02272	.02185
17	.02709	.02595	.02490	.02391	.02300
18	.02839	.02721	.02610	.02507	.02410
19	.02971	.02846	.02730	.02621	.02520
20	.03108	.02977	.02855	.02741	.02635
21	.03251	.03114	.02986	.02866	.02755
22	.03402	.03258	.03123	.02998	.02880
23	.03562	.03410	.03269	.03137	.03014
24	.03735	.03577	.03428	.03290	.03159
25	.03927	.03761	.03605	.03459	.03322
26	.04141	.03966	.03803	.03649	.03505
27	.04377	.04194	.04023	.03861	.03710
28	.04639	.04447	.04267	.04098	.03938
29	.04922	.04721	.04532	.04354	.04187
30	.05228	.05017	.04819	.04633	.04457
31	.05554	.05334	.05126	.04930	.04746
32	.05904	.05674	.05456	.05251	.05058
33	.06279	.06038	.05810	.05595	.05392
34	.06677	.06435	.06187	.05962	.05750
35	.07102	.06839	.06590	.06355	.06132
36	.07553	.07278	.07019	.06773	.06540
37	.08030	.07745	.07474	.07217	.06974
38	.08534	.08237	.07955	.07687	.07433
39	.09065	.08755	.08462	.08182	.07917
40	.09624	.09302	.08996	.08706	.08429
41	.10212	.09878	.09560	.09258	.08970
42	.10833	.10486	.10156	.09842	.09543
43	.11484	.11125	.10783	.10456	.10145
44	.12167	.11795	.11441	.11102	.10779
45	.12880	.12495	.12128	.11777	.11442
46	.13625	.13227	.12847	.12484	.12137
47	.14402	.13991	.13599	.13223	.12863
48	.15214	.14791	.14385	.13997	.13626
49	.16060	.15625	.15207	.14806	.14422
50	.16944	.16496	.16065	.15653	.15257
51	.17862	.17401	.16959	.16534	.16126
52	.18816	.18343	.17888	.17451	.17031
53	.19805	.19320	.18853	.18404	.17972
54	.20825	.20328	.19850	.19390	.18946
55	.21878	.21370	.20881	.20409	.19954
56	.22963	.22443	.21943	.21460	.20994
57	.24081	.23551	.23040	.22546	.22069
58	.25231	.24691	.24170	.23665	.23178
59	.26418	.25868	.25336	.24822	.24325
60	.27640	.27081	.26540	.26016	.25509
61	.28899	.28332	.27782	.27249	.26733
62	.30197	.29622	.29064	.28523	.27998
63	.31533	.30950	.30385	.29836	.29304
64	.32905	.32316	.31743	.31188	.30648
65	.34311	.33716	.33138	.32576	.32030
66	.35751	.35151	.34568	.34001	.33449
67	.37221	.36618	.36030	.35459	.34902
68	.38723	.38116	.37526	.36950	.36390
69	.40257	.39649	.39056	.38478	.37914
70	.41826	.41217	.40623	.40043	.39478
71	.43435	.42827	.42233	.41652	.41086
72	.45084	.44478	.43885	.43305	.42739
73	.46765	.46161	.45571	.44994	.44429
74	.48460	.47861	.47274	.46700	.46138
75	.50155	.49561	.48979	.48409	.47851
76	.51841	.51253	.50677	.50112	.49559
77	.53514	.52934	.52364	.51806	.51258
78	.55177	.54605	.54043	.53492	.52951
79	.56837	.56273	.55720	.55177	.54643
80	.58497	.57944	.57401	.56866	.56341
81	.60148	.59606	.59073	.58548	.58033
82	.61775	.61245	.60723	.60210	.59705
83	.63381	.62863	.62354	.61852	.61358
84	.64974	.64470	.63973	.63484	.63002
85	.66558	.66068	.65586	.65110	.64641
86	.68096	.67622	.67154	.66692	.66236
87	.69542	.69082	.68628	.68180	.67738
88	.70891	.70445	.70005	.69570	.69141
89	.72172	.71739	.71312	.70891	.70474
90	.73422	.73004	.72591	.72182	.71779
91	.74632	.74229	.73829	.73435	.73045
92	.75763	.75373	.74988	.74606	.74229
93	.76791	.76414	.76042	.75673	.75308
94	.77710	.77345	.76983	.76626	.76272
95	.78510	.78155	.77804	.77457	.77113
96	.79183	.78837	.78494	.78155	.77819
97	.79783	.79445	.79110	.78779	.78450
98	.80306	.79975	.79647	.79322	.79000
99	.80797	.80471	.80149	.79830	.79514
100	.81283	.80964	.80648	.80335	.80025
101	.81708	.81394	.81082	.80774	.80468
102	.82165	.81856	.81550	.81247	.80946
103	.82754	.82452	.82153	.81857	.81563
104	.83312	.83017	.82723	.82433	.82144
105	.84165	.83880	.83597	.83316	.83038
106	.85562	.85297	.85034	.84772	.84512
107	.87523	.87288	.87054	.86822	.86591
108	.90652	.90471	.90291	.90111	.89932
109	.95788	.95704	.95620	.95537	.95455

Table G—Table, Single Life, Unisex, Showing the Present Worth of the Remainder Interest in Property Transferred to a Pooled Income Fund Having the Yearly Rate of Return Shown. Source, Internal Revenue Service, *Code of Federal Regulations,* Vol. 26, Part I, Sec. 1.641 to 1.850, April 1, 1985, p. 40.

pect to receive annual or monthly income. It also depends upon the expected payout rate measured by the highest rate of return to the pool in the preceding three years. The higher the expected payout rate, the lower the deduction because the greater the income that a donor will receive. Also the younger the donor, the lower the deduction because income may be flowing to him or her for a considerable period of time. The tax savings depend upon the tax bracket of the donor; the higher the tax bracket the greater the savings. As will be shown by the following illustration, it also depends upon the number of noncharitable beneficiaries and their ages regardless of sex.

Illustration 2

Let us add another complication to the pooled income trust. Assume that Simon decides he would like to make a contribution of $100,000 to a pooled income trust but that the income should go to his two daughters prior to the remainder being turned over to the charity. What will his deduction be?

Assume that his two daughters, Emeline and Celes, are 35 and 30 years of age, respectively. Then we must take both of these ages into account because we are concerned not only with the life expectancy of one person, but of two persons jointly. Assume also that the highest rate of return experienced by the pooled trust in the preceding three years was 9.2 percent. Turn to Table E(2) Part 4, on p. 261. The factor is .02043 so his deduction would be $2,043. But both of his children will receive annual incomes equalling their share of the earnings of the pooled trust for the remainder of their lives.

Note that in both of these cases, the nonprofit gets $100,000 and its payments to the donor or his designees are dependent upon the earnings of the investment made with the $100,000. In a pooled trust, the annuity to the donor or his designees is for life. Recall that the income that noncharitable beneficiaries get will be taxable as ordinary income.

Illustration 3

Let's assume that Roy decides to make a gift of $100,000 to a charitable remainder unitrust. The trust instrument requires that the trustee pay at the end of each taxable year of the trust 5 percent of the fair market value of the trust assets as of the beginning of the trust's taxable year to his son, Rene, for life, and then to his son, Robert, for life. Robert is 35, and Rene is 30. What will the deduction be for Roy? The factor in Table E(2) Part 2 on p. 262 is .09193 so the deduction will be $9,193. All of the arguments stated above about Myra and Simon apply except that in the case of income flowing to the noncharitable beneficiaries, Rene and Robert, are not necessarily treated as ordinary income. They may be totally or partially tax free.

Table E(2)—Part 4

Yearly Rate of Return

O	Y	8.2%	8.4%	8.6%	8.8%	9.0%	9.2%	9.4%	9.6%	9.8%	10.0%
34	5	00890	00812	00742	00679	00622	00570	00523	00481	00443	00408
34	6	00936	00855	00782	00715	00656	00602	00552	00508	00468	00431
34	7	00985	00900	00824	00754	00692	00635	00583	00537	00494	00456
34	8	01037	00948	00868	00796	00730	00670	00616	00567	00523	00482
34	9	01092	00999	00915	00839	00771	00708	00651	00600	00553	00510
34	10	01150	01053	00965	00886	00814	00748	00689	00635	00585	00540
34	11	01210	01109	01017	00934	00859	00790	00728	00671	00620	00572
34	12	01274	01168	01072	00985	00907	00835	00769	00710	00656	00606
34	13	01339	01229	01129	01039	00956	00881	00813	00750	00693	00641
34	14	01407	01293	01188	01094	01007	00929	00857	00792	00732	00678
34	15	01477	01358	01249	01150	01060	00978	00903	00835	00772	00715
34	16	01548	01424	01311	01208	01114	01028	00950	00879	00813	00753
34	17	01622	01492	01375	01268	01170	01080	00999	00924	00856	00793
34	18	01697	01563	01440	01329	01227	01134	01049	00971	00899	00834
34	19	01775	01635	01508	01392	01286	01189	01100	01019	00945	00876
34	20	01855	01711	01579	01458	01348	01247	01154	01070	00992	00921
34	21	01938	01789	01652	01527	01412	01307	01211	01122	01041	00967
34	22	02025	01869	01728	01598	01478	01369	01269	01177	01093	01015
34	23	02114	01953	01806	01671	01548	01434	01330	01235	01147	01066
34	24	02206	02040	01888	01748	01620	01502	01394	01294	01203	01119
34	25	02302	02130	01972	01827	01695	01572	01460	01357	01262	01174
34	26	02401	02223	02060	01910	01773	01646	01530	01423	01323	01232
34	27	02503	02320	02151	01996	01854	01723	01602	01490	01388	01293
34	28	02609	02419	02245	02085	01938	01802	01677	01561	01455	01357
34	29	02717	02522	02342	02177	02024	01884	01754	01635	01524	01422
34	30	02828	02627	02442	02271	02114	01969	01834	01711	01596	01491
34	31	02942	02735	02544	02368	02205	02055	01917	01789	01670	01561
34	32	03057	02844	02648	02467	02299	02144	02001	01869	01747	01633
34	33	03175	02956	02754	02568	02395	02236	02088	01952	01825	01708
34	34	03295	03070	02863	02671	02493	02329	02177	02036	01906	01785
35	0	00871	00803	00741	00685	00634	00588	00546	00508	00473	00442
35	1	00752	00686	00627	00574	00526	00482	00443	00407	00375	00346
35	2	00785	00716	00654	00599	00548	00503	00462	00425	00391	00360
35	3	00823	00751	00686	00628	00575	00528	00485	00446	00410	00378
35	4	00864	00789	00722	00660	00605	00555	00510	00469	00432	00398
35	5	00909	00831	00760	00696	00638	00585	00538	00495	00456	00420
35	6	00957	00875	00801	00733	00673	00618	00568	00523	00482	00444
35	7	01007	00921	00844	00774	00710	00652	00600	00552	00509	00470
35	8	01061	00971	00890	00816	00749	00689	00634	00584	00539	00497
35	9	01117	01023	00938	00861	00791	00728	00670	00618	00570	00527
35	10	01177	01079	00990	00909	00836	00770	00709	00654	00603	00558
35	11	01239	01137	01044	00959	00883	00813	00749	00692	00639	00591
35	12	01305	01198	01101	01012	00932	00859	00792	00732	00676	00626
35	13	01373	01261	01160	01067	00983	00907	00837	00774	00715	00662
35	14	01443	01327	01221	01124	01037	00957	00884	00817	00756	00700
35	15	01515	01394	01283	01183	01091	01008	00931	00861	00798	00739
35	16	01589	01463	01348	01243	01147	01060	00980	00907	00840	00779
35	17	01665	01533	01414	01305	01205	01114	01030	00954	00884	00820
35	18	01743	01606	01482	01368	01264	01169	01082	01003	00930	00863
35	19	01823	01682	01552	01434	01326	01227	01136	01053	00977	00907
35	20	01907	01760	01625	01503	01390	01287	01193	01106	01026	00953
35	21	01994	01841	01701	01574	01457	01350	01251	01161	01078	01002
35	22	02083	01925	01780	01648	01526	01415	01312	01218	01132	01052
35	23	02176	02012	01862	01725	01598	01482	01376	01278	01188	01105
35	24	02272	02103	01947	01805	01674	01553	01443	01341	01247	01161
35	25	02372	02197	02036	01888	01752	01627	01512	01406	01309	01219
35	26	02476	02295	02128	01975	01834	01704	01585	01475	01373	01280
35	27	02583	02396	02223	02065	01919	01785	01661	01546	01441	01344
35	28	02694	02500	02322	02158	02007	01868	01740	01621	01512	01411
35	29	02808	02608	02424	02255	02099	01954	01821	01698	01585	01480
35	30	02924	02718	02529	02354	02192	02043	01906	01778	01661	01552
35	31	03044	02832	02636	02456	02289	02135	01993	01861	01739	01626
35	32	03166	02947	02746	02560	02388	02229	02082	01946	01820	01703
35	33	03290	03066	02858	02667	02490	02326	02174	02033	01903	01782
35	34	03416	03186	02973	02776	02593	02424	02268	02123	01988	01863
35	35	03545	03308	03089	02887	02699	02525	02364	02214	02075	01946
36	0	00896	00827	00764	00707	00655	00609	00566	00527	00492	00460
36	1	00769	00702	00642	00588	00539	00495	00455	00419	00386	00357
36	2	00802	00732	00670	00613	00562	00516	00474	00437	00402	00371
36	3	00841	00768	00702	00643	00590	00542	00498	00458	00422	00390
36	4	00883	00807	00738	00677	00621	00570	00524	00482	00445	00410
36	5	00929	00849	00778	00713	00654	00601	00553	00509	00469	00433
36	6	00978	00895	00820	00752	00690	00634	00584	00538	00496	00458
36	7	01030	00943	00864	00793	00728	00670	00617	00568	00524	00484
36	8	01085	00994	00911	00837	00769	00708	00652	00601	00555	00513

O	Y	8.2%	8.4%	8.6%	8.8%	9.0%	9.2%	9.4%	9.6%	9.8%	10.0%
36	9	01143	01048	00961	00883	00812	00748	00689	00636	00587	00543
36	10	01204	01104	01014	00932	00858	00790	00729	00673	00622	00575
36	11	01268	01164	01070	00984	00907	00836	00771	00712	00659	00610
36	12	01336	01227	01129	01039	00958	00883	00816	00754	00698	00646
36	13	01406	01291	01190	01096	01011	00933	00862	00797	00738	00684
36	14	01479	01361	01253	01155	01066	00984	00910	00842	00780	00723
36	15	01553	01430	01318	01216	01123	01037	00960	00889	00823	00764
36	16	01630	01501	01385	01278	01181	01092	01010	00936	00868	00805
36	17	01708	01575	01453	01342	01240	01148	01063	00985	00914	00848
36	18	01789	01650	01523	01408	01302	01205	01117	01035	00961	00892
36	19	01872	01728	01596	01476	01366	01265	01173	01088	01010	00939
36	20	01959	01809	01672	01547	01433	01327	01231	01143	01061	00987
36	21	02049	01893	01751	01621	01502	01393	01292	01200	01115	01037
36	22	02142	01981	01833	01698	01574	01460	01356	01260	01171	01090
36	23	02238	02072	01919	01778	01650	01531	01422	01322	01230	01145
36	24	02339	02166	02007	01862	01728	01605	01492	01388	01292	01203
36	25	02443	02264	02100	01949	01810	01682	01565	01456	01356	01264
36	26	02551	02366	02196	02040	01896	01763	01641	01528	01424	01328
36	27	02663	02472	02296	02134	01985	01847	01720	01603	01495	01395
36	28	02779	02582	02400	02232	02077	01935	01803	01682	01569	01466
36	29	02899	02695	02507	02333	02173	02026	01889	01763	01647	01539
36	30	03021	02811	02617	02437	02272	02119	01978	01847	01726	01615
36	31	03147	02930	02729	02545	02374	02216	02070	01934	01809	01693
36	32	03275	03052	02845	02655	02478	02315	02164	02024	01894	01774
36	33	03406	03176	02964	02767	02585	02417	02261	02116	01982	01857
36	34	03539	03303	03085	02882	02695	02521	02360	02211	02072	01943
36	35	03675	03432	03208	03000	02808	02628	02462	02308	02165	02032
36	36	03813	03564	03333	03119	02921	02737	02566	02407	02259	02122
37	0	00922	00852	00788	00730	00678	00630	00587	00547	00511	00478
37	1	00785	00718	00657	00602	00553	00508	00468	00431	00398	00368
37	2	00819	00749	00685	00628	00576	00530	00487	00449	00414	00382
37	3	00858	00785	00719	00659	00605	00556	00511	00471	00434	00401
37	4	00902	00825	00755	00693	00636	00585	00538	00496	00457	00422
37	5	00949	00868	00796	00730	00670	00616	00568	00523	00483	00446
37	6	00999	00915	00839	00770	00707	00651	00599	00553	00510	00472
37	7	01052	00964	00884	00812	00747	00687	00633	00584	00540	00499
37	8	01108	01016	00933	00857	00789	00726	00670	00618	00571	00528
37	9	01168	01072	00984	00905	00833	00768	00708	00654	00605	00560
37	10	01231	01130	01039	00956	00881	00812	00749	00693	00641	00593
37	11	01297	01192	01097	01010	00933	00862	00797	00733	00679	00629
37	12	01367	01257	01157	01066	00983	00908	00839	00776	00719	00666
37	13	01440	01325	01220	01125	01038	00959	00887	00821	00761	00706
37	14	01514	01395	01286	01186	01095	01013	00937	00868	00805	00747
37	15	01591	01466	01353	01249	01154	01067	00988	00916	00850	00789
37	16	01670	01540	01421	01313	01214	01124	01041	00965	00896	00832
37	17	01751	01616	01492	01379	01276	01182	01095	01016	00943	00876
37	18	01835	01694	01565	01448	01340	01241	01151	01068	00992	00922
37	19	01921	01775	01641	01518	01406	01303	01209	01123	01043	00970
37	20	02011	01859	01720	01592	01475	01368	01270	01180	01097	01020
37	21	02104	01946	01802	01669	01548	01436	01333	01239	01153	01073
37	22	02201	02037	01887	01749	01623	01507	01400	01302	01211	01128
37	23	02301	02131	01975	01832	01701	01580	01469	01367	01273	01186
37	24	02405	02229	02068	01919	01783	01657	01542	01435	01337	01246
37	25	02514	02332	02164	02010	01868	01738	01618	01507	01405	01310
37	26	02627	02438	02265	02105	01958	01822	01697	01582	01476	01377
37	27	02744	02549	02369	02204	02051	01911	01781	01661	01550	01448
37	28	02865	02664	02478	02306	02148	02002	01868	01743	01628	01522
37	29	02990	02782	02590	02412	02249	02098	01958	01829	01709	01598
37	30	03119	02904	02705	02522	02353	02196	02051	01917	01793	01678
37	31	03253	03029	02824	02635	02460	02298	02148	02009	01880	01761
37	32	03385	03157	02946	02750	02570	02402	02247	02103	01970	01846
37	33	03533	03288	03070	02869	02683	02510	02349	02201	02063	01935
37	34	03663	03422	03198	02990	02798	02620	02454	02301	02158	02025
37	35	03807	03558	03328	03115	02917	02733	02562	02403	02256	02119
37	36	03952	03697	03461	03241	03037	02848	02672	02509	02356	02215
37	37	04099	03838	03595	03370	03160	02966	02784	02616	02459	02313
38	0	00949	00877	00813	00754	00701	00652	00608	00568	00531	00498
38	1	00802	00734	00672	00617	00567	00521	00480	00443	00409	00379
38	2	00836	00765	00701	00643	00590	00543	00500	00461	00426	00394
38	3	00876	00802	00735	00674	00619	00570	00525	00484	00447	00413
38	4	00920	00843	00772	00709	00652	00599	00552	00509	00470	00435
38	5	00968	00887	00814	00747	00687	00632	00583	00537	00496	00459
38	6	01020	00935	00858	00788	00725	00667	00615	00568	00525	00485
38	7	01074	00985	00905	00832	00765	00705	00650	00600	00555	00514
38	8	01132	01039	00955	00878	00808	00745	00688	00635	00588	00544

Source: Actuarial Values I: Valuation of Last Survivor Charitable Remainders, Part D: Two-Life Last to Die Pooled-Income Fund Factors, Internal Revenue Service, Publication 723D (9–84), p. 128.

Table E(2)—Part 2

Adjusted Payout Rate

O	Y	4.2%	4.4%	4.6%	4.8%	5.0%	5.2%	5.4%	5.6%	5.8%	6.0%
34	5	06343	05505	04857	04388	03887	03447	03059	02718	02417	02151
34	6	06558	05803	05139	04554	04040	03586	03187	02834	02523	02248
34	7	06780	06007	05326	04726	04198	03731	03319	02955	02634	02349
34	8	07008	06217	05520	04905	04361	03881	03457	03081	02749	02455
34	9	07243	06434	05720	05089	04531	04037	03600	03212	02869	02565
34	10	07484	06657	05926	05279	04706	04198	03748	03348	02994	02679
34	11	07731	06886	06138	05474	04886	04364	03901	03489	03124	02798
34	12	07984	07121	06355	05675	05072	04535	04059	03635	03258	02922
34	13	08241	07360	06577	05881	05262	04711	04221	03785	03396	03049
34	14	08502	07603	06802	06090	05456	04890	04387	03938	03537	03179
34	15	08767	07849	07031	06302	05652	05073	04555	04093	03681	03312
34	16	09033	08097	07262	06517	05852	05258	04727	04252	03827	03447
34	17	09303	08349	07497	06735	06054	05446	04901	04413	03977	03585
34	18	09575	08603	07734	06956	06260	05637	05078	04578	04129	03726
34	19	09850	08861	07974	07181	06469	05831	05259	04745	04284	03871
34	20	10129	09122	08219	07409	06682	06029	05443	04917	04444	04018
34	21	10411	09387	08467	07641	06899	06232	05632	05092	04607	04170
34	22	10697	09655	08719	07876	07119	06437	05824	05271	04774	04325
34	23	10985	09926	08973	08115	07343	06647	06019	05454	04944	04484
34	24	11276	10201	09231	08358	07570	06860	06219	05640	05118	04646
34	25	11570	10478	09493	08604	07801	07076	06422	05830	05296	04813
34	26	11866	10758	09757	08853	08036	07297	06629	06024	05478	04983
34	27	12165	11041	10024	09105	08273	07520	06839	06222	05663	05156
34	28	12465	11325	10293	09359	08513	07747	07052	06422	05851	05333
34	29	12765	11610	10564	09615	08755	07975	07267	06625	06042	05513
34	30	13065	11895	10835	09872	08998	08205	07484	06830	06235	05694
34	31	13364	12180	11105	10129	09242	08436	07702	07036	06430	05878
34	32	13661	12464	11376	10386	09486	08667	07922	07243	06626	06063
34	33	13957	12747	11645	10643	09730	08899	08142	07452	06823	06250
34	34	14250	13027	11913	10898	09973	09130	08361	07660	07021	06437
35	0	05746	05075	04489	03977	03528	03134	02789	02485	02218	01983
35	1	05602	04929	04341	03828	03378	02985	02641	02339	02074	01841
35	2	05783	05094	04492	03964	03502	03098	02743	02431	02157	01916
35	3	05977	05272	04654	04112	03637	03220	02854	02532	02249	01999
35	4	06180	05458	04824	04267	03779	03349	02972	02639	02346	02088
35	5	06392	05652	05002	04430	03928	03485	03096	02752	02449	02182
35	6	06610	05853	05186	04600	04083	03625	03225	02871	02558	02281
35	7	06836	06060	05377	04775	04244	03775	03361	02994	02671	02384
35	8	07068	06274	05574	04956	04410	03928	03501	03123	02789	02492
35	9	07307	06495	05778	05144	04583	04087	03647	03257	02912	02605
35	10	07552	06722	05988	05338	04762	04251	03798	03396	03039	02722
35	11	07804	06956	06204	05538	04946	04421	03955	03541	03172	02844
35	12	08062	07195	06426	05743	05136	04597	04117	03690	03310	02971
35	13	08325	07440	06653	05953	05331	04777	04283	03843	03451	03102
35	14	08592	07688	06884	06167	05529	04960	04453	04000	03596	03235
35	15	08862	07940	07118	06385	05731	05147	04626	04161	03744	03372
35	16	09135	08195	07355	06606	05936	05337	04802	04324	03895	03512
35	17	09411	08452	07595	06829	06144	05530	04981	04489	04049	03651
35	18	09690	08713	07839	07056	06355	05727	05164	04659	04206	03799
35	19	09973	08978	08086	07287	06570	05927	05350	04832	04366	03948
35	20	10260	09247	08338	07522	06790	06132	05540	05009	04531	04101
35	21	10550	09520	08594	07761	07013	06340	05735	05190	04699	04257
35	22	10844	09796	08853	08004	07241	06553	05933	05375	04872	04418
35	23	11142	10076	09116	08251	07472	06769	06136	05564	05048	04582
35	24	11443	10360	09383	08502	07707	06990	06342	05757	05229	04751
35	25	11747	10647	09654	08757	07947	07215	06553	05955	05414	04924
35	26	12054	10937	09928	09016	08190	07444	06768	06157	05603	05101
35	27	12363	11231	10205	09278	08437	07676	06987	06362	05796	05282
35	28	12675	11526	10485	09542	08687	07912	07209	06571	05992	05467
35	29	12987	11823	10767	09809	08940	08150	07434	06783	06192	05655
35	30	13300	12121	11050	10077	09193	08391	07661	06997	06394	05845
35	31	13612	12418	11333	10346	09448	08632	07889	07213	06598	06037
35	32	13924	12716	11616	10615	09704	08875	08119	07431	06804	06232
35	33	14233	13011	11898	10884	09960	09118	08350	07650	07011	06428
35	34	14541	13306	12179	11152	10216	09361	08581	07869	07219	06625
35	35	14846	13598	12459	11420	10471	09604	08812	08089	07428	06823
36	0	05797	05125	04537	04023	03572	03177	02829	02524	02256	02019
36	1	05640	04966	04376	03861	03411	03016	02670	02367	02100	01866
36	2	05823	05133	04528	03999	03536	03129	02773	02460	02184	01942
36	3	06060	05309	04676	04129	03652	03253	02882	02552	02277	02026
36	4	06225	05501	04865	04307	03816	03385	03005	02671	02377	02117
36	5	06439	05705	05045	04472	03967	03523	03132	02786	02482	02213
36	6	06661	05901	05233	04644	04125	03667	03264	02907	02592	02313
36	7	06890	06112	05427	04822	04289	03818	03401	03033	02707	02419
36	8	07126	06330	05627	05007	04458	03974	03544	03164	02828	02529

Adjusted Payout Rate

O	Y	4.2%	4.4%	4.6%	4.8%	5.0%	5.2%	5.4%	5.6%	5.8%	6.0%
36	9	07369	06554	05835	05198	04635	04136	03693	03301	02953	02644
36	10	07618	06786	06049	05396	04817	04303	03848	03443	03084	02765
36	11	07875	07024	06269	05599	05005	04477	04008	03591	03220	02890
36	12	08138	07268	06496	05809	05199	04657	04174	03744	03361	03020
36	13	08406	07518	06727	06024	05398	04841	04344	03901	03506	03154
36	14	08679	07771	06963	06243	05601	05029	04518	04062	03655	03291
36	15	08955	08029	07203	06466	05808	05221	04696	04227	03807	03432
36	16	09234	08290	07446	06692	06018	05416	04877	04394	03962	03575
36	17	09517	08553	07692	06921	06231	05614	05060	04565	04120	03721
36	18	09803	08821	07942	07154	06448	05815	05248	04739	04281	03871
36	19	10093	09092	08196	07391	06669	06021	05439	04917	04447	04024
36	20	10387	09369	08454	07633	06895	06232	05635	05099	04616	04182
36	21	10686	09649	08717	07879	07125	06447	05836	05286	04790	04344
36	22	10988	09934	08984	08130	07360	06666	06041	05477	04969	04510
36	23	11295	10222	09256	08385	07599	06890	06250	05673	05151	04680
36	24	11605	10515	09532	08644	07842	07118	06464	05873	05338	04855
36	25	11919	10812	09812	08908	08090	07351	06683	06078	05530	05035
36	26	12237	11113	10096	09176	08343	07589	06906	06287	05727	05219
36	27	12558	11417	10383	09447	08599	07830	07133	06501	05928	05407
36	28	12881	11724	10674	09723	08859	08076	07365	06719	06133	05600
36	29	13206	12032	10967	10000	09122	08324	07599	06940	06341	05796
36	30	13531	12342	11262	10280	09387	08575	07836	07164	06552	05995
36	31	13857	12653	11557	10560	09653	08827	08075	07390	06765	06196
36	32	14182	12963	11853	10842	09920	09081	08315	07617	06981	06400
36	33	14506	13272	12148	11123	10188	09336	08557	07847	07198	06606
36	34	14827	13581	12443	11405	10457	09591	08800	08077	07417	06813
36	35	15147	13887	12736	11685	10724	09846	09043	08308	07637	07022
36	36	15464	14191	13028	11964	10991	10101	09286	08540	07857	07231
37	0	05848	05175	04585	04069	03616	03219	02870	02564	02294	02055
37	1	05678	05002	04411	03894	03442	03046	02699	02394	02126	01891
37	2	05862	05170	04564	04034	03569	03161	02803	02488	02211	01968
37	3	06061	05352	04730	04185	03707	03286	02917	02592	02306	02053
37	4	06269	05542	04905	04345	03853	03420	03038	02703	02406	02145
37	5	06486	05742	05088	04512	04006	03560	03167	02820	02513	02243
37	6	06711	05949	05278	04687	04166	03707	03301	02943	02626	02345
37	7	06942	06163	05475	04868	04333	03859	03441	03071	02743	02453
37	8	07182	06384	05679	05056	04505	04018	03587	03205	02866	02566
37	9	07429	06612	05890	05251	04685	04183	03739	03345	02994	02683
37	10	07683	06847	06108	05452	04870	04355	03897	03490	03128	02806
37	11	07944	07090	06332	05660	05063	04532	04060	03641	03267	02935
37	12	08212	07339	06563	05874	05261	04715	04230	03797	03412	03068
37	13	08485	07593	06800	06093	05464	04904	04404	03958	03560	03205
37	14	08763	07852	07041	06317	05672	05096	04582	04123	03713	03346
37	15	09045	08115	07286	06545	05884	05293	04764	04292	03869	03490
37	16	09331	08382	07534	06776	06099	05492	04949	04463	04028	03637
37	17	09619	08652	07786	07011	06317	05695	05138	04638	04190	03788
37	18	09912	08926	08042	07250	06539	05902	05331	04817	04356	03942
37	19	10209	09204	08302	07493	06766	06114	05527	05000	04526	04099
37	20	10511	09487	08568	07741	06998	06330	05729	05188	04701	04262
37	21	10817	09775	08838	07994	07235	06551	05936	05381	04880	04429
37	22	11128	10068	09113	08252	07477	06778	06147	05578	05064	04600
37	23	11443	10365	09392	08515	07723	07008	06363	05780	05253	04777
37	24	11763	10667	09677	08783	07975	07244	06584	05987	05447	04958
37	25	12087	10973	09966	09055	08231	07485	06810	06199	05646	05144
37	26	12416	11284	10260	09332	08492	07731	07042	06417	05850	05335
37	27	12748	11599	10558	09614	08758	07982	07278	06639	06058	05531
37	28	13083	11917	10860	09900	09028	08237	07518	06865	06271	05732
37	29	13420	12238	11164	10188	09301	08495	07762	07095	06488	05936
37	30	13758	12560	11470	10479	09577	08756	08009	07329	06709	06144
37	31	14097	12883	11778	10772	09855	09020	08258	07565	06932	06355
37	32	14436	13207	12087	11065	10134	09285	08510	07803	07157	06568
37	33	14774	13530	12395	11360	10415	09552	08763	08043	07385	06784
37	34	15110	13852	12704	11654	10695	09819	09018	08285	07615	07001
37	35	15445	14174	13011	11948	10976	10087	09273	08528	07851	07211
37	36	15777	14492	13317	12241	11256	10354	09528	08771	08077	07441
37	37	16105	14809	13621	12533	11535	10621	09783	09014	08309	07662
38	0	05899	05224	04633	04115	03661	03262	02912	02603	02332	02092
38	1	05714	05037	04445	03927	03473	03076	02727	02421	02152	01916
38	2	05900	05207	04599	04067	03603	03192	02832	02516	02238	01993
38	3	06101	05390	04767	04220	03740	03319	02948	02621	02330	02080
38	4	06311	05583	04944	04382	03888	03454	03071	02734	02436	02173
38	5	06531	05785	05129	04552	04044	03596	03201	02853	02545	02273
38	6	06758	05995	05322	04729	04207	03745	03338	02978	02659	02377
38	7	06993	06212	05522	04913	04376	03900	03480	03108	02779	02487
38	8	07236	06436	05729	05104	04551	04062	03629	03245	02904	02602

Source: Actuarial Values I: Valuation of Last Survivor Charitable Remainders, Part C, Two-Life Last to Die Unitrust Factors, Publication 723C (9–84), Internal Revenue Service, p. 46.

Illustration 4

Henry decides to create a charitable remainder trust. The trust instrument requires that 10 percent of the market value of its assets on June 30 of each year be paid to Camila for a period of 15 years. The adjusted payout rate is 10 percent. Turn to the table below. The factor for 10 percent for 15 years is .205891 so the deduction will be $20,589. Notice in this case the trust must pay a specific percentage and that the valuation date of the trust, once chosen, is fixed; in this case, June 30 of each year. Thus, the amount that is received depends upon the value of the trust on that date. If the trust does exceedingly well, say its market value is $400,000 on that date, Camila would receive $40,000. Henry might only have put in a small fraction of the $400,000 which is based on his initial investment, plus the compound rate of growth in the value of the assets. Moreover, only part or possibly all of the $40,000 may be received untaxed.

Table D–Table Showing the Present Worth of a Remainder Interest Postponed for a Term of Years in a Charitable Remainder Unitrust Having the Adjust Payout Rate Shown. Internal Revenue Service, *Code of Federal Regulations,* Vol. 26, Part I, Sec. 1.641 to 1.850, April 1, 1985, p. 119.

TABLE SHOWING THE PRESENT WORTH OF A REMAINDER INTEREST POSTPONED FOR A TERM OF YEARS IN A CHARITABLE REMAINDER UNITRUST HAVING THE ADJUSTED PAYOUT RATE SHOWN

(1) Years	(2) Adjusted payout rate				
	9.2%	9.4%	9.6%	9.8$	10.0%
1	.908000	.906000	.904000	.902000	.900000
2	.824464	.820836	.817216	.813604	.810000
3	.748613	.743677	.738763	.733871	.729000
4	.679741	.673772	.667842	.661951	.656100
5	.617205	.610437	.603729	.597080	.590490
6	.560422	.553056	.545771	.538566	.531441
7	.508863	.501069	.493377	.485787	.478297
8	.462048	.453968	.446013	.438180	.430467
9	.419539	.411295	.403196	.395238	.387420
10	.380942	.372634	.364489	.356505	.348678
11	.345895	.337606	.329498	.321567	.313811
12	.314073	.305871	.297866	.290054	.282430
13	.285178	.277119	.269271	.261628	.254187
14	.258942	.251070	.243421	.235989	.228768
15	.235119	.227469	.220053	.212862	.205891
16	.213488	.206087	.198928	.192001	.185302
17	.193847	.186715	.179830	.173185	.166772
18	.176013	.169164	.162567	.156213	.150095
19	.159820	.153262	.146960	.140904	.135085
20	.145117	.138856	.132852	.127096	.121577

It should be noted that in this example, the income is to flow not for the life of an individual or individuals, but for a specific term. Remainder trusts, unlike pooled trusts, can be set up either for a life or for a specific term. Notice from the table above that the amount that can be deducted varies inversely both with the length of the term and the rate.

These are four simple examples. How a trust operates depends upon the nature of the trust, whether it is a pooled, remainder unitrust or remainder annuity trust, a guarantee trust, or a charitable lead trust and the terms specified in the trust document. For example, a creator of a charitable lead trust could get either a one time or an annual deduction. The latter will depend upon the earnings of the trust and the amount transferred each year to the charity. But to do this, the donor has to report the income of the trust as his or her income. Therefore, the net effect of an improperly constructed trust agreement could be to raise the tax liability of the donor.

Furthermore, each trust has a different set of annuity tables and each annuity table defers according to the age and the number of noncharitable beneficiaries. What is important is for the reader to have a firm grasp of the descriptions and applications of each trust as described in this text. With a good tax and legal consultant specializing in estates and trusts, it is possible to construct trusts that yield a donor a higher rate of return on the gift than he or she was receiving prior to the gift.

Table 11.1 compares and summarizes some of the basic features of the trusts we have discussed. This summary may provide a quick reference to the advantages and disadvantages of these trusts. There are features they have in

TABLE 11.1   Comparison of Advantages and Disadvantages of Trusts by Type

	Type of Trust	Advantages	Disadvantages
Income Flow to Donor, Remainder to Charity	Pooled Income	Small gifts can be placed in pool for more efficient investment management.	Income must flow for life of one or more individuals; not for term. Income usually is fully taxed.
	Remainder Unitrust	Income flows for life of one or more noncharity recipients or for a specified term; some or all of income may be untaxed. Income keeps pace with growth of value.	Because income is percentage of value year to year, income declines if value declines.
	Remainder Annuity	Same as above except income is fixed percentage of initial value. Income is protected against decline in value.	Income does not keep pace with growth.
Income Flow to Charity, Remainder to Donor	Guaranteed (Gift) Annuity	Income is assured.	Assets of nonprofit exposed to need to pay donors guaranteed income.
	Charitable Lead Unitrust	Flow of income to nonprofit keeps pace with growth of trust.	Exposes recipient to tax liability if annual deduction chosen.
	Charitable Lead Annuity	Flow of income to charity not jeopardized by slow growth.	Same as above.

Source: Author.

common. Each provides for a gift to the nonprofit that is deductible by the donor. Some provide for an annuity to the donor or beneficiaries while the remainder goes to the nonprofit. This remainder, depending upon the financial and investment management of the gift, can be substantially larger than the initial gift. This is so because only a portion of the income in many cases will go to the donor. The remainder accumulates and grows with the investment experience of the fund and the appreciated gift by the time it is turned over to the nonprofit.

THE USES OF WILLS: GIFTS DEFERRED UNTIL DEATH

A gift through a will (a bequest) can be easily arranged. All that is basically necessary is a statement in the will to the effect that "I give, devise, and bequeath to. . . . .the. . . . . . .(amount of dollars or name of property)." It is the execution of the will at the time of death that becomes confounding and this can occur for several reasons. Let us start with the well-known case of Howard Hughes. At least 40 wills have turned up as being allegedly written by him. Most are declared forgeries. Hughes died in 1979 and in 1986, after the Supreme Court of the United States had appointed Wade McCree, former Solicitor General, as special master, settlements were being made but not yet complete.

There was even confusion about where Howard Hughes lived and this had an impact on his will. Thus, the estate of Howard Hughes had to pay inheritance taxes to the states of Texas ($50 million in cash) and California ($119 million in cash and real estate), even though the lawyers for the estate had argued that his residence was in the state of Nevada which had no inheritance taxes. Hughes had lived four of his last ten years in Nevada, 40 years in California and was born in Texas, leaving when he was 20 years old and had not been in the state for 48 hours in the 50 years before he died. He had, in an attempt to escape California state taxes, frequently filed papers indicating that Texas was his state of residence.[5]

In a recent case before the Chester County Courthouse in Westchester, Pennsylvania, the 33-year old widow of a millionaire was said to have spent her 90-year old deceased husband's $4 million fortune on personal expenses, travel and gifts. His children and the charities which were named as beneficiaries in his will allegedly lost out because of her spending.[6]

Similarly, upon the death of Ron Hubbard, founder of the Church of Scientology, his will was challenged by a son who was disinherited because he had denounced his father and his church. The will provided for a trust for his wife and four other children and a trust for the church.[7]

A will specifies how an individual's estate (all properties in which the decedent had an incidence of ownership) is to be distributed. A will must generally be written, signed, dated and witnessed. Under some conditions, an oral will may have the force of law. Like a trust and a nonprofit corporation, a will must abide by the laws of the individual state. State laws also determine how property will be treated. For example, some properties are subject to taxation and valuation on the basis of their location (situs) while others are determined on the basis of the domicile of the deceased. State laws vary.

A will names an executor (male) or executrix (female) who is responsible for collecting all properties, paying all taxes and debt, preserving the value of the property, and distributing it according to the desires of the deceased. The executor or executrix, unlike the trustee, is nominated by the deceased but serves at the pleasure and approval of the court.

The court may or may not require that the executor or executrix be bonded. It is customary that the testator (the person to whom the will belongs) would not require bonding. Bonding is insurance to protect the creditors of the estate against the errors of the executor. Executors can be held liable for losses but cannot share in the gains made as a consequence of their actions. Thus, the incentive for most executors is to do the minimum required to expeditiously settle an estate in a reasonable period.[8]

Estates are comprised of probate and nonprobate property. Probate property is distributed according to the terms of a will. Nonprobate property is distributed by the operation of the law or by contract or by agreement. If a property is owned through joint tenancy with the right of survivorship, or through tenancy in the entirety (as these terms were defined in Chapter 10), or subject to claims of the government or creditors, or a spouse, such claims are honored without regard to the instructions in a will.

Wills can lead to disappointments. One source of disappointment is that the property supposedly given by bequest may not be probate property and may pass to another through the operation of the law, some previous agreement, or contract. It may not be the deceased's to give, for example, if the property is owned with rights of survivorship being held by another person.

Disappointment might occur for another reason. Promises in a will are not obligations of the testator. A person might change his or her will at will, so to speak. A nonprofit that was once a beneficiary can be dropped whenever the testator wishes.

Furthermore, the will may be too generous. Rene, who is married, decided to leave all his property to his favorite nonprofit, but this will not work. A spouse, and often children, no matter how disliked, cannot be left with nothing. The spouse may go to court to "take against the will." The court may permit the spouse to take between one-third to one-half of the estate despite the will. The nonprofits might be left out, have a reduced share of the estate and have to wait a long time as legal battles are fought.

Worse yet, the entire will could be invalid. This may result if the will or any codicle (amendment) does not conform with the law. The will may not be signed, dated, or prepared by a person mentally competent and acting freely. There might be a later will. Any of these could cause the will to be invalidated. Even if the will is valid, it may be rescinded if written at the point of death and testator does not die. And even if death occurs, such a will may be rescind-ed if the cause of death is different than anticipated.

Still other problems could occur. If the amount being given is a residual after all other donees and legal and tax matters are taken care of, there might be nothing left. Here again state laws come into play. These laws, known as abatement laws, govern how an estate is distributed when it is not large enough to cover all distributees. When the amount going to a nonprofit is the residual rather than a specific amount taken off the top, there might be nothing for the nonprofit to receive.

Despite these uncertainties, wills are necessary if deathtime gifts are to be made. If a person dies without a will, intestate, no provisions are made by state law for contributions to nonprofits. Distributions are made to a legally married spouse, to children, to parents and to the state. Brothers and sisters may, like nonprofits, get nothing.

Also, gifts occurring at death are more favorably treated than gifts made during one's lifetime. The latter is subject to deductible limits as described in Chapter 10, but there are not limits to how much one may give to a charity at time of death.

Hence, if the property has appreciated substantially, a deathtime rather than a lifetime gift may be advantageous to the donor since there are no limits to the amount that can be given at death and still receive a tax deduction. But there are also advantages to the nonprofit. This is particularly true if the non-profit would be subject to unrelated business income tax on the appreciated value of the property when sold because the property was subject to debt as described in Chapter 7.[9] To illustrate, if Rene purchases a property for $50,000 but paid only $25,000 so that the property is subject to debt and the property appreciated to $200,000, and if he bequeathed the property to his favorite non-profit, the nonprofit will receive it at the value at the time of his death.[10] This value would be $200,000. On the other hand, if the gift were made just before his death, the appreciation upon which the tax would be calculated would be $175,000 ($150,000 in appreciation plus the $25,000 owed).

Finally, deathtime gifts give the donor a lifetime to decide among poten-tial donees and to enjoy the property, secure in the knowledge that he or she will have no use for it after death. Little wonder that the largest single gifts take effect at death.

LIFE INSURANCE: MAGNIFYING THE VALUE
OF SMALL GIFTS

Through life insurance policies, it is possible for persons of modest means to make gifts of hundreds of thousands of dollars. Through insurance, anyone can give well above his or her means. Death benefits are many times larger than the premiums paid.

Many persons have so-called paid-up life insurance policies. These are policies for which the potential donor does not have to pay any annual premiums because they have long been paid up. Hence, a gift of these policies to a nonprofit means that the donor gets a deduction without actually making an out-of-pocket transfer of cash. The organization gets a future value (the face value of the insurance) upon the death of the donor. In the period prior to the death of the donor, the organization gets the cash value (the cash accumulated in the policy over the years).

Insurance also provides a means through which the donor can make regular installment donations. This is the case where the donor makes a gift of a policy that still requires annual payments of premiums; that is, one that is not paid up. In this way, the organization gets a regular commitment for an annual payment—a donation. If the policy is one that accumulates cash value, the organization also gets a valuable pool of funds so that the benefits from the policy are not dependent upon the death of the donor.

Even term policies, those that do not accumulate cash values, are suitable gifts because they are inexpensive. In dealing with term policies, the organization would want to know the term; is it 10, 20, 30, or 100 years? Is it level or decreasing? A ten-year term means that if the donor does not die within ten years, the institution gets nothing. The same holds true for 20, 30 or other similar years. Since most people will not live to be 100, such a term policy does assure some benefits to the organization. The amount of benefits depends upon whether the term is level or decreasing. If the term is level, then the face value at the time the policy is issued is the amount that the organization may expect any time the person dies within the term of the contract.

If the insurance contract is a decreasing term, then the amount that the organization is due upon the death of the donor decreases the older the donor gets. A decreasing 100-year term policy with a face value of $100,000 would be worth approximately $10,000 if the person dies at age 65. Yet the person would only have paid about $7,000 in premiums during that time.

For this small difference, would it not be better to make a direct annual contribution to the nonprofit giving it the advantage of having the money on hand to invest rather than waiting? Not necessarily. The advantages of insurance—even term—over regular donations is that it immediately magnifies the gift. In the above case, if the donor paid the annual premium of say $300 and then died after the first, second, or third or even fifth year, the organization would get approximately $100,000. It would only have cost the donor $300, $600, $900, $1500 in premiums. The organization would have foregone anywhere from $98,500 to $99,700 if instead of an insurance policy the donor had made a direct gift of cash to the organization.

Moreover, an annual premium shifts the burden of fund-raising to the insurance company which sends the donor notices of when the premium is due. It replaces the telephone call from the nonprofit.

Between the paid-up policy and the term policies are other options. The universal life policies are ones that give the donor the option of making the gift in one, four or eight payments. Such policies usually pay very high rates of interest on the cash they accumulate. The amounts accumulated are available to the nonprofit for loans. These loans, with interest usually at approximately 8 percent, never have to be repaid. Neither the interest nor the principal have to be repaid and if not, the amount owed the company is deducted from the face value at the time of the death of the donor. Hence, with a universal life policy, it is possible for the donor to make a single payment that pays up all of the premiums. A female can purchase a $100,000 policy for $22,000 at age 46. In ten years at 12 percent, this policy is worth about $70,000. Universal life policies are flexible and they accumulate sums rapidly both for withdrawals in the form of loans and in the form of proceeds at the time of death. A policy that has a $110,000 value in the first year could double in about six years if the rate of interest paid is 12 percent.

An insurance policy may be used to make a joint gift. Frequently a man and his wife may want to make a joint gift to a nonprofit. If each bought an insurance policy separately, it would be more expensive than if they bought it jointly. The could both give the policy to the nonprofit. This strategy has some peculiarities that call for caution. One is that joint policies often pay only after the last of the two persons has died. Some pay only a portion of the face value after the first has died. Although the death of the first spouse could yield no immediate benefit to the nonprofit, this does not make such a strategy useless. The nonprofit will get some or all of the proceeds eventually; both parties will eventually die and the cash value and collateral value of the policy are always available as long as the organization owns the policy.

Insurance policies also have another advantage. They are safe. Insurance companies are required to carry reserves to cover their potential claims and most insurance companies also engage in reinsurance. This is a process through which companies try not to keep too many high-risk policies on their books. By prior agreement, through reinsurance they sell some of these to other companies. Insurance policies and premiums are also calculated and designed based upon actuarial calculations (the probability that a person of a certain age, sex, health condition would die within a given period). The insurance company is not taking a wild gamble when it insures someone; it is taking a calculated risk.

A gift of insurance must be carefully planned, for an insurance policy that is owned by the donor even if it is being held by the nonprofit is subject to the control of the donor. The beneficiary can be changed. Nothing bars an owner from dropping the name of the nonprofit as beneficiary. If this happens, the nonprofit could not collect even though it may have the policy in its possession. Furthermore, if the policy is owned by the donor he or she may borrow on it. Should that be done and the loan was not repaid prior to the death of the donor, the proceeds that will go to the nonprofit will be the face value minus the amount of indebtedness. In short, the nonprofit could end up with less than the face value if there is outstanding indebtedness.

The outcome could be worse if the owner used the policy as collateral for a loan. In that case, depending upon state law, the creditor of the donor may have first claim. Not only will the amount gotten by the nonprofit be less than the face value, but the nonprofit could get nothing at all if in the process of getting the loan the donor made a permanent assignment of the policy to the creditor. A permanent assignment cannot be reversed; the creditor owns the policy.

Also, an insurance policy that is owned by the donor must be included in his or her estate even though it is in the physical possession of the nonprofit. This could mean that some or all of the proceeds may be taxed, and some or all of the proceeds could be subject to the claims of the creditors or the donor and to claims of the donor's spouse, should the latter choose to take against the will.

These difficulties may not be resolved in favor of the nonprofit even if it could prove that it paid the premiums. Ironically, one possible interpretation of this eventuality is that the nonprofit in its charitable benevolence made a gift to the insured. The point simply is that the nonprofit should own, not merely possess, the policy. It does this by being sure that its name appears on the policy not only as beneficiary but also as owner.

Ownership and possession of the policy by the nonprofit also have another benefit. The nonprofit does not have to wait for the donor to die; for as owner, the nonprofit may assign the policy, use it as collateral for loans, or borrow the cash value of the policy.[11] The nonprofit will also be able to avoid the creditors of the donor and legal fights over the instructions in the will. The policy will be nonprobate property, meaning that it will escape the legal hassle, delays and claims that are likely in the settlement of an estate in accordance with the terms of a will.

From the donor's point of view, when a policy is given makes a considerable amount of difference in the value for tax deduction purposes and in the cost to the donor. The value of an insurance policy that has just been issued is the gross premium paid. If a policy has just been issued to the donor and the premium on it is $500, all that can be deducted is $500. But $500 can buy over a $100,000 in insurance for a person below 35 years of age. The gift to the nonprofit is therefore $100,000.

The tax deductible value of a policy that is fully paid up is its replacement cost at the time the gift is made. Giving a paid-up policy might be a superior strategy for an older person than a younger one, particularly if the policy is one that was taken out many years before and is no longer needed. A newly paid-up policy is expensive.[12]

In between these two extremes, is a policy that is presently being paid for and the value of such a policy is the gross premiums paid by the owner in the past minus the dividends received by the owner, plus the net premiums (gross premiums minus dividends) that will be paid in the future, plus interest earned. This is the amount that can be deducted.

The donor does not have to purchase insurance or use a paid-up policy in order to make a gift. It is possible to make a gift of insurance in the form of the face value in excess of $50,000 in a qualified employee insurance contract as discussed in Chapter 9. Such a gift is not likely to bring any deduction to the donor, but the excess premium is not taxable as income. The employer who pays the excess may deduct it if it is a customary policy of the firm to give in this fashion.

A gift of insurance can also be made in the form of an outright gift of the contract itself. Or, the policy could be placed in a trust. The trust should be irrevocable permitting an immediate tax deduction for the gift.[13] The deduction of premiums can be lost, however, if the trust is not properly set up because an insurance policy in a trust is a future interest since the gift cannot be obtained until the person dies. To qualify the premium payments for immediate tax deduction, the trust agreement should contain a promise to make the premium available to the nonprofit at the time premiums are paid. The nonprofit need not take the money; it must simply have the option to do so.

If the insurance policy is in a trust, there is a second concern; the policy could be considered to have been acquired by debt and, as discussed earlier, lead to unrelated business income tax. To avoid this, the trust agreement should not permit a person who is a noncharitable beneficiary to have an interest in the income of the trust that exceeds that person's lifetime. That is, all such interests should cease upon that person's death so that the remainder goes to the charitable beneficiary rather than being bequeathed by the person to some other beneficiary.

A gift of insurance may also be made through a will at the time of death. The will might provide for the formation of a trust, or for outright gifts of the insurance proceeds to the nonprofit. One of the disadvantages of giving at the time of death is that the proceeds could be taxed as part of the donor's estate. As part of the estate, it is also exposed to the claims of the creditors of the deceased. Also, if the gift is made by a trust that becomes irrevocable at the time of death, the charity is less protected since there is some passage of time after the federal taxes are paid before the trust becomes a charitable trust and subject to the rules covering private foundations. These rules protect the corpus of a trust for charitable purposes.

There is no single best strategy. The best strategy requires sensible financial planning taking the needs of the organization and the desires and financial position of the donor into account. Each strategy that has been mentioned should be considered.

ANNUITIES: PROVIDING INCOME FLOWS

Annuities are merely payments that must be made over a period of time. Unitrust, annuity trusts and pooled trusts all pay annuities. Sometimes the annuity is paid to the donor or a noncharitable designated beneficiary and sometimes it is paid to a charity, as in charitable lead trusts.

In Chapter 9 we discussed the possibilities of a worker giving his or her pension annuity to a nonprofit. Let us return to that discussion briefly. In the giving or receiving of annuities, care must be taken that the potential donor actually owns the annuity. Most pension annuities have a period that must lapse before the accounts are vested and owned by the future annuitant. Until that time has elapsed, the person does not own the balance in the account and is not legally able to donate it, even though the account may be in his or her name. Also, the surviving spouse may have a legal claim on the annuity.

The value of annuities for tax deduction purposes is determined by finding its present value after discounting at a rate (currently 10 percent) recommended by the IRS. Basically, that value is the amount that would have to be invested today at a specific interest rate given by the IRS so that the annuity would be worth the amount promised at a time in the future. This formula is used in calculating an annuity provided by an employer. If there is a going market for the type of annuity to be donated, that is, if the annuity is a commercial one, then the value is its replacement cost.

A final type of annuity, gift annuities, must be mentioned. In the case of gift annuities, the donor gives the nonprofit a large amount of money or property with the understanding that the nonprofit will guarantee a specific annual payment to the donor. The promise to make this payment is backed by all of the assets of the nonprofit. Can you see what happens when the earnings of the pool of money given to the nonprofit are too small to make the payments promised? Yes, the assets have to be liquidated in order to meet the payments.

ENDOWMENTS: PERPETUATING A GIFT

Any of the mechanisms discussed in this chapter and in Chapter 10 may be used for funding an endowment. An endowment is an account that is established to have perpetual life and to finance a specified set of activities. To fund an endowment is merely to put the money or property in it. An endowment can therefore be funded singularly or in combination with outright gifts and contributions, annuities, life insurance, trusts or testamentary gifts.

An endowment serves at least two important purposes. One purpose is to provide a pool of funds to which the organization can turn to in an emergency. As such, it gives some financial basis or stability to the organization.

A closely related use occurs when the endowment is used to cover shortfalls between the expenditures and revenues of the organization. Continuous invasion of an endowment for this purpose, however, is not to be encouraged. This problem should be solved by better financial management.

Second, endowments provide a source of funds that the organization may use to finance activities that are important to it but for which it cannot readily obtain support from outside sources. Many organizations use endowments to finance activities that are innovative, experimental and developmental. When used this way, the endowment serves to push the organization forward. It helps the organization to carry out its mission without having to meet the constraints and demands of an outside funding agency.

All of these ideal uses of endowments can be defeated, however, if the endowment is not properly structured and negotiated with the persons who are its donors. The central problem of most endowments is that they carry restrictions. These restrictions may prohibit certain types of investments, certain uses of the money in the endowment, and so on. Some observers may suggest that small nonprofits ought to avoid endowments because they may be too restrictive. A better alternative is to wisely structure the endowment, to negotiate its terms with the donors, and to manage the endowment well.

Because an endowment is a pool of funds intended to support a set of activities in perpetuity, it has to be managed well. From a financial planning perspective, several important issues must be resolved. A decision has to be made about a custodian. The custodian is the entity, usually a bank, that holds the account and assets of the endowment. A separate decision has to be made about the trustees—who they will be and what powers they will have. These are the persons who, as discussed earlier, are responsible for the administration of the funds such as disbursements and receipts. The funds are entrusted to them. Another decision, often made by the trustees, is who will be the investment managers of the funds. These managers are the persons responsible for determining how the funds will be invested; that is, what securities will be bought and sold and when. Yet another decision is what powers the investment managers will have. Will they have discretionary powers that permit them to use their best judgment without obtaining authorization from the trustees? Should there be more than one investment advisor, each with a portion of the endowment portfolio to manage? This technique is used with large endowments because it generates competition among the investment advisors.

Aside from these issues relating to the structure of the endowment, there are financial issues. Obviously, if an endowment is to provide funds, a target rate of return should be set on the investment of the endowment funds. This target range determines the rate of growth in these funds and the amount that may be expected to be available to the organization. Having set a target rate to guide the investment advisor, a decision must be made as to whether or not only the income of the fund will be available annually to the institution or whether the institution will also be permitted to invade the principal. The most conservative answer is to make only a portion of the earnings (not the prin-

Endowed and Special 4-H Funds

*T*he continuation of the 4-H legacy—developing strong, effective and self-directed citizens—can be guaranteed only by building an endowment that will help insure against fluctuations in government funding and the ability of friends to provide current support. Through THE CAMPAIGN FOR 4-H more than $11,000,000 must be added to the National 4-H Council endowment fund to sustain programs and support new ventures in 4-H work to meet the needs of future generations.

National 4-H Council currently has eight named funds which are part of the endowment and help perpetuate specific 4-H programs.

Kenneth H. Anderson Fund

Established and added to by many friends in honor of this long time staff member of the National 4-H Service Committee who continues to provide volunteer leadership to 4-H youth programs in Arizona and throughout the United States. Income from the fund goes to citizenship and leadership training programs.

Becky and Jay Kaiserman Scholarship Fund

Established in 1984 by Mr. and Mrs. Kaiserman to honor more than 33 years of involvement in 4-H. The income from this fund will be awarded as college scholarships to assist 4-H'ers in pursuing their educational and career goals.

Norman C. Mindrum 4-H Education Fund

Established by friends on the occasion of his retirement in 1981 in honor of the first president of National 4-H Council who continues to provide outstanding service and significant leadership to 4-H. Income from this fund is used to strengthen 4-H programs and to recognize and honor outstanding qualities of leadership and citizenship in 4-H'ers.

Onizuka 4-H Fund For Excellence

4-H members, leaders, parents, staff and friends established this fund to honor Lt. Col. Ellison S. Onizuka, a former 4-H member, and other crew members aboard the space shuttle Challenger. The purpose of the fund is to help 4-H boys and girls develop the pioneering characteristics and personal qualities epitomized in the life of Col. Onizuka. Income from the fund will provide science and technology scholarships to young people and support 4-H leadership development initiatives in the states.

Gertrude L. Warren Memorial Scholarship Fund

Established in 1979 to honor the late pioneer in the 4-H movement and augmented by a gift from her sister, Mary Margaret Warren. This fund provides income for advancing the education of 4-H members.

Thomas E. Wilson Fund

Established in 1948 to honor the late chairman of the National Committee on Boys and Girls Club work, this fund provides income for annual scholarships to 4-H members who achieve good citizenship.

Elaine R. and Paul E. Pitts Fund

To be established through a charitable trust created by Elaine R. Pitts in 1984. This fund honors Mrs. Pitts' many years of 4-H involvement beginning as a Sperry and Hutchinson Company donor representative, as well as her and her late husband's commitment to youth development. Future income from the fund will support teen and adult volunteer leadership development programs.

Edward R. Tinker Charitable Trust

Established by Mr. Tinker, late member of the Board of Trustees of Wilson & Company. One-half of the income goes to the Thomas E. Wilson Fund and one-half to promote Americanism through 4-H programs.

Endowed and Special 4-H Funds, National 4-H Council, Annual Report 1985, Donors Report, Washington, D.C., 1985.

cipal) of the funds available. In that way the fund will not be totally used up and it can still grow even while it is providing ongoing support to the organization.

If this is the decision, the following should be computed: Given the rate of growth in the portfolio, how much can be extracted every year if the endowment is to last forever? Obviously, the structuring and management of endowments are both very technical. Few if any of the most successful managers of nonprofits can by themselves structure and manage an endowment portfolio and none should try. The shrewd ones form good finance committees, appoint savvy trustees and learn the importance of constantly raising the issues as previously stated. They also learn the roles of custodians, trustees, investment managers or advisors and the restrictions placed on them and on the use of the endowments. We shall say more about managing endowments and setting targets for them in Chapters 12, 13, and 14.

VALUATION OF FUTURE GIFTS

The valuation of gifts is of interest to the donor because it determines the amount that can be deducted from federal and state income taxes. It is of interest to the nonprofit financial manager because (1) it must be included among the organization's assets at value. As we shall see in Chapter 13, contributions are assets appearing on the balance sheet of the organization. (2) It may lead to tax and liability consequences if the gift is subject to debt or if it has been so depreciated by the donor that its value in transfer is decreased. For example, a gift that has a market value of $400,000 would be less if the donor owes money on it and the nonprofit assumes the donor's debt. Being a debt-acquired property, it would lead to unrelated business income tax if the property generates income. See our earlier discussion of unrelated business income. (3) Its value, as discussed in Chapter 6 and earlier in this chapter, may be used in the calculation of public support which must be demonstrated in order to retain the tax-exempt status of the organization. (4) Since tax considerations are a major impetus for giving, the amount of deductibility which is directly determined by the value of the gift may be used by the nonprofit to encourage the potential donor to make the gift.

A financial manager of a nonprofit would be unwise to try to determine the value of a gift for a potential donor. Donations are often part of an overall tax strategy of a person or corporation, and the valuation of specific gifts is a special skill. It is, however, important that the manager understand the key variables that determine the values of gifts and how they interact to determine the level of deduction that a taxpayer may take. Knowing this will help the manager to make a deal by appealing to the tax motive for making the gift. As a general rule, the dollar value of the gift in the hands of the donor is its dollar value to the nonprofit at the time of the transfer to the organization. For accounting and tax purposes, the good does not change value simply because it is now in the hands of a nonprofit, although it may change value later due to market appreciation or depreciation.

The basic rule is that the value of the gift is its fair market value. This is the amount that a knowledgeable buyer would voluntarily pay a knowledgeable seller for the property at the time and under the conditions that the property was transferred from the donor to the nonprofit organization. Note that you cannot presume an extraordinary past or future situation to inflate the value of the gift and you cannot assume laissez faire to mean that the property could be sold to an ignorant buyer or to a buyer acting under duress for more. If the property is one that is usually sold through classified ads, then the value is that appearing in such ads on the day of the transfer. If the property is normally subject to retail sale, then its value is the retail price on that date. Further, the transfer between the nonprofit and the person must represent an arm's-length agreement. That is to say, they cannot conspire or use influence to set an artificially high value.

The simple term "fair market value" can be very complex when the gift is made in a form other than an outright and immediate transfer of cash from the donor to the nonprofit organization. A check written for $1,300 by Orvin to his church is a gift valued at $1,300. But what if the gift is in some form other than cash? What if the gift is to pass to the nonprofit at a time in the distant future? What if the nonprofit will be permitted to get the income from a gift and then pass the gift on to Orvin's children upon his death?

There are several factors which would affect the answers to these questions: the age of the donor; the term of the gift; the kind of property being transferred; whether the gift is being transferred to the nonprofit first and then to a noncharity or whether the nonprofit gets the gift only after a noncharitable beneficiary has enjoyed it; the payout rate; and the discount or interest rate that is presumed and the kind of trust being used. Let us discuss some of these factors. Our discussion of trusts introduced their importance to us.

Age is a determinant of the value of the gift whenever the transfer of the gift to the nonprofit is keyed to life expectancy. This is so if the gift is to pass to the nonprofit at the death of the donor or some other person or persons before being transferred to the nonprofit; or if the gift must first be used by the nonprofit and then passed on to some other noncharitable entity or person under the death of the donor. For example, Margaret may elect that a gift be passed on to her church only after her death and her husband's death. This gives both of them the opportunity to enjoy the property during their lifetimes. In this case, the life expectancy of both persons must be taken into account. On the other hand, she may elect to have the church enjoy the benefits of the gift during her lifetime, but require that it be passed on to her husband upon her death since he would need it to sustain life. In this case, only her life expectancy is important.

Life expectancy affects valuation because the longer the noncharitable beneficiary is likely to live, the smaller the contribution that is being made to the charity. If Margaret's gift is to pass to her church at the time of her death and she is only 25 years old, she could live many more years and the contribution to the church, barring a growth in the value of the property, could be very little at the time of her death. Similarly, if Margaret's gift is to pass to the church only after her death and the death of her daughter who is 2 years old, it could be another 60 years before the gift is passed. However, if she is 80 years old and the transfer of the property to the nonprofit will occur at the time of her death, it is conceivable that at her age, the transfer could take place in a reasonably short time. Therefore, the value of the gift for purposes of deduction is closer to its present market value.

The term or the specific number of years that must pass before the gift is transferred works similarly to the age variable. Sometimes a donor will make the gift conditional on the passage of a number of years rather than upon death. The donor may require that 5, 10, 12, etc. years must pass before the gift can be transferred to the nonprofit, or that the nonprofit may have use of the gift for a specific number of years before it must pass it on to a noncharitable beneficiary. The longer the term that the nonprofit may possess the gift, or the shorter the term it has to wait to receive it, the closer is the present market value to its value for the purposes of deduction.

The kind of property determines how its value is calculated. Unimproved real property, land that does not have building and developments that increase its value, is valued at the price paid for it or at comparable sales price of similar geographically located and geologically constituted undeveloped land, subject to the same zoning limitations and development rights on the date of the transfer to the nonprofit. Stocks and bonds are valued at the midpoint between their highest and lowest selling price on the stock exchange on the date of the transfer. If the stock exchanges are closed on that date (weekends and holidays), the most recent last date of its opening is used. Unpaid dividends may also be included in the valuation of the security. If the security is a share of a mutual fund, then the valuation price is the redemption price on the date that the funds are transferred. If the stock or interest in a business is not sold on the exchange, then the price is based upon such factors as its book value (assets minus liability).

If the gift is an annuity regularly sold by a financial company, then the value of the annuity is the price that it is usually sold for by the company. But often the value of an annuity, life estate, remainder of reversionary interests must be calculated by special tables issued by the IRS. An annuity is merely a contract that agrees to pay an annual payment over a number of years. Pension plans are annuities. A remainder interest refers to the transfer of the property to the nonprofit after a passage of time either expressed in a specific number of years (term) or the lifetime of one or more persons. A life estate is an interest for payment during the life of an individual.

The way the good is transferred also affects its valuation for purposes of deduction. As stated earlier, a gift of a future interest, a gift that does not take effect until a time in the future, has no deductible value unless the gift is a conservation property or is transferred through a trust. In the case of an annuity, this is handled by an insurance company. But if a trust is used, the value also differs if the transfer is made through a pooled income, a unitrust or an annuity trust and if it is a charitable lead or charitable remainder trust. The latter usually has very limited deductible value since it often requires that the donor include the income of the trust in his or her own taxable income. These considerations were discussed earlier in this chapter.

Also as stated earlier in this chapter the payout rates have a considerable bearing on the value of the gift. The higher, longer and more frequent the payout to a noncharitable beneficiary, the lower the deductible value of the gift. While we did not demonstrate it earlier, payout must be at least once a year, but can be monthly, quarterly, or semiannually.

The assumed interest rate or discount rate also affects the value of the property. In gifts of future interests, the IRS stipulates that the rate to be used for gifts made after August 8, 1984 is 10 percent; prior to that 6 percent is to be used. It is a mathematical fact that the higher the discount rate, the lower the present value of a gift because the value is being discounted by a greater number.

To understand how these concepts work or interact to determine value, please refer to Table A. Note that the table is based on a 10 percent discount rate (a presumption that the rate of return on an investment is 10 percent). Note that the annuity factors (column 2) get smaller the older the age. A person who is 109 years old is not expected to live very long; therefore, an annuity contract promising to pay such a person a specific sum for the remainder of his or her life is not likely to be worth very much. A gift of such a contract would have a very small present value. Hence, a gift of an annuity of $100,000 payable annually over the lifetime of such a person would be valued at ($100,000 × .4545) or $45,540. On the other hand, a similar $100,000 annuity payable each year over the life of a 25-year-old person would be valued at ($100,000 × 9.6678) or $966,780. Thus, an annuity may provide either a large or small deduction depending upon the age of the donor or the person for whom it is designed.

A life estate given to a nonprofit through a charitable lead trust means that the donor gives the charity the earnings from the property for the duration of a lifetime with the property to revert to a noncharitable donor such as an heir at the time of the donor's death. A donor who is 109 years old is not expected to live much longer. Therefore, a gift of a life estate of $100,000 is worth ($100,000 × .04545) or $4,545.

The value of remainder interest (column 4 of Table A) is also affected by age. Take a gift appraised at $100,000 that is to be enjoyed by a noncharitable beneficiary who is 25 years of age and then pass on to a charity upon the death of that beneficiary. The present value of that gift ($100,000 × .03322) is $3,322 for purposes of tax deduction. The same gift would be worth ($100,000 × .95455) $95,455 if the person is 109 years old. Being that old, the

Table A—10%

1 Age	2 Annuity	3 Life Estate	4 Remainder	1 Age	2 Annuity	3 Life Estate	4 Remainder
0	9.7188	.97188	.02812	55	8.0046	.80046	.19954
1	9.8988	.98988	.01012	56	7.9006	.79006	.20994
2	9.9017	.99017	.00983	57	7.7931	.77931	.22069
3	9.9008	.99008	.00992	58	7.6822	.76822	.23178
4	9.8981	.98981	.01019	59	7.5675	.75675	.24325
5	9.8938	.98938	.01062	60	7.4491	.74491	.25509
6	9.8884	.98884	.01116	61	7.3267	.73267	.26733
7	9.8822	.98822	.01178	62	7.2002	.72002	.27998
8	9.8748	.98748	.01252	63	7.0696	.70696	.29304
9	9.8663	.98663	.01337	64	6.9352	.69352	.30648
10	9.8565	.98565	.01435	65	6.7970	.67970	.32030
11	9.8453	.98453	.01547	66	6.6551	.66551	.33449
12	9.8329	.98329	.01671	67	6.5098	.65098	.34902
13	9.8198	.98198	.01802	68	6.3610	.63610	.36390
14	9.8066	.98066	.01934	69	6.2086	.62086	.37914
15	9.7937	.97937	.02063	70	6.0522	.60522	.39478
16	9.7815	.97815	.02185	71	5.8914	.58914	.41086
17	9.7700	.97700	.02300	72	5.7261	.57261	.42739
18	9.7590	.97590	.02410	73	5.5571	.55571	.44429
19	9.7480	.97480	.02520	74	5.3862	.53862	.46138
20	9.7365	.97365	.02635	75	5.2149	.52149	.47851
21	9.7245	.97245	.02755	76	5.0441	.50441	.49559
22	9.7120	.97120	.02880	77	4.8742	.48742	.51258
23	9.6986	.96986	.03014	78	4.7049	.47049	.52951
24	9.6841	.96841	.03159	79	4.5357	.45357	.54643
25	9.6678	.96678	.03322	80	4.3659	.43659	.56341
26	9.6495	.96495	.03505	81	4.1967	.41967	.58033
27	9.6290	.96290	.03710	82	4.0295	.40295	.59705
28	9.6062	.96062	.03938	83	3.8642	.38642	.61358
29	9.5813	.95813	.04187	84	3.6998	.36998	.63002
30	9.5543	.95543	.04457	85	3.5359	.35359	.64641
31	9.5254	.95254	.04746	86	3.3764	.33764	.66236
32	9.4942	.94942	.05058	87	3.2262	.32262	.67738
33	9.4608	.94608	.05392	88	3.0859	.30859	.69141
34	9.4250	.94250	.05750	89	2.9526	.29526	.70474
35	9.3868	.93868	.06132	90	2.8221	.28221	.71779
36	9.3460	.93460	.06540	91	2.6955	.26955	.73045
37	9.3026	.93026	.06974	92	2.5771	.25771	.74229
38	9.2567	.92567	.07433	93	2.4692	.24692	.75308
39	9.2083	.92083	.07917	94	2.3728	.23728	.76272
40	9.1571	.91571	.08429	95	2.2887	.22887	.77113
41	9.1030	.91030	.08970	96	2.2181	.22181	.77819
42	9.0457	.90457	.09543	97	2.1550	.21550	.78450
43	8.9855	.89855	.10145	98	2.1000	.21000	.79000
44	8.9221	.89221	.10779	99	2.0486	.20486	.79514
45	8.8558	.88558	.11442	100	1.9975	.19975	.80025
46	8.7863	.87863	.12137	101	1.9532	.19532	.80468
47	8.7137	.87137	.12863	102	1.9054	.19054	.80946
48	8.6374	.86374	.13626	103	1.8437	.18437	.81563
49	8.5578	.85578	.14422	104	1.7856	.17856	.82144
50	8.4743	.84743	.15257	105	1.6962	.16962	.83038
51	8.3874	.83874	.16126	106	1.5488	.15488	.84512
52	8.2969	.82969	.17031	107	1.3409	.13409	.86591
53	8.2028	.82028	.17972	108	1.0068	.10068	.89932
54	8.1054	.81054	.18946	109	.4545	.04545	.95455

See *Valuation* in both the *Estate Tax* and *Gift Tax* sections of this publication to determine whether you should use the 6% or 10% tables to value these items.

Table A-10. Source: Federal Estate and Gift Taxes, Publication 448, rev. Sept. 1984, Internal Revenue Service, p. 17.

gift would be expected to pass on very soon and therefore close to its present market value.

Let us assume that instead of using age, we use a specific term; that is, a number of years. Please turn to Table B. First, we see that the upper panel

Table B—6%

Number of Years	Annuity	Term Certain	Remainder	Number of Years	Annuity	Term Certain	Remainder
1	0.9434	.056604	.943396	31	13.9291	.835745	.164255
2	1.8334	.110004	.889996	32	14.0840	.845043	.154957
3	2.6730	.160381	.839619	33	14.2302	.853814	.146186
4	3.4651	.207906	.792094	34	14.3681	.862088	.137912
5	4.2124	.252742	.747258	35	14.4982	.869895	.130105
6	4.9173	.295039	.704961	36	14.6210	.877259	.122741
7	5.5824	.334943	.665057	37	14.7368	.884207	.115793
8	6.2098	.372588	.627412	38	14.8460	.890761	.109239
9	6.8017	.408102	.591898	39	14.9491	.896944	.103056
10	7.3601	.441605	.558395	40	15.0463	.902778	.097222
11	7.8869	.473212	.526788	41	15.1380	.908281	.091719
12	8.3838	.503031	.496969	42	15.2245	.913473	.086527
13	8.8527	.531161	.468839	43	15.3062	.918370	.081630
14	9.2950	.557699	.442301	44	15.3832	.922991	.077009
15	9.7122	.582735	.417265	45	15.4558	.927350	.072650
16	10.1059	.606354	.393646	46	15.5244	.931462	.068538
17	10.4773	.628636	.371364	47	15.5890	.935342	.064653
18	10.8276	.649656	.350344	48	15.6500	.939002	.060998
19	11.1581	.669487	.330513	49	15.7076	.942454	.057546
20	11.4699	.688195	.311805	50	15.7619	.945712	.054288
21	11.7641	.705845	.294155	51	15.8131	.948785	.051215
22	12.0416	.722495	.277505	52	15.8614	.951684	.048316
23	12.3034	.738203	.261797	53	15.9070	.954418	.045582
24	12.5504	.753021	.246979	54	15.9500	.956999	.043001
25	12.7834	.767001	.232999	55	15.9905	.959433	.040567
26	13.0032	.780190	.219810	56	16.0288	.961729	.038271
27	13.2105	.792632	.207368	57	16.0649	.963895	.036105
28	13.4062	.804370	.195630	58	16.0990	.965939	.034061
29	13.5907	.815443	.184557	59	16.1311	.967867	.032133
30	13.7648	.825890	.174110	60	16.1614	.969686	.030314

Table B—10%

Number of Years	Annuity	Term Certain	Remainder	Number of Years	Annuity	Term Certain	Remainder
1	.9091	.090909	.909091	31	9.4790	.947901	.052099
2	1.7355	.173554	.826446	32	9.5264	.952638	.047362
3	2.4869	.248685	.751315	33	9.5694	.956943	.043057
4	3.1699	.316987	.683013	34	9.6086	.960857	.039143
5	3.7908	.379079	.620921	35	9.6442	.964416	.035584
6	4.3553	.435526	.564474	36	9.6765	.967651	.032349
7	4.8684	.486842	.513158	37	9.7059	.970592	.029408
8	5.3349	.533493	.466507	38	9.7327	.973265	.026735
9	5.7590	.575902	.424098	39	9.7570	.975696	.024304
10	6.1446	.614457	.385543	40	9.7791	.977905	.022095
11	6.4951	.649506	.350494	41	9.7991	.979914	.020086
12	6.8137	.681369	.318631	42	9.8174	.981740	.018260
13	7.1034	.710336	.289664	43	9.8340	.983400	.016600
14	7.3667	.736669	.263331	44	9.8491	.984909	.015091
15	7.6061	.760608	.239392	45	9.8628	.986281	.013719
16	7.8237	.782371	.217629	46	9.8753	.987528	.012472
17	8.0216	.802155	.197845	47	9.8866	.988662	.011338
18	8.2014	.820141	.179859	48	9.8969	.989693	.010307
19	8.3649	.836492	.163508	49	9.9063	.990630	.009370
20	8.5136	.851356	.148644	50	9.9148	.991481	.008519
21	8.6487	.864869	.135131	51	9.9226	.992256	.007744
22	8.7715	.877154	.122846	52	9.9296	.992960	.007040
23	8.8832	.888322	.111678	53	9.9360	.993600	.006400
24	8.9847	.898474	.101526	54	9.9418	.994182	.005818
25	9.0770	.907704	.092296	55	9.9471	.994711	.005289
26	9.1609	.916095	.083905	56	9.9519	.995191	.004809
27	9.2372	.923722	.076278	57	9.9563	.995629	.004371
28	9.3066	.930657	.069343	58	9.9603	.996026	.003974
29	9.3696	.936961	.063039	59	9.9639	.996387	.003613
30	9.4269	.942691	.057309	60	9.9672	.996716	.003284

See *Valuation* in both the *Estate Tax* and *Gift Tax* sections of this publication to determine whether you should use the 6% or 10% tables to value these items.

Table B–6. Source: Federal Estate and Gift Taxes, Publication 44B, rev. Sept. 1984, Internal Revenue Service, p. 18.

of that table presumes a 6 percent discount rate and the lower a 10 percent. The latter is used to value all gifts made after August 8, 1984. By comparing the same cells in both panels, we observe that with a 10 percent discount rate, the value of the property is reduced. Thus, for a term of 20 years at 6 percent, the factor is 11.4699 for an annuity, compared to 8.5136 for 10 percent; .688195 for a term certain period (a specific term rather than a lifetime which is an uncertain term) compared to .851356, and .311805 compared to .148644 for a remainder interest.

Also notice that the factors in the 10 percent panel are different from the factors in Table A which also assume a 10 percent rate of discount. One reason is that the latter has an element of uncertainty. To make a gift contingent on someone's death involves an uncertainty about how long the person may live. The estimates are based on actuarial tables which are estimates of the life expectancy of persons at specific ages. When a specific term is used, the length of time is for a term certain or a period of time that is certain. A 109-year-old person may live one month, one year, one day. To make a gift after a specific period is to set a specific term regardless of whether or not the person lives.

Large gifts are often induced by applying the right combinations of factors to bring about a high valuation when a tax motive is important to the potential donor. A couple of simple rules may help: (1) Age works inversely with value when the charity gets a remainder interest and positively with value when the charity gets a life estate (an income interest). (2) The longer the time the nonprofit has the benefits of the property the greater the deductible value. (3) The deductible value must be consistent with the fair market value of the property. (4) The higher the payout rate to the noncharitable beneficiary, the lower the value of the property as a charitable deduction.

This last point is revealing of the kinds of trade-offs that must often be made by the donor. A high payout rate may attract a potential donor because it offers a good income to the donor or a loved beneficiary; but it is at the expense of a higher tax deduction. Thus, the tax problem is one of coming up with a trade-off between a present benefit (tax deduction) or a flow of income (the payout) that suits the donor's needs.

SUMMARY AND CONCLUSIONS

This chapter has presented techniques and tools that every manager of a nonprofit organization should know if the organization is to be successful in raising big money. These techniques allow the donor to have a deduction on present income tax, avoid estate taxes on gifts made, have a current income from the earnings of the gift or to make a gift of that current income to someone such as a relative or friend. The techniques also allow the nonprofit to receive annual income from a property only temporarily in its possession; or in the reverse, to finally take possession of a property that was providing an annual income to the donor. Basically, these tools and techniques are ways to strike a deal when the objectives of the potential donor and those of the organization may be in conflict; or, if not in conflict, may be in conflict with the laws governing the usual ways of making gifts, such as outright gifts discussed in Chapter 10. All of the tools discussed are in keeping with the 1986 law.

The tools that were discussed were charitable remainder trusts of the unitrust, annuity trust, and pooled trust types. These permit the income interest to go to someone other than the nonprofit. The nonprofit gets the remainder or corpus. The other type of trusts are charitable lead trusts, also of the unitrust or annuity trust types. These permit the nonprofit to get an annual payment with the principal eventually going to someone else.

Life insurance policies are also instruments for getting large gifts. Insurance policies can magnify the size of the gift thousands of times larger than the actual money outlay of the donor and they shift the burden of periodic reminders of donations to the insurance companies in the form of premium notices. Annuities are yet another tool. These range from gifts of pension plans, including private plans such as indiviudal retirement accounts (IRAs) to gift annuities. The latter exposes the organization to default or bankruptcy.

The chapter closes with a discussion of the valuation of future gifts and endowments, a special fund set aside for financing a special program or set of programs. An endowment may be funded by any one or (where permitted by law) any combination of the techniques discussed here and in Chapters 7 or 10. We say permitted by law because once a trust is established, sometimes no further contributions can be made and some trusts must be separate and independent. Indeed, one of the motives for a donor's setting up a trust or an endowment is to maintain identity. This is why trusts and endowments usually carry the names of persons or corporations. It is their memorial. Regardless of how funded, each endowment requires a separate set of financial records. How we read these records is the subject of Chapter 13.

APPENDIX 11: INTERNAL REVENUE SERVICE EXAMPLE OF DECLARATION OF TRUST

In the first part of this chapter and in Chapter 5, it was said that a nonprofit could operate as a trust or as a corporation. The Appendix of Chapter 6 is an example of an acceptable charter. This appendix is an example of a trust declaration that is acceptable to the IRS. This is an elaboration of the principles discussed in this chapter.

The ——— Charitable Trust. Declaration of Trust made as of the — day of ——— 19—, by — , of ——— , and ——— of ——— ., who hereby declare and agree that they have received this day from ——-, as Donor, the sum of Ten Dollars ($10) and that they will hold and manage the same, and any additions to it, in trust, as follows:

First: This trust shall be called "The ——— Charitable Trust."

Second: The trustees may receive and accept property, whether real, personal, or mixed, by way of gift, bequest, or devise, from any person, firm, trust, or corporation, to be held, administered, and disposed of in accordance with and pursuant to the provisions of this Declaration of Trust; but no gift, bequest or devise of any such property shall be received and accepted if it is conditioned or limited in such manner as to require the disposition of the income or its principal to any person or organization other than a "charitable organization" or for other than "charitable purposes" within the meaning of such terms as defined in Article Third of this Declaration of Trust, or as shall in the opinion of the trustees, jeopardize the federal income tax exemption of this trust pursuant to section 501(c)(3) of the Internal Revenue Code of 1954, as now in force or afterwards amended.

Third: A. The principal and income of all property received and accepted by the trustees to be administered under this Declaration of Trust shall be held in trust by them, and the trustees may make payments or distributions from income or principal, or both, to or for the use of such charitable organizations, within the meaning of that term as defined in paragraph C, in such amounts and for such charitable purposes of the trust as the trustees shall from time to time select and determine; and the trustees may make payments or distributions from income or principal, or both, directly for such charitable purposes, within the meaning of that term as defined in paragraph D, in such amounts as the trustees shall from time to time select and determine without making use of any other charitable organization. The trustees may also make payments or distributions of all or any part of the income or principal to states, territories, or possessions of the United States, any political subdivision of any of the foregoing, or to the United States or the District of Columbia but only for charitable purposes within the meaning of that term as defined in paragraph D. Income or principal derived from contributions by corporations shall be distributed by the trustees for use solely within the United States or its possessions. No part of the net earnings of this trust shall inure or be payable to or for the benefit of any private shareholder or individual, and no substantial part of the activities of this trust shall be the carrying on of propaganda, or otherwise attempting, to influence legislation.

No part of the activities of this trust shall be the participation in, or intervention in (including the publishing or distributing of statements), any political campaign on behalf of any candidate for public office.

B. The trust shall continue forever unless the trustees terminate it and distribute all of the principal and income, which action may be taken by the trustees in their discretion at any time. On such termination, the trust fund as then constituted shall be distributed to or for the use of such charitable organizations, in such amounts and for such charitable purposes as the trustees shall then select and determine. The donor authorizes and empowers the trustees to form and organize a nonprofit corporation limited to the uses and purposes provided for in this Declaration of Trust, such corporation to be organized under the laws of any state or under the laws of the United States as may be determined by the trustees; such corporation when organized to have power to administer and control the affairs and property and to carry out the uses, objects, and purposes of this trust. Upon the creation and organization of such corporation, the trustees are authorized and empowered to convey, transfer, and deliver to such corporation all the property and assets to which this trust may be or become entitled. The charter, bylaws, and other provisions for the organization and management of such corporation and its affairs and property shall be such as the trustees shall determine, consistent with the provisions of this paragraph.

C. In this Declaration of Trust and in any amendments to it, references to "charitable organizations" or "charitable organization" mean corporations, trusts, funds, foundations, or community chests created or organized in the United States or in any of its possessions, whether under the laws of the United States, any state or territory, the District of Columbia, or any possession of the United States, organized and operated exclusively for charitable purposes, no part of the net earnings of which inures or is payable to or for the benefit of any private shareholder or individual, and no substantial part of the activities of which is carrying on propaganda, or otherwise attempting, to influence legislation, and which do not participate in or intervene in (including the publishing or distributing of statements), any political campaign on behalf of any candidate for public office. It is intended that the organization described in this paragraph C shall be entitled to exemption from federal income tax under section 501(c)(3) of the Internal Revenue Code of 1954, as now in force or afterwards amended.

D. In this Declaration of Trust and in any amendments to it, the term "charitable purposes" shall be limited to and shall include only religious, charitable, scientific, literary, or educational purposes within the meaning of those terms as used in section 501(c)(3) of the Internal Revenue Code of 1954 but only such purposes as also constitute public charitable purposes under the law of trusts of the State of——————.

Fourth: This Declaration of Trust may be amended at any time or times by written instrument or instruments signed and sealed by the trustees, and acknowledged by any of the trustees, provided that no amendment shall authorize the trustees to conduct the affairs of this trust in any manner or for any purpose contrary to the provisions of section 501(c)(3) of the Internal Revenue Code of 1954 as now in force or afterwards amended. An amendment of the provisions of this Article Fourth (or any amendment to it) shall be valid only if and to the extent that such amendment further restricts the trustees' amending power. All instruments amending this Declaration of Trust shall be noted upon or kept attached to the executed original of this Declaration of Trust held by the trustees.

Fifth: Any trustee under this Declaration of Trust may, by written instrument, signed and acknowledged, resign his office. The number of trustees shall be at all times not less than two, and whenever for any reason the number is reduced to one, there shall be, and at any other time there may be, appointed one or more additional trustees. Appointments shall be made by the trustee or trustees for the time in office by written instruments signed and acknowledged. Any succeeding or additional trustee shall, upon his acceptance of the office by written instrument signed and acknowledged, have the same powers, rights and duties, and the same title to the trust estate jointly with the surviving or remaining trustee or trustees as if originally appointed.

None of the trustees shall be required to furnish any bond or surety. None of them shall be responsible or liable for the acts of omissions of any other of the trustees or of any predecessor or of a custodian, agent, depositary or counsel selected with reasonable care.

The one or more trustees, whether original or successor, for the time being in office, shall have full authority to act even though one or more vacancies may exist. A trustee may, by appropriate written instrument, delegate all or any part of his powers to another or others of the trustees for such periods and subject to such conditions as such delegating trustee may determine.

The trustees serving under this Declaration of Trust are authorized to pay to themselves amounts for reasonable expenses incurred and reasonable compensation for services rendered in the administration of this trust, but in no event shall any trustee who has made a contribution to this trust ever receive any compensation thereafter.

Sixth: In extension and not in limitation of the common law and statutory powers of trustees and other powers granted in this Declaration of Trust, the trustees shall have the following discretionary powers:

a) To invest and reinvest the principal and income of the trust in such property, real, personal, or mixed, and in such manner as they shall deem proper, and from time to time to change investments as they shall deem advisable; to invest in or retain any stocks, shares, bonds, notes, obligations, or personal or real property (including without limitation any interests in or obligations of any corporation, association, business trust, investment trust, common trust fund, or investment company) although some or all of the property so acquired or retained is of a kind or size which but for this express authority would not be considered proper and although all of the trust funds are invested in the securities of one company. No principal or income, however, shall be loaned, directly or indirectly, to any trustee or to anyone else, corporate or otherwise, who has at any time made a contribution to this trust, nor to anyone except on the basis of an adequate interest charge and with adequate security.

b) To sell, lease, or exchange any personal, mixed, or real property, at public auction or by private contract, for such consideration and on such terms as to credit or otherwise, and to make such contracts and enter into such undertakings relating to the trust property, as they consider advisable, whether or not such leases or contracts may extend beyond the duration of the trust.

c) To borrow money for such periods, at such rates of interest, and upon such terms as the trustees consider advisable, and as security for such loans to mortgage or pledge any real or personal property with or without power of sale; to acquire or hold any real or personal property, subject to any mortgage or pledge on or of property acquired or held by this trust.

d) To execute and deliver deeds, assignments, transfers, mortgages, pledges, leases, covenants, contracts, promissory notes, releases, and other instruments, sealed or unsealed, incident to any transaction in which they engage.

e) To vote, to give proxies, to participate in the reorganization, merger or consolidation of any concern, or in the sale, lease, disposition, or distribution of its assets; to join with other security holders in acting through a committee, depositary, voting trustees, or otherwise, and in this connection to delegate authority to such committee, depositary, or trustees and to deposit securities with them or transfer securities to them; to pay assessments levied on securi-

ties or to exercise subscription rights in respect of securities.

f) To employ a bank or trust company as custodian of any funds or securities and to delegate to it such powers as they deem appropriate; to hold trust property without indication of fiduciary capacity but only in the name of a registered nominee, provided the trust property is at all times identified as such on the books of the trust; to keep any or all of the trust property or funds in any place or places in the United States of America; to employ clerks, accountants, investment counsel, investment agents, and any special services, and to pay the reasonable compensation and expenses of all such services in addition to the compensation of the trustees.

Seventh: The trustees' powers are exercisable solely in the fiduciary capacity consistent with and in furtherance of the charitable purposes of this trust as specified in Article Third and not otherwise.

Eighth: In this Declaration of Trust and in any amendment to it, references to "trustees" mean the one or more trustees, whether original or successor, for the time being in office.

Ninth: Any person may rely on a copy, certified by a notary public, of the executed original of this Declaration of Trust held by the trustees, and of any of the notations on it and writings attached to it, as fully as he might rely on the original documents themselves. Any such person may rely fully on any statements of fact certified by anyone who appears from such original documents or from such certified copy to be a trustee under this Declaration of Trust. No one dealing with the trustees need inquire concerning the validity of anything the trustees purport to do. No one dealing with the trustees need see to the application of anything paid or transferred to or upon the order of the trustees of the trust.

Tenth: This Declaration of Trust is to be governed in all respects by the laws of the State of ———.

Trustee—

Trustee—

Declaration of Trust. Source: Internal Revenue Service. Tax Exempt Status of Your Organization, Publication 557 (Revised January 1982) U.S. Government Printing Office, 1982, p. 10.

NOTES

1. American Bar Endowment v. U.S., 56 AFTR 2d 85–5005 (5-10-85), aff'g and rev'g, in part, 53 AFTR 2d 84–942. The Claims Court also concluded that the income derived by the American Bar Association was not taxable to them; that is, it was not unrelated business income. But on April 28, 1986, the Supreme Court ruled that this was an unrelated business and was taxable. (Supreme Court of the United States, United States v. American Bar Endowment, No. 85–599, April 28, 1986.)

2. The laws on income, estate and gift taxes state that if the creator of a trust has any incidence of ownership in the property that is in the trust, that person is deemed to derive economic benefits from it and therefore must pay both income and estate taxes on the earnings and value of the property. This rule, as we shall see, is relaxed in the case of charitable trusts.

3. There are some differences in the treatment of irrevocable and revocable trusts at the time of death. If, for example, a trust is revocable and becomes irrevocable at the time of death through the estate, then a "reasonable" period is granted to transform the trust to a charitable one. The basic point to keep in mind is that a revocable transfer even through a trust is not a gift.

4. The reader should recall the discussion in Chapter 10 on the treatment of real property and other partial gifts.

5. Paul Taylor, "Hughes Settlement," *The Washington Post*, Thursday, August 30, 1984, p. C18

6. See The Ellsworth B. Warner Estate, file 15–81–1118, in the office of the Register of Wills, Chester County Courthouse, Westchester, Pennsylvania.

7. Associated Press story appearing *The Washington Post*, February 8, 1986, page A2.

8. A "reasonable period" is that period required for the trustees to perform the ordinary duties of the trust. This includes the collection of assets, the payment of debt, the payment of taxes and the determination of the rights of the subsequent beneficiaries.

9. Chapter 10 discusses capital gains and charitable contributions and organizations.

10. Normally, a property is valued on the date of death. An alternate date is six months after that period, or anytime within the first six months that the property is first distributed. If the value of the property is affected by the mere lapse of time, such as a savings account or an annuity because it increases in value over time, then the property is valued as of the time of death.

11. Loans from the policy to purchase income-producing assets will lead to an unrelated business income tax because the assets would have been acquired through debt. Mose & Garrison Sisken Memorial Foundation, Inc. v. U.S., 55 AFTR 2d 85-1024, (12-4-84). See also Chapter 7 of this book.

12. A single premium is roughly equal to the value of the policy, discounted at a rate of interest and probability of death. This amount is large because it is paid over several years.

13. An irrevocable trust is not required, but a revocable trust does not provide an immediate tax deduction.

SUGGESTED READINGS

BAETZ, TIMOTHY W., "Tax Planning for Sophisticated Charitable Transfers: The Divide Between Downright Doable and Dangerous," *TAXES—The Tax Magazine*, 62, no. 12 (December 1984), 997–1009.

Internal Revenue Service, Department of the Treasury, Federal Estate and Gift Taxes, Publication 448, rev. May 1982, (Washington, D.C.: U.S. Government Printing Office, 1982).

Internal Revenue Service, Department of Treasury, Tax Information for Private Foundations and Foundation Managers, Publication 578, rev. October 1981, (Washington, D.C.: U.S. Government Printing Office, 1981).

KIRCHICK, CALVIN B., and EDWARD J. BECKWITH, "The Internal Revenue Service Changes the Odds on Death and Taxes." TAXES—*The Tax Magazine*, 62, no. 10 (October 1984), 699–713.

MELFE, THOMAS A., "Effective Planning for Charitable Giving," 40th Annual New York University Institute on Federal Taxation, 1982, Nicolas Liakas, ed., (New York: Mathew Bender, 1982), pp. 1–36.

McCOY, JERRY J. and LYNDA S. MOERSCHABECHER, "Modern Martial/Charitable Estate Planning," TAXES—*The Tax Magazine*, 61, no. 1 (January 1983), 3–12.

STERN, SUE S. and PATRICK D. MARTIN, "Gifts to Private Foundations and Trusts and Property Contributions Are Affected by DRA," *The Journal of Taxation*, 6, no. 4, (October 1984), 211–12.

SCHMOLHA, LEO L., "Income Taxation of Charitable Remainder Trusts and Decedents' Estates: Sixty-Six Years of Astigmatism," *Tax Law Review*, 40, no. 1 (Fall 1984), New York University School of Law (Warren Gortham and Lamont, Inc., Fall 1984), pp. 1–350.

VERES, JOSEPH A., "Using Pooled Income Funds to Pass ITC and Depreciation Through to Life-Income Donors," *The Journal of Taxation*, 61, no. 1 (July 1984), pp. 28–33.

TWELVE

Setting and Controlling Targets: The Role of the Budget

Budgeting is more than balancing expected revenues and expenditures. Chapter 1 of this book noted that one of the functions of management is the determination of how the organization's resources will be allocated among alternative uses. Another function mentioned in that chapter is the raising of money to fund the organization's mission. The budget, a financial plan for the organization, is the document which shows how the management hopes to meet both of these objectives.

The budget is also a tool of management control. Once the budget has been adopted, it can be used periodically to compare actual performance with budgeted or planned performance. Variance between actual and planned expenditures or receipts indicates the organization is off course and should sound an alarm to management. This chapter discusses central budget concepts and describes how the budget can be used as an aid to management of nonprofit organizations.

THE CENTRAL PURPOSES OF BUDGETING

Budgets are important tools of planning and management. The process of budget formulation is part of the planning process. The budget is the monetary expression of the strategic plan described in Chapter 5. First, a preliminary budget for each program the organization is considering in its strategic planning is necessary so that the organization may compare benefits and costs before choosing among programs.

Second, before the chosen programs can be implemented, a final budget must be adopted so that the managers may know the amount of resources that is planned for their programs, the sources of those dollars (from grants, fees, and so on), the way those dollars are expected to be allocated among competing uses within each program and a schedule of expenditures and receipts over the life of the program. As a planning document, a budget has no legal force.

The budget is a political document. It expresses a policy decision about the priority of some programs over others, and increases the power of some managers over others. Programs can be dropped or added, weakened or strengthened by using the budget as the rationale such as "it is not in the budget."

The budget also serves as an instrument for managerial control. Actual spending and receipts can be tracked against planned targets. Variance between actual and budgeted performances signal the need to slow spending or increase receipts, or to shift resources from one category to another, or the need to raise more funds.

Variance from budgeted amounts should be of concern to management, even though the variance may be positive.[1] When actual spending is lower than planned amounts, this could be the result of laggard performance in program implementation. But it could also indicate greater than expected cost savings in program implementation. In short, all variances in spending or in revenues that are more than incidental departures from the planned amounts demand some attention. Variances are often an early warning that something could go wrong. They can alert managers to the possibilities of cost overruns for which the organization may not be reimbursed. These overruns can create serious financial problems. Much of the deficit nonprofits experience may well represent sloppy financial and operating management rather than benevolent overspending.

While not audited, the budget as an instrument of control may be used by auditors to judge the extent to which the organization exercises forethought and control over its spending and revenues. Does the organization display reasonable management that plans and sets targets? Does it keep regular and systematic track of its financial performance?

For those nonprofits that are complex running several different programs, endowments, or businesses, the organization's final budget may be a composite of several subbudgets (1) one for each activity within a program or functional area, (2) one for each program or functional area and (3) one for the organization as a whole which is a composite of all functional or program areas plus general administration. A functional or program budget merely refers to one that is set up according to programs or activities rather than according to objects such as paper, pencil, books and other items. Thus, each function will have its own detailed budget, and the organization's budget will be a composite of these individual functional budgets.

As a special element of control, budgets in nonprofits should distinguish between restricted and unrestricted sources and uses of funds and show any anticipated transfer from one to the other. This is important because the management of the nonprofit has no discretionary use over the restricted funds. These funds must be used for the purposes for which they were obtained. To use them otherwise is to violate the contract under which the funds were obtained. Therefore, it is imperative that when the amounts of restricted funds are shown as receipts in the budget, it is similarly shown that they are restricted; that is, their planned use is predetermined. We shall say more about restricted funds in Chapters 13 and 14.

Restricted funds do not always come from outside the organization. Sometimes the board of directors may choose to set aside a certain portion of the annual revenues of the organization for some special purpose and restrict the management from using it for any other purpose. Here again, it makes no sense to include such funds as revenues without indicating that their use is restricted. Nonprofits without an independent flow of funds from investments, unrelated or related businesses or from institutional gifts frequently find themselves with relatively little discretionary budgetary power. They function, but with little budgetary discretion.

It is frequently helpful to put the current year's budget into a historical perspective. That can be done by showing the budget for the previous five or ten years. By so doing, the board of the organization can get a picture of where the organization has been, how it is growing or declining, and how resources have shifted from one functional use to another. Is the organization changing emphasis or direction? Have some programs been sufficiently funded and emphasized such that now they should be less dependent upon the organization's general funds?

She points out that, at a time when reduced government spending on social programs has forced greater competition among private agencies for financial support, the New York league last year increased its budget for special programs by 109 percent, to $2.7 million from about $1.3 million.

A $2 Million Aid Cut

However, despite the dramatic gain, the New York league still had almost $400,000 less for programs than it did in fiscal 1982-83.

Carlyle C. Douglas, "Urban League Is Rebounding After Cuts in Government Aid," *The New York Times,* page 60 Sunday, September 15, 1985. Copyright 1985 by the New York Times Company. Reprinted by permission.

This historical perspective can also provide a basis for forecasting and projecting financial changes in the organization. By comparing how far off previous planned amounts were from actual experience in the amount of funds received and spent for each function, senior management can obtain a picture of how realistic their subordinate managers' projections are. Are they consistently overoptimistic and by how much?

To facilitate comparisons over time, budget figures should be shown in current and constant dollars. Constant dollars are current dollars adjusted for inflation. The fact that current budget is 20 percent higher than last year's would not mean that the organization is expanding in real terms if the inflation rate is 20 percent. The organization is standing still.

Another useful presentation in some nonprofits is between capital and operating budgets. Capital budgets, to be discussed later in this book, relate only to the acquisition or disposition of assets that have a useful life of more than one year. Planned acquisition or disposition of cars, buildings, furniture and computers will be included in the capital budget. Operating budgets, the subject of this chapter, are prepared annually for showing expected revenues, support, and expenses for the year. Nonprofits that are on a cash basis with very little capital plans will not need to separate capital from operating budget but nonprofits with large capital programs must separate these two. Failure to do so would distort the annual operating budget. For example, a building purchased for $1,000,000 is paid for over several years. In an operating budget, this transaction would be shown as a planned expenditure of $1,000,000 in the current year.

PRINCIPLES UNDERLYING BUDGETS

Budgets of nonprofits should be formed using two distinct principles: policy and efficiency. On the policy level, the governing body should be concerned with what programs will be undertaken, how much of the organization's resources will be allocated to each program, and what will be the sources of funds for financing each program. As we saw in Chapter 6, the sources of support and the nature of the programs have implications beyond the budget. They affect the tax-exempt status of the organization and are therefore policy questions.

The other principle that should influence budget formulation in nonprofit organizations is efficiency. Questions here are: How much will it cost? How much money must be raised? What will be the schedule of disbursements and expenditures over the life of the program? These are questions that are not resolvable by policy debates without specific technical estimates.

When capital budgets are being considered, additional questions must be raised. How many dollars must the organization raise today or on a periodic basis if it is to meet a certain target funding level by some specific date in the future?[2]

Other types of capital budgeting questions are: How much can a nonprofit extract annually from an endowment which is earning interest at a specific rate before the endowment runs out?[3] How should the capital budget be funded? Should the organization borrow? If so, by note, bond, and of what maturity?

Would industrial development revenue bonds be wise?[4] How will the loan be amortized? What percentage of the project should be paying for itself? How should the nonprofit invest the funds for the capital project while waiting to start the project?

These are examples of tough questions that pertain to capital planning. They are technical in nature and should be resolved first in a technical manner. We shall show how in Chapter 14. From this technical information, a policy choice can be made. To illustrate, some questions require a clear understanding of discounting, present value, and annuity techniques. Without an understanding of these, no sensible policy decision can be made; the objective will not be met and the endowment will be wiped out. Indeed, if the organization is a private foundation it could be liable for taxes on unwarranted accumulations if it overshoots its mark and does not have permission for accumulation, as discussed in Chapter 6.

These two principles, policy and efficiency, undergird all budget formulation processes and techniques.

One technique is zero-based budgeting (ZBB). This technique requires the organization to pretend that it is starting from scratch. Thus, in every budget formulating period, each activity must be ranked in terms of its expected contribution to the organization's mission. Programs that cannot be justified or are of low priority are dropped or their resources are decreased. Another technique is program budgeting (planning, programming and budgeting, systems or PPBS). PPBS rests heavily on measures of costs and benefits. Programs are ranked and those with the highest ratio of benefits to costs are assumed to be superior. Even when these two techniques are used, the ultimate decisions are based on policy and efficiency considerations as described in Chapter 5 and in the preceding paragraphs. Accordingly, it is conceivable that the program with the highest benefit-cost ratio may be rejected because it does not fall within the policy range preferred by the organization. Similarly, the most justified program in a zero-based planning exercise may not be one that the organization can implement with the level of efficiency required.[5]

EFFICIENCY: COSTS AND SUPPORT

In earlier chapters we dealt with policy questions. What should the organization's mission be? How should it be funded? What type of tax-exempt status is most appropriate? Let us focus for a moment on the efficiency aspect of the budget. Efficiency may be technological or economic. Technological efficiency refers to the use of the most advanced and appropriate techniques, machines, and tools for getting a job done. The other type of efficiency, economic efficiency, is concerned not merely with dollar costs but with benefits. Thus, economic efficiency means lowering costs and increasing benefits. Technological efficiency, as opposed to economic efficiency, is concerned only with lowering costs. When constructing its budget, a nonprofit must be concerned with economic efficiency; that is, it wants to provide the greatest amount of help (benefits) at the least cost.

Costs

Let us look at the cost aspect of efficiency. What are the important concepts from the point of view of budget making? Costs may be direct or indirect. Direct costs are those that relate to a specific project or activity. A nonprofit may, for example, hold a concert. The payment to the musicians to perform is a direct cost of that activity.

Indirect costs are costs which do not relate to specific activities but to the administration and management of the organization. These costs, usually called overhead costs, cut across all activities and would exist even if one or the other activity is discontinued. For example, even without a concert the nonprofit would have to pay salaries and benefits to a core staff (the management of the nonprofit), pay rent, and buy supplies and equipment for the general operation of the organization. John Jones' salary as secretary would have to be paid but his payment as a musician in the concert is due solely to the concert. Thus, part of John's work is a direct cost and part is indirect from the perspective of the concert.

For accounting and contracting purposes, overhead or direct costs are usually stated as a percentage of direct labor costs, or total direct cost (labor, materials and other costs directly and exclusively caused by an activity). This is referred to as an overhead rate. For example, based on the previous year's experience, the organization may find that its indirect cost was $200,000 and its direct labor cost was $100,000. Its overhead rate would be 200 percent of direct labor costs. If total indirect costs were used as the base and we presume that it amounted to $150,000, the overhead rate would be 150 percent.

These concepts are so important to managers of nonprofits that the federal government has written regulations about how they should be treated. The reader may proceed to page 300 if these specific rules are not of interest at this time. At some point, however, the following insert should be read.

B Direct Costs

1. Direct costs are those that can be identified specifically with a particular final cost objective: i.e., a particular award, project, service, or other direct activity of an organization. However, a cost may not be assigned to an award as a direct cost if any other cost incurred for the same purpose, in like circumstances, has been allocated to an award as an indirect cost. Costs identified specifically with awards are direct costs of the awards and are to be assigned directly thereto. Costs identified specifically with other final cost objectives of the organization are direct costs of those cost objectives and are not to be assigned to other awards directly or indirectly.

2. Any direct cost of a minor amount may be treated as an indirect cost for reasons of practicality where the accounting treatment for such cost is consistently applied to all final cost objectives.

3. The cost of certain activities are not allowable as charges to Federal awards (see, for example, fund raising costs in paragraph 19 of

Attachment B). However, even though these costs are unallowable for purposes of computing charges to Federal awards, they nonetheless must be treated as direct cost for purposes of determining indirect cost rates and be allocated their share of the organization's indirect costs if they represent activities which (1) include the salaries of personnel, (2) occupy space, and (3) benefit from the organization's indirect costs.

4. The costs of activities performed primarily as a service to members, clients, or the general public when significant and necessary to the organization's mission must be treated as direct costs whether or not allowable and be allocated an equitable share of indirect costs. Some examples of these types of activities include:

a. Maintenance of membership rolls, subscriptions, publications, and related functions.

b. Providing services and information to members, legislative or administrative bodies, or the public.

c. Promotion, lobbying, and other forms of public relations.

d. Meetings and conferences except those held to conduct the general administration of the organization.

e. Maintenance, protection, and investment of special funds not used in operation of the organization.

f. Administration of group benfeits on behalf of members or clients including life and hospital insurance, annuity or retirement plans, financial aid, etc.

C. Indirect Cost

1. Indirect costs are those that have been incurred for common or joint objectives and cannot be readily identified with a particular final cost objective. Direct cost of minor amounts may be treated as indirect costs under the conditions described in paragraph B.2. above. After direct costs have been determined and assigned directly to awards or other work as appropriate, indirect costs are those remaining to be allocated to benefiting cost objectives. A cost may not be allocated to an award as an indirect cost if any other cost incurred for the same purpose, in like circumstances, has been assigned to an award as a direct cost.

2. Because of the diverse characteristics and accounting practices of nonprofit organizations, it is not possible to specify the types of costs which may be classified as indirect cost in all situations. However, typical examples of indirect cost for many nonprofit organizations may include depreciation or use allowances on buildings and equipment, the costs of operating and maintaining facilities, and general administration and general expenses, such as the salaries and expenses of executive officers, personnel administration, and accounting.

D. ALLOCATION OF INDIRECT COSTS AND DETERMINATION OF INDIRECT COST RATES

1. *General.*

a. Where a nonprofit organization has only one major function, or where all its major functions benefit from its indirect costs to approximately the same degree, the allocation of indirect costs and the computation of an indirect cost rate may be accomplished through simplified allocation procedures as described in paragraph 2 below.

b. Where an organization has several major functions which benefit from its indirect costs in varying degrees, allocation of indirect costs may require the accumulation of such costs into separate cost groupings which then are allocated individually to benefiting functions by means of a base which best measures the relative degree of benefit. The indirect costs allocated to each function are then distributed to individual awards and other activities included in that function by means of an indirect cost rate(s).

c. The determination of what constitutes an organization's major functions will depend on its purpose in being; the types of services it renders to the public, its clients, and its members; and the amount of effort it devotes to such activities as fund raising, public information and membership activities.

d. Specific methods for allocating indirect costs and computing indirect cost rates along with the conditions under which each method should be used are described in paragraphs 2 through 5 below.

e. The base period for the allocation of indirect costs is the period in which such costs are incurred and accumulated for allocation to work performed in that period. The base period normally should coincide with the organization's fiscal year, but in any event, shall be so selected as to avoid inequities in the allocation of the costs.

2. *Simplified allocation method.*

a. Where an organization's major functions benefit from its indirect costs to approximately the same degree, the allocation of indirect costs may be accomplished by (i) separating the organization's total costs for the base period as either direct or indirect, and (ii) dividing the total allowable indirect costs (net of applicable credits) by an equitable distribution base. The result of this process is an indirect cost rate which is used to distribute indirect costs to individual awards. The rate should be expressed as the percentage which the total amount of allowable indirect costs bears to the base selected. This method should also be used where an organization has only one major function encompassing a number of individual projects or activities, and may be used where the level of Federal awards to an organization is relatively small.

b. Both the direct costs and the indirect costs shall exclude capital expenditures and unallowable costs. However, unallowable costs which represent activities must be included in the direct costs under the conditions described in paragraph B.3. above.

c. The distribution base may be total direct costs (excluding capital expenditures and other distorting items, such as major subcontracts or subgrants), direct salaries and wages, or other base which results in an equitable distribution. The distribution base shall generally exclude participant support costs as defined in pargraph 29 of Attachment B.

d. Except where a special rate(s) is required in accordance with paragraph D.5 below, the indirect cost rate developed under the above principles is applicable to all awards at the organization. If a special rate(s) is required, appropriate modifications shall be made in order to develop the special rate(s).

3. *Multiple allocation base method.*

a. Where an organization's indirect costs benefit its major functions in varying degrees, such costs shall be accumulated into separate cost groupings. Each grouping shall then be allocated individually to benefiting functions by means of a base which best measures the relative benefits.

b. The groupings shall be established so as to permit the allocation of each grouping on the basis of benefits provided to the major functions. Each grouping should constitute a pool of expenses that are of like character in terms of the functions they benefit and in terms of the allocation base which best measures the relative benefits provided to each function. The number of separate groupings should be held within practical limits, taking into consideration the materiality of the amounts involved and the degree of precision desired.

c. Actual conditions must be taken into account in selecting the base to be used in allocating the expenses in each grouping to benefiting functions. When an allocation can be made by assignment of a cost grouping directly to the function benefited, the allocation shall be made in that manner. When the expenses in a grouping are more general in nature, the allocation should be made through the use of a selected base which produces results that are equitable to both the Government and the organization. In general, any cost element or cost related factor associated with the organization's work is potentially adaptable for use as an allocation base provided (i) it can readily be expressed in terms of dollars or other quantitative measures (total direct costs, direct salaries and wages, staff hours applied, square feet used, hours of usage, number of documents processed, population served, and the like) and (ii) it is common to the benefiting functions during the base period.

d. Except where a special indirect cost rate(s) is required in accordance with paragraph D.5 below, the separate groupings of indirect costs allocated to each major function shall be aggregated and treated as a common pool for that function. The costs in the common pool shall then be distributed to individual awards included in that function by use of a single indirect cost rate.

e. The distribution base used in computing the indirect cost rate for each function may be total direct costs (excluding capital expenditures and other distorting items such as major subcontracts and subgrants), direct salaries and wages, or other base which results in an equitable distribution. The distribution base shall generally exclude participant support costs as defined in paragraph 29, Attachment B. An indirect cost rate should be developed for each separate indirect cost pool developed. The rate in each case should be stated as the percentage which the amount of the particular indirect cost pool is of the distribution base identified with that pool.

4. *Direct allocation method.*

a. Some nonprofit organizations, treat all costs as direct costs except general administration and general expenses. These organizations generally separate their costs into three basic categories: (i) General administration and general expenses, (ii) fund raising, and (iii) other direct functions (including projects performed under Federal awards). Joint costs, such as depreciation, rental costs, operation and maintenance of facilities, telephone expenses, and the like are prorated individually as direct costs to each category and to each award or other activity using a base most appropriate to the particular cost being prorated.

b. This method is acceptable provided each joint cost is prorated using a base which accurately measures the benefits provided to each award or other activity. The bases must be established in accordance with reasonable criteria, and be supported by current data. This method is compatible with the Standards of Accounting and Financial Reporting for Voluntary Health and Welfare Organizations issued jointly by the National Health Council, Inc., the National Assembly of Voluntary Health and Social Welfare Organizations, and the United Way of America.

c. Under this method, indirect costs consist exclusively of general administration and general expenses. In all other respects, the organization's indirect cost rates shall be computed in the same manner as that described in paragraph D.2 above.

5. *Special indirect cost rates.* In some instances, a single indirect cost rate for all activities of an organization or for each major function of the organization may not be appropriate, since it would not take into account those different factors which may substantially affect the indirect costs applicable to a particular segment of work. For this purpose, a particular segment of work may be that performed under a single award or it may consist of work under a group of awards performed in a common environment. The factors may include the physical location of the work, the level of administrative support required, the nature of the facilities or other resources employed, the scientific disciplines or technical skills involved, the organizational arrangements used, or any combination thereof. When a particular segment of work is performed

in an environment which appears to generate a significantly different level of indirect costs, provisions should be made for a separate indirect cost pool applicable to such work. The separate indirect cost pool should be developed during the course of the regular allocation process, and the separate indirect cost rate resulting therefrom should be used provided it is determined that (i) the rate differs significantly from that which would have been obtained under paragraph D.2, 3, and 4 above, and (ii) the volume of work to which the rate would apply is material.

E. Negotiation and Approval of Indirect Cost Rates.

1. *Definitions.* As used in this section, the following terms have the meanings set forth below:

a. "Cognizant agency" means the Federal agency responsible for negotiating and approving indirect cost rates for a nonprofit organization on behalf of all Federal agencies.

b. "Predetermined rate" means an indirect cost rate, applicable to a specified current or future period, usually the organization's fiscal year. The rate is based on an estimate of the costs to be incurred during the period. A predetermined rate is not subject to adjustment.

c. "Fixed rate" means an indirect cost rate which has the same characteristics as a predetermined rate, except that the difference between the estimated costs and the actual costs of the period covered by the rate is carried forward as an adjustment to the rate computation of a subsequent period.

d. "Final rate" means an indirect cost rate applicable to a specified past period which is based on the actual costs of the period. A final rate is not subject to adjustment.

e. "Provisional rate" or billing rate means a temporary indirect cost rate applicable to a specified period which is used for funding, interim reimbursement, and reporting indirect costs on awards pending the establishment of a final rate for the period.

f. "Indirect cost proposal" means the documentation prepared by an organization to substantiate its claim for the reimbursement of indirect costs. This proposal provides the basis for the review and negotiation leading to the establishment of an organization's indirect cost rate.

g. "Cost objective" means a function, organizational subdivision, contract, grant, or other work unit for which cost data are desired and for which provision is made to accumulate and measure the cost of processes, projects, jobs and capitalized projects.

2. *Negotiation and approval of rates.*

a. Unless different arrangements are agreed to by the agencies concerned, the Federal agency with the largest dollar value of awards with an organization will be designated as the cognizant agency for the negotiation and approval of indirect cost rates and, where necessary, other rates such as fringe benefit and computer charge-out rates. Once an agency is assigned cognizance for a particular nonprofit organization, the assignment will not be changed unless there is a major long-term shift in the dollar volume of the Federal awards to the organization. All concerned Federal agencies shall be given the opportunity to participate in the negotiation process, but after a rate has been agreed upon it will be accepted by all Federal agencies. When a Federal agency has reason to believe that special operating factors affecting its awards necessitate special indirect cost rates in accordance with paragraph D.5 above, it will, prior to the time the rates are negotiated, notify the cognizant agency.

b. A nonprofit organization which has not previously established an indirect cost rate with a Federal agency shall submit its initial indirect cost proposal to the cognizant agency. The proposal shall be submitted as soon as possible after the organization is advised that an award will be made and, in no event, later than three months after the effective date of the award.

c. Organizations that have previously established indirect cost rates must submit a new indirect cost proposal to the cognizant agency within six months after the close of each fiscal year.

d. A predetermined rate may be negotiated for use on awards where there is reasonable assurance, based on past experience and reliable projection of the organization's costs, that the rate is not likely to exceed a rate based on the organization's actual costs.

e. Fixed rates may be negotiated where predetermined rates are not considered appropriate. A fixed rate, however, shall not be negotiated if (i) all or a substantial portion of the organization's awards are expected to expire before the carry-forward adjustment can be made; (ii) the mix of Government and non-government work at the organization is too erratic to permit an equitable carry-forward adjustment; or (iii) the organization's operations fluctuate significantly from year to year.

f. Provisional and final rates shall be negotiated where neither predetermined nor fixed rates are appropriate.

g. The results of each negotiation shall be formalized in a written agreement between the cognizant agency and the nonprofit organization. The cognizant agency shall distribute copies of the agreement to all concerned Federal agencies.

h. If a dispute arises in a negotiation of an indirect cost rate between the cognizant agency and the nonprofit organization, the dispute shall be resolved in accordance with the appeals procedures of the cognizant agency.

i. To the extent that problems are encountered among the Federal agencies in connection with the negotiation and approval process, the Office of Management and Budget will lend assistance as required to resolve such problems in a timely manner.

The major conceptual task in calculating the overhead rate is the proper classification of costs between direct and indirect. For this reason an independent judgment, perhaps through an audit, of how the organization classified costs is necessary before an overhead rate is etablished. In federal government contracting, agencies may differ among themselves as to what is an appropriate overhead rate for the nonprofit. Further, even though an agency may accept an overhead rate at the inception of a contract, it may change it if an audit of the organization's books by the agency shows that the classification of direct and indirect costs or the amounts assigned to each were incorrect or inconsistent with the actual cost experience of the organization. Unlike the government, many foundations do not pay overhead when financing specific programs. These programs are financed by restricted funds and overhead must be covered by unrestricted funds (sometimes called general funds) from other sources.

Two types of costs, common and joint, are indirect costs that are particularly important for nonprofits seeking to enter into a business. Two products are said to have a common cost when they share an identical cost factor so that the production of one of the products means incurring part if not all of the costs of producing the other. The same thing is true with joint costs. However, with joint costs, unlike common costs, the ratio of the output of the two products remains the same. To illustrate, the production of beef and hide are joint costs because they have the same cost factors (the production of cattle) and they occur roughly in the same ratio: so many pounds of beef and so much hide in an animal.

The important thing about both common and joint costs is that they provide ways of exploiting the charitable mission of the nonprofit for business purposes. The selling of advertising space in the nonprofit's publication is an example. The advertising (business) and the articles (nonbusiness) activities share printing, editorial, circulation, material, and space costs. (See Chap. 3–8.)

These costs are important in budgeting if the costs are to be allocated among the activities, as they must be for accounting purposes. In addition, a careful review of major costs items may reveal opportunities for producing a money-making product or service at very little additional cost.

Costs can also be classified as variable or fixed.[6] These concepts are closely related to direct and indirect costs but they are not synonymous. A fixed cost is one that does not vary with the number or amount of product or services produced. Thus, if the concert is to be held in Harmony Hall, the cost of Harmony Hall is fixed. If Harmony Hall has a capacity of 590 people, the rental for the hall is the same whether 590, or 400, or zero persons attend the concert. The rental does not vary by the number of attendees. It is also a direct cost to the concert, for without the concert there would be no need to rent the hall. This says that in budgeting a program should be fully charged for its direct cost, part of which could be fixed.

In contrast to fixed costs, there are variable costs. These are costs that vary with the number or quantity of a product or service produced. The number of tickets printed is a variable cost; usually, the more tickets printed the higher the total printing bill. It is less expensive to print 100 tickets than 500. Thus, in planning the budget for the concert we must add the direct variable costs to the direct fixed costs.

Let's pause to take note. When the decision is made to hold the concert, all costs are variable. The nonprofit has not yet selected a hall; it may choose among many. But once the hall is chosen it is a fixed cost—not simply because it is chosen, but because it holds 590 people and rents for a fixed fee. The nonprofit cannot change the fee or vary the capacity of the hall. It is fixed. But it can certainly affect costs by varying the number of tickets it prints. This reveals two principles: (1) that both direct fixed and direct variable costs should figure in the budgetary plans for an activity; and (2) once the decision has been made, the only discretion is over variable costs.

But who pays for the indirect cost? Who pays the overhead? Someone has to pay the salaries of the nonprofit management and for the office space in which the nonprofit works. Indirect costs are those that exist even in the absence of the particular activity. These costs are not the result of the concert. Ah, but the concert is being conducted by the nonprofit and the latter needed a staff and offices to function—not only for the concert but for the general mission of the organization. Thus, the indirect costs are allocated (when possible) among all projects of the nonprofit. All projects benefit from the existence, operation and management of the nonprofit. The concert is charged its share of indirect cost, its full share of direct fixed costs and its full share of direct variable costs.

Again, the allocation of overhead among all projects in a nonprofit organization is not always possible or necessary, as in the case of firms, because some funding agencies will not pay overhead. General or unrestricted funds are needed to meet these overhead costs which arise from the cost of the organization's being. We shall elaborate in Chapter 13.

In short, using the budget as a mangement tool means being able to separate various types of costs, looking at variances and making adjustments, and understanding that once the program is in operation, the only control is over the variable costs. Fixed costs cannot be affected and indirect costs whether fixed or variable are outside the control of program managers. The latter costs fall within the purview of the management of the organization.

Related to variable costs are marginal or incremental costs. This is the increment in cost due to the production of an additional unit of good or service. By how much does variable cost increase if one more unit of the good is produced? This is marginal or incremental cost. When marginal cost is increasing rapidly, variable cost and total costs are increasing rapidly. By knowing something about marginal costs, we can know by how much to cut output in order to keep variable costs and hence total costs from rising rapidly. In the example of Harmony Hall, the manager knows that costs can only be affected once the decision to use Harmony Hall is made by reducing variable costs. But how much can he save by printing one less ticket? This is marginal cost. In other words, by knowing marginal cost the manager will know how much can be saved by reducing the variable costs (the tickets) one by one, and how much costs will increase should the number of tickets be increased one by one.

Marginal cost is important for another reason. It tells the manager how much additional support may be needed as the output of goods or services increases. If a nonprofit produces housing units and the marginal cost of a unit is known to be $4,000 (that is, the next unit will add $4,000 to total costs), then the minimum amount of support that the nonprofit must raise to fully cover the cost of that additional unit is $4,000. By knowing how much variable costs increase as output increases (marginal cost), the manager can tell how much must be raised to cover that cost. Any additional amount contributes to the reduction of overhead or fixed costs.

Marginal costs show only the variation in variable costs as the number of goods and services produced varies. Another concept of costs is average cost. This tells the unit cost of each output. Average cost is found by dividing total costs by the number of units produced. Total costs is the sum of variable and fixed costs or the sum of direct and indirect costs. For most planning purposes, a nonprofit manager may find it easier to calculate average costs rather marginal costs. Furthermore, for many reporting purposes, average costs are requested. Often marginal and average costs are about equal so that one is a good approximation of the other. The astute manager should realize, however, that there is a difference between the two concepts and a conceptual familiarity with both helps to make better decisions.

The total cost of goods or services produced is the sum of variable and fixed costs, just as the total cost from an earlier perspective is the sum of direct and indirect costs. One perspective shows how cost varies as output varies. The other distinguishes between costs directly and exclusively due to a specific project and, therefore, a direct cost of that project, and those due to the existence and operation of the organization. Both perspectives give important information to the manager.

Another concept of cost is opportunity cost. This is the true economic cost of a project. Because every organization has a limited amount of resources, any decision to undertake one project means that another project has to be reduced or totally sacrificed. Opportunity cost tells the management in monetary or programmatic terms the consequence of its decisions on the ability of the nonprofit to meet all facets of its mission. We saw in Chapter 8 that opportunity cost can be measured in financial terms when choices are being made about alternative investment opportunities.

In a similar manner when measurement permits, opportunity cost can be measured in terms of the net present value of benefits foregone by choosing one program over another. Even when measurement is not fully possible, the concept of opportunity cost is important in reminding decision makers that the choice of one program over another is not costless. This realization should be an explicit part of the decision. What are we giving up to pursue this course of action?

Opportunity cost is applicable every time the management thinks, "we could have done X if we didn't have to do Y," or "in order to do X we cannot do Y." Opportunity cost forces management to see the consequence of its decisions on the ability of the organization to fully meet its mission or the targets decided upon in the strategic planning process as seen in Chapter 5.

Costs are not always instantaneous. Some costs flow over several years. This is not simply because the cost is associated with a capital item, the payments of which extend over years, but because once a project has been launched it sets into place a stream of costs from which the organization may not be able to extricate itself. Once a building has been bought, the mortgage must be paid regardless of whether or not the building is used. This is related to an initial capital expenditure which also sets off the need for various types of operating expenses—insurance, janitorial, utility, security. Similarly, once a journal or newsletter has been launched, the organization must be prepared to carry it through for some time or lose face (a small price to pay compared to bankruptcy.)

In planning, programming and budgeting, it is important to take into account the operating as well as capital expenditures that flow over time. Often these costs increase rather than decrease as time passes. Inflation and deterioration requiring maintenance are two reasons why these costs increase.

This brings us to another element of costs—replacement costs. It is beyond the purpose of this book to discuss the actual measurement of costs and cost accounting. But what is important for the purpose of this book is for the reader to appreciate that the term "cost" could refer to the original cost of the item or the replacement cost at a given period in time. The replacement cost of a machine today would be the price one has to pay for it today. The replacement cost tomorrow may be higher. The original cost (what one paid for it in the past) is lower. In capital (*not* operating as in the discussion here) budgeting, repacement cost is sometimes better to consider than original cost because the organization is looking into the future. In accounting, original cost is used because the organization is depreciating or recovering its expenditure on a capital item for which it has already paid. This means that the cost in the balance sheet of an organization may be quite different to the cost in its capital budget for a similarly named property.

Another concept is sunk cost. Once an expenditure has been made it represents a sunk cost. It cannot be retrieved or changed. It therefore has no impact on what the financial opportunities are today or tomorrow. Tomorrow's choices should not be burdened by yesterday's. Therefore sunk costs are ignored when choosing among programs (capital or operating) to be financed by an organization in the future.

All of the concepts described are helpful, at least conceptually, even if they cannot be precisely measured and even if in some organizations the activity and budgetary levels are so small and simple that they do not justify expensive calculations. In many of these organizations, what appears as costs are really expenditures. That is to say, the organization spends in every year roughly what it has as revenues from all sources. These organizations are said to be on a cash basis.

Other nonprofits are on an accrual basis. They record costs when they are incurred, not necessarily when they are paid. Thus, what they would show in their budgets will be the costs they will incur during that period. The actual payment may be made in the future. Similarly, the revenues shown are those to which they have a firm commitment, even though the revenues may not be received until the future. The advantage of this approach to budgeting and accounting is that management can get a more accurate picture of what costs it actually incurred and what revenue commitments it actual had during a period in time. How much did it actually cost to operate in this period even though we do not pay the bills until the next period? What will be the limit on our cost commitments this period? An organization on the accrual basis seeks to avoid financial difficulties by controlling its commitments.

Organizations on a cash basis seek to answer the questions: How much will we spend and pay for in cash this period? How much will we receive in cash this period? A cash-oriented organization seeks to avoid financial difficulties by controlling its cash flow, cash revenues and expenditures.

Finally, it should be pointed out that there is another way in which costs are reported for purposes of control and accountability. Many organizations find it wise to set up cost centers, mission centers, support centers or responsibility centers. Accordingly, instead of showing costs simply by function or object, costs are shown by centers of program activity. The center of activity might be a department or a unit that conducts more than one program or project. By doing this, the senior management can hold subordinate managers responsible for cost variations. In very large and complex organizations this decentralization into centers is often preferred since the central management cannot keep track of all the details of a program or unit. Within each unit, however, there might be a functional and an object budget so that the manager of that unit can keep track of financial and operating details.

Support

It is intentional that the word "support" is used. For nonprofits, the critical revenue data for the organization are sources of support. In Chapter 6 we described what is included in support for different types of tax-exempt qualifications. We now take a budgetary perspective on the same concepts.

In the for-profit sector, firms have only one principal source of revenues and that is from sales. In the public sector, the principal source of revenues is from taxation. In the nonprofit sector, revenues may come from a variety of sources. What is critical is the balance. Good budgeting for a nonprofit means more than showing numbers; it means being alert to the balance required to maintain the nonprofit's classification as discussed in Chapter 6.

For the management of the nonprofit, this balance has an important effect not intended by the law. The law intended this balance to assure itself that the nonprofit was not a sham for a profit or private money-making activity designed to avoid taxes. It turns out that this balance also means that support can be diversified. The more diversified support is, the better because it means that the nonprofit is not overly exposed to the influence of one supporter and to the risk that it would collapse if that supporter declines to make gifts or contributions.

Support falls into several categories. First, there are fees from membership. These can be a steady base of support and can be seen as analogous to fixed costs. Fees do not ordinarily go up or down depending upon the amount of output of the organization. Obviously, fees relate to the kinds of service the membership gets but small variations in that quantity do not appreciably affect the number of members. Disputes over particular services do affect membership and recession does cause a drop in membership as members or the agency or corporation that pays their membership dues fall on hard times. Not all nonprofits have membership and therefore not all get membership fees.

Other sources of support are gifts and contributions. In writing a budget, estimates from past experience should be made concerning amounts of gifts and contributions and their sources. This book should enable the manager to broaden the organization's base for more lucrative gifts and contributions. As stated earlier, in dealing with gifts and contributions, it is important to distinguish between those gifts that are made to the general fund of the organization and are unrestricted and those made with restrictions about the uses to which they may be put.

Another source of support is revenues from related and unrelated businesses. One advantage of revenues from these sources is that their use is totally at the discretion of the board of directors of the organization. They are also reasonably predictable in the same sense (and using the same techniques) that for-profit businesses project their earnings. The simplest way for a nonprofit to make these projections is by evaluating past trends and asking if there are any reasons to believe that there would be significant variations from past trends. If there are not, the trend line would be adequate. If variations are expected, then a judgment can be made to adjust the trend line. This is a judgment call. When the issue is more complex than this, then it is up to the management of the business to supply its nonprofit owners with better information. As a matter of fact, this information should always be demanded from the business manager.

Contracts and grants are another source of revenues. These may be from the federal, state or local governments or from a for-profit firm or from another organization. Some grants are unrestricted and are given to enable an organization to get off the ground by having resources that the management needs to build and support the organization. Other grants and all contracts are awards for performing a specific task. The task may be broadly defined but the money cannot be shifted from the intent of the contract or grant. Even these elements of revenues have a degree of predictability because many are multiyear grants or contracts.

Investments in securities and royalties produce revenue. Many securities have fixed terms and set rates of interest or dividends to be paid over a specified period. Some organizations (such as those in research) get royalties which are also predictable. The royalties that may be less predictable are production royalties that come from oil, gas and other materials. Gains and losses in the sale or purchase of securities are unpredictable.

INTEGRATION OF STRATEGIC PLANNING, PROGRAMMING AND BUDGETING

Conceptual, our previous discussion of costs and support can be integrated into our earlier discussion of strategic planning. Budgets are expressions of a plan. In strategic planning, programming begins at the point that a decision has been made about the type of programs that the organization will undertake to carry out its mission. The specific choice of programs can only be made after each program has been financially appraised; that is, what will it cost, and what will it yield in benefits? Consequently, strategic planning, programming and budgeting is a symbiotic process with constant feedback.

Referring to Figure 5.1 and reading it backwards rather than forward, we can say that: Programming is the process through which programs are designed to execute the strategies that will enable the organization to meet the management's chosen objectives because these are internally and externally compatible with the organization, enabling the organization to carry out the mission for which it was created.

Programming begins when programs to realize the strategies and objectives are being designed. Any rational choice of programs should be based partly on economic factors. Which program has the greater benefit-cost ratio? Can the organization raise the money to meet the cost? Can it afford the program? Answers to these questions can only be obtained through developing and comparing a standard budget for each alternative. Thus, budgeting and programming are linked and in the ideal case, when the choice of a program is made, a choice of a budget is also intrinsically a part of that choice.

While it is not necessary to go over the entire strategic planning exercise every year, it is necessary to do a budget every year. In those years when a new strategic plan is not developed and the existing plan remains operative, the budgeting exercise implies the continuation of the organization's strategies and objectives.

Any number of factors make annual budgeting imperative. Changes in the prices of labor, materials, and equipment, increases or decreases in revenues, changes in the size and scope of the activity, errors in the previous budget, the requirements of most major sponsors for annual budgets, and the bylaws of the organization are some of the most important forces leading to the pressures for an annual budget.

Let us see how some of the concepts learned earlier in this chapter apply in planning, programming and budgeting. We begin by noting that at the point of choosing among programs, we also compare their costs and revenues. This is what is referred to as a differential analysis. We are comparing the difference between one set of costs and revenues against others. This is how we compare costs and benefits as in Figure 5.2.

We get these costs and revenues by estimating what we can expect. For example, we know that if the average secretary costs $4.00 per hour and we need 2,000 hours of secretarial time, that we can expect to spend $8,000 in secretarial salaries plus benefits. Thus, we calculate standard costs for labor. We do the same for materials by multiplying the price of the material times the quantity that we expect to use. Less precisely, we can guess future revenues based upon projections from past experiences and by netting new and continued commitments and promises from those that will terminate.

Given dollar limitations and the limitations of the organization, a choice must be made because all programs cannot be adopted. Thus, we are comparing opportunity costs. How much are we giving up by adopting one program over another?

From a decision-making and operating perspective, however, it is not sufficient to know what the total costs or revenues would be. As we saw earlier, the composition of revenues by source is important to the maintenance of tax-exempt status. It is also important in giving management a clue as to whether the revenue flow can be sustained sufficiently into the future to finance any commitments they may make. It is pure folly to make a five-year cost commitment for a gift that will last only one year. In the same vein, it is important to know the structure of costs, for if the program has a high proportion of direct fixed costs, then this is tantamount to saying that the organization is committing itself to a cost structure over which it will have little control in subsequent years. Fixed costs are usually long-term costs (such as furniture, automobiles, buildings, equipment) which the organization must pay even if the program fails.

Therefore, management must distinguish between direct variable costs of each program (labor, materials, supplies that are used directly and solely for each program within their mission or responsibility center). These costs are within their managerial control. Management can reduce the number of persons employed or increase the number of hours worked, knowing that by so doing they change both the center's production and costs. For example, since labor that is a direct cost to a program is variable, the amount of work done can be increased by increasing the number of workers assigned exclusively to that project, and the reverse is also true.

Similarly, managers must be able to isolate the direct fixed costs. By so doing, the manager can know what proportion of costs and what cost factors he or she has relatively no control over once the program gets underway. If the program requires a printing machine or a computer, no marginal or slight variation in output is going to affect costs. These costs must be met regardless of the level of effort making them fixed. Such costs are directly and exclusively the result of a specific program.

Management should also be aware of the indirect costs or overhead associated with a responsibility center. Overhead costs are those that are indirectly associated with each program in the center. If any one program was dropped, these costs would still exist. A good example is the salary paid to the director of the center and to the secretary, accounting clerk, receptionist, and so on. These people serve the entire mission center, not just one program in it. Obviously, indirect costs can be variable—the more programs, the more central staff that is needed. Indirect costs can also be fixed.

In addition to the indirect costs associated with the mission itself is the indirect cost of the support centers that are allocated or assigned to the responsibility center. For example, if the organization has a president and a central administration, part of the cost of this central administration is allocated to each one of the mission centers. These two parts of the indirect cost (those generated by the responsibility center and those assigned or allocated to it) make up the total overhead cost that the center must meet.

This is done by setting an overhead rate that is charged to every program operated by the center. Thus, every program contributes to paying the organization's overhead. The overhead rate can be a percentage of direct labor costs or a percentage of total direct costs (labor and materials) or some percentage of volume of output. That rate is charged to every program in the center to the extent that the funding agency permits. Some foundations do not pay overhead. Some donors may subsidize the overhead of a nonprofit by giving money to cover general support either of a center or of the entire organization. Generally, government contracts cover overhead (See the insert on page 293.)

Overhead must be allocated between the exempt and nonexempt (including unrelated business) activities of the organization. Thus, a university operating a fieldhouse that is used both for exempt and unrelated business is permitted to allocate the overhead between the two based upon the amount of time the facility is used for the two purposes.[7] The effect of this is to reduce the amount of taxes the university pays on unrelated business income because overhead expenses are deducted.

FORECASTING

Implicit in much of the previous discussion is the question: How do we know what future revenues and expenditures will be? Answers to this type of question requires forecasting or projecting.

The science of revenue and expenditure forecasting can be very complex or very simple. For most nonprofit organizations, simple methods are applicable. One method is to assume that last year's accomplishment will be the same or increase or decrease by a certain percent. This percent can be based on the previous year's performance adjusted by expectations of some unusual event. For example, just by taking a look at how the receipts have grown per year over the past five years is an indication. The simple average of that amount could be used.

Going up the ladder of sophistication one step, the management could look at the weighted average of the past five years. For example, the management may say that we are less likely to perform as we did in the first years, and more likely to perform as we did in the most recent ones. Thus, last year's performance may be multiplied by 5, the year before that by 4, the year before that by 3, the one before that by 2, and the last by 1. The average of this gives us a weighted average.

A third level of sophistication may involve some form of an equation. The simplest form is a linear regression model but we will not discuss that here. However, imagine that the organization has ten years of experience. It may plot its performance each year such as in Figure 12.1. Then it may run or calculate

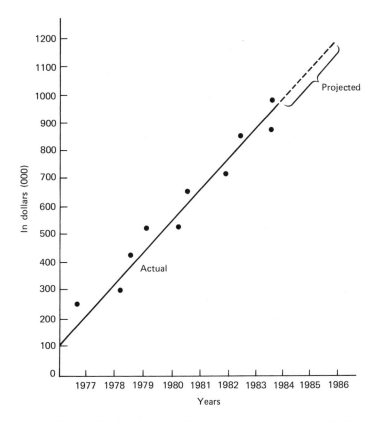

Figure 12.1 Scatter Diagram of Annual Receipts or Expenditures and Projections into Future. Source: Author.

a straight line through these points. The slope of this line is the average rate that the performance may be expected to change over time. This slope can then be used to project the future. Simply move up along the line.

However this is done, it is to be appreciated that forecasting is judgmental. A new organization may simply make a modest guess year after year, and this experience over the years becomes the basis for its projections. Projections should never yield to mathematics even though the latter is important in avoiding wild guesses. Comparing the actual with the projected we get a variance that tells us how good our forcasting is. But the past is not necessarily prologue.

For most organizations there is an element of stability. From past experience of commitment, a bottom level of revenues to be received is known. Several grants are multiyear. Some costs are so critical to the organization that they will never run to zero. If it cannot afford office space, it cannot function. Hence, it is impossible to approach forecasting with the notion: "We have no idea." The management may not know it all, but it most surely know the minimum performance in revenues beyond which it must close down and the minimum performance in expenditures below which it is a useless organization.

BUDGET FORMATS: FORMS AND FUNCTIONS

The purpose of this section is to discuss formats that can be used to set up and analyze budgets and for presentation to the board. This is not a difficult task once the basic aim, as discussed earlier, is understood.

Combinations of Program and Item Budgets

Table 12.1 shows a combination of a functional or program budget with an object or item budget. Such a display gives management a view of how much of the organization's dollars are being spent on each program and their distribution among various items. In accounting, each program is referred to as a cost objective. It is the set of actions that generates costs. Each unit that generates these costs or runs a program is called a cost center. Thus, we can see that through a form such as Table 12.1 it is possible to pinpoint which cost center (staff units) is mostly responsible for each type of expenditure.

Each program, may have more than one objective. For example, we show that program C has three objectives. Suppose that program C is for operating a new site for a nonprofit organization that runs a chain of day care centers. Each objective under program C may be a site. Note that other programs are given no objectives. Whether or not each should be broken down into objectives is a matter of judgment. In general, a program should not be broken down into objectives if each cannot be clearly defined and if each cannot be clearly and separately evaluated.

Table 12.2 is an example of a form that may be used to analyze the inflow of expected or budgeted money into the organization. This inflow may

TABLE 12.1 Example of Program or Functional Budget and Object or Item Budget Combined

Object or Item Budget

Classification of Program	Salaries and Benefits	Rent and Utility	Supplies and Materials	Travel	Equipment	Totals
Program A						
Program B						
Program C Objective 1 Objective 2 Objective 3						
Program D						
Program E						
Totals						

Source: Author

TABLE 12.2 Example of Horizontal and Vertical Presentations of Actual and Budgeted Receipts

Classification of Support	Actual Receipts		Budgeted Receipts 1986	Change in Receipts		Distribution of Dollars by Sources (in percent)	
	1984	1985		1984–1985	1985–1986	1985	1986
Restricted							
Total							
Unrestricted							
Total Unrestricted							
Total						100.0	100.0

Source: The author

be divided between restricted funds such as gifts, contracts, and endowments over which the nonprofit has no discretionary control and unrestricted funds. The latter are inflows from fees, business income, investments, gifts and contributions which have not been designated exclusively for some specified purpose. The ratio of the two gives an indication of the amount of discretionary authority the management has over its budget. It is possible to have a wealthy nonprofit with minimal discretionary authority.

The first two columns give a historical backdrop for the budgeted amount in the third column. By doing this, management has some basis for judging the reasonableness of the budgeted amount. Why should we expect this amount of money from gifts and contributions when we have not had anything close to it in the past? Is the staff serious, or do they have something planned? What is it? Is it feasible? Will it generate that much revenue? Is it consistent with the mission of the organization? Will it infringe on the organization's tax-exempt status? Is it desirable?

The next two columns give the rate of growth in past years as well as the budgeted rate of growth. Rates of growth (occurring across columns) are examples of what accountants refer to as horizontal analysis; that is, one column is divided by another. Again, by setting up the budgeted rate of growth next to the past rate of growth, it is possible to judge the reasonableness of the expectation. By looking down the rows, it is possible to ascertain which sources of support are expected to grow fastest.

The last two columns show the percentage that each source will contribute to the overall expected revenues of the organization during the year for which the budget is made. This is called a vertical analysis because it shows how much each row contributes to the total. Each of these columns will add up to approximately 100 percent. Again, reasonableness can be disclosed by comparing the budgeted amount with the past year's performance. It is important to indicate that once these figures are accepted by the board they become targets. Accordingly, in the next budget cycle, an appropriate question would be: Why did we not attain our financial objectives? If we outdid our expectations, can we do it again?

A similar type of analysis can be done in Table 12.3 for expenditures. Note that in both the cases of expenditures and revenues we are concerned with the rates and distribution of growth or decline. Variances to be discussed below, are concerned with actual performance.

Variances

Variance analysis is a highly technical field and most quantitative approaches would have limited use in nonprofits. Here we present the most basic idea which has the greatest usefulness. Earlier we discussed variances from planned amounts and other types of variances. In this section, we show some forms that may be used. From a policy perspective, management should be concerned with at least three types of variances: variances in overall program expenditures from the budgeted amount, variances in receipt from the expected amount, and variances from alternatives, especially those that would have been

TABLE 12.3   Example of Horizontal and Vertical Presentation of Actual and Budgeted Expenditures

Classification Programs	Actual Expenditures		Budgeted Expenditures	Change		Distribution of Dollars by Programs (percent)	
	1984	1985	1986	1984 to 1985	1985 to 1986	1985	1986
Program A							
Program B							
Program C							
Program D							
Program E							
Totals						100.0	100.0

Source: Author

acceptable if the expected expenditures were lower. Operationally, managers may also be interested in variances in actual costs from standard costs where standard costs may be the list price of an item or the usual and reasonable current cost multiplied by the number of the item used.

Table 12.4 shows a format that may be used to look at variances in expenditures. Note that the advantage of putting all of this information on one sheet is that it is easily read. Each program being implemented (A to E) is assessed at least every six months by comparing the budgeted amount with the actual expenditure. The difference is the variance which should be shown both in dollars and in percentages. At the end of each year, this is also done so that an annual summary is available.

There is no hard and fast rule saying this analysis must be done every six months. In some cases, it might be wise to do it quarterly or even monthly. The critical factor is that it is done with sufficient frequency that the information needed to generate corrective action is available in time for action to be taken. There is little value in knowing that a program is off target when the program is already ended. The trade-off is interruption in the flow of work and the resistance of many managers to report data accurately and frequently.

At the bottom of the form is room for explanation. This may not be sufficient room. Both positive and negative variances (undershooting or overshooting targets) need to be explained. As stated earlier, spending less than budgeted may be a sign that the program has been delayed and will not meet its deadline. Overshooting may mean that the program was badly designed and needs revamping and will lead to a deficit. To appreciate this latter point, recall that contracts are often negotiated at a fixed price. This means that if the organiza-

TABLE 12.4 Example of Variance Between Budgeted (Expected) and Actual Expenditures

Classification of Programs	First Six Months			Second Six Months			Cumulative Year End		
	Budgeted	Actual	Variance	Budgeted	Actual	Variance	Budgeted	Actual	Variance
Program A									
Program B									
Program C									
Program D									
Program E									
Comments: Explanation:									

Source: Author

tion overshoots and results in a deficit there is no way to recover the money from the donor or the contracting agency.

A similar type of form can be used for analyzing variances of expected from actual receipts, Table 12.5. In this case, the receipts should be divided into the two basic groups of unrestricted and restricted funds. Restricted funds are from endowments, gifts or decisions of the board to set aside funds to be used only for specific designated purposes. Unrestricted funds are those that go into the general account of the organization and can be used in the way management chooses. These are discretionary funds. Here, too, the arguments of the previous paragraphs including the frequency of collecting and reporting these data pertain. It is apodictic that if receipts are lagging behind expenditures, the organization is heading for trouble. The purpose of these forms is to give an early warning of what is ahead.

For this reason, a separate summary sheet is necessary for the end of every period to show what the projected deficit or surplus is likely to be based on that period and the past period's performance. An example is Table 12.6. The unrestricted account shows the individual program period and a cumulative deficit or surplus, since all funds in that account may be used for any general purpose. Not so with the restricted account and, therefore, each has an expected deficit or surplus.

A RECOMMENDED FORMAT FOR USING THE BUDGET AS A CONTROL TOOL

Let us consider the difficulty placed on an executive whose organization conducts many programs. Each responsibility center or mission center in the organization may oversee several cost objectives or programs. If the manager oversees ten mission centers and if each has ten programs, such a manager would either have to look at 100 different budgets, or ten summary budgets—one for each responsibility center summarizing all of the activities in that center. One hundred budgets are too many to consider in detail and ten summary budgets are, by definition, too broad to grasp the essential details.

From a control point of view, the financial manager needs to identify quickly and flag those programs that are in jeopardy of overspending in order to meet their targets, those that have overspent and, if possible, cut losses by terminating them, and those that are moving so laggardly that they are not likely to spend the money committed to them in the time period allotted and may therefore need an extension lest the money allocated to them be lost.

I would like to recommend a way in which this can be done for each program and yet not be burdensome. Please turn to Table 12.7. It shows a list of over a 100 programs according to the responsibility centers under which they fall. Each program has a control number to identify it. The first two digits identify the responsibility center and the other digits identify the specific program within the center; i.e., 0110 is a program in the responsibility center designated

TABLE 12.5 Example of Variance Between Budgeted (Expected) and Actual Receipts

Classification of Support	First Six Months			Second Six Months			Cumulative		
	Budgeted	Actual	Variance	Budgeted	Actual	Variance	Budgeted	Actual	Variance
Restricted									
Total Restricted									
Unrestricted									
Total Unrestricted									
Total									
Explanation									

Source: Author

TABLE 12.6   Example of Summary Showing Deficit or Surplus
by Program

Classification of Programs	Summary First Six Months		Summary Second Six Months		Summary Cumulative	
	Deficit	Surpluses	Deficit	Surpluses	Deficit	Surpluses
Unrestricted						
Program A						
Program B						
Program C						
Total unrestricted						
Restricted						
Program D						
Program E						
Explanation:						

Source: Author

01. The number 10 identified the program. In this display we show each responsibility center having 27 programs. It is not necessary for purposes of financial flagging to deal with specific program names.

The program code is followed by a code such as 2/4/80/70. The first number represents the current year of the program, i.e., 2 would mean that the program is in its second year—the year for which the present budget is being submitted. The second number indicates the expected life of the program, i.e., 4 means that the program is planned for four years. The third number is the percentage of the total allocation that will be consumed by the end of the year for which the budget is being submitted, i.e., 80 means that by the end of this year, 80 percent of the budget allotment would have been used up. The fourth number indicates the program manager's assessment of the amount of work that will have been done by the end of the budget year, i.e., 70 percent means that by the end of this present budget year, only 30 percent of the promised activities will be left to be done.

This technique provides several advantages. First, the financial manager can focus on the possibilities of cost overruns on each program within the organization because the pertinent information is given in simple form. Second, it gives the individual program manager, the manager of the responsibility center in which the program falls, and management of the organization an early warn-

TABLE 12.7 Format for Flagging Potential Budgetary Problems

Program Code	Responsibility Center-01 Status	Flag	Program Code	Responsibility Center-02 Status	Flag	Program Code	Responsibility Center-03 Status	Flag	Program Code	Responsibility Center-04 Status	Flag
0100			0200			0300			0400		
0101			0201			0301			0401		
0102			0202			0302			0402		
0103			0203			0303			0403		
0104			0204			0304			0404		
0105			0205			0305			0405		
0106			0206			0306			0406		
0107			0207			0307			0407		
0108			0208			0308	1/2/110/60		0408		
0109			0209			0309			0409		
0110	3/4/10/90		0210			0310			0410		
0111			0211			0311			0411		
0112			0212			0312			0412		

Source: Author

319

TABLE 12.7 (Continued)

	Responsibility Center-01			Responsibility Center-02			Responsibility Center-03			Responsibility Center-04	
Program Code	Status	Flag	Program Code	Status	Flag	Program Code	Status	Flag	Program Code	Status	Flag
0113			0213	3/4/99/50		0313			0413		
0114			0214			0314			0414	3/5/80/60	
0115			0215			0315			0415		
0116			0216			0316			0416		
0117			0217			0317	2/4/80/70		0417		
0118			0218			0318			0418		
0119			0219			0319			0419		
0120			0220			0320			0420		
0121			0221			0321			0421		
0122			0222			0322			0422		
0123			0223			0323			0423		
0124			0224			0324			0424		
0125			0225			0325			0425		
0126			0226			0326			0426		
0127			0227			0327			0427		

Source: Author

ing of trouble. Third, it forces the program manager to assess how much has been accomplished and how much is still left to be done; and, consequently, to be accountable as to how the tasks remaining to be done will get done.

Now, it is not unusual to find program managers who would try to escape this responsibility by saying that it is hard to ''measure how much is left to be done.'' Such a plea is itself often a sign of incompetence. The fact is that one cannot manage a multi-year program under a budget constraint, if one cannot see the end of the project and cannot ascertain where one is, where one is going and roughly what it will take to get there. The judgement does not have to be 100 percent accurate. It has to be reasonable. The users of such information should keep in mind that an objective of all control systems is to be able flag and avoid potential problems. Control systems do not give answers as much as they flag situations where managerial attention ought to be focused and questions raised.

In addition to reducing the probability of cost overruns, this system also alerts managers to projects that are lagging behind the funding schedule. Some contracts are written such that they terminate at a specific period in time and must be re-negotiated at the risk that they will not be extended. Unspent funds may be lost. Thus a program that shows 3/4/10/90 is as much a potential problem as one that shows 3/4/99/50. The first has to find a way to justifiably use 90 percent of the funding in one year when only 10 percent of the job is left to be done. This is not a problem only if the last 10 percent can justifiably use the remaining funds. The latter has to do 50 percent of the work with 1 percent of the funds.

A display such as 1/2/110/60 would raise serious questions about cutting losses. This is a two-year program which at the end of its first year it would have overspent its budget by 10 percent and still has 40 percent of the expected work to be completed. One that shows 3/5/80/60 is a five-year program that already in its third year there is a sign of a potential need for more funding. This process of seeking additional funding can be started well before the project enters into serious cost overruns.

A Budget Format for the Board

The formats we have discussed are well suited for daily management. The board of directors need less detailed information, and can request it if they do. They need to evaluate the overall direction of the organization.

One format for presenting a budget to directors is to show simultaneously the revenue, support and expense expectations and how they are distributed by program and support categories. This is shown in Table 12.8.

This format shows the revenues and support by source and how they are distributed across programs and support activities by the organization at the same time that it shows how the organization plans to allocate its dollars not only by expense category but simultaneously by program or support category. This budget format is akin to Table 12.2, but it omits considerations of the dif-

TABLE 12.8 A Budget Format for the Board of Directors

| | Program Services | | | | | Supporting Services | | | Total Expenses | |
	Program 1	Program 2	Program 3	Program 4	Total	Fund Raising	Management and General	Total	1985	1986
Support and revenue:										
Support-contributions and grants and contracts										
Revenue-fees and investment income										
Total support and revenue										
Expenses:										
Salaries										
Employee benefits and payroll taxes										
Fees to consultants and contracted services, including expenses										
Fees to authors and speakers, including expenses										
Rent										
Printing and production										
Postage and mailings										
Office supplies and expenses										
Telephone										
Conference on-site expenses										
Committee meetings										
Travel and other meetings										
Books and periodicals										
Advertising and promotion										
Depreciation										
Other										
Total expenses										

ferent objectives of each program. The objectives can be given as part of the supporting document accompanying the budget.

The advantage of this format is that it provides the key information needed by top-level decisions makers at a glance. It gives the following information:

1. It shows the total revenues that are expected during the year, how much will be distributed to each of the various programs or responsibility centers, how much will be allocated to support activities, and the composition of revenues by type. For example, it shows how much the organization expects to receive from contributions. Is this reasonable? Does this help the organization maintain its one-third support requirements? How will these revenues be distributed across programs? Is this consistent with the mission of the organization and the directive of the board? Should some programs be more self-supporting?

2. It shows the major expense categories of the organization and how much the organization plans to allocate to each category by program.

3. It shows annual changes in allocated amounts by type of expenses.

One of the principal advantages of such a format is that it comes close to the statement of revenues, support and expenses that records the actual dollars that were received and spent by the organization during the year. Hence, it would be easy to compare actual with planned performance. In a later chapter we shall look at statements of revenues and expenses and come back to this discussion.

SUMMARY AND CONCLUSIONS

This chapter focuses on different views of costs as the other parts of this book focused on revenues. Specifically, the chapter looks at direct, indirect, fixed, variable, overhead opportunity and other cost concepts and indicates how they may be used by the managers of nonprofit organizations.

The chapter also shows the managers various forms that may be used in the presentation of budgets and how these may be analyzed both from the perspective of receipts and the expenditures. The budget is not only an expression of the strategic plan showing how dollars are to be allocated among various cost objectives or programs, but it is also a political tool and an instrument to exercise control over the functioning of the organization.

In order to utilize the control feature of budgets, it is imperative that standard forms be set up by each organization such that variances of all types may be analyzed. If this is done properly and on a periodic basis, the management will have an opportunity to take corrective action before it is too late.

NOTES

1. The reader is referred to any standard text on the mathematics of finance and to Chapter 14 of this book.
2. Ibid.

3. Industrial revenue bonds are issued by local government authorities to finance projects of private firms including nonprofit hospitals and housing authorities. These bonds are backed by the property and income stream of the project rather than by the local government's taxing powers. They are tax-exempt. Borrowing can also occur through nonprofit notes or institutional bonds.

4. Some levels of efficiency are required by law. Day care centers, hospitals, housing providers are all subject to legal regulations which affect their productivity. Housing providers, for example, must meet housing codes; hospitals and day care centers must meet health and zoning codes.

5. The reader is again referred to the Appendix 7.1 and to standard texts in the mathematics of finance.

6. Rensselaer Polytechnic Institute v. Commissioner, Docket k# 7024–79, 79 Tax Court #60, 12/1/82.

7. Accounts also refer to semivariable costs. These are costs that are partly fixed and partly variable. Thus, a worker represents both fixed and variable costs. The amount that a hired worker must be paid even during the hours that he or she does not work is a fixed cost, and overtime pay is variable. For most analytic purposes, the fixed portion of the labor costs is simply categorized as fixed and the variable as variable. Hence, we can speak correctly to two types of costs—fixed and variable.

8. Revenue Ruling 79-18 and Revenue Ruling 72-124.

SUGGESTED READINGS

American Institute of Certified Public Accountants, *Audit of Certain Nonprofit Organizations* (New York: American Institute of Certified Public Accountants, 1981).

American Institute of Certified Public Accountants, *Accounting Principles and Reporting Practices for Certain Nonprofit Organizations* (New York: American Institute of Certified Public Accountants, 1978).

ANTHONY, ROBERT N. and REGINA HERZLINGER, *Management Control in Non-Profit Organizations,* rev. ed. (Homewood, Illinois: Richard D. Irwin, 1980).

CRESS, WILLIAM P. and JAMES PETTIJOHN, "A Survey of Budget-Related Planning and Control Policies and Procedures," *Journal of Accounting Education*, Vol. 3 #2. Fall 1985, p. 61–80.

GROSS, MALVERN J., JR. and WILLIAM WARSHAUER, JR., *Financial and Accounting Guide for Nonprofit Organizations*, rev. ed. (New York: John Wiley, 1983).

HENKE, EMERSON O., *Introduction to Nonprofit Organization Accounting* (Boston: Kent Publishing Company, 1980).

JONES, REGINAL L. and H. GEORGE TRENTON, rev. ed. *Budgeting: Key to Planning and Control* (New York: American Management Association, AMACOM, 1971).

MONTGOMERY, THOMPSON A., *Financial Accounting Information,* 2nd ed. (Reading, Massachusetts: Addison-Wesley Publishing Company, 1982).

STOECH, JOHN, "What Human Services Managers Need to Know about Basic Budgeting Strategies," *Administration in Social Work,* 4, (Spring 1980), pp. 88–97.

TRAUB, JACK, *Accounting and Reporting Practices of Private Foundations* (New York: Praeger, 1977).

TRUMPELER, MARGO C. and RICHARD S. ROUNDS, *Basic Budgeting Practices for Librarians* (Chicago: American Library Association, 1985).

VINTER, ROBERT D. and RHEA K. KISH, *Budgeting for Not-for-Profit Organizations* (New York: The Free Press, 1984).

THIRTEEN

Recognizing Financial Opportunities and Impending Difficulties: Interpreting Financial Statements

Budgets are financial plans indicating the level at which the nonprofit plans to operate, how its resources will be allocated among various programs within its mission, and from where those dollar resources are expected to come. Budgets have no legal force in nonprofit organizations and they are usually never audited.

This is not so with the other financial documents that will be studied in this chapter. These documents are audited, they have some legal force and unlike the budget, they are made up of actual numbers rather than projections or estimates. These documents have legal force in the sense that to propagate them knowing that the numbers are wrong is an act of misrepresentation. It is these documents, not the budget, that creditors and donors to the organization often require. They are also often required by sponsors of single programs within the organization. While sponsors may ask for a budget of the program they expect to support, they usually also ask for a picture of the overall financial condition of the organization to be sure that they are not pouring their donation into a sinking ship. Moreover, it is these documents that provide the management with an early warning of impending financial disaster and signal the possibilities of financial opportunities. Let us begin with the balance sheet.

THE BALANCE SHEET

The balance sheet, Figure 13.1, is a statement of the financial position of the nonprofit on a given date, in this case, December 31, 1985. This balance sheet as presented assumes that the nonprofit sells a product in a related business.

326

There are also alternative presentations of a balance sheet.[1] These highlight certain points. As a basic rule, the information in the balance sheet is divided into two major categories; assets and liabilities and fund balances. Assets may be divided into two subgroups: current and fixed or long-term.

FIGURE 13.1   Example of a Balance Sheet of a Nonprofit Corporation, 12/31/85

Assets		Liabilities	
Current Assets		Current Liabilities	
Cash	$ 1,000	Current notes payable	$ 8,000
Pledges of contribution	50,000	Accounts payable	600
(minus allowance for		Wages and salaries	55,500
uncollectibles)	(5,000)	Deferred revenues	700
Marketable securities	5,000	Total current liabilities	64,800
Receivables	400		
(less uncollectibles)	(40)		
Inventory	900		
Supplies	500		
Prepaid items	1,000		
Total current assets	53,760		
Long-lived assets			
Long-term investments	3,000	Long-term debt	1,000
Property and equipment	8,000	Total liabilities	65,800
(less accumulated			
depreciation)	(800)		
Leasehold improvements	3,000	Funds balance; excess (deficit)	
Deferred charges	1,500	of assets over liabilities	5,260
Other long-term assets	2,600		
Total long-term assets	17,300		
		Total liabilities and fund balance	$71,060

Source: Author

Current assets include:

1. Cash and accounts on which checks may be drawn

2. Marketable securities (Treasury bills, certificates of deposit, repurchase agreements or any security with a fixed date, usually no more than a year for its redemption)

3. Pledges of contributions showing the amount that may not be received as pledges are not kept

4. Prepaid items such as insurance when payments are made in advance usually to cover the current year's costs

5. Supplies—paper, pencils, pens that are consumable in the work process

6. Accounts receivable—payments expected from others for goods or services rendered minus the uncollectibles

7. Inventory—the stock of goods and services the organization has to sell

Since all claims are not collectible because some clients do not pay, the accounts receivable should be adjusted to reflect the uncollectibles. The same is true for pledges. All other assets are listed at fair market value except that marketable equity securities (stocks) are either listed at fair market value or cost whichever is lower, and bonds are listed at amortized cost or fair market value whichever is lower.[2] Inventory may be listed according to the latest or earliest price of the item making up the inventory.[3]

Fixed or long-term assets include such items as:

1. Buildings and equipment. These items are listed at cost and the depreciation on them is shown in an accumulation account just below their entry on the balance sheet. The cost (the amount paid for it by the organization) minus the depreciation is known as the book value of the asset.

2. Another long-term asset is deferred charges which are advance payments by the organization for goods and services which will not be delivered to it during the year.

3. Other fixed assets include copyrights, leasehold improvements (long-term leases on real property where the nonprofit maintains the property and remodels it as if it were the owner).

The total assets owned by the organization is the sum of the current and long-lived or fixed assets. In the balance sheet shown in Figure 13.1, this amounts to $71,060. Some balance sheets will show items 2 and 3 as intangible assets—meaning that the organization does not possess a physical asset.

Other major areas of information in a balance sheet are liabilities of the nonprofit and funds balance. Liabilities are claims against the nonprofit and may be divided into current and long-term claims.

1. Current notes payable are payments to be made this year. These might be short-term notes or the current portions of long-term debt that are payable in the current year such as mortgage payments to be made this year.

2. Accounts payable are payments due creditors who have extended goods and services to the organization.

3. Wages and salaries include payments to the employees for services rendered and accrued vacation time.

4. Deferred revenues are amounts received but not yet earned by the nonprofits. The nonprofit may receive subscription dollars for a publication not yet produced and distributed. Such revenues are said to be deferred and create a liability or claim of the subscribers against the organization until such time that the goods or services are produced and delivered.

Long-term liabilities include debt and other obligations that must be paid to others in future years. (Note that current year's amortization of debt is listed as current liability). Total liabilities are the sum of long-term and current claims. For this organization on December 31, 1985 it is $65,800.

The difference between total liabilities (current and long term) and total assets (current and fixed) is the fund balance which may be an excess or a deficit. This nonprofit has an excess of $5,260. Its liabilities are less that its assets.

Interpretation of the Balance Sheet

The balance sheet tells how financially sound the organization is on a specific date. We know from Figure 13.1 that as of December 31, 1985, the assets of this organization exceed its liabilities. For most uninformed observers this nonprofit is economically sound. If it had to close down tomorrow it could meet all of its liabilities and still have $5,260 left over. But there is more to the story.

A balance sheet can give other critical information about a nonprofit. It tells how liquid or solvent the organization is on a given date. Can it pay its current bills? Does it have enough cash or liquid assets that it can sell easily in order to raise enough cash to pay its current liabilities? In short, is the organization solvent? This organization is not.

There are several ways to use the information in the balance sheet to determine how liquid or solvent the organization is. One test is the size of the net working capital. This is the difference between current assets and current liabilities. By definition, the larger the net working capital, the greater the liquidity. The net working capital for this organization is a deficit of $11,040. This is the amount by which its current liabilities exceed its current assets. It cannot pay its bills this year.

Another way of expressing the same dilemma in which this organization finds itself is to calculate the current or the working capital ratio. This is the current assets divided by the current liabilities for the two years in question. Ratios are better than absolute numbers for making comparisons. This year's ratio is 0.826, meaning that the current assets are about 83 percent of the current liabilities. The organization is 17 percent short of just covering its current debts including paying its employees.

Liquidity is also measured through what is called a quick ratio or acid test. Instead of using all current assets, as is done in calculating working capital, only cash and assets that are easily converted to money (those that have a fixed redemption date preferably in the current year) are used. In the balance sheet of Figure 13.1 this would include cash, marketable securities, pledges (minus the expected uncollectibles) and accounts receivable (minus the uncollectibles). The amount, $51,360 in this example, is divided by the current liabilities ($64,800). The ratio is 0.792. It is worse than the working capital ratio. The amount of money or near money the organization has is $51,360, but it is 20 percent short of what it needs to pay its current debt. The amount of cash or near cash the organization has must be viewed in terms of the current claims against it. Can it pay the monthly bills?

Note that we speak of monetary assets—cash and assets easily converted into money—and not just cash. As we discussed in Chapter 8, a large amount of cash on hand is not necessarily good cash management. The excess cash could be invested in marketable securities. On the other hand, a shortage of cash portends a serious solvency problem if the organization does not have marketable securities which it could readily sell to raise the needed cash. Like the working capital, the quick ratio is a warning signal. There is no magical level that is good or bad. Obviously, however, the lower the cash or working capital relative to the current liabilities, the greater the risk of insolvency.

Here are some illustrations of the use of working capital or quick ratios. Would you be willing to lend a nonprofit money if its quick ratio is less than one or its working capital is negative? You probably would not without substantial collateral because a negative working capital figure or a quick ratio that is less than one is a sign of probable insolvency because current liabilities exceed current assets.

As a matter of fact, short-term borrowing would not help because it increases current liabilities by the amount of the debt and interest, thus increasing the demand for cash. But long-term borrowing may be helpful. It increases long-term rather than current liabilities and provides cash that increases current assets. The debt ratio of this organization (long-term debt divided by total assets) is 0.014. Not bad. Over the long run the organization is not overleveraged in excess debt relative to its assets. But would you still want to make the loan? How will the organization pay the interest and the principal? One possibility would be to use the long-term loan to meet its current obligations and begin to restructure its balance sheet so that it will avoid the same dilemma in the future.

One way of restructuring the organization is to increase revenues from its business. Another way is to sell some of its assets and another is to increase gifts and contributions. In all cases the objective of the organization should be to increase its cash or near-cash items. To illustrate, a gift in the form of a building would not help. It increases fixed assets rather than current assets. Furthermore, if a debt is assumed or if there are current operating costs exceeding current revenues from the building (a negative cash flow), the situation is worsened.

Comparative Balance Sheets

The critical differences between the balance sheet of a for-profit and a nonprofit corporation are in the line items referring to gifts and contributions and in the balancing entry. For-profits do not attract gifts and contributions even when they are insolvent. Nonprofits do not have stockholders and, therefore, there is no stockholder's or owner's equity (net worth) shown on their balance sheets. This is central to the definition of a nonprofit: Its income and assets may not be distributed to individuals. Thus, any excess of assets over liabilities is reflected in fund balances and not in stockholder's equity.

However, even this is a matter of degree. Some nonprofits have members who are not owners in the sense of stockholders, because they cannot cash in their shares. Yet, the organization may be thought of as having earnings that are at the disposal of the membership as a group. Thus, the excess shown in the balance sheet may be labeled "funds balance and membership equity."

STATEMENT OF SUPPORT, REVENUES AND EXPENSES

Another important financial statement for nonprofits is the statement of activity or statement of expense, revenues and support as in Figure 13.2. This is an annual statement produced by the nonprofit and is analogous to the income statement of a for-profit firm. The statement is a depiction of the financial operation of the organization during a year.

FIGURE 13.2 Statement of Support, Revenues and Expenses
of a Nonprofit Corporation, 1/1/85 to 12/31/85

Support and Revenue		
Admissions	$ 2,235	
Government contracts	20,000	
Gifts and grants	230,000	
Membership	38,000	
Investment income	10,000	
Net realized investment gains (losses)	4,000	
Revenue from sales	5,000	
Total		$309,235
Expenses		
Programs	290,000	
Supporting services	48,000	
Cost of sales	1,000	
Total		339,000
Excess (Deficit) Revenues and Support over Expenses		(29,765)
Capital Additions		
Gifts	300,000	
Net investment income	34,000	
Net realized investment gain (loss)	4,000	
Total		338,000
Excess (deficit) Support and Revenues and Capital Additions		308,235
Fund Balance at Beginning of Period		(30,000)
Fund Balance at End of Period		278,235

The statement of support, revenues and expense show the income of the organization. The support and revenues of the organization may include:

1. Fees from admissions to events
2. Government contracts—state, local or federal

3. Gifts and grants from institutions and from individuals

4. Membership fees (if applicable)

5. Investment income (dividends and interest) on marketable and long-term securities

6. Net realized investment gains or losses from the sale of the securities

7. Revenues from sales of publications and the like

Generally, these revenues and support are available for use by the organization in an unrestricted manner. This nonprofit had unrestricted support and revenues during the year January 1, 1985 to December 31, 1985 of $309,235 minus the $20,000 for government contracts restricted to their specific performance. This was the difference available for its general operations.

There are also expenses to consider. For nonprofit organizations, expenses are generally classified by function or program, general administration or supporting services, and the cost of sales (items sold in a related business). This organization had a total operating expense of $339,000. Its operating expenses exceeded its revenues and support by $29,765. It operated in the red.

This operating deficit had nothing to do with the related business that yielded sales of $5,000, for the cost of such sales was $1,000 giving a gross profit (defined as the difference between the two) of $4,000. As these businesses become larger, it will be important for the organization to actually itemize such costs as insurance, wages, rents, and interests specifically attributed to the business as for-profits do. A more accurate measure of the profitability of the business can then be obtained.[4]

This organization has two strategies available to it. It can seek to bring its expenses into line or increase its revenues and support. This latter approach would work only if the organization increases its unrestricted funds. Restricted funds cannot be applied to general operations which is where this organization is in trouble.

There is a special class of revenues and support that is called capital additions. These are receipts, usually in the form of endowments, the use of which are restricted by the donor. The restrictions are expressed in the agreement that leads to the gift, bequest, or contribution. The use of the funds may be restricted in several ways. The restriction may apply to specific purposes such as the construction of a building. The restriction may require the lapse of time or the occurrence of an event such as the passage of 20 years or the death of the donor.

The concept of "capital additions" includes:

1. The restricted gifts received during the year

2. Net investment income earned on these gifts and similar ones received earlier

3. Gains or losses realized from the sale of assets related to these restricted gifts

For the organization in this example, the capital additions amounted to $338,000. Taking both operating costs and capital additions into account, the overall performance of the organization during the year is given by the figure of $308,235. This is the amount by which revenues and support exceeded expenses when capital additions were taken into account. This surplus in the restricted fund balance was so high that it was sufficient to make up the deficit ($30,000) with which the organization started the year. Hence, at the end of the year, the fund balance is $278,235.

This balance of $278,235 indicates that the overall performance of the organization led to a surplus. Note, however, that this surplus occurs in the restricted segment. Unless the individual contracts that created these accounts permit, the surplus is not available to the organization to stay alive. We shall say more about restricted funds in Chapter 14.

It is important to recognize that the statement of activity gives hard facts, not estimates such as the budget. The data in the statement of activity can therefore be used to compare the actual with the projected figures shown in the budget. Thus, the statement of activity tells whether or not the organization operated efficiently, whether it met its budgetary targets and limits, and how. Moreover, as we can see here, the statement of actual activity if used properly would also form the basis for budgetary targets. This organization needs to review its revenue and expense performance and set new achievable budgetary targets on each if it is to escape the fate now facing it.

Comparative Statement of Activities

There are differences between the income statement of a for-profit firm and the statement of activity of the nonprofit. The revenues of a firm are earned from the sale of goods or services (called revenues from operation) or from the earnings on investment or the sale of assets (called other revenues). For-profit firms do not get support from gifts and contributions.[5]

In many nonprofits, the support is the only meaningful form of income. In others, there are both support and earned revenues very much in the same vein as in for-profit firms. It is the ability to rely on support that permits the nonprofit to operate and sell its goods and services below market price. The price might even be zero indicating that the nonprofit does not charge at all. It can do this because of its reliance on gifts and other contributions. A for-profit firm cannot do the same. It must operate at or above market price because it must bear all costs and provide a fair rate of return to its investors.

At the risk of being repetitious, another difference between for-profit and nonprofits is in the bottom line. The income statements of for-profits normally end with an entry that is called net income. This is the bottom line because it shows whether or not the organization operated at a loss or a gain during the course of the year. If there is a gain, that amount can be retained by the firm, distributed to the shareholders in the form of dividends, used to purchase other assets, and pay off debt at the discretion of the board of directors.

A nonprofit has as its bottom line "funds deficit or excess" or a similar phrase. Note that in both the case of a for-profit and nonprofit, the possibility of having a positive or negative bottom line exists. Either may have a surplus (called a profit in for-profit firms) or a deficit (called a loss in a for-profit firm). The major difference is in the use of the surplus or profit. Of all of the possible uses, one does not pertain to nonprofits: Nonprofits may not distribute their surplus to individuals. Of all the possible ways of dealing with a deficit, the one that cannot be done by nonprofits is that they cannot sell shares of stocks, but they may rely upon support. Just the reverse is true of a for-profit firm: They may raise additional funds by selling stocks but cannot rely on support.

A final difference between the for-profit and nonprofit statement of activity is that the former will have an allowance for taxes while the latter, unless a private foundation or the operator of an unrelated business, would not normally have such a line item.

STATEMENT OF CHANGES IN FINANCIAL POSITION

The principal purpose of the statement of changes in the financial position of the organization is to show how resources were acquired and how they were used during the year and, consequently, why the organization finds itself in either a favorable or unfavorable financial position at the end of the year. Unlike a budget, it is not a projection of the sources and uses of resources. It is an actual accounting of major resource uses and acquisition during the fiscal year of the organization. And, unlike a budget, this statement is subject to audit.

The statement of changes in the financial position of the organization also differs from the balance sheet. The latter describes the financial status of the organization at a point in time. The former shows the flows that contributed to the attainment of that financial status. In short, what are the major financial flows that resulted in the picture portrayed in the balance sheet? Both statements are subject to audit.

The statement of changes in the financial position of the organization differs from the statement of activities just analyzed. The latter shows the dollar expenditures of each set of activities by type of expenditure (salaries, rent, supplies, and so on) and the sources of revenues by type. The latter focuses on broader categories of resource flows.

Sometimes the statement of changes in financial position may be combined with the statement of activities. Instead of a statement of changes in financial position, an organization may report a statement of changes in working capital. This latter statement merely shows the changes in current assets and liabilities which the organization experienced during the year. A statement of changes in financial position is broader than a statement of changes in working capital because it includes all major resource flows, not just those in current assets and liabilities.

Like all financial statements, the statement of changes in the financial position of the organization is one that contains numbers, and the interpretation of these numbers is an art. Instead of looking at an example of a statement of changes in financial position (we shall see a specific example later), we focus our attention on some of the major resource flows that may appear in the statement. In other words, what are some of the major uses and sources of financial resources for the nonprofit organization during the course of its fiscal year? What resource flows may bring about a change in its financial position?

1. The operating excesses from the organization's performance during the year arise because the organization's revenues and support from operations exceeded its expenditures. These revenues and support may include sales and contributions that are unrestricted; that is, available to be used for the general operation of the organization. An excess implies that the organization did not spend more than it brought in during the year so that the excess can be used to strengthen its financial position. If the organization operated at a deficit, this too would represent a change in financial position implying, at least in the short term, a weakening of the financial position of the organization.

2. Decrease in inventories (when the organization runs a related business) implies that sales were made. Therefore, a reduction in inventories implies a positive change in the financial position of the organization. An increase in inventories particularly if such increases were unintended and merely represent the inability to make planned sales implies a weakening of the financial position of the organization. The organization is less liquid and had to use its resources to build up unintended inventories which it has been unable to sell.

3. Increases in deferred amounts (such as taxes or unfilled orders such as for the organization's publications) represent changes in the financial position of the organization. By deferring payments or the fulfillment of orders, the organization has more financial resources available to it now. On the other hand, a decrease in these amounts implies that payments were made and, therefore, the organization has less cash available to it.

4. The financial position of the organization is also changed by returns on its investments. These may be from the sales of investments, from interest earned, and from dividends received from corporations in which it owns stocks. This may or may not be a solely owned corporation. Returns on investments represent a positive increase in the financial position of the organization and an improvement in its ability to advance its mission. On the other hand, losses represent a deterioration of the financial position of the organization.

5. Increases in contributions and bequests that are restricted to specific purposes such as a building fund or a scholarship fund represent improvements in the financial position of the organization. These are known as capital additions. One aspect of capital additions is that the funds may not be used for operating purposes at the time they are given and that their uses are restricted to those stipulated by the donor. Thus, while capital additions improve the long-term financial position of the organization, they do little to improve its liquidity unless the terms of the gift provide for borrowing of these funds for operating purposes.

6. Sales of the long-term assets of the organization also bring about a change in the financial position of the organization. Such sales bring in cash. This is not to imply that selling the assets of the organization is necessarily good. In some cases it might be a strategy forced by the need to raise cash. But in others, it might be the result of a decision that the assets are no longer needed.

7. Depreciation is another source of resources for the organization. Recall that the organization deducts depreciation every year in determining whether or not it operated at a deficit or a surplus. But unlike other expenses, the organization does not pay out any money to anyone when it incurs a depreciation expense. Technically, it withholds the amount depreciated to be used to finance the replacement of the equipment or property depreciated. Thus, the depreciation is a "source" of resources.

Another way of looking at depreciation as a source of resources is to recall that when the organization recorded a depreciation expense, it did not make a payment to anyone such as it does when it incurs salary and benefit expenses. In these latter cases, payments are made. Because no payments are made in depreciation even though it is deducted as an expense, this deduction represents a source of resources.

8. Another source of financial resources that results in a fundamental change in the financial position of the organization is the acquisition of debt. By borrowing, the organization increases the amount of resources available to it in the short run. At the same time, it increases the claims of others over the future resources of the organization. Debt may be necessary because the organization does not have needed resources. If debt is incurred to purchase an asset that appreciates, then the effect is to increase the total financial resources of the organization by more than the debt.

What are some of the major uses of resources of the organization that result in a change in its financial position? These include the following:

1. Resources may be used to purchase new assets such as buildings and equipment. To say that such a transaction represents a change in the financial position of the organization is not to imply that the organization is worse off. The organization is merely less liquid by using its cash to purchase long-term assets; or it may have limited effect on its immediate liquidity position if the purchase is financed totally by long-term debt such as a mortgage. Future liquidity will be affected because the interest and principal on the notes will have to be paid. Whatever method is used to finance the purchase, a change in the financial position has occurred.

2. Reductions in short-term and long-term debt also represent a change in the financial position of the organization. A reduction in debt implies a payment; that is, a use of the organization's resources.

3. A change in the financial position of the organization is brought about by the purchase of investments such as bonds and certificates of deposit. The change represents the use of cash for the acquisition of an income-producing asset.

4. The resources of the organization are also used to the extent of increasing receivables including pledges of contributions not received. To understand this, consider that a receivable whether it is called accounts receivable or pledges due is really a payment due to the organization. Technically, that payment is due because the organization expended resources either to create and sell a product or service or to create a situation to which a donor wishes to give. The act of creating the product, the service, or the purpose to which the donor wishes to give could only occur by the use of the organization's resources. Put another way, the organization's resources may be used to create a product or service or to create a purpose for giving. If an immediate sale were made or if the donation had been received, then this would have represented an increase (a source) of resources. Since no money is received by the organization, technically all the organization has done is expended its resources in expectation of receiving money. These expectations are receivables.

Another major flow of resources is the transfer of funds from restricted accounts to the unrestricted operating account (a source of resources) or vice versa (a use or application of resources). This flow is unlike the others because it does not represent bringing in additional resources to the organization or transferring the organization's resources to an outsider. It is a flow of funds between one set of accounts of the organization and another. Thus, the organization changes its financial position without necessarily adding or subtracting from the total amount of resources it commands. These interfund transfers are governed not only by accounting principles but by the legal agreements that set up the funds. For example, the organization may transfer funds from an endowment to the operating fund either because the terms of the endowment provide for such an amount to be transferred at that time, or because the organization is borrowing the funds for operating purposes as long as the terms of the agreement that set up the endowment permit such loans.

The net effect of providing and applying resources is the increase or decrease in resources. If more resources are provided than used, this may be represented by an increase in the cash position of the organization. If the reverse is true, then the cash position of the organization would decrease.

Comparative Statements of Changes in Financial Position

A principal difference between the for-profit firm's statement of changes in financial position and that of a nonprofit is that the former can bring about changes by selling stocks. This produces cash and it can also use funds to pay dividends. Neither of these entries will appear on the books of a nonprofit. The nonprofit may not issue stocks to increase its cash and may not pay dividends. It has no individual owners.

GENERAL ASPECTS OF INTERPRETATION

In interpreting financial statements, the management must know whether the accounting is on a cash or an accrual basis. If it is on a cash basis, this means that all accounting entries represent actual cash receipts or outlays. If the organization is on an accrual basis, this means that there is a definite commitment to pay or to receive payment. The transaction may be completed but no cash has been transferred. In this case, the amounts shown as accounting entries represent commitments rather than cash. Small nonprofits tend to operate on a cash basis, while the larger more complex ones like for-profit firms operate on an accrual basis.

When interpreting financial statements, managers should also be aware that, as in budgets, vertical and horizontal analyses can be helpful. This is especially true if the data are presented for more than one year. For example, in the support, revenue and expense statement, a horizontal analysis for more than one year could reveal if the proportion that each line item contributes to expense or revenues has changed. Similarly, a vertical analysis of the same factors over the same number of years could reveal which line items are growing fastest and which are declining. The questions for management: Why? Is this in the best interest of the organization? Is this what we planned in our strategic planning process? Do we need to change our plans?

Interpreting financial statements may also involve comparisons with other organizations. This is not necessary, but it is often advisable. Needless to say that in so doing the underlying differences in the organizations ought to be kept in mind. Moreover, when possible, ratios rather than absolute numbers ought to be used to reflect the differences in size of the organization. Because nonprofits tend to be so different from each other and data and accounting procedures are less standardized, comparisons among organizations ought to be done with utmost care.

On the point of standardization of accounting procedures, it should be reiterated that the examples given in this chapter are intended to highlight problems. All nonprofits do not use exactly the same accounting procedures or reporting format. The mastery of the information as presented in this chapter, however, would be a firm basis for dealing with individual organizations.

FUND ACCOUNTING

Fund accounting refers to a system of financial record keeping and reporting that is common among nonprofit organizations. The basic characteristic of fund accounting is that certain accounts must be kept separate, that funds cannot be co-mingled except in an approved investment pool or through authorized and documented transfer of funds from one account to another, and that the financial activity in each separate fund is subject to its own independent accounting.

For the purposes of fund accounting, funds may be classified as expendable or nonexpendable. Expendable funds are those that may be totally spent. Unexpendable funds are those where typically only the income to the fund may be spent but the principal and sometimes the gains from sales of the assets of the funds must not be spent so that the fund may have a perpetual life. Most endowments are examples of nonexpendable funds.

Endowments, as we discussed earlier, are of several types. A university may have an endowment fund for scholarships, for land acquisition and building construction, for athletic purposes and facilities, for lectureships and for professorships. Thus, while we may speak of the endowments of Harvard or Columbia universities to be a certain dollar amount, we are actually speaking of the composite of several separate endowments.

Within any category of endowments, there are numerous separate accounts. For example, Syracuse University has a modest endowment of $100 million. This is made up of over 1,023 separate restricted accounts.[6] Some are restricted for scholarships, some for academic prizes, and some for financing academic events. Each account represents a specific donor or cause for which a specific endowment has been established—not just a gift but an endowment; that is, a gift that is expected to have a lengthy life whose principal would not generally be spent, but the income of which will be used to support a specific cause specified by the donor or donors.

Each one of these separate accounts technically has a balance sheet, an income statement, a financial report and perhaps a statement of changes in financial position. Each one must be kept separate and generally bears the name of the donor. Thus, the Simon and Myra Bryce chair, the Orvin and Sylvia Gaustad chair and the Mabel and Mary Laporte chair may be in the same university but each is a separate endowment subject to separate accounting. Each is also subject to a separate agreement between the donor and the donee. It is this separate, written, legal document that determines how a fund may be used.

Fund accounting uses another important classification of funds. Funds may be restricted or unrestricted. Restricted funds are those that can be used only for specified purposes which are specified in the agreement at the time the gift was made or the contract was signed. A grant or payment to a nonprofit to provide research on the topic of AIDS uses its restricted funds. An unrestricted fund is one that can be used to finance activities at the discretion of the board of directors of the organization. As one Syracuse University official pointed out, unrestricted funds are the backbone of the growth of the university. These unrestricted funds can be used to pay salaries, provide scholarships, make investments, take advantage of unanticipated opportunities, meet emergencies, fund scholarships, begin new programs, and to finance general activities.[7]

Sometimes the phrases "general funds" or "operating funds" are used to denote unrestricted funds but this may not be correct. Operating funds may consist both of unrestricted funds used for general operations and restricted funds used in current operations but for the specifically restricted purpose for which they are given. Thus, in a current year a university uses restricted funds to finance scholarships and lectures and also uses unrestricted funds for these and other purposes including salaries and maintenance.

It should be kept in mind that the terms "restricted" and "unrestricted" are not synonymous with budgeted. An organization may budget $1 million for salaries and benefits. What makes the amount restricted is a legal force. A restricted amount cannot be used for any other purpose than those for which it was given. Variations from this intended purpose legally occur only by an act of the board of directors and the donor. Again, a budgeted amount is a planned or anticipated amount. It is not a legal restriction. There are no legal contracts or consequences from their variations. The misuse of a restricted fund is a violation of a contract and can be subject to both civil and criminal penalties.

The fact that the funds are unrestricted does not mean that discretion is absolute. These funds cannot be used for purposes which contravene the mission of the organization or violate the terms discussed in Chapter 6. Unrestricted merely means that the management may use its discretion about how the funds can be used as long as the use is consistent with the mission of the organization and the terms under which it was given legal and tax-exempt status.

Unrestricted funds come from gifts and contributions of donors and the earnings of the nonprofit. Many nonprofits conduct special campaigns to increase the size of their unrestricted funds. Others such as the University College, the University of Maryland, obtain unrestricted funds almost exclusively through tuitions. They receive no state aid and have very small endowments.

In addition to giving the organization fiscal discretionary powers, unrestricted funds also have the advantage that there is no legal limit on how much unrestricted funds a nonprofit may have or any legal ratio of unrestricted to restricted funds that it must maintain. Hence, financially skillful nonprofit management can maintain the support ratios discussed in Chapter 6 and still maintain discretion. For example, it is possible to meet the one-third public support test and still have a large percentage of the assets of the organization being discretionary. It is possible, for example, to emphasize unrestricted gifts in any contribution campaign the organization may conduct.

Many nonprofits do run campaigns for unrestricted gifts at the same time they seek out funds for endowments. They are two different tracks upon which

Chapters 10 and 11 of this book were based. We shall say more about fund accounting in our discussion of the American Red Cross.

AUDIT

The various sectors in the nonprofit world apply different accounting standards. One standard is "Audits of Voluntary Health and Welfare Organizations" of the American Institute of Certified Public Accountants; another is *Accounting Principles and Reporting Practices for Churches and Church Related Organizations* by the Catholic bishops.

Audits are done to determine if the accounting procedures used by the organization conform with the Generally Acceptable Accounting Principles (GAAP). The aim of these principles is to be sure that the accounting of the organization is objective, fair, complete, and accurate. These are the four criteria used to judge the accounting practices of the organization.

In assessing the organization's conformity with these four standards, the auditors look at both expenses and revenues of the organization. In investigating the expenses, the auditors seek clear evidence that the expenses were authorized and approved by a responsible person of the management team, are correctly classified by function (program) or object, are recognized in the correct accounting period, and are justified or supported by documents such as invoices. Auditors are instructed to pay particular attention to the existence of controls over expenditures. These controls include the existence of an organizational chart and a clear line of responsibility for decision making, recording, and monitoring expenses. The auditor may also compare the extent to which actual expenditures deviate from planned or budgeted expenditures. The auditors may also be expected to see if the factors that are included in the overhead of the organization are properly classified as such or whether they should be classified as part of the direct cost of a specific project. Conversely, they will check to see that those items treated as direct costs are properly classified and charged to the correct project. The auditors can be expected to look at business expenses to be sure that they are properly classified as unrelated or related and that there is compliance with the payment of taxes.

On the revenue side, the auditors will be concerned with the accurate recording of the amounts of revenues, in the proper time period and in the proper classification by type such as fees, gifts and contributions, income from investments, sales, and so on. The auditors will also check to be sure that there are proper controls set over the receiving of revenues including the persons who are so authorized and that there is a chain of command within the organization to control the receiving, recording and accountability for such revenues. Where applicable such as in the case of endowments, the auditors will assure that accounts are segregated and independently recorded.

Where cash is involved the auditors may want to be sure that there are physical safeguards for keeping cash and that there are procedures that control and limit petty cash to a reasonable amount. Where securities are concerned, the auditor will verify the type, and the reasonableness of their reported cost and return.

In carrying out their function, the auditors focus on financial statements such as the balance sheet which tell them about the treatment of assets and liabilities of the organization. They focus on the revenue and expense statements which tell them about the flow of revenues from various sources and the expenditures of the organization for various purposes. They examine those and other statements that explain how the financial position of the organization has changed over a period that is usually one year. Their only use of the budget is as a standard through which they may judge departures from the organization's commitments or what the organization thought was reasonable and as evidence that there is some creditable attempt to control both the revenues and expenses of the organization.

At the end of the audit, the auditors may render an opinion in writing to the organization. The opinion is divided into a section which describes the scope of the audit, a disclaimer, an explanatory paragraph, and an opinion. The scope tells what financial statements were audited and for what time period; the disclaimer tells what was omitted from the audit and why; the explanatory statement explains departures or peculiar aspects of accounting by the nonprofit and why they may be justified; and the opinion is the judgment of the auditors as to the conformity of the organization with generally acceptable accounting practices. An opinion may be "clean," meaning that the organization conforms with the GAAP, while a "qualified" opinion expresses concern about the practices of the organization. An example of an auditor's report follows.[8]

The Scope

"We have examined the statement of assets, liabilities, and fund balance of the Endowment Fund of XYZ Nonprofit Organization as of September 30, 19x2, and the related statement of changes in the fund balance for the year then ended. Our examination was made in accordance with generally accepted auditing standards and, accordingly, included such tests of the accounting records and such other auditing procedures as we considered necessary in the circumstances."

The Explanation

"As explained in Note 1, the financial statements being presented are only for the fund referred to above and do not include the assets, liabilities, and fund balances and the support, revenue, expenses, and capital additions of XYZ Nonprofit Organization that are recorded in its funds not intended to present the financial position of the XYZ Nonprofit Organization as of September 30, 19x2, or its results of operations for the year then ended in conformity with generally accepted accounting principles."

The Opinion

"In our opinion, the financial statements referred to above fairly present the assets, liabilities, and fund balance of the Endowment Fund of the XYZ Nonprofit Organization at September 30, 19X2, and the changes in the fund balance for the year then ended, in conformity with generally accepted accounting principles applied on a basis consistent with that of the preceding year."

The reader will note several features of this auditors' report. In the scope statement the time period and the specific fund being audited are given and the basis for the audit. Note that the scope is limited to a time period and in this case to a particular fund. So, we know that the audit does not cover an earlier period; that it does not cover the entire nonprofit; and some specific other endowments are not included and that there was no specifically stated purpose for the audit. Audits may be conducted for a variety of reasons including conformity with the conditions of a grant. If that were its purpose, it would have so stated.

The explanatory paragraph further defines the scope. In this case, it emphasizes that the audit is not of the entire organization which is not unusual. As we recall, endowments are accounted for separately and often periodic auditing may be called for in the contract. Alternatively, the audit could have been for the organization in general rather than for a specific endowment alone.

Finally, the opinion is a clean opinion. There are no qualifying statements. The auditors state, "In our opinion, the financial statements referred to above fairly present. . . ." Take note that the opinion does not use words that imply that the financial status of the organization is strong or weak or precarious. An audit does not make judgments about the financial strength of the organization. Only those who interpret financial statements make such judgments. Note also that the audit does not say that the numbers used by the accountant or bookkeepers for the nonprofit are right or wrong. Even a clean audit does not verify that the numbers are right. An audit gives an opinion about the soundness and merits of the procedures and practices used.

In assessing the practices used, the auditors attempt to establish what is known as an audit trail. That is, it tries to trail each revenue item and each expense item from its inception. In an audit trail, auditors may discover sloppiness and embezzlement as the perpetrator fails to provide acceptable evidence of the justification, authorization, and disposition of the nonprofit's money.

ILLUSTRATION OF INTERPRETATION OF FINANCIAL STATEMENTS

The rules provide for affiliated organizations to report a combined financial statement. Thus, the statement to be shown for the American Red Cross is one that combines the financial situation of the entire 2,908 chapters, 57 regional blood services, and the national sector.

As stated in the earlier part of this chapter, there are a variety of ways in which financial statements are presented in the nonprofit world. Each format depends upon the nature of the organization and the requirements of its board and financial needs. There are, however, some basic principles to which good financial statements adhere. To demonstrate, let us turn to three of the financial statements used by the American Red Cross. We begin with the balance sheet for the organization's fiscal year that ended June 30, 1985. Refer to Figure 13.3.

1. Note that the total assets of the organization are greater than the total liabilities; i.e., $1,067,605,000 compared to $296,004,000 for net assets of $771,601,000. In a for-profit firm, this total amount of $771,601,000 would be stockholder's equity. It would belong to the owners. In a nonprofit this must be maintained for benefit of the public.

2. Relatively little of the organization's monetized assets (cash and investments) is in cash. Most of it is invested and earning interest for the organization. Some of these investments may have been donated.

3. Most of the assets of the organization fall into the categories of unrestricted amounts available for current operations of the organization permitting the organization to function on a daily basis; land, buildings and equipment needed to carry on the organization's business and also representing a long-term investment. Buildings and equipment also increase the organization's borrowing ability because they can serve as collateral for loans.

4. The organization is very liquid and very solvent; it can pay its current bills and the total of its current assets of cash, investment and receivables of about $692,700,000 well exceed its current liabilities (less than $296,004,000). Note that the Red Cross does not separate current from noncurrent liabilities. However, the notes that accompany this balance sheet show that only about half of the notes, capital lease obligations, and mortgages payable are current.

5. Note the book value of the land, buildings, and equipment is $308,939,000. This is the book value which is calculated by taking the original cost of these properties and subtracting the amount of depreciation that has accumulated over the years. As you know, the typical building appreciates; hence, the true value of the buildings is likely to be higher than reported. On the other hand equipment does lose value and may even become obsolete; therefore, the true value of the equipment is likely to be less than reported. The law does not permit depreciation on land, but land is listed at its original cost even though it usually appreciates. The point is that the book value figure that appears is likely to

Combined Statement of Net Assets
June 30, 1985, With Comparative Totals for 1984
(Includes the operations of 2,908 chapters, 57 regional blood services, and the national sector for 1985)

(in thousands)	Notes	Current Operations Unrestricted	Current Operations Donor Restricted	Land, Buildings, and Equipment	Endowment	Totals 1985	Totals 1984
Assets							
Cash and time deposits at chapters and regional							
blood services		$ 36,281	$ 6,243	$ 3,206	$ 53	$ 45,783	$ 38,734
Investments—at cost:	1,6						
Chapters and regional blood services		197,212	9,016	19,414	5,520	231,162	211,741
National sector		80,411			112,467	192,878	167,452
Receivables:							
Fund campaign and other pledges		119,956		8,977		128,933	122,553
Blood services products	2	51,817				51,817	49,534
Service members' loans		9,484				9,484	10,015
Due from other funds			9,680			9,680	1,785
Grants and other		17,717	2,636		2,583	22,936	21,485
Inventories:	1						
Blood services products and related supplies	2	52,872				52,872	51,261
Program and educational materials, and other supplies		8,785				8,785	9,261
Land, buildings, and equipment—less							
accumulated depreciation	1,7,8,9			308,939		308,939	269,010
Other		3,953	383			4,336	4,259
Total Assets		578,488	27,958	340,536	120,623	1,067,605	957,090
Liabilities and Deferred Public Support							
Accounts payable and accrued liabilities		62,311	1,088	3,669		67,068	57,840
Notes, capital lease obligations, and mortgages payable	7	645		56,495		57,140	47,125
Due to other funds		4,938		4,216	526	9,680	1,785
Deferred public support—funds received and receivable							
required for subsequent years' operations	1	159,777	1,785	554		162,116	147,616
Total liabilities and deferred public support		227,671	2,873	64,934	526	296,004	254,366
Net Assets		$350,817	$25,085	$275,602	$120,097	$ 771,601	$702,724
Net assets—as follows:							
Donor restricted for specific services			$25,085			$ 25,085	$ 14,058
Land, buildings, and equipment—expended				$244,559		244,559	220,423
Land, buildings, and equipment—unexpended				31,043		31,043	29,194
Endowment					$120,097	120,097	111,682
Designated by board actions for:							
Disaster revolving fund	5	$ 13,550				13,550	12,450
Blood services operations	2	187,512				187,512	170,832
Replacement and improvements of buildings and equipment		18,006				18,006	13,967
Other specific purposes		50,546				50,546	49,491
Net assets required for remaining operations		81,203				81,203	80,627
Net assets—as above		$350,817	$25,085	$275,602	$120,097	$ 771,601	$702,724

(See notes to combined financial statements.)

Figure 13.3   Balance Sheet of the American Red Cross. Source: American Red Cross, Annual Report 1985, Washington, D.C., p. 27.

reflect the market value of these assets very poorly. But the accounting used by the Red Cross is in keeping with Generally Acceptable Accounting Principles (GAAP).

In a complex organization, it is worth going beyond the knowledge that the organization has a positive net asset. It is worth knowing how the net assets of the organization are distributed among its various missions or responsibility centers. This information is given in the bottom of the balance sheet under the caption, "Net Assets—as follows." It shows that $350,817,000 or 45 percent of the $771,601,000 total net assets of the organization is allocated to its unrestricted annual budget; of this amount, $187,512,000 is to be found in its Blood Services Operations.

Recall that net assets is the difference between total assets and total liabilities. It is a measure of the net worth or wealth of the organization. Therefore, we see based on the totals for 1985 that the wealth of the Red Cross is in its land, buildings and equipment ($275,602,000), blood services operations ($187,512,000), and endowments ($120,097,000).

How does this statement differ from a similar balance sheet of a for-profit firm? In a for-profit firm, the net worth or net assets would be owned by private individuals and would, in the case of a corporation, show the amount owned by common and preferred stock owners and the amount retained in the corporation but owned by the stockholders. In a nonprofit organization, there are no stockholders.

Let us look at the income and revenue statement for the American Red Cross for the fiscal year ending June 30, 1985, Figure 13.4.

1. The bottom line shows an operating excess of $59,248,000. In the for-profit sector, this is known as a profit. However, in the nonprofit sector, such excesses must be used either in the current period or accumulated for advancing the mission of the organization. In 1985, the Red Cross used this excess to purchase property and equipment. These are long-lived assets which can generate income, appreciate in value, and be used to advance the mission of the organization for many years to come.

2. The columns are divided into current and capital accounts (land, buildings and equipment and endowments). The current operations are divided into restricted and unrestricted. Note that the unrestricted support and revenues are nearly ten times as much as the restricted. This gives the organization financial flexibility. It has discretion over the use of unrestricted funds permitting the organization to be responsive to a variety of needs within its mission. Consequently, its expenditures are nearly ten times greater in the unrestricted category than in the restricted. There are no rules that specify how much of a nonprofit's revenues or expenditures must be in the restricted category; only that the expenditures must be consistent with the mission of the organization. Thus, the Red Cross provides disaster relief, blood services, services to the members of the armed forces, veterans and their families as the need arises.

3. An organization acquires such flexibility only if its income is not obtained in a manner that restricts its use. Note in the current operations columns that unrestricted support and revenues are nearly ten times as great as restricted; i.e., $753,009,000 to $73,563,000.

4. How did the Red Cross acquire such sizable unrestricted funds? They earned it. While public support is important to the organization, it accounted for only one-third of the organization's total income (the minimum required by law to maintain the status as a publicly supported organization). The remainder comes from revenues including fees charged to hospitals to process blood, investment income, and gains from sales of assets and program materials. These are related business income.

Combined Statement of Public Support, Revenues, and Expenses and Changes in Net Assets
for the Year Ended June 30, 1985, With Comparative Totals for 1984
(Includes the operations of 2,908 chapters, 57 regional blood services, and the national sector for 1985)

(in thousands)	Notes	Current Operations Unrestricted	Current Operations Donor Restricted	Land, Buildings, and Equipment	Endowment	Totals 1985	Totals 1984
Public Support and Revenues							
Public support:							
Contributions:							
Fund campaign	1	$211,450				$211,450	$198,550
Disaster relief operations	5		$26,835			26,835	21,630
Other		8,565	12,061	$ 6,372	$ 42	27,040	26,518
Legacies and bequests	3	9,689	3,038	292	4,717	17,736	15,429
Total public support		229,704	41,934	6,664	4,759	283,061	262,127
Revenues:							
Blood services processing	2	455,597				455,597	437,014
Investment income		30,326	1,032	1,589		32,947	27,286
Income from endowment funds		9,926	70			9,996	7,993
Government and private foundation grants		2,785	29,166	1,546		33,497	21,846
Program materials		14,689	45			14,734	11,832
Gain on sale of assets and other		9,982	1,316	5,934	3,663	20,895	18,441
Total revenues		523,305	31,629	9,069	3,663	567,666	524,412
Total public support and revenues		753,009	73,563	15,733	8,422	$850,727	$786,539
Expenses							
Program services:							
Services to members of the armed forces, veterans, and their families		64,454	2,370	1,531		$ 68,355	$ 65,440
Disaster	5	50,403	32,653	1,865		84,921	69,629
Blood services	2	435,213	1,964	15,725		452,902	423,989
Health services		48,524	5,428	2,246		56,198	49,848
Youth		6,338	753	309		7,400	7,609
Community volunteer		22,079	17,152	2,154		41,385	36,166
International		3,448	192	17		3,657	2,808
Total program services		630,459	60,512	23,847		714,818	655,489
Supporting services:							
Membership and fund raising		17,804	264	1,043		19,111	14,061
Management and general		45,498	599	1,824		47,921	42,923
Total supporting services		63,302	863	2,867		67,032	56,984
Total expenses		693,761	61,375	26,714		$781,850	$712,473
Excess (deficiency) of public support and revenues over expenses before property and equipment acquisitions and other		59,248	12,188	(10,981)	8,422		
Property and equipment purchased with current funds, net of proceeds from sales of property and equipment and other		(35,798)	(1,161)	36,966	(7)		
Net Excess of Public Support and Revenues Over Expenses and Transfers							
Donor restricted			11,027				
Land, buildings, and equipment				25,985			
Endowment					8,415		
As to the current unrestricted operations:							
Increase in designated balances approved by Board action for:							
Disaster revolving fund	5	$ 1,100					
Blood services operations	2	16,680					
Replacement and improvements of buildings and equipment		4,039					
Other specific purposes		1,055					
Net operating assets required for remaining operations		576					
		23,450					
Net Assets, Beginning of Year		327,367	14,058	249,617	111,682		
Net Assets, End of Year		$350,817	$25,085	$275,602	$120,097		

(See notes to combined financial statements.)

Figure 13.4 Statement of Revenues and Support of the American Red Cross. Source: American Red Cross, Annual Report 1985, Washington, D.C., p. 25.

In short, despite its worthy charitable and compassionate mission the Red Cross could not survive or conduct that mission as laudably as it does if it could not generate the business revenues that have been the emphasis of this book.

Note that the Red Cross operated with an excess or surplus of $59,248,000 in 1985. Some $35,798,000 was used to cover the purchase of equipment and property. The other $23,450,000 was designated by the board of directors to be used for various Red Cross programs, including $16,680,000 for blood services. Finally, observe that the final two lines show how much the net assets increased during the year. At the beginning of the year, for example, the unrestricted net assets were $327,367,000 and this amount increased to $350,817,000. This increase in the unrestricted net assets was the result of two factors: (1) efficiency in the operation of the organization that led to an excess; and (2) a decision of the board of directors about how such excesses are to be allocated.

In addition to revealing the general good financial health of the Red Cross, these statements reveal several principles alluded to in this book:

1. A nonprofit may produce a surplus or excess through its annual operations.

2. All excesses must be used in a manner that is consistent with the tax-exempt mission of the organization.

3. There are no legal limits to the size of unrestricted funds; and an efficient organization tends to have unrestricted funds that are several times the size of their restricted funds because this gives them flexibility.

4. The term "unrestricted" does not imply that excesses may be spent on matters outside of the mission of the organization. Even though fund accounting requires strict separation of funds, there may be interfund transfers approved by the board of directors and consistent with the advancement of the mission of the organization.

5. Unlike a for-profit business, net assets (equivalent to net worth) cannot be distributed to or possessed by owners. They may be accumulated; that is, transferred into a capital fund (such as a building or endowment fund) or placed in the unrestricted fund for meeting annual operating expenses.

Let us look at the statement of changes in the financial condition of the American Red Cross for the fiscal year which ended June 30, 1985. See Figure 13.5.

1. The most important source of funds for the American Red Cross during that year was internal. Internal financing was more than twice as much as external ($97,300,000 compared to $41,638,000). These internally generated funds came from selling property and equipment and from a paper transaction involving depreciation.

Depreciation is always a source of funds because it is deducted as an expense, although it is never paid. The external source of funding occurred by increasing the liability of the organization. What was done is that instead of paying for certain goods or services during that period, it promised to pay for it at a later date and not deplete its cash immediately. Available funds are increased if they are not used to make immediate payments on purchases. As we said earlier, good cash management always involves some delay in making payments.

Combined Statement of Changes in Financial Position
for the Year Ended June 30, 1985, With Comparative Totals for 1984
(Includes the operations of 2,908 chapters, 57 regional blood services, and the national sector for 1985)

(in thousands)	Current Operations Unrestricted	Donor Restricted	Land, Buildings, and Equipment	Endowment	Totals 1985	1984
Internal Sources of Financing						
Operations:						
Excess (deficiency) before property and equipment transfers and other	$59,248	$12,188	$(10,981)	$ 8,422	$68,877	$74,066
Add items not requiring cash and investments:						
Depreciation of buildings and equipment			25,399		25,399	21,566
Net book value of property disposals			3,024		3,024	3,086
Total internal sources of financing	59,248	12,188	17,442	8,422	97,300	98,718
Application (Source) of Internal Financing						
Purchase of land, buildings, and equipment and other	35,798	1,161	31,386	7	68,352	53,421
Increase (decrease) in:						
Receivables	11,488	7,183	(1,626)	433	17,478	12,010
Inventories	1,135				1,135	(6,132)
Other assets	346	(269)			77	671
Total application of internal financing	48,767	8,075	29,760	440	87,042	59,970
Balance of internal financing	10,481	4,113	(12,318)	7,982	10,258	38,748
External Financing						
Increase (decrease) in:						
Accounts payable and accrued liabilities	12,514	97	5,684	(1,172)	17,123	4,126
Notes, capital lease obligations, and mortgages payable	(94)		10,109		10,015	836
Deferred public support—funds received and receivable required for subsequent years' operations	15,639	(1,077)	(62)		14,500	6,339
Total external financing	28,059	(980)	15,731	(1,172)	41,638	11,301
Increase in Cash and Investments	$38,540	$ 3,133	$ 3,413	$ 6,810	$51,896	$50,049
Increase in Cash and Investments Represented by:						
Chapters and regional blood services	$19,876	$ 3,133	$ 3,413	$ 48	$26,470	$22,408
National sector	18,664			6,762	25,426	27,641
Total as above	$38,540	$ 3,133	$ 3,413	$ 6,810	$51,896	$50,049

(See notes to combined financial statements.)

Figure 13.5 Statement of Changes in Financial Position of the American Red Cross.
Source: American Red Cross, Annual Report 1985, Washington, D.C., p. 28.

2. What were the generated funds used to do? We see that $1,135,000 were used to increase inventories of blood, blood products, and program materials. Some $17,478,000 were used to increase receivables. What this means is that the Red Cross had received certain promises that it would be paid. In the meantime, it satisfied a need or request based on that promise. The money has not yet been received but it cost the Red Cross to fulfill the request. In other words, the Red Cross financed the request; that is, it paid the workers, transportation and material costs to meet the request. It financed these by applying its own funds. The principal use of the funds, however, was to purchase property and equipment.

Another major use of funds was to increase the cash available to the national organization as well as to the chapters and to invest part of that cash. The total increase in cash and investments was $51,896,000.

How does this statement of changes in financial position differ from one in the for-profit sector? Note that in this statement for the Red Cross, there is no indication that the organization has changed its financial position through the sale or purchase of its own stocks. There are no stocks in a nonprofit organization.

AUDITORS' OPINION

After reviewing the financial statements of the American Red Cross the auditors rendered the following opinions:

Auditors' Opinions

Deloitte Haskins+Sells

DEPARTMENT OF THE ARMY
HEADQUARTERS, U.S. ARMY AUDIT AGENCY
3101 PARK CENTER DRIVE
ALEXANDRIA, VIRGINIA 22302

1101 Fifteenth Street, N.W.
Washington, D.C. 20005
(202) 862-3500
TWX 710-822-9289

The American Red Cross:

We have examined the combined statement of net assets of the American Red Cross as of June 30, 1985 and the related combined statements of public support, revenues and expenses and changes in net assets, of functional expenses, and of changes in financial position for the year then ended. Our examination was made in accordance with generally accepted auditing standards and, accordingly, included such tests of the accounting records and such other auditing procedures as we considered necessary in the circumstances. The financial statements of certain Chapters and Regional Blood Services, which statements include 31% of the combined total assets and 37% of the combined public support and revenues, were examined by other auditors whose reports thereon have been furnished to us. Our opinion expressed herein, insofar as it relates to the amounts included for such Chapters and Regional Blood Services, is based solely upon the reports of such other auditors. We previously examined the combined financial statements of the American Red Cross as of June 30, 1984 and for the year then ended, from which the accompanying comparative totals for 1984 were derived. Our unqualified opinion dated October 2, 1984, on such financial statements was based, in part, on the reports of other auditors.

In our opinion, based upon our examination and the reports of other auditors referred to above, the combined financial statements referred to above present fairly the financial position of the American Red Cross at June 30, 1985 and the results of its operations, and the changes in its financial position for the year then ended, in conformity with generally accepted accounting principles applied on a basis consistent with that of the preceding year.

Deloitte Haskins & Sells

September 30, 1985

The American Red Cross:

Pursuant to the Act of Congress, January 5, 1905, and Department of Defense Directive Number 1330.5, August 16, 1969, we have reviewed the Combined Statement of Public Support, Revenues, and Expenses and Changes in Net Assets; and the Combined Statement of Functional Expenses of the American Red Cross for the year ended June 30, 1985. The American Red Cross employs a firm of certified public accountants (principal auditor) to audit its combined financial statements. The financial statements of certain chapters and regional blood services, which statements include 37 percent of the combined public support and revenues, were examined by other auditors whose reports thereon were furnished to the principal auditor. The opinion of the principal auditor as it relates to the amounts included for such chapters and regional blood services was based solely upon the reports of such other auditors. Our opinion expressed herein is based primarily on observation of the audit work performed by the principal auditor and such tests of the accounting records and such other auditing procedures as we considered necessary in the circumstances.

In our opinion, the accompanying Combined Statement of Public Support, Revenues, and Expenses and Changes in Net Assets; and the Combined Statement of Functional Expenses present fairly the results of operations of the American Red Cross for the year ended June 30, 1985, in conformity with generally accepted accounting principles applied on a basis consistent with that of the preceding year.

U. S. Army Audit Agency

21 October 1985

Auditors' Opinion. Source: American Red Cross, Annual Report, 1985, Washington, D.C., p. 28.

AN ALTERNATIVE PRESENTATION OF FINANCIAL REPORTS

The Combined Statement of Support, Revenue and Expenses and Changes in Fund Balance for the National Multiple Sclerosis Society for 1985 shows a diversification of support from gifts and contributions and dues from members, and a respectable income from investment. Notice the transfer of $3,771,450 which was the excess of public support and revenues from an unrestricted classification to a restricted one and the transfer from one restricted fund of $20,000 to make up a total transfer of $3,791,450 for research, fellowships and grants. This is the financial expression of a policy decision. It is evidence that transfers can be made between categories—unrestricted to restricted and vice versa, if permitted.

NATIONAL MULTIPLE SCLEROSIS SOCIETY (HEADQUARTERS AND CHAPTERS)

COMBINED STATEMENT OF SUPPORT, REVENUE AND EXPENSES AND CHANGES IN FUND BALANCES

Year Ended September 30, 1985, With Comparative Combined Totals For The Year Ended September 30, 1984

	Unrestricted General Funds	Research and Research Fellowship Grants Fund	Other Restricted Funds	Total All Funds September 30, 1985	September 30, 1984
PUBLIC SUPPORT AND REVENUE:					
PUBLIC SUPPORT:					
Received directly:					
Dues and contributions from members and others	$17,504,589		$ 16,500	$17,521,089	$16,180,611
Contributions for research and development		$1,451,298		1,451,298	1,853,379
Legacies and bequests	1,966,851	78,831		2,045,682	3,320,162
Special events (net of direct benefit costs (1985—$3,507,137; 1984—$2,225,075)	12,028,272			12,028,272	10,627,850
Total received directly	31,499,712	1,530,129	16,500	33,046,341	31,982,002
Received indirectly:					
Federal Services Campaign for National Health Agencies	1,416,228			1,416,228	903,095
Allocated by federated fund raising organizations	1,220,856			1,220,856	1,125,324
Total received indirectly	2,637,084			2,637,084	2,028,419
Total public support	34,136,796	1,530,129	16,500	35,683,425	34,010,421
REVENUE:					
Investment income	1,087,742	53,121		1,140,863	1,043,350
Miscellaneous	299,456			299,456	201,429
Total revenue	1,387,198	53,121		1,440,319	1,244,779
Total public support and revenue	35,523,994	1,583,250	16,500	37,123,744	35,255,200
EXPENSES:					
PROGRAM SERVICES:					
Research and research fellowships	806,117	5,374,700		6,180,817	6,276,607
Patient services	9,314,062			9,314,062	8,299,316
Community services	3,998,941			3,998,941	3,570,928
Professional education and training	2,560,933			2,560,933	2,268,688
Public education	5,055,045			5,055,045	4,687,043
Total program services	21,735,098	5,374,700		27,109,798	25,102,582
SUPPORTING SERVICES:					
Fund raising	5,025,688			5,025,688	4,580,186
Management and general	3,970,745			3,970,745	3,692,688
Total supporting services	8,996,433			8,996,433	8,272,874
Total expenses	30,731,531	5,374,700		36,106,231	33,375,456
Excess (deficiency) of public support and revenue over expenses	4,792,463	(3,791,450)	16,500	1,017,513	1,879,744
Other changes in fund balances: Transfers (from) to funds	(3,771,450)	3,791,450	(20,000)		
	1,021,013	—	(3,500)	1,017,513	1,879,744
FUND BALANCES, beginning of year	11,759,537	—	322,890	12,082,427	10,202,683
FUND BALANCES, end of year	$12,780,550	—	$319,390	$13,099,940	$12,082,427

See notes to combined financial statements.
Note: Expenses have been allocated to various classifications on the basis of time records and/or estimates.
Note: These statements have been prepared by the National Office from the individual audit reports of each Chapter and are not covered by the report of Ernst & Whinney.

Figure 13.6 Combined Statement of Support, Revenue and Expenses and Changes in Fund Balances, Source: National Multiple Sclerosis Society, Annual Report, 1985, p. 28.

The Combined Balance Sheet segregates unrestricted from restricted funds and shows many of the entries that we have discussed earlier in this chapter. Notice that the cash, investments, deferred income and other entries are segregated.

COMBINED BALANCE SHEETS

NATIONAL MULTIPLE SCLEROSIS SOCIETY
(HEADQUARTERS AND CHAPTERS)
September 30, 1985 With Comparative
Amounts For September 30, 1984

	September 30	
	1985	1984
ASSETS		
UNRESTRICTED GENERAL FUND		
Cash	$ 6,554,832	$ 3,949,533
Investments—at cost (approximate market)	5,808,514	7,311,422
Furniture and equipment, at cost less allowance for depreciation (1985—$2,391,213; 1984—$2,002,834)	1,462,028	1,443,306
Campaign materials	433,090	412,397
Prepaid expenses and other assets	1,524,233	1,121,111
	15,782,697	14,237,769
RESTRICTED FUNDS		
Cash	115,185	81,226
Investments—at cost (approximate market)	400,772	413,497
Mortgage note receivable	149,434	150,932
	665,391	645,655
	$16,448,088	$14,883,424
LIABILITIES AND FUND BALANCES		
UNRESTRICTED GENERAL FUND		
Accounts payable and accrued expenses	$ 2,323,208	$ 1,718,771
Deferred income	678,939	759,461
Fund balances:		
Funds designated and committed by the Board for research and research fellowship grants— Note 3	11,007,861	8,502,806
Undesignated general fund (deficit)	1,772,689	3,256,731
Unrestricted general fund balance	12,780,550	11,759,537
	15,782,697	14,237,769
RESTRICTED FUNDS		
Research grants payable	292,042	246,101
Deferred income	53,959	76,664
	346,001	322,765
Fund balances:		
Research and research fellowship grants fund balance	0	0
Other restricted funds—Note 6	319,390	322,890
Restricted fund balance	319,390	322,890
	665,391	645,655
	$16,448,088	$14,883,424

See notes to combined financial statements.

Figure 13.7 Combined Balance Sheets, Source: National Multiple Sclerosis Society, Annual Report, 1985, p. 29.

Some organizations, such as the National Multiple Sclerosis Society, provide an additional set of financial data which permits the analysis of the distribution of expenses by type and across program lines. This is a useful tool for giving management a clear picture of how the organization's resources are being allocated in meeting its overall mission. Turn to Figure 13.8.

Figure 13.8 shows that the society, a 501 (c) (3) organization, directly serves over 132,494 registered persons with multiple sclerosis. A 1985 combined statement for the national and its chapters shows the society's five major program areas and how its resources are allocated by type of expense across program lines. Patient services gets $9,314,062 or one-third of all program dollars which amounted to $27,109,798 in 1985. Salaries, amounting to $4,073,251, or 15 percent of all program services dollars, is the largest expense in providing patient services; and at $10,047,282 is the largest program expense across program lines.

NATIONAL MULTIPLE SCLEROSIS SOCIETY (HEADQUARTERS AND CHAPTERS)

COMBINED STATEMENT OF FUNCTIONAL EXPENSES

Year Ended September 30, 1985 With Comparative Totals For The Year Ended September 30, 1984

	Program Services						Supporting Services			Total Expenses	
	Research and Research Fellowships	Patient Services	Community Services	Professional Education and Training	Public Education	Total	Fund Raising	Management and General	Total	September 30, 1985	September 30, 1984
Research and research fellowship grants	$5,374,700					$ 5,374,700				$ 5,374,700	$ 5,400,514
Clinics		$ 289,845				289,845				289,845	244,859
Salaries	324,735	$4,073,251	1,952,166	$1,301,266	$2,395,864	10,047,282	$1,720,653	$1,994,618	$3,715,271	13,762,553	12,964,886
Employee health and retirement benefits	74,132	339,253	155,235	115,911	217,008	901,539	166,670	273,348	440,018	1,341,557	1,113,932
Payroll taxes	19,667	329,991	164,151	101,505	210,086	825,400	173,205	157,942	331,147	1,156,547	1,097,135
Professional fees and contract service payments	104,553	465,265	226,512	180,590	264,097	1,241,017	351,104	344,207	695,311	1,936,328	1,385,012
Office supplies	8,458	184,278	80,555	56,992	128,033	458,316	170,477	88,004	258,481	716,797	708,272
Telephone and telegraph	11,907	402,284	136,028	107,553	210,126	867,898	189,826	136,060	325,886	1,193,784	1,155,405
Postage	38,121	314,307	147,837	85,616	220,558	806,439	239,498	99,804	339,302	1,145,741	964,687
Rent	32,436	485,232	222,172	153,905	293,790	1,187,535	217,673	269,372	487,045	1,674,580	1,529,607
Electricity	8,246	12,238	7,245	7,248	11,411	46,388	9,535	15,317	24,852	71,240	66,719
Maintenance and cleaning		34,970	7,075	5,231	14,374	61,650	19,387	12,767	32,154	93,804	116,058
Outside printing and visual aids	96,603	507,593	279,858	196,858	585,318	1,666,230	1,039,538	133,385	1,172,923	2,839,153	2,467,473
Travel	55,306	374,900	185,296	145,880	262,716	1,024,098	346,158	120,278	466,436	1,490,534	1,432,345
Conferences, conventions and meetings	11,055	151,521	40,891	32,104	86,447	322,018	127,662	78,066	205,728	527,746	439,229
Awards and other grants	2,116	2,251	1,681	1,830	3,222	11,100	2,463	903	3,366	14,466	15,279
Membership dues and support payments	10,518	38,111	19,512	14,636	24,882	107,659	26,797	21,232	48,029	155,688	121,417
Miscellaneous equipment		144,067	20,203	8,404	27,782	200,456	22,854	24,925	47,779	248,235	171,439
Specific assistance to individuals		1,222,293				1,222,293				1,222,293	1,211,575
Miscellaneous	5,162	90,314	31,497	24,899	49,529	201,401	155,117	112,852	267,969	469,370	426,364
Total expenses before depreciation	6,177,715	9,172,119	3,967,759	2,540,428	5,005,243	26,863,264	4,978,617	3,883,080	8,861,697	35,724,961	33,032,207
Depreciation of furniture and equipment	3,102	141,943	31,182	20,505	49,802	246,534	47,071	87,665	134,736	381,270	343,249
TOTAL EXPENSES	$6,180,817	$9,314,062	$3,998,941	$2,560,933	$5,055,045	$27,109,798	$5,025,688	$3,970,745	$8,996,433	$36,106,231	$33,375,456

Figure 13.8 Combined Statement of Functional Expenses, Source: National Multiple Sclerosis Society, Annual Report 1985, p. 28.

Recall that in our discussion of budgets we distinguished between program and support services (generally overhead). Figure 13.8 also shows the amount allocated to various services that support the programs of the National Multiple Sclerosis Society. Over half of the total expenditures needed to support the programs and operation of the organization goes to fund-raising. The Society is heavily dependent upon gifts, contributions and special events for generating the support it needs to carry out its mission.

Let us go back for a moment to labor costs. Recall that earlier in this book we dedicated an entire chapter to labor costs because it is a high-cost item among nonprofits. The total labor expenses including benefits for the National

Multiple Sclerosis Society for 1985 is in excess of $18,000,000 (the amounts for salaries, benefits and payroll taxes added together). This is about 50 percent of the total expenses of the organization. Hence, we see evidence of a point made earlier in this book: The word "voluntary" hardly describes the costs confronting nonprofits. The National Multiple Sclerosis Society has over 450,000

NOTES TO COMBINED FINANCIAL STATEMENTS

NATIONAL MULTIPLE SCLEROSIS SOCIETY
(HEADQUARTERS AND CHAPTERS) Year Ended September 30, 1985

NOTE 1-The combined financial statements include the accounts of National Multiple Sclerosis Society Headquarters and all of its Chapters. All transactions between National Headquarters and the Chapters have been eliminated in the combined financial statements.

NOTE 2-The significant accounting policies followed by the Society conform to the requirements of the Industry Audit Guide entitled "Audits of Voluntary Health and Welfare Organizations" published by the American Institute of Certified Public Accountants.

The Society's financial statements are prepared on the accrual basis of accounting.

Investments are carried at cost or, if donated, the fair value on the date received.

Campaign materials are carried at the lower of cost (first-in, first-out method) or estimated realizable value.

Furniture and fixtures are carried at cost. The provision for depreciation is computed on the straight-line method over the estimated useful lives of the assets.

Contributions received are considered to be available for unrestricted use unless specifically restricted by the donor.

The Society recognizes income from legacies and bequests when an unassailable right to the gift has been established by the court and the proceeds are measurable in amount.

Where objectively determinable, the fair value of donated services is recorded as revenues and expenses ($113,671) for 1985 and ($74,650) for 1984.

NOTE 3-Commitments are subject, among other things, to revocation rights by the Society, to the continued qualifications of grantees and to the satisfaction by the grantees of prior conditions before payment. Research and Fellowship projects are scheduled as follows: 1986— $4,904,161; 1987—$3,474,973; 1988—$2,014,815; 1989—$349,548; 1990—$264,364.

NOTE 4-The Society's retirement plan for qualified employees is non-contributory with benefits provided under a group annuity contract with an insurance company. Pension expense for the year ended September 30, 1985 was $286,827 ($257,706—1984), including amortization of past service cost over approximately 40 years. The Society's policy is to fund accrued pension costs. Accumulated plan benefits and net assets of the Society's retirement plan are presented below:

	January 1	
	1984	1983
Actuarial present value of accumulated plan benefits:		
Vested	$1,349,551	$1,212,068
Nonvested	165,258	115,834
	$1,514,809	$1,327,902
Net assets available for plan benefits	$1,648,378	$1,383,370

The assumed rate of return used in determining the accumulated plan benefits was 7 percent for 1984 and 1983.

NOTE 5-Minimum rental payments required under long-term lease commitments for office space are as follows:

1986-	$ 741,130
1987-	638,867
1988-	477,091
1989-	221,961
1990-	129,393
	$2,208,442

Rent expense for the year ended September 30, 1985 was $1,674,580.

NOTE 6-Other restricted funds of the Society at September 30, 1985 are as follows:

Ralph I. Straus Award Fund	$180,000
Louise Mellen Research Fund	90,000
Ray and Joan Kroc Fund for Research on the Symptomatic Treatment of Multiple Sclerosis	12,890
John A. Alexander and Elyza C. Alexander Fund	20,000
Wilfred B. Doner Multiple Sclerosis Student Scholarship Fund	16,500
	$319,390

NOTE 7—GIFTS OF NOTES RECEIVABLE

During 1985, the Society received a gift of Notes Receivable (the "Notes") with a face value of $1,034,000 and bearing interest rates of 9½% to 10½%. The Notes are receivable from limited partnerships which purchased and operate low income housing projects. Repayment provisions require the payment of nominal amounts annually plus additional amounts related to excess cash distributions, as defined, by the partnerships through maturity generally in 1994. The maturities, at the option of the partnerships, may be extended for an additional five years to 1999. Because the Society has been unable to identify any clearly measurable and objective basis for determining the fair value of the Notes, they have been recorded at the nominal value of $1, and income will be recorded as proceeds are received.

Figure 13.9 Notes to Combined Financial Statements, Source: National Multiple Sclerosis Society, Annual Report 1985, p. 29.

member-volunteers according to its 1985 Annual Report. Yet, its combined labor costs in order to run the organization efficiently and to carry out its mission exceeds $18,000,000. The performance of the most laudable charitable mission can be expensive.

The last document to be considered for the National Multiple Sclerosis Society are the notes. These notes explain entries and tell a lot about the organization and its performance. Notes of this type accompany all financial statements discussed in this chapter. Because of space, we have chosen only to reproduce this one. The reader would do well not to overlook notes in interpreting financial statements.

COMPARATIVE SUPPORT STATEMENTS

Let us consider two other 501 (c) (3) organizations. Figure 13.10 shows the Condensed Statement of Support, Revenue and Expenses of The Salvation Army World Service Office for 1983 and 1984. The organization was incorporated in 1977 to carry the Salvation Army's service to the poorest of developing countries. Its programs are in five areas: health, employment, community

THE SALVATION ARMY WORLD SERVICE OFFICE

Condensed Statement of Support, Revenue and Expenses

Year ended December 31, 1984 with comparative amounts
for the year ended December 31, 1983

	Total All Funds	
	1984	1983
Public support and revenue:		
Public support:		
Contributions	$ 8,895,369	$4,057,378
Grants from government agencies	3,170,634	3,058,192
Total public support	12,066,003	7,115,570
Revenue — investment income	71,091	27,960
Total support and revenue	12,137,094	7,143,530
Expenses:		
Program services:		
Health care in refugee settlement	413,255	249,297
Village reconstruction programs	926,819	700,629
Development programs	3,022,904	2,061,530
Operational grants to affiliates	5,976,140	3,249,791
Total program services	10,339,218	6,261,247
Supporting services — management and general ...	252,467	302,436
Total expenses	10,591,658	6,563,683
Excess (deficiency) of public		
support and revenue over expense	1,545,409	579,847
Fund balances:		
Beginning of year	1,775,106	1,195,259
End of year	$ 3,320,515	1,775,106

Figure 13.10   Condensed Statement of Support, Revenue and Expenses, Source: The Salvation Army World Service Office's Annual Report 1984, p. 13.

development, disaster aid and leadership development. We see that in the fiscal year ending December 31, 1984, some 99 percent of the total support of the organization came from contributions and from grants from government agencies. The remainder came from investment income. Understandably, raising revenues from sales to its client population is less possible for an organization with the mission of SAWSO. But good management, as in this case, gets an additional stream of income by properly investing cash between the time of their receipt and their disbursement. We shall further discuss cash management in the next chapter. Again, this organization avoids a deficit and its surplus, partly restricted and committed, helps to finance SAWSO's mission.

The Council on Foundations, Inc., is a 501 (c) (3) founded in 1949. Its goals are to promote responsible and effective grant-making, develop and maintain a supportive environment for philanthropy; encourage and support collaboration among grantmakers, and to promote the formation of new foundations.

STATEMENT OF SUPPORT, REVENUE AND EXPENSES
AND CHANGES IN FUND BALANCES

For year ended December 31, 1985
(with comparative totals for 1984)

	Unrestricted		Restricted			Total all funds	
	Core programs	Long-term reserve fund	Specially funded projects	Robert W. Scrivner fund	Property and equipment fund	1985	1984
Support and revenue:							
Support—contributions and grants	$ 65,239	—	675,794	122,695	—	863,728	783,695
Revenue:							
Membership dues and contributions	2,198,591	—	—	—	—	2,198,591	1,828,357
Annual conference	504,164	—	—	—	—	504,164	436,801
Workshops and seminars	68,835	—	16,415	—	—	85,250	126,228
Foundation News	375,542	—	—	—	—	375,542	289,808
Investment income and other	386,394	90,326	10,683	4,781	—	492,184	447,723
Total revenue	3,533,526	90,326	27,098	4,781	—	3,655,731	3,128,917
Total support and revenue	3,598,765	90,326	702,892	127,476	—	4,519,459	3,912,612
Expenses:							
Core programs and specially funded projects:							
Member services	691,534	—	—	—	7,455	698,989	628,770
Workshops and seminars	105,893	—	—	—	642	106,535	131,415
Annual conference	519,711	—	—	—	2,165	521,876	507,817
Research and information services	162,693	—	—	—	1,475	164,168	—
Communications and public affairs	468,473	—	—	—	4,504	472,977	256,018
Foundation News	595,118	—	—	—	2,891	598,009	482,092
Legislative activities	90,093	—	—	—	411	90,504	199,412
Administrative and management	782,331	—	—	—	8,868	791,199	818,954
Specially funded projects	—	—	702,892	—	—	702,892	779,590
Robert W. Scrivner fund	—	—	—	12,500	—	12,500	—
Total expenses	3,415,846	—	702,892	12,500	28,411	$4,159,649	3,804,068
Excess (deficiency) of support and revenue over expenses	182,919	90,326	—	114,976	(28,411)		
Fund balances, at January 1, 1985	89,953	845,657	—	—	160,333		
Transfers—furniture and equipment acquisitions	(113,040)	—	—	—	113,040		
Fund balances, at December 31, 1985	$ 159,832	935,983	—	114,976	244,962		

See accompanying notes to financial statements.

Figure 13.11   Statement of Support, Revenue and Expenses and Changes in Fund Balances, Source: Council on Foundations, Annual Report 1985, p. 57.

The Council's membership is composed of independent, community, operating and public foundations, corporate grantmakers and trust companies.

Figure 13.11 shows its statement of support, revenue and expenses for the year ending December 31, 1985. Approximately 80 percent of its $4,519,459 income comes from membership dues and revenues from related businesses such as annual conferences, workshops and seminars, and its newsletter.

Its portfolio, acquired at a cost of $4,171,867 has produced a healthy income of $492,184 in 1985. Its portfolio, according to its Annual Report of 1985, is made up of certificates of deposit, government bonds, corporate bonds, and commercial paper. In the next chapter we shall see various types of investment instruments. We shall see that these are reasonably safe.

From the above statements we should learn: (1) that operating with an annual surplus is not uncommon among well operated nonprofits; (2) that investment income is an important source of revenues for these nonprofits; (3) that related business income can contribute substantially to the amount of dollars the nonprofit has to work with; (4) that nonprofits use these sources of income along with contributions and unrelated business income to increase their capacity to carry out their missions.

SUMMARY AND CONCLUSIONS

The budget, as discussed in the last chapter, and the financial statements are similar in the sense that both are expressed in dollars and cents. The budget, however, is a financial plan and it may or may not be realized. If there are variances from the plan, the manager will wisely ask why. The financial statements discussed in this chapter, on the other hand, are factual representations of what occurred financially in the organization during a given period of time. The budget charts the course, and the financial statements reveal if the course was actually maintained.

Unlike the budget, the financial statements must conform to Generally Acceptable Accounting Principles (GAAP). These principles are intended to ensure consistency, objectivity, fairness and completeness in the reporting of financial data. The purpose of an audit is to ascertain if the practices of the organization conform to good practices. In conducting an audit, auditors seek evidence to confirm that accounting entries are supported by the facts and by authoritative decision making on the part of responsible managers.

NOTES

1. The reader is referred to the references in accounting at the end of this text for alternative treatments of the financial statements of nonprofit organizations.
2. Bonds are bought usually at a discount or premium. At maturity the full face value of the bond is paid. During the period between purchase and maturity, the difference between the full face value and the amount paid for the bond is amortized; that is, paid in increments.

3. We refer to the "first-in-first-out" and "last-in-last-out" methods of valuing inventory.

4. The reader may look at a standard accounting text for ratio measures of profitability.

5. While for-profits do not generally receive gifts and contributions, this does not mean that they cannot receive them or be deemed to have received them. But no deduction is allowed. For our purposes, however, it is safe to ignore gifts and contributions to corporations or to their shareholders in the case of closely held corporations.

6. *Syracuse University Leadership Report,* 1., no. 2 (March 1986), p. 7.

7. Ibid., p. 2.

8. The source of this discussion is the American Institute of Certified Public Accountants, *Audits of Certain Nonprofit Organizations* (New York: AICP, 1981), pp. 53–54.

SUGGESTED READINGS

AMERICAN INSTITUTE OF CERTIFIED PUBLIC ACCOUNTANTS, *Audit of Certain Nonprofit Organizations* (New York: American Institute of Certified Public Accountants, 1981).

AMERICAN INSTITUTE OF CERTIFIED PUBLIC ACCOUNTANTS, *Accounting Principles and Reporting Practices for Certain Nonprofit Organizations* (New York: American Institute of Certified Public Accountants, 1978).

HENKE, EMERSON O., *Introduction to Nonprofit Organization Accounting* (Boston: Kent Publishing Company, 1980).

MONTGOMERY, THOMPSON A., *Financial Accounting Information,* 2nd ed. (Reading, Massachusetts: Addison-Wesley Publishing Company, 1982).

TRAUB, JACK, *Accounting and Reporting Practices of Private Foundations* (New York: Praeger, 1977).

```
┌─────────────────────┐
│      FOURTEEN        │
└─────────────────────┘
          │
┌─────────────────────────────────────────────┐
│                                               │
│         Evaluating and Setting                │
│         New Financial Goals                   │
│                                               │
│                                               │
└─────────────────────────────────────────────┘
```

After the financial statements have been interpreted, decisions have to be made about how the organization will proceed. Should new financial objectives be set? What should be the new targets? With a good system of reporting information, the board of directors and managers of the nonprofit should have financial statements at least every six months. On the basis of the information in these statements, financial goals and targets can be modified. These modifications feed right back into the system and in this sense, financial management is a loop. Periodic evaluation at mid-year or at the end of the fiscal year leads to the setting of new targets or the affirmation of old ones which themselves will later be reaffirmed or modified. This chapter is about evaluating old targets and setting new ones and the menu of short-term investment opportunities that are available in this process. It is also about capital budgeting and endowment planning—both of which involve setting long range targets.

EVALUATING OLD TARGETS

The end of every fiscal period marks the commencement of a new one. Thus, a new fiscal year begins at the very moment that the old one ends, immediately giving an uninterrupted continuity to the financial function. Having the financial data from the closing period means that the managers of the nonprofit organization are now armed with real data indicating the actual performance of the organization. One way in which this data can be used is to amend old targets. The first step is asking the right questions.

The following are examples of the questions that must be answered in evaluating targets:

1. Was the revenue target in the budget met? If not, by how much was it missed and what was the reason? Does it make sense, in light of recent experience, to continue believing that such a target is reasonable? Should it be increased or decreased, or should it remain the same? Why?

2. What form and sources of giving showed the greatest increase? Is this a promising new area of emphasis? Is this where the organization has its best shot? In what form of giving did the organization underachieve? What can be done to get greater support from this form of giving or from this sector?

3. What is the distribution of support by source? Is there too much dependence on one source or form of giving? Should the organization diversify its base of support? Does the mix of support leave the organization in jeopardy of its tax-exempt status?

4. What are the major cost factors in operating the organization? Can anything be done to contain costs without reducing the productivity and commitment of the organization to its mission?

5. What cost factors are rising and at what rate? Why? Is there a less expensive substitute?

6. What cost centers are exceeding their budgets? Why? Was the budget allocation unreasonable? Should these allocations be realigned? Do some centers need less while others need more? What programs should be dropped?

7. Is it time to put some functions on a self-financing basis? Could they survive? Could they provide revenues for the organization?

8. If there is a deficit, how will it be financed? How long can it be sustained before destroying the organization?

9. Is it time to change investment advisors? Is it time to change banks, insurance companies, or the financial committee of the organization?

10. Is there is a cash surplus and how can it be used to the best interest of the organization?

These questions feed back into the strategic planning process from the interpretation of the hard facts in the financial statements. Once decisions are made about targets for the new year, renewed efforts will be made to utilize the concepts in earlier chapters to raise money and contain costs, to gather financial data, interpret them and then begin the cycle all over again setting new targets. The process continues as long as the organization exists.

A FRAMEWORK FOR SETTING NEW TARGETS

Based on the answers to such questions, the management may set new targets and restrictions.

1. First, there are policy considerations based upon the mission and philosophy of the organization. An example is that this organization will not invest in overly risky investments, investments in South Africa, and the like.

2. Second, there are legal considerations. New targets should not jeopardize the tax-exempt status of the organization or its charter.

3. A third type of consideration is one based upon contractual arrangements of the organization such as those prohibiting or requiring certain specific performance in endowment funds. Although it is not common now, nonprofits used to guarantee donors an annual rate of return as an annuity to them based on their gifts. This guarantee was backed by the assets of the organization. If the guarantee was not met, the assets ultimately had to be sold to meet the guarantee. Such extreme promises are rare today but the restrictions placed on gifts, grants and contracts must still be met.

On this latter point, one must note that there are also opportunities. For example, it is not uncommon for a nonprofit that has a promise of an annual gift for perhaps three years to negotiate to receive it all in one or two years and to invest the amount so that not only do they get the gift but the interest too.

4. A fourth consideration is the capacity or knowledge of the organization. Hopefully, this book has broadened the horizon of management so that it can view itself as having more money-making opportunities. Yet, some may not have learned, others would fear, and yet others would reject. The point as noted in the strategic planning chapter is that an organization is constrained not only by what occurs externally but by its own internal capacity, imagination and initiative.

5. A fifth and realistic type of concern is that the organization may simply not have the financial resources to be flexible. It is common for an organization to receive a high percentage of its support in the form of restrictive gifts, grants or contracts. Hence, the room for discretionary decision is limited. Ironically, however, it is these very organizations that need to push toward the development of unrestricted money to be used for the general support and development of the organization in the conduct of its growing mission.

Within this broad set of constraints, decisions have to be made and targets set. This chapter gives examples of six common types of financial target-setting problems in nonprofits and shows how they can be resolved.

To set these targets, the organization has to have a firm vision of what it is and what it can do (Chapters 1, 2, 3, 4, and 6), because this shapes its range of possible financial or other options to meet the targets. The management will want to consider these options systematiclly (Chapters 5 and 12), decide what investments to make (Chapters 7 and 8), or how to strengthen their fundraising activities (Chapters 10 and 11). Management must also know how to control costs and attract good managers to their programs (Chapter 9). After these managers have had a chance to implement the programs, they must evaluate the fiscal performance of the organization (Chapter 13) and then reassess targets, set new ones and make new investment decisions to help meet the targets (Chapter 14). The process is continuous and circular.

CASH MANAGEMENT AND INVESTMENT
OPPORTUNITIES

One set of options that must be continuously assessed is what to do with the organization's money (cash management) so that it might multiply to meet the organization's targets. This book places considerable emphasis on related and unrelated businesses as potential sources of additional funds for nonprofits. The potential for related businesses is as extensive as the number of programs, for a related business is one that is directly connected to the exercise of the tax-exempt mission of the organization.

However, the choice for most nonprofits is not between the extremes of going into business and soliciting more gifts and contributions. The intermediate point is making productive use of cash regardless of its source. To appreciate the challenges of cash management, it is necessary to repeat the sources and uses of cash. In Chapter 13 we looked at sources and uses of cash for detecting the changes in the financial condition of the organization. Now we shift from analyzing past actions to the planning of present and future ones.

1. A source of cash is the operation of the organization. The organization may operate at a deficit or surplus. To this deficit or surplus we add depreciation since it was an expense charged but no cash was actually spent. Thus, two sources of cash are the surplus (revenues and support—including gifts and contributions, and fees—over expenses) and the depreciation.

2. A third source of cash is the net decrease in all current noncash assets. A decrease in inventory implies that the organization had sales that yielded cash; a decrease in marketable securities implies they were sold for cash. The inserts on the next page illustrate the impact of selling stocks. A decrease in accounts receivable means that cash was received. A decrease in prepaid items and supplies is a source of cash savings and therefore a source of cash. If the organization had increased these current assets instead of decreased them, this would imply a decrease in its cash position. It can only buy more marketable securities by spending cash and it can only prepay items by spending cash.

3. A fourth source of cash is the increase in current liabilities. An increase in notes payable implies a loan of cash. An increase in accounts payable means that the organization has increased its cash position by not paying for its purchases. Similarly, an increase in salaries and wages owed implies that the organization has kept cash by postponing the payment of these expenses. If it had paid any of these expenses, its cash position would have decreased. Expenses can only be paid with cash.

4. A fifth source of cash is the sale of fixed or long-term assets. The sale of the organization's furniture, automobile and building will all lead to an increase in the organization's cash.

5. A sixth way to increase cash is to enter into long-term loans. These loans may even be from insurance policies given to the organization or they may be from a lending institution such as a bank.

By a WALL STREET JOURNAL *Staff Reporter*

BOSTON—The Howard Hughes Medical Institute said it will use proceeds from its sale last year of Hughes Aircraft Co. to fund at least $1 billion of medical research during the next five years.

The Bethesda, Md.-based nonprofit concern became the world's richest independent research institute in December when it completed the sale of Hughes Aircraft to General Motors Corp. for $5 billion. The institute had been expected to boost its spending for basic medical research by about $200 million a year after the sale.

At 72, the Altman Foundation has acquired new wealth, a new director and emerging plans to blend its traditional style of giving to local charities and cultural institutions with fresh initiative to benefit New Yorkers.

The foundation's support will continue for museums, libraries and cultural centers in the city as well as for Catholic, Protestant and Jewish charities. It has been spending about $800,000 yearly on such undertakings, with total assets of $7 million.

But with an additional $86 million in assets from the sale on Friday of the seven B. Altman department stores to a group of real-estate investors, the foundation intends to spend $5 million to $6 million each year.

All of these approaches lead to an increase in the cash position of the organization. Please note that receipt of gifts and contributions is not ignored. As stated in item 1, an excess from operations is a source of cash. This excess is defined as the amount of all revenues and support (including gifts and contributions) minus all expenses. So, the organization does increase its cash by increasing its receipt of gifts and contributions and other forms of support. But the actual amount of cash available at the end of any fiscal year depends upon the timing of disbursements and receipts and their volumes. We shall say more. But, first, what are the competing uses of cash?

The organization can do the following:

1. It can increase its fixed assets by buying more or better types of plants, equipment, or buildings.

2. It can increase its current assets by buying more marketable securities, making more prepayments, increasing inventory, buying more supplies, and financing more accounts receivables.

3. It can decrease its current liabilities by paying notes, accounts payable, salaries and wages, and its deferred revenues by spending what it takes to produce and deliver those items for which it had been paid but had not delivered the goods or services bought.

4. It can pay its long-term debt.

5. The organization could also use cash to finance the operating deficit. The fact that an organization has a deficit does not mean that it does not have to pay bills. The deficit may be financed by using previous years' cash accumulations, or what would have been this year's cash accumulation.

6. Alternatively, if there is a surplus, cash could be saved. As we discussed in Chapter 8 under cash management, holding idle cash is unwise.

Cash management is a skill. It involves increasing the total volume (sources) and the rate (acceleration) at which cash flows into the organization. At the same time the volume (uses) and the rate (deceleration) at which cash flows out must be prudently tempered to meet the obligations and missions of the organization. Unlike government agencies, nonprofits are not "required" to disburse or obligate their funds at the end of the fiscal period. Some surplus shown in the financial statements of nonprofits results from expenditures lagging behind receipts. This is good management and it provides cash for investment opportunities. The lag might be due to time needed to build the organization's capacity to carry out a program successfully or because of interest arbitrage (the interest earned is higher than that to be paid).

Liquidity vs. Investment and Risk vs. Safety

The following steps may be taken once cash is available:
1. The board of directors of the organization may elect to have a part of the cash placed in a restricted fund. This fund may be restricted so that withdrawals can occur only at the discretion of the board or to finance some specific activity in the future. Accumulation of this type is generally no prob-

lem for public charities as discussed in Chapter 6. For private foundations, any attempt to set aside large amounts of cash should be done only after getting specific authorization from the IRS. Obviously, if accumulation is the choice, holding cash and currency makes no sense. The money ought to be placed in an interest-earning account.

2. An amount of cash of approximately six months of the organization's cash need should be kept in a highly liquid asset earning interest with a very low risk of losses. Negotiable order of withdrawals (NOW) and money market accounts available at banks and savings institutions meet these conditions.

3. Beyond this amount, cash should be invested such as to stagger maturity dates. That is to say, some cash should be placed into instruments that have a 30, 60, 90, 360-day maturity. Repurchase agreements (as explained in Chapter 8), certificates of deposit, Treasury bills, and commercial paper (short-term loans to corporations) are examples. These instruments pay higher rates of interest than NOW and money market accounts but are less liquid.

One possible use of cash is to hold it to meet the known cash needs of the organization and to meet emergencies. There is no formula to determine what this amount should be. This depends upon the experience of the organization. Holding enough to meet the organization's cash needs for approximately six months would not be unreasonable. Holding cash does not necessarily mean holding currency. There are accounts that pay interest and permit the organization to draw checks to meet its bills. Two of these are negotiable order of withdrawals (NOW accounts) that are available only to nonprofits and to individuals, and money market mutual funds. Holding cash in either of these two forms means that the organization can earn interest while remaining in a position to readily pay its bills.

Treasury bills are the lowest risk instruments on the market but newly issued ones must be held for six months to a year. Redemption in a shorter period of time may lead to a loss. Repurchase agreements are reasonably safe, especially if the agreement is backed by Treasury bills. The risk of loss of any portion of the investment in commercial paper can be reduced by buying only the shortest term papers of the strongest companies. The risk of loss from buying certificates of deposit can be reduced by buying them from institutions covered by federal insurance.[1]

For longer term investments, U.S. Treasury notes or bonds from the Treasury, a government agency, state and local governments or from a corporation may be bought. Except for Treasury notes that mature in five years, newly issued units of these other instruments mature in 20 to 30 years. This is a long time to commit the organization's money and while we would like to think of bonds as having little risk, this is not the case. There are risks of default and there is a risk of inflation with not only a decline in the real value of the interest earned, but a fall in the bond prices as investors seek to make up for the low interest by lowering the price they will pay for it. Why pay $1,000 for a bond that offers 7 percent, when one can get 10 percent on another bond?

Thus, if the organization needs to sell before maturity, it will have to take a loss unless interest rates have declined.

Low grade corporate bonds (rated B or under) pay attractive rates but are highly risky not only of default, but of loss of principal if the corporation collapses. True, bondholders have a claim on the assets of the corporation but this claim may be long in exercising and may be worthless.

Another risk that bondholders face is that the bond may be called by the issuers. Bonds are called when the issuer sees that it can issue a new bond at a lower rate of interest. Consequently, a bondholder who is getting abnormally high rates of interest may not have that bond for very long.

Even some state and local government bonds have this risk. Not all are backed by the full faith and credit of the issuing government. That is, not all are backed by the full taxing powers of the jurisdiction. Those that are reduce the risk of loss of principal investment because the issuing juridiction is required by law to fully utilize its taxing powers to pay the bondholders. But the fastest growing type of jurisdictional bonds have no such backing. These are called revenue bonds because they are backed only by the revenues from the project they financed. To reduce the exposure to risk, the managers of the nonprofit may obtain information on how the bonds are rated, keep to AAA or AA ratings, and take an additional precaution by being sure that the bond is insured.

Listed stocks are easily marketable because they can be bought and sold every working day. Stocks are highly volatile. Preferred stocks (stocks that are given preference in the receiving of dividends and in the settlement of claims should the business collapse) are less risky than common stocks. The latter has lowest priority in exercising claims if the firm folds, and no preference in the payment of dividends. Usually, the dividends paid are low and may be changed at any time by the board of directors of the corporation. Both types of stocks offer the possibility of appreciation in their prices as the company becomes more favorably sought after by investors. They also have the possibility of decline as they become less favored and common stocks are more volatile than preferred.

While stocks are dubious investments for most nonprofits, they have served many others well. One of the country's top 20 holders of stocks is a nonprofit: Teachers Insurance and Annuity Association and College Retirement Equities Fund (TIAA–CREF). Moreover, a number of nonprofits and foundations have sizable ownerships of businesses and indeed were originally founded by gifts of stocks in these businesses. Playing the stock market, however, requires a lot more expertise and involvement than most nonprofits have. For most, their involvement should not go further than accepting gifts of stocks, and investing in mutual funds.

Mutual funds, other than money market funds, are of all types. There are corporate bond funds, municipal bond funds, energy funds, gold funds, aggressive common stock funds, to name a few. There is virtually a mutual fund for every investment taste. Mutual funds are marketable in that they can be bought and sold with relative ease. They avoid the need for investment expertise on the part of the organization because they are managed by professional investment advisors. Mutual funds reduce the risks of losses associated with individual common stocks because they are very large and highly diversified. Even a mutual fund that specializes only in gold will carry the stocks of several firms involved in gold. Mutual funds do not generally invest more than 10 percent of their portfolio in any one company so that the individual investor in one of these funds is not overexposed to the risks of collapse by any one company.

There is also the option of investing in tax-sheltered partnerships, but this serves no useful purpose to most nonprofits except pension funds. These partnership interests cannot be redeemed without considerable penalty and only in the amounts and at the times stated in the contract. Moreover, the need of nonprofits for a shelter is less than it is for tax-paying entities; and the use of such shelters may be challenged by the IRS.

Notice that in the above paragraph we were referring to partnerships for tax purposes. These are very different from the types of partnerships dicussed in Chapters 4 and 8 where the partnership is for productive purpose or for producing rental income, discussed in Chapter 7. Several nonprofits including the American Medical Association engage in the latter types of partnerships.

There are ratings that can be used as a guide to determine the investment quality of bonds, commercial paper, municipal notes and stocks. These ratings are not recommendations and they are not forecasts of how well the security will perform in the future. They are evaluations of the financial integrity of the issuer and the issue. In the following, we summarize certain ratings, beginning with the Moody's rating of corporate bonds.

Aaa: These bonds are judged to be of the highest quality. The interests are believed to be protected by exceptionally stable profit margins and the principal is deemed to be secure. The chances that the fundamental financial qualities of the issuer will deteriorate are deemed to be unlikely.

Aa: These bonds, like Aaa bonds, are considered high-grade bonds. They are not graded Aaa because their underlying financial position is subject to wider changes than the Aaa bonds but they are of high quality.

A: These bonds are backed by a sound financial situation of the issuer but some of these conditions may be subject to change in the future. These bonds are said to be of medium grade.

Baa: These are also medium-grade bonds but they are more speculative since it is believed that some of the underlying factors that protect principal and interest could deteriorate in the forseeable future.

TABLE 14.1 Securities: Their Typical Minimum Maturities and Risks

Securities	Typical Minimum Maturity Period	Comments
Negotiable Order of Withdrawal*	immediate	Low risk especially if institution is federally insured
Money Market Mutual Fund	immediate	Low risk especially if portfolio is weighted toward U.S. Treasury paper
Repurchase Agreements	1–90 days	Risk depends upon security backing agreement
Commercial paper	20 days or more	Risk depends upon issuing corporation
Certificate of Deposit	90 days	Low risk especially if institution is federally insured
U.S. Treasury Bills	90 days	Low risk
Negotiable Certificates of Deposit	90 days	Low risk, but requires large initial amount of $100,000
U.S. Treasury Notes	3 years	Low risk, but long holding period
U.S. Treasury Bonds	30 years	Low risk, but long holding period
State and Local Government Bonds	30 years	Varying risk depending upon issuer. Long waiting period
Mutual Funds (other than money market)	immediate	Risk depends upon investment philosophy of fund
Corporate Bonds	20 years	Risk depends upon issue
Stocks	immediate	Wide fluctuation
Tax-sheltering partnerships	indefinite	Risky and redemption depends upon terms set in contract. Early redemption will lead to losses

*By law, available only to individuals and nonprofits.

Source: Author.

Ba: These bonds are characterized as uncertain. They are speculative with very moderate protection of principal and interest.

B: These bonds are speculative and there is limited assurance that the principal or interest will be forthcoming in the future or that even the terms of the contract under which the bonds were purchased can be met.

Caa: These bonds may either be in default (interest has not been paid) or there are visible dangers that a default or the inability to pay principal may be imminent.

Ca: These are very speculative. They are either in default or seriously flawed.

C: These bonds have little likelihood of ever being upgraded to investment standing. They are the most speculative.

Sometimes Moody will show the letter grades and a numerical grade. An Aaa 1 rating means that the security is in the top of the Aaa ratings and a C3 means that it is the lowest of the C-rated bonds.

Standard and Poors has a similar rating system except that it uses pluses and minuses instead of a numerical grade to indicate the standing of each security within its generic class and the letter grades are somewhat different. Thus, instead of Aaa, it uses AAA and instead of Baa, it uses BBB.

Again, the major purpose of these rating systems as far as the financial manager is concerned is an indication of the investment worthiness of securities. It is often unnecessary, unwise and sometimes illegal to invest the dollars of a nonprofit organization in a highly risky (below A) security. Another way to reduce risk is to purchase securities that are insured. Even municipal bonds may be insured so that the purchaser's risk is reduced.

A good investment strategy is an excellent source of unrestricted income for running an organization. The earnings can generally be used at the discretion of the management to carry out the mission of the organization. The significance of earned revenues, including those from investments is revealed by the chairman and president of The Foundation Center:

During the fiscal year 1984–1985, the Foundation Center earned $1,338,657 from publication revenues which was slightly over a third of its support and revenues. But it also did well with its investments. All of the nonprofits we have looked at thus far have had healthy investment incomes. Let's look at the portfolio of the Foundation Center.

The portfolio of The Foundation Center, a 501(c)(3) organization specializing in the collection, preparation, and dissemination of information on philanthropy and which maintains public libraries on philanthropy is shown. The portfolio reveals the exercise of a prudent strategy of asset diversification. It contains income-producing assets that provide a steady base of investment income to the organization and a known date of maturity. The numbers such as 7.95, 10/21/96, are the rates of interest and date of maturity. First, a word from the president and chairman of the board:

> Every nonprofit organization serving a broad public, whether it be a college or university with an annual budget in the tens of millions of dollars or a smaller organization such as The Foundation Center with an annual budget of about $4,000,000, faces the challenge of how to meet operating expenses of a good program designed to meet the needs of the community it serves.
>
> How has the Center met the challenge of funding? First, by attracting a few large donors and holding their interest in a simple but compelling idea: providing "a place to go" for information on private giving. Then, by broadening that base of initial support to include other interested donors across the country, while gradually expanding earned income to a high level unusual in nonprofit organizations. The record is one of accomplishment, and an occasion for celebration. Prior to 1971, we sought support from only a few large foundations; after 1971, in a new climate, a much broader base of grant support seemed desirable, not just from a few grantmakers in the East, but from large and small foundations all over the country. Similarly, prior to 1971, earned income was a welcome windfall; after 1971, it was actively pursued as a means of multiplying the value of grant dollars to improve the delivery of service to the field.

Daniel Herrick and Thomas R. ɒuckman, "From the Chairman and the President" Annual Report 1985, Source: The Foundation Center, p. 1.

The portfolio shown on the next page also contains common stocks which permit the organization to participate in the growth of companies. These common stocks are generally of good investment quality and therefore do not expose the organization to unusually high risks. The bottom line shows that the market value of the portfolio exceeds its costs by $175,661 ($2,019,387 minus $1,843,726) an unrealized gain of just under 10 percent. This does not include the revenues it receives periodically from dividends earned on the stocks and interest earned on the bonds and notes and net capital gains resulting from the sale of securities during the year. Its statement of support, revenues and ex-

Investments

December 31, 1985 — Schedule 1

Description	Face value	Cost	Quoted market value
Bonds and notes:			
U.S. Government and Agencies:			
Federal National Mortgage Assn. 7.80% SM-1991-A 10/10/91	$ 20,000	20,000	19,025
GNMA Pool No. 23841 9% 1/15/2009 Gulf Coast Investment Mtg. backed Ctf. Ser. 2009A	21,586	18,428	20,776
Twelve Federal Land Banks Cons. 7.95% 10/21/96	20,000	20,450	17,925
U.S.A. Treasury bonds:			
8½ % 5/15/99	50,000	51,469	47,313
U.S.A. Treasury notes:			
10¾ % 8/15/90	50,000	47,562	53,938
12⅜% 1/15/88	25,000	24,875	27,031
14½ % 5/15/91	50,000	49,844	62,094
10⅞% 2/15/93	25,000	24,109	27,547
11¼ % 2/15/95	50,000	49,797	56,656
12⅜% 8/15/87	25,000	25,156	26,641
11⅝% 11/15/94	50,000	50,406	57,719
11¾ % 11/15/93	25,000	24,344	28,828
12¾ % 11/15/89	75,000	75,422	84,938
9½ % 8/15/88	50,000	50,367	51,485
11⅜% 9/30/88	50,000	49,970	53,766
11⅜% 2/15/89	100,000	100,313	108,062
Corporate bonds and notes:			
General Motors Acceptance Corp., undivided interest in demand note	93,000	93,000	93,000
CIT Financial Corp. Series A, undivided interest in demand note	20,000	20,000	20,000
General Electric Co., undivided interest in demand note	10,000	10,000	10,000
Nordstrom Credit Inc., undivided interest in demand note	1,000	1,000	1,000
Citicorp notes:			
8.45% 3/15/2007	50,000	50,438	42,062
12⅞% 10/15/89	50,000	49,615	53,615
Southwestern Bell Telephone Co. 9⅝% 3/15/2019	25,000	22,187	23,629
Tenneco Inc. 8⅜% 4/01/2002	50,000	50,562	42,805
Total bonds and notes		**979,314**	**1,029,855**
Preferred stock:			
R. J. Reynolds Industries Inc.	100	12,876	13,138
Common stocks:			
Allied Signal Inc.	576	21,229	26,928
Ampco Pittsburgh Corp.	1,100	21,724	15,538
Atlantic Richfield Co.	600	26,211	38,250
B. F. Goodrich Co.	1,000	32,245	32,875
Burlington Northern Inc.	400	23,173	27,300
Chase Manhattan Corp.	500	24,103	36,313
Citicorp	500	18,790	24,688
Crystal Brands Inc.	80	—	1,820
Eagle Pitcher Industries Inc.	1,000	21,116	29,875
Ford Motor Co.	400	19,382	23,200
General Electric Co.	300	18,398	21,825
General Mills Inc.	400	20,742	24,450
Genstar Corp.	1,400	26,587	33,425
Georgia Pacific Corp.	1,000	23,154	26,500
Hospital Corp. of America	550	25,293	19,663
International Business Machines Corp.	712	66,627	110,716
J. C. Penney Co.	600	35,165	33,300
J. P. Stevens & Co. Inc.	600	11,247	18,600
Kansas City Power & Light Co.	900	18,847	20,363
Kenner Parker Toys Inc.	120	—	1,890
Mapco Inc.	600	21,510	22,800
Marriott Corp.	200	8,260	21,800
Melville Corp.	500	20,639	25,250
Motorola Inc.	700	23,110	27,213
Northern Indiana Public Service Co.	1,000	12,310	9,875
Philip Morris Companies Inc.	300	25,737	26,513
Phillips Petroleum Co.	1,200	16,225	14,550
Ralston Purina	300	13,952	14,100
Schlumberger Ltd.	600	26,602	21,900
Smithkline Beckman Corp.	300	20,193	22,688
Southwestern Bell Corp.	200	19,470	25,650
Tandon Corp.	2,400	34,369	11,700
Tech Sym Corp.	1,100	23,208	15,263
Tenneco Inc.	500	17,615	19,875
Texas Commerce BancShares, Inc.	500	20,335	14,000
Texas Oil & Gas Corp.	1,100	17,152	16,913
Union Camp Corp.	400	13,889	15,900
Union Electric Co.	1,000	13,776	21,375
United Technologies Corp.	600	24,506	26,250
U.S. West Inc.	240	13,603	21,360
White Consolidated Industries	400	11,042	13,900
Total common stocks		**851,536**	**976,394**
Total investments		**$1,843,726**	**2,019,387**

Investment Schedule 1, December 31, 1985, Annual Report 1985. Source: The Foundation Center, 1985, p. 32.

penses reveals an investment income of $144,110 during the year—all of which was unrestricted.

Managers of small organizations may wonder whether investment strategies such as those used by larger organizations may be available to them. The answer is yes if through an investment pool. Such pools provide for several organizations to invest as a group. By doing this, they share risks, are able to diversify among several investments, are able to hire an investment advisor, and trade at a lower commission rate. The National Conference of Catholic Bishops, the United States Catholic Conference, the American Board of Catholic Missions, The Campaign for Human Development, the Committee for the Church in Latin America and the Catholic Communication Campaign, for example, have a short-term and a long-term investment pool for themselves.[1] This assists them in conducting a wide range of charitable missions here and abroad including financial support of other charities.

CAPITAL BUDGETING AND ENDOWMENT PLANNING— SETTING TARGETS

The operating budget that we described in Chapter 12 is concerned with the annual operation of the organization. It shows planned inflow and outflow of the organization's resources during the course of the coming year. Some organizations, not many, have a multi-year operating budget. These budgets show the plan for annual operation of the organization for each of the next five years.

A capital budget shows the planned acquisition, disposition, or reconstruction of capital items. A capital item is one that has a useful life of more than one year. Furniture, equipment, buildings, automobiles, computers, are examples of capital items. They have a useful life of more than one year.

Expenditures on capital items are called investments or capital expenditures. These are different from expenditures planned in the operating budget which are operating expenses. An investment is an expenditure on a item that may change in value over time and that is not all consumed or used up in one year. A building is not used up in one year. It has a useful life of decades. But each year, a portion of the building, the computer, and the automobile is used up, i.e., there is wear and tear. The dollar approximation of this wear and tear is called depreciation. Because depreciation arises as a result of annual operation, depreciation is shown as an annual expense in the operating budget and financial statements of the organization.

Furthermore, once the capital item is placed in service, it requires maintenance and the principal and interest on the loan used to purchase the asset (mortgage in the case of a building and car loan in the case of an automobile) must be paid annually. These become annual operating expenses.

Thus, capital planning and budgeting requires analyses not only of when and how the capital asset will be obtained, but how it would impact on the annual operating budget. Two routes through which this impact occurs are by way of maintenance and amortization costs (payment of principal and interest). Another source is through insurance premiums. Credit and liability insurance premiums are examples. A credit insurance policy protects the organization against the eventuality that it cannot pay off the loan; liability protects it against claims such as those arising from automobile accidents, fire, or injury of a person while on the premises of the building. We saw in an earlier chapter that the inability to acquire liability insurance through no fault of their own can cripple the use of certain capital items owned by nonprofits and sharply increase their costs of annual operation.

From a financial point of view, several questions arise in capital budgeting. Let us put ourselves in the position of the board of directors of a nonprofit organization considering the acquisition of a building. What are some of the questions that may arise?

One question is what will be the source of the required funds? Potential sources are gifts and contributions, including a large gift obtained in trust or the running of a special gift campaign, i.e., a capital campaign.

A second potential source is through the accumulation and setting aside of part of its annual earnings of the organization. Recall that with private foundations, such accumulations must be authorized by the IRS. A related source that provides the basis of systematic accumulation is depreciation. By depreciating existing assets, an expense is written off current operations. But depreciation does not represent the kind of expense that requires the organization to draw a check. It is a paper expense. Therefore, one way to finance new acquisitions is to accumulate these paper expenses—actually setting aside each year the amount of depreciation so that these amounts may subsequently be used to purchase new assets. Of course, running the organization so that it produces an annual excess or surplus and dedicating a part of that amount to a capital account is another source of organizational savings.

A third source of capital acquisition may be the physical gift of a building which may be used, sold, or leased by the organization. Be reminded, however, that if the building is gotten through a gift and has a mortgage on it, the income from the rental is subject to an unrelated business income tax and this annual tax payment would impact on the organization's operating budget. A fourth source is to enter into debt, i.e., to borrow the money. This source would also have an impact on the organization's operating budget since the principal and interest on the debt must be paid annually. Any one or a combination of these approaches may be used.

As we stated earlier in this book, nonprofits may not sell stocks. Therefore, this source of financing capital projects is not available to them as it is to for-profit corporations.

A related set of questions has to do with the schedule of accumulating the funds needed to acquire the building. For example, the organization could collect all the money it needs in one year or it could collect it over a number of years. How much does it need to collect in each year if it chooses the latter course? How much does it need to collect by the end of the first year if it chooses to collect all the money it needs at the end of that year?

Both of these answers depend upon the rate of interest; for the smart financial manager would invest the collected sum in a safe investment paying a relatively predictable (fixed rate). By doing this, the amount that has to be collected, borrowed or taken from the organization's savings or shifted from the moneys available for the daily operation of the organization would be lessened.

Let us assume that the rate of interest is 10 percent and the planning horizon, the time over which to accumulate the money, is four years and the amount needed to acquire the building is $5,000,000. What are some of the alternative targets for accumulating the funds?

Present Value of Single Sum

One option is to have a fund raising drive that ends at the end of the first year and to put that money into the bank so that, at 10 percent, it will accumulate the money needed to acquire the building over a five-year period. If the organization can be successful in doing this, it will be able to avoid debt, shift its fund-raising efforts to another program, and avoid using any of its operating income or savings from operations to buy the building. How much must it raise in the first and only year of its fund-raising effort in order that this strategy may be successful? What is its target amount?

A strategy such as this is obviously dependent upon the amount of money that must be collected in the first year so that when it is invested at 10 percent over a 4-year period would be equal to $5,000,000. This is called the present value of a single sum. It is the dollar value of a single amount of money which, if invested, would yield the targeted amount at the end of some specified period (in this case 4 years) when the rate of interest per year is some specific amount (in this case 10 percent).

This problem can be solved by going to a table such as Table 14.2 which can be found in interest rate books. We look under the column called single payment present worth, and the row that applies to 4 years and we find a factor 0.6830. We multiply $5,000,000 by this factor and get $3,415,000. This is the amount that must be raised and invested in the first year at 10 percent annual rate of return each year if the $5,000,000 target is to be met by the fourth year. Of course, the board could significantly reduce this amount and still not take a greater risk by looking for a higher rate of return by stretching out the time it has to accumulate the funds. If they chose to wait 8 rather than 4 years, their fund-raising target would be (0.4665 × $5,000,000) or $2,332,500.

TABLE 14.2 Time Value of Money Assuming 10% Interest Factor

n Years	Single-payment compound-amount — Future value of $1	Single-payment present-worth — Present value of $1	Uniform-series compound-amount — Future value of uniform series of $1	Sinking-fund payment — Uniform series whose future value is $1	Capital recovery — Install-ment to amortize $1	Uniform-series present-worth — Present value of uniform series of $1
1	1.100	0.9091	1.000	1.00000	1.10000	0.909
2	1.210	0.8264	2.100	0.47619	0.57619	1.736
3	1.331	0.7513	3.310	0.30211	0.40211	2.487
4	1.464	0.6830	4.641	0.21547	0.31547	3.170
5	1.611	0.6209	6.105	0.16380	0.26380	3.791
6	1.772	0.5645	7.716	0.12961	0.22961	4.355
7	1.949	0.5132	9.487	0.10541	0.20541	4.868
8	2.144	0.4665	11.436	0.08744	0.18744	5.335
9	2.358	0.4241	13.579	0.07364	0.17364	5.759
10	2.594	0.3855	15.937	0.06275	0.16275	6.144
11	2.853	0.3505	18.531	0.05396	0.15396	6.495
12	3.138	0.3186	21.384	0.04676	0.14676	6.814
13	3.452	0.2897	24.523	0.04078	0.14078	7.103
14	3.797	0.2633	27.975	0.03575	0.13575	7.367
15	4.177	0.2394	31.772	0.03147	0.13147	7.606
16	4.595	0.2176	35.950	0.02782	0.12782	7.824
17	5.054	0.1978	40.545	0.02466	0.12466	8.022
18	5.560	0.1799	45.599	0.02193	0.12193	8.201
19	6.116	0.1635	51.159	0.01955	0.11955	8.365
20	6.727	0.1486	57.275	0.01746	0.11746	8.514
21	7.400	0.1351	64.002	0.01562	0.11562	8.649
22	8.140	0.1228	71.403	0.01401	0.11401	8.772

TABLE 14.2

n Years	Single-payment compound-amount Future value of $1	Single-payment present-worth Present value of $1	Uniform-series compound-amount Future value of uniform series of $1	Sinking-fund payment Uniform series whose future value is $1	Capital recovery Installment to amortize $1	Uniform-series present-worth Present value of uniform series of $1
23	8.954	0.1117	79.543	0.01257	0.11257	8.883
24	9.850	0.1015	88.497	0.01130	0.11130	8.985
25	10.835	0.0923	98.347	0.01017	0.11017	9.077
26	11.918	0.0839	109.182	0.00916	0.10916	9.161
27	13.110	0.0763	121.100	0.00826	0.10826	9.237
28	14.421	0.0693	134.210	0.00745	0.10745	9.307
29	15.863	0.0630	148.631	0.00673	0.10673	9.370
30	17.449	0.0573	164.494	0.00608	0.10608	9.427
35	28.102	0.0356	271.024	0.00369	0.10369	9.644
40	45.259	0.0221	442.593	0.00226	0.10226	9.779
45	72.890	0.0137	718.905	0.00139	0.10139	9.863
50	117.391	0.0085	1,163.909	0.00086	0.10086	9.915
55	189.059	0.0053	1,880.591	0.00053	0.10053	9.947
60	304.482	0.0033	3,034.816	0.00033	0.10033	9.967
65	490.371	0.0020	4,893.707	0.00020	0.10020	9.980
70	789.747	0.0013	7,887.470	0.00013	0.10013	9.987
75	1271.895	0.0008	12,708.954	0.00008	0.10008	9.992
80	2048.400	0.0005	20,474.002	0.00005	0.10005	9.995
85	3298.969	0.0003	32,979.690	0.00003	0.10003	9.997
90	5313.023	0.0002	53,120.226	0.00002	0.10002	9.998
95	8556.676	0.0001	85,556.760	0.00001	0.10001	9.999

Future Value of a Single Sum

Alternatively, the organization may already have a large gift that it can invest in the first year. The question that the board of directors are faced with is will this be sufficient when invested at 10 percent over the 4-year period to meet our target? Would we have to raise more money? How much more? This type of problem is called finding the future value of a single sum, i.e., how much is a single sum invested today at, say 10 percent, worth in the future, say 4 years? Once we have found the answer to this, we can subtract this amount from our required amount and determine if we are going to meet, exceed, or fall short of the target.

To answer this question, turn to Table 14.2 and look under the single-payment compound amount. Assume that the amount the board of directors has on hand is $2,000,000. What would this amount be worth in 4 years invested in a manner that yields 10 percent per year? The factor is 1.464. Multiply $2,000,000 by this factor and get $2,928,999. Since $5,000,000 is needed, the board knows that it cannot rely merely on its initial investment. It must raise more money to meet its target.

Future Value of a Uniform Series of Payments

The board of directors may conclude that they prefer not to deal with a single sum. Rather, they would prefer to have a fund-raising campaign that is annual and stretches over a 4-year period. This has the advantage of being less pressing on them and on the staff. They can assume, based on past experience, and on their contacts, that they could raise a specific amount of money every year; i.e., say $800,000 per year. Would they meet their target if they collected that amount every year and put it into an investment paying 10 percent per year? Would they overshoot their target, fall short of it, or just meet it?

This type of problem requires finding the dollar value that a series of uniform payments made at the end of every year for a specified number of years would be worth on a specific future date. To solve this we go to Table 14.2 and the column that shows a uniform series compounded amount. We see the factor 4.641. Multiply this by $800,000 and get $3,712,800 which is how much $800,000 raised and invested at the end of each of 4 years will be worth at the end of the fourth year. The board will fail to meet its $5,000,000 target unless it raises more money or stretches out the period of raising and investing funds.

Sinking Fund

The reciprocal of the same uniform series of payments problem stated above is a sinking fund problem. In this case, the board of directors are less interested if they would exceed, fall short, or miss their target. They wish to give a clear and specific annual target to the fund-raising manager. "We have a target of $5,000,000 that we must have in 4 years. We know that the safest rate of return we can get on our money is 10 percent. To accomplish this we give you a directive to set a fund-raising target of X number of dollars per year." The director of fund-raising retorts: "I shall be happy to follow your orders if you could specify how much must be raised each year under the conditions you have set."

The answer can be found by resorting to Table 14.2. The column entitled "Sinking Fund Payment" tells how much money must be sunk into a fund each year if a specific target is to be met over a specific number of years and when the rate is 10 percent. Multiply the factor shown for 4 years, 4.641, by $5,000,000. The fund-raising team must come up with $2,325,000 per year. Notice that this is substantially lower than the fund-raising target when the money is expected to be raised only in one year—the example given earlier— but to accomplish the objective, the fund-raising campaign must last at the same intensity for 4 years.

Capital Recovery

The board of directors may follow another option. They may decide that they would rather go out and borrow the money to acquire the building. They know that if they do this they will have to pay principal and interest on the loan each year until the loan is paid off. This is called amortization; i.e., the paying off of a debt. They will borrow the entire $5,000,000. How much will be their annual payment in principal and interest? In other words, how much will the lender charge per year so as to recover the full amount loaned plus the interest charged? This is called a capital recovery problem.

To solve this problem, go to Table 14.2 and locate the column showing capital recovery. The factor is 0.31547 which when multiplied by $5,000,000 gives $1,577,350. This is how much the organization would have to come up with if it chooses to borrow the funds at 10 percent and try to pay off the mort-gage in 4 years. More realistically, it may choose a 30-year mortgage. The factor there is 0.10608. Multiply it by $5,000,000 and get $530,400, the amount it must come up with each year (its target) to pay off its principal and interest.

Present Value of a Uniform Series

The reciprocal of the capital recovery problem is one that involves find-ing out how much money the organization could borrow given its capacity to pay a total sum of money each year. Would the amount of money we can afford to pay each year for the next specific number of years be sufficient to pay both principal and interest on our loan so that at the end of that period our loan would be paid off?

In this case, the board of directors are willing to commit themselves to a specific annual payment, but only if it would be enough to pay off the prin-cipal and interest on the debt. To answer the question, turn to Table 14.2 and the column showing the present worth of a uniform series. Assume that the organization is willing to come up with $200,000 per year for the next 10 years, what size mortgage could it afford assuming a mortgage rate of 10 percent? The factor is 6.144 which when multiplied by $200,000 gives $1,228,800—the maximum mortgage it can afford.

Perpetual Endowment

Now once a building is built it has to be maintained for the remainder of its life. It has to be painted, remodeled, refitted with heating and air conditioning systems, and so on. Good planning will involve the kind of strategy used by the Colonial Williamsburg Foundation. They decided that they would not only raise the funds to construct a building but raise the funds to do the maintenance for the life of the building. Hence, once the building is in service, they do not have to be searching for funds to keep it maintained. It is a far-sighted and wise strategy. A precious building will not stand in jeopardy of being ruined, as did the Statue of Liberty, for the lack of money to do maintenance and repairs.

Since a building could conceivably last forever, the board may well ask: Assuming that we have a fund of $4,000,000 which we intend to last forever, how much would we have per year to take care of maintenance and repairs if we use just the earnings of the fund for repairs. By using only the earnings, the principal amount we invested in the fund would last forever. It will always be there earning money to pay for the maintenance and repairs. This is called a perpetual endowment problem. Funding scholarships and professorships are of this type. Thus, Chapter 11 refers to endowments as lasting forever.

The answer to this problem is not found in Table 14.2. It is simple. Multiply the principal amount by the rate of interest expected per year and we get the target. Hence, if the rate of return on the invested $4,000,000 is 10 percent, $400,000 would be available each year to maintain and operate the building.

Capitalization

Capitalization is the opposite of a perpetual endowment. In capitalization, the board of directors are asking: How much must we put up in an endowment if we know that the annual cost of repairs and maintenance or scholarship awards is $200,000 per year? In other words, how much capital must we put in an endowment if we intend never to use any portion of the endowment so that it will last forever, earning the required amount of money we need to do maintenance and repairs or to award scholarships so that we might never have to undertake (unless in an unusual circumstance) to borrow, use operating funds, or have another fund-raiser for this specific purpose.

To answer this question, let us assume that the expected rate of return on the investment is 10 percent. Divide this required amount of $200,000 by

10 percent and get $2,000,000. This is the target amount by which an endowment would have to be capitalized if it is to yield sufficient money annually to pay for the repairs and maintenance of the building.

Other Aspects of Capital and Endowment Planning

In the above case we used the example of a building. Scholarships are another form of capital planning. In fact, endowments are capital plans and the same principles which we described above apply. Scholarships and chairs are often set up in the form of perpetual endowments; i.e., to provide a perpetual flow of funds by using only the interest to make annual awards.

The law requires that endowments be prudently administered to preserve the intent of the donor and that the trustees act with loyalty toward the public purpose of the endowment. The list of actions given in Chapter 9 that could be cause for suit applies to endowments.

When we say that endowments must be administered by the terms of the contracts that create them, we are making reference to law. The borrowing of money that is in an endowment, shifting it to some other use, closing an endowment are all legally prohibited transactions unless allowed in the endowment contract. Otherwise, the management, trustees or board can be sued by the donors or their public beneficiaries. To make such unspecified transactions legal, the trustees or board may have to get permission from a court. Such permission is usually granted if a financial crisis that cannot be satisfied in some other manner can be demonstrated, if the purpose of the endowment no longer exists or is impracticable or financially infeasible, and when actions required by the endowment would lead to its destruction. Under what the lawyer's call a cy pres ruling the court may give authority for the funds to be used in some manner other than that stipulated in the contract but consistent with the mission of the organization.

The above paragraph applies to restricted funds—an endowment being a type of restricted fund—although the rules may be relaxed when the restricted fund is created by the board of directors or trustees and not through a contract with a donor. There are many law suits involving university trustees and their use of endowment or restricted funds.[2]

Some endowments are set up so that they will not commence making awards or cash payments until the passage of some time. This gives the fund an opportunity to grow, to establish some critical level based on a calculation of the future value of a single payment, and then to make perpetual awards based on some calculation and the capitalized value; i.e., the amount that is needed to sustain a perpetual gift at some specific amount.

It should be obvious from what has been said in this section that capital planning and endowment management are related to sustaining the growth and performance of the organization over several years. It has not only to do with buying buildings, equipment and machines but in creating funds that can finance the mission of the organization well into the future.

In all capital planning problems, as we saw above, the pressures on the fund-raising campaign can be reduced by stretching out the time required to accumulate a targetted amount of money or investing it in assets that pay a higher rate of return. Let us consider each of these. A higher rate of return always implies a greater risk (the rate may decline, the investment is risky and that is why it must pay a high rate so as to attract money, the issuer may default or go bankrupt because of its inability to meet high expenses including the high rates it must pay and so on). Because securities of the Federal Treasury are generally considered to be the lowest risk, a rate approximating their prevailing rate is what should be used as a basis of judging the relationship between risk and return. For most legal purposes, the IRS requires the presumption of a rate around 10 percent.

Moreover, because the rate has to be presumed to prevail for the length of the planning horizon, in the above case 4 years, the investment that should be made is one that is likely to keep a relatively fixed rate for that period of time. The accumulated funds should be invested in reasonably safe, fixed-rate assets that mature at about the time the money is needed. Notes, bonds, U.S. Treasury securities, securities of government agencies, certificates of deposits, even high-grade zero-coupon bonds and municipal bonds are examples.

Stretching out the time reduces the pressures on the fund-raising efforts and may perhaps make the project more realistic. This has to be weighed against other factors. Stretching out the time increases risk: Inflation would cause the cost of the project to rise. If the assets held are fixed rate, then their value will decline or probably will not keep pace with the rise in inflation. Thus, the earnings to finance the project will not keep pace with its rising costs and more, not less, fund-raising will be necessary.

Stretching out time also risks loss of interest on the part of donors; and, in the case of buildings, changes in zoning or building codes that could increase costs. On the other hand, stretching out time does have an advantage when there is rapid technological change. Waiting some years to buy a computer or copier meant getting more efficient and cheaper machines. When equipment is undergoing significant technological change, it is often better to lease than to buy.

SETTING TARGET PRICES

For a nonprofit organization to do well selling its goods and services requires a rational approach to the setting of prices and fees. In this section, we describe some approaches. Before doing so, however, it is essential to note that all prices are determined by the market, some prices more so than others. In a very competitive market, the price or fee that a nonprofit will be able to charge will depend upon the prices or fees being charged by its competitors. Even in a monopoly situation where the nonprofit sets a price and does not have to worry about competition, market forces will determine how much of that good or service will be sold. If there is no demand for the product, it will not sell. If the demand is limited by a very high price, only a few will be purchased. If the price is low enough and consumers are very sensitive to prices, more will be sold. This is the basic law of supply and demand.

Not only does the market set limits on prices, but so too do the laws and regulations from federal, state or local authorities. For example, where there is rent control, nonprofits may not exceed it unless by special exemption.

In short, whatever the price or fee level set by the nonprofit and whichever of the methods it uses to determine those prices or fees, they must eventually adjust to the realities of the market and the law. Therefore, the methods to be discussed may best be viewed as rational ways to determine target prices or fees.

The rational setting of prices and fees means that they should have some relationship to costs. To simplify matters, let us describe the full costs of producing a good or service as composing (1) of direct costs resulting solely from the production of the good or service, and (2) indirect costs only partly related to the production of the good and service. Put another way, direct costs exist only because the good or service is being produced. Indirect costs would exist whether or not a specific good is being produced because the organization has to incur costs to exist and to carry on its nonprofit mission.

Various price or fee targets can be set depending upon the amount of the direct and indirect costs that the organization wishes to recover. On one level, the nonprofit may set a fee or price that does not meet even its direct costs. It can do this only to the extent that gifts and contributions make up the difference. This is in fact what many nonprofits do. When they set the price of their goods or service at zero (or no charge), they are totally dependent upon gifts and contributions to pay for the cost of the service they provide.

On a second level, the nonprofit may set a price or fee that only recovers its direct costs. When this is done, less pressure is placed on gifts and contributions to support that particular activity. Gifts and contributions would be needed only to cover the indirect costs, a portion of which would exist even if the good or service were not being produced.

On a third level, the price or fee could be set so that the full costs, both direct and indirect, are being covered by the price. In this case, the activity is self-supporting. The gifts and contributions can be used to advance other missions of the organization.

On yet another level, the price or fee may be set so that the organization not only recovers its full costs (direct and indirect) but more. It can do this by adding a percentage to its full costs. In the for-profit world, this percentage reflects a profit or a return on the investment to owners. This margin is also permitted to nonprofits. In the General Council Memorandum 39346, dated

3-15-85, the IRS concluded that the provision of veterinary service for a fee of cost plus a percent was not in violation of the tax-exempt status of 501(c)(3) organizations formed to provide veterinary services. Moreover, the IRS concluded that, given the facts and circumstances of that organization, the markup did not constitute an unrelated business and therefore it was not taxable.

The significance of this last level of setting a target price or fee is that this extra percentage can be (and virtually must be if it is not to be taxed as an unrelated business) used to support the advancement of the mission of the organization. Hence, the pricing levels described progress from losses which impose a burden on the organization to one that provides a legal surplus helping to support the organization in its mission.

Setting of prices or fees does not necessarily subvert or destroy the charitable character of the organization or its mission. The fees or prices may be set according to some means test. Clients are charged according to their ability to pay. Those who cannot pay are served without charge, and the charge rises as the ability to pay increases. Thus, in setting rental levels in homes for the elderly, the nonprofit must set the prices so that they fall within the financial reach of a significant proportion of the elderly population in the community. Should a resident not be able to pay, the organization should be prepared to make necessary arrangements to continue to provide housing even in a housing project operated by another organization. Further, the organization should operate at the lowest feasible cost. This does not mean that it does not provide amenities but that the cost of these plus other necessary costs should not become so high that the subsequent price is out of reach of a large segment of the elderly population.[3]

SUMMARY AND CONCLUSIONS

The final chapter of this book has shown how the financial function of the non-profit organization is continuous and feeds back into the planning of the future of the organization and the continuous search for new opportunities.

The successful search rests on the ability of management to expand its view of what the organization can and cannot do legally and the identification of appropriate niches within and outside the boundaries of the marketplace. However, merely identifying these potential niches is not enough. The organization needs to have a well thought out set of financial strategies and targets that are consistent with its mission and capabilities and objectives. This chapter focused on setting targets and the management of cash to meet these financial targets. Best wishes for the mission and future of your organization.

NOTES

1. United States Catholic Conference, *Reports on Examinations of Financial Statements and Additional Information,* 1983 and 1984 (Washington, D.C. April 19, 1985), p. 6.

2. For a summary of this literature, see Edward Johnson and Kent M. Weeks, "To Save a College: Independent College Trustees and Decisions on Financial Exigency, Endowment Use, and Closure," *The Journal of College and University Law,* Vol. 12, No. 4, Spring 1986, pp. 455–488.
3. Rev. Rul. 79–18, Rev. Rul. 72–124.

SUGGESTED READINGS

FABOZZI, FRANK J. & LESLIE MASON, *Corporate Cash Management,* (Homewood, Illinois: Dow-Jones Irwin, 1985).

JOHNSON, EDWARD A. AND KENT M. WEEKS, "To Save A College: Independent College Trustees and Decisions on Financial Exigency, Endowment Use, and Closure," *The Journal of College and University Law* Vol. 12, No. 4, Spring 1986, pp. 455–488.

VIGELAND, CARL A., *Great Good Fortune, How Harvard Makes Its Money,* (Boston, Mass.: Houghton-Mifflin, 1986).

Index

Page numbers in *italics* indicate illustrations.

Page numbers followed by *t* indicate tables.

A

Accidental death and dismemberment insurance as benefit, 203–4
Accounting, fund, 339–41
Activities, comparative statement of, 333–34
Annuity, 272
Annuity trusts, 252, 253–55
Asset test in private nonoperating foundations, 154–55
Audit, 341–43
Auditors' opinion in financial statements, 350

B

Balance sheet, 326–31
  comparative, 330–31
  interpretation of, 329–30
Bargain sales and losses as gifts, 235–36
Benefits for employees, 198–219
  accidental death and dismemberment insurance as, 203–4
  cafeteria plan as, 212–13
  disability income insurance as, 199–201
  liability insurance as, 215–17
  life insurance as, 201–3
  medical and hospitalization insurance as, 204–7
  pension plan as, 207–12
  profit-sharing plan as, 213–14
  retirement plan in, 207–12
Blue Cross as benefit, 206

This hands-on new book provides valuable insight into the all-important financial underpinnings of nonprofit organizations. Whether used as a training tool for managers and board members, or as a desk reference for professionals, those charged with the responsibility for the direction and health of a non-profit organization will find this book an indispensible tool.

By frankly discussing the course of a nonprofit organization's problem — money — it is able to present a variety of creative, practical solutions. For starters, you'll discover how a nonprofit organization can increase its revenues, including the sale of goods and services and gifts and contributions from individuals and corporations, and how the resulting inflow of cash can be managed successfully. A number of examples of successful organizations are included.